Gramophone
Records
of the
First World War

Gramophone Records of the First World War

An HMV Catalogue 1914–1918

Introduced by Brian Rust

DAVID & CHARLES
Newton Abbot London North Pomfret (VT) Vancouver

0 7153 6842 7

Library of Congress Catalog Card Number 74-20448

© EMI Limited
Reprinted by permission of EMI Limited

Published in the United States of America
by David & Charles Inc   North Pomfret
Vermont 05053 USA

Published in Canada by Douglas David
& Charles Limited   3645 McKechnie Drive
West Vancouver BC

Printed in Great Britain
by Redwood Burn Limited Trowbridge & Esher
for David & Charles (Holdings) Limited
South Devon House Newton Abbot Devon

Introduction

As the Archduke Ferdinand of Austria and his wife Sophia were driving through the Serbian town of Sarajevo on the morning of Sunday, June 28, 1914, they were hit by shots from a gun fired by a nineteen-year-old Serbian anarchist, Gavrilo Prinzip. Within six weeks, Europe was engulfed in the Great War, as it was known in the two decades of uneasy peace that followed it. The political machinations, the military and naval build-up and the incredible arrogance and stupidity of the leaders of most of the warring nations have long been a matter for the history books. The work presented here is also a history book, with a great difference: it shows not only the general trend of events reflected by the speeches recorded by statesmen and politicians, but also the changing taste and mood of the public of Great Britain, in the light of those events.

The Gramophone Company Ltd. of Hayes, Middlesex, England, had been producing disc records for exactly sixteen years prior to the cataclysm of August, 1914; the first known record made in London is dated August 2, 1898. By 1914 'His Master's Voice' was established as one of the world's best-known trade-marks. With branches and factories throughout the entire globe, the company could publish, month by month, recordings of the topmost professional artists and entertainers, most of them under exclusive contracts. The greatest tenor of all time, in the balanced estimation of many leading authorities, was Enrico Caruso; he had sung at

Covent Garden—as it happened, for the last time there—in June and July, 1914. His records were awaited with as much enthusiasm as if they had been popular songs of the day. In a sense, they were; his magnetic personality and extraordinary vocal method turned operatic arias into songs that the man in the street knew and recognised. His friend and fellow-tenor John McCormack was equally well loved, and his records, which ranged from Irish folk songs to opera, sold even at their relatively high prices to people whose libraries of records were otherwise filled with military bands, drawing-room ballads and popular numbers in the new American ragtime style. (At least, it was considered ragtime; when Murray Johnson's record of *Pack Up Your Troubles In Your Old Kit-Bag* was announced in April, 1916, it too was described as 'a tuneful little tickler for which ragtime is directly responsible'!)

For the few months immediately preceding the outbreak of war, the record-buying public had been treated to the issue, two single-sided records at a time, of the first recording of Beethoven's Fifth Symphony, played by the Berlin Philharmonic Orchestra conducted by Arthur Nikisch, one of the greatest conductors of the time. By a curious irony, this pioneering work was completed in the issue for August, 1914. Up to 1914, recordings of symphonies simply did not exist in any but the most absurdly edited and truncated form, usually offering no more than a bowdlerised version of one movement, or as much of it as could be squeezed on to one side of a twelve-inch record. The Nikisch set, edited though it was, at least was a step forward: a top conductor, a 'name' orchestra, a major work by a major composer, and you could buy all eight parts for 5s. 6d. each.

You could, that is, if your patriotic sensitivity allowed you to invest in anything so patently belonging to what the popular press termed 'the Hun'. If not, you could console yourself with some truly exquisite records by the New Symphony Orchestra, later re-named the Royal Albert Hall Orchestra, under its British conductor, Mr Landon Ronald, who had been employed as accompanist, arranger, impresario and composer to the Gramophone Company since 1900. Most of these were of music by Allied composers, Camille Saint-Saëns and Jules Massenet featuring among some of the first issues. There was also a remarkably good example of how brilliant acoustic recording could be in the issue of Järnefeldt's *Praëludium*. Another British conductor and composer also visited the studios in Hayes during the war years, and made records of his own works, and that was Sir Edward Elgar.

Patriotic feeling ran extremely high, of course, especially during the early months of hostilities, and American soi-disant 'ragtime' numbers vied with flag-waving, unashamed jingoism for popularity. Everyone knows how *Tipperary* was an unremarkable music-hall-Irish number for two years until the British Expeditionary Force took it up and made it into a classic of its kind, but Ivor Novello's *Keep The Home Fires Burning (Till The Boys Come Home)* and *Belgium Put The Khibosh On The Kaiser* are better guides to the way most people liked their songs in 1915.

That is to say, those who could not bring themselves to listen to anything other than escapist dream-fantasies couched in somewhat archaic poetic language! There were also those who responded to the publicity of 'Opera in English' launched by HMV in 1915. This venture succeeded as it deserved to do; there were superb records by fine artists such as Nora d'Argel, Flora Woodman, George Baker, Edna Thornton, Charles Mott, the ill-fated William Samuell—who died of typhoid early in 1916 at the outset of a most promising career in music—and of course the ever-reliable Peter Dawson, who could and did cope equally well with excerpts from operas by Rossini, Bizet and Handel and with popular ballads and even vocal arrangements of dance tunes. The firmament of British opera was also lit by the scintillating brilliance of two sopranos, both of whom recorded copiously during and after the war, on HMV records and under their own and other names. These were Bessie Jones and Violet Essex. Bessie Jones had sung with Caruso at Covent Garden; Violet Essex had been trained by Herman Klein amongst others, and both were to become members of the great cast of artists that made the ambitious, and highly successful albums of Gilbert and Sullivan operas, starting with *The Mikado* in 1917. As Louise Leigh, Bessie Jones also made delightful records of revue and musical comedy songs, including one of *Peter Pan* from the 1918 show at the Comedy Theatre; it was written by an eighteen-year-old soldier named Noël Coward. Violet Essex recorded Arditi's famous *Il Bacio* for the May, 1915 issue, and followed this with magnificent recordings of *Musetta's Waltz Song* from *La Bohème*, the *Jewel Song* from *Faust* (including the recitative), *Deh! vieni, non tardar* (*Oh come, my heart's delight*) from Mozart's *The Marriage Of Figaro*, all in English under her own name, and exquisite popular numbers under the name of Vera Desmond.

George Baker was re-named Walter Jefferies, and his colleague, the tenor Ernest Pike, became Eric Courtland, when they sang popular songs that ranged from the sentiment of *There's A Long, Long Trail* (March, 1916) to the stuttering, tongue-twisting nonsense of *Indianapolis* (November, 1918), the latter being a duet by both of them. By contrast, 'Walter Jefferies' made as a coupling to his *Long Trail* record a number called *Everybody's Crazy On The Fox Trot*, a statement that reflected what was nothing less than the truth. After a succession of strange contortionate dances bearing the names of animals and birds—the Turkey Trot, the Bunny Hug, the Grizzly Bear, amongst others—the Fox Trot was at first regarded as just another in a line that was already too long, especially for those whose idea of dance music was confined to the Viennese waltz, the regimentation of the Lancers and Quadrille, and the daring brazen exhibitionism of the Boston Two-Step. It was the great and genuinely loved American comedienne and revue artist Elsie Janis who introduced the Fox Trot to London, in stage partnership with the man who became her fiancé, Basil Hallam. Her record of *Balling The Jack*, from *The Passing Show of 1915* at the Palace Theatre, shows her giving her reluctant and sceptical (and very British) partner rudimentary lessons in dancing the Fox Trot.

The first instrumental record of the Fox Trot must be the one released in December, 1915 by the Van Eps Trio. This consisted of the American banjoist Fred van Eps, with Felix Arndt, the composer of the very popular 'novelty' piece *Nola*, at the piano, and an exuberant drummer named Eddie King. Comparing this with the smooth, sophisticated sleekness of fox-trots that followed in their thousands over the next thirty or more years, there seems little similarity, but it is possible to understand how and why the Fox Trot became so popular by listening to it. It was said that if you could walk in time to the music, you could Fox Trot.

The banjo was a very popular instrument in concerts of lighter music, and there was even an unaccompanied banjo solo of *Home, Sweet Home*, played by a violinist named Helen Sealy. Novelties in instrumental recording were not confined to music-hall artists, either; early in 1915 a Russian tympanon player named Sacha Votitchenko came to Hayes and recorded a strange work of his own called *Douleur (Sadness)*. A few months later, in June, the recording equipment was moved to the Cadbury Model Village in Bourneville, near Birmingham, to perpetuate the sound of the carillon there in old English melodies, and from America there came records by the Florentine Quartet, the Neapolitan Trio and the Venetian Trio, comprising between them violin, 'cello, flute and harp, playing delightfully restful music, much of it hitherto not recorded, some of it barely recorded since. On a more classical plane, the company issued in 1915 a series of records by Fritz Kreisler and Efrem Zimbalist, two of the greatest violinists of the time, playing Bach's Concerto in D minor for two violins, with string quartet. This was progress indeed; if Caruso, Melba and the other great singers had failed to convince anyone a decade or so earlier that the gramophone was not a raucous toy, but a musical instrument, here was surely proof indeed!

The Kreisler-Zimbalist records enjoyed a remarkable sale over the years; and other, perhaps less advanced but still high-grade instrumental records followed. There were piano records by Benno Moiseiwitsch, the great Ignace Jan Paderewski, Arthur de Greef and the young Australian composer Percy Grainger; Marie Hall, Maud Powell and Isolde Menges, three brilliant young girl violinists, were joined by Helen Sealy and Marjorie Hayward, the latter providing in 1918 the first recording of Beethoven's *Kreutzer* Sonata, with piano by the Australian girl Una Bourne, who had accompanied Nellie Melba on one of her tours in their homeland. The Philharmonic String Quartet on the middle-priced black label records matched in grace and artistry the Elman String Quartet on the red label celebrity series, and even a casual perusal of this catalogue and supplements reveals an awakening of public interest in music that was neither opera nor quasi-ragtime.

Nevertheless, if German and Austrian music was out of favour with some, American popular music was very much in favour with many. It is true that customers did not flock to buy the record of Will Halley singing *I'm Glad My Wife's In Europe* at the time of its issue in November, 1915—the American neutrality of that time was a sore point with many Britons who considered the sinking of the *Lusitania* by a

German torpedo off the Irish coast on May 7, 1915 was sufficient cause for an instant declaration of war on Germany by the American President Woodrow Wilson—but leaving aside such considerations, this remains as an excellent example of what might be termed a song-cartoon. (There were others, more patriotically inclined, in the repertoire of Tom Clare, the great entertainer at the paino, whose satirical comments on then-current events and the people in the public eye, usually sung to a well-known tune, rank as the audible equivalent of a cartoon from *Punch* by Sir Bernard Partridge or F. H. Townsend.) When America eventually declared war on the Central Powers on April 6, 1917, the record catalogues burgeoned with issues of a suitably patriotic flavour to welcome the 'doughboys', and the backbone of the military band section of the monthly lists, H. M. Coldstream Guards under their ramrod-backed musical director Capt. J. Mackenzie-Rogan, recorded *Hands Across The Sea* by Sousa. The public fairly ate it up as they had records of the same band playing *Colonel Bogey*—issued in August, 1914. Records of American patriotic songs, such as *What Kind Of An American Are You?* and *My Own United States*, however, made far less appeal than did the glorious-voiced Alma Gluck singing *Carry Me Back To Old Virginny* on a single-sided red label celebrity disc costing more than twice as much.

Submarine warfare claimed not only the *Lusitania* in major ships that were not outwardly at least concerned with hostilities, but the *Arabic*, on her way to America on August 18, 1915 and including on her passenger list the British actor Kenneth Douglas, who survived to record his experiences a month later. Another interesting eye-witness account of history in the making was provided six months later by 'The Man Who Dined With The Kaiser', an Italian journalist named Antonio Cippico who, with others of his profession, was invited to attend a royal luncheon during a tour of occupied Serbia, prior to Italy's entry into the war on the side of the Allies in May, 1915. Dr Cippico was never named on publicity material or the label of the record at the time, but his description of what he saw and his reactions to being in a position to observe the All-Highest and his entourage provide a unique historical document, albeit a somewhat biased one.

British record enthusiasts cared little for such things at the time, however; they vanished from the catalogue very shortly, for the best-sellers, especially among the younger customers, and those involved in the actual fighting, were often to be found among the original-cast recordings by stage favourites such as W. H. Berry (in *Tina*, *High Jinks* and *The Boy*), Gwendoline Brogden (*The Passing Show of 1915*), the incomparable Alice Delysia (*Carminetta*), Teddie Gerrard (*5064 Gerrard*), Lee White (*Cheep*) and Courtice Pounds (*Chu Chin Chow*).

The year 1917 witnessed the downfall of the Czarist régime in Russia as well as the entry of the USA into the battlefields; only a few months earlier, HMV records had been issued giving a language course in Russian, in the hope that commercial ties with Russia after the war would be strengthened. It was the year of compulsory military service, of food shortages (although rationing did not come into effect until early the following year), of torrential rain through the summer (ascribed by very amateur meteorologists to the heavy bombardments in Flanders), and of the first murmurs from America of a new musical craze called 'jazz'. (They sometimes spelt it jas, jass, jasz or jaz, but it meant the same thing.) Elsie Janis told us all about it in her revue *Hullo, America* in September, 1918; ten days after the German surrender of November 11, she went to Hayes and recorded *The Jazz Band* and other numbers from the same show. (They included *Give Me The Moonlight, Give Me The Girl*, four decades prior to Frankie Vaughan's adopting—and adapting—the same number.) The session was evidently interrupted to allow a prominent MP named Winston Churchill to record his suggestions and beliefs for the best ways of winning the peace. A month before, recording equipment had been transported to a farmhouse near Lille, which was then under attack by gas shells from a detachment of the Royal Garrison Artillery, and there, on October 9, the only authentic sounds of World War I were recorded and preserved forever. Before it could be edited and issued, however, Kaiser Wilhelm II had abdicated and fled to neutral Holland, where he died.

The theme of the first post-war Christmas was 'On with the dance, let joy be unconfined!' King Fox Trot ruled, and his principal courtiers, the Original Dixieland Jazz Band, were coming to play in London in the New Year. The man who had assassinated the heir to the Austrian throne four and a half years before, and had thus changed the world forever, was long dead himself; so were millions of his contemporaries. The world had changed indeed; with it, public taste. Nostalgia with a jazz flavour took over from flag-waving and drum-beating; serious music on records meant more than well-worn and oft-repeated arias from repeatedly staged operas or slices from symphonies by military bands, and complete works on several records in handsome albums were a proven commercial and artistic possibility. Radio, electric recording, television were still a little way in the future. Some preserve old newspapers and magazines in an effort to retain the authenticity of history; those who collect records such as those listed in these pages can preserve history with equal accuracy.

BRIAN RUST

Publisher's note
The publishers wish to thank EMI Limited for their kind help and co-operation.

THIS Catalogue of "His Master's Voice" Records is arranged under the following headings:

ALPHABETICAL LIST OF BANDS AND ORCHESTRAS

ALPHABETICAL LIST OF ARTISTS

Alphabetical List of Artists—*continued.*

Alphabetical List of Artists—*continued.*

Alphabetical List of Artists—*continued*.

Names commencing with the definite article in French, Italian and Spanish, *l*, *la*, *las*, *les*, *lo*, *los*. should be looked for under the word following the article.

Names commencing with the Italian definite article *i* and *il* should be looked for under the word following the article; for example, "Il Conte d' Essex" will be found indexed as "Conte d' Essex, il."

ABBREVIATIONS.

Mil. = Military.	**Roy.** = Royal.	**B.** = Band.
Orch. = Orchestra.	**Pat.** = Patrol.	**R.** = Regiment.
Gal. = Galop.	**Fin.** = Finale.	**Imit.** = Imitations.

Ovt. = Overture.	**M** = March.
Sel. = Selection.	**Med.** = Medley.
P.P. = Pot Pourri.	**Min.** = Minuet.

A — BANDS and ORCHESTRAS		Record No.	Page
Abanico, el	*Coldstream Gds.*	C 107	109
Abide with me	*Coldstream Gds.*	B 209	106
Aïda, Sels. I and II	*Coldstream Gds.*	C 870	113
"Airs and Graces"— Assyrian Scene—Two dances from: I, Cup Bearer's Dance; II, Bacchanale	*Palace Theatre Orch*	122 C 810	
"Airs and Graces"— Passionate Puppets— Sel. of music from: I, Doll Waltz, II, Harlequin Motif, III, Jack-in-the-box Dance, IV, Duet Dance "Doll and Jack"	*Palace Theatre Orch.*	122 C 810	
A la Hongroise	*De Groot's Orch.*	B 502	116
Alethea	*Bijou Cinema Orch.*	C 807	115
All aboard for Dixieland —One step	*Metropolitan Dance Band*	C 385	113
All people that on earth	*Coldstream Gds.*	B 209	106
"All the Winners," Parts I and II.	*Mayfair Orch.*	C 754	120
All we like sheep	*Coldstream Gds.*	C 106	109
Allies in Arms (Sels.)	*Metropolitan Mil. Band*	C 378	114
American Fantasia— Happy days in Dixie	*Coldstream Gds.*	C 825	112
American National Airs (a) Yankee Doodle; (b) Dixie; (c) Hail, Columbia	*Coldstream Gds.*	B 809	107
American National Airs (a) Red, White and Blue; (b) The Star Spangled Banner	*Coldstream Gds.*	B809	107
Amerinda Intermezzo	*Mayfair Orch.*	B 872	119
Amina—Egyptian Serenade	*Coldstream Gds.*	C 194	110
Amina Serenade	*Lincke's Orch.*	C 141	119

BANDS and ORCHESTRAS		Record No.	Page
Among the flowers	*Coldstream Gds.*	C 614	112
And the Glory of the Lord ("Messiah")	*Coldstream Gds.*	C 211	110
Angelus—"Scènes pittoresques"	*Albert Hall Orch.*	2-0599	28
Any Old Thing, Sels. I and II.	*Mayfair Orch.*	C 843	121
Any place is Heaven if you are near me	*De Groot and the Piccadilly Orch.*	C 816	117
Any time's kissing time ("Chu Chin Chow")	*De Groot and the Piccadilly Orch.*	C 778	117
Apache Rag, The ("Tails Up")	*De Groot and the Piccadilly Orch.*	B 982	116
Arabia March	*Opal Mil. Band*	B 849	114
Arcadians, The, Gems from	*Bohemian Orch.*	C 143	115
Arcadians, The (Sels.)	*Coldstream Gds.*	C 124	110
Arizona	*De Groot and the Piccadilly Orch.*	B 770	116
Arizona —Foxtrot	*Metropolitan Dance Band*	C 818	113
Arlésienne Suite, L', Adagietto for Strings.	*Albert Hall Orch.*	0837	28
Arlésienne Suite, L', Farandole	*Albert Hall Orch.*	0834	28
Arlésienne Suite, L', Prelude and Minuet	*Albert Hall Orch.*	0828	28
Arlette, Sels. I and II.	*Mayfair Orch.*	C 831	121
As you like it, Masque from, Nos. 1 and 2.	*Symphony Orch.*	2-0661	30
As you like it, Masque from, No. 3.	*The Symphony Orch.*	2-0665	30
"As you were," Sels. I and II	*Mayfair Orch.*	C874	121
At a Georgia Camp Meeting	*Sousa's Band*	B 246	114
At the Foxtrot Ball	*Mayfair Orch.*	B 287	119
Austria March	*Coldstream Gds.*	B 236	107
Automne Mélodie, L'	*Bijou Cinema Orch.*	C 653	115
Autumn Voices Waltz	*Gottlieb's Orch.*	C 179	117

C

Song	Artist	Record No.	Page
Kind Captain ("H.M.S. Pinafore")	Peter Dawson and Thorpe Bates	B 440	89
King Charles	K. Rumford	02197	35
King Neptune ("Merrie England")	George Baker	D 23	14
King's Song ("Lohengrin")	Journet	3-42550	13
Kipling Walk, The	Nat. D. Ayer	C 677	75
Kirchner Girl, The ("Vanity Fair")	Teddie Gerard	2-3218	54
Kiss me! ("Going up")	Marjorie Gordon and H. de Bray	04234	57
Kiss that made you min', The	Blanche Dare and E. Courtland	B 884	85
Kiss, The ("Il Bacio")	Violet Essex	03398	34
Kiss Waltz, The ("Soldier Boy")	Leigh and Courtland	C 864	87
Kitty! ("What a pity")	Charles Tree	4-2330	38
Kitty, what a pity	Topliss Green	B 564	61
Kyrie and Gloria	Westminster Cathedral Choir	04781	47

L

Song	Artist	Record No.	Page
La-bas dans la montagne ("Carmen")	Calvé and Dalmores	034023	2
La ci darem la mano ("Don Giovanni")	Eames and Gogorza	054071	5
La ci darem la mano	Battistini and Corsi	054104	2
La ci darem la mano	Ruffo and Pareto	054229	6
La Marseillaise	Chaliapin	032 61	10
La Marseillaise	Journet	032033	13
La Marseillaise (in English)(Rouget de L'Isle)	Robert Radford	02738	24
Lack-a-day	Ernest Crampton and Marjorie Vernon	C 457	67
Lad with the carrotty poll, The	Ernest Butcher	4-2899	32
Laddie in khaki	Renee Mayer	B 541	66
Lads who fought and won, The	Lauder	02688	55
Lady mine	Stewart Gardner	02475	34
Land of Delight	Hubert Eisdell	C 740	61
Land of Hope and Glory	Clara Butt	03239	7
Land of Hope and Glory	Clara Butt	03510	8
Land of Roses, A	Edna Thornton	2-3181	38
Land of the Long Ago, The	Hubert Eisdell	B 742	60
Land o' the Leal, The	Kirkby Lunn	03447	23
Land of the mountains (An teid thm leam arighinn og)	Phemie Marquis	B 974	66
Lang, lang syne	Lizzie Hunter	B 787	65
Langley Fair ("Songs of the Fair")	Thorpe Bates	C 434	59
Larboard Watch	John Harrison and Robert Radford	4453	40
Largo—"Rest" (Ombra mai fu)	Kirkby Lunn	03272	22
Largo (Ombra mai fu)	Edna Thornton	2-053051	38
Lascia ch'io pianga ("Rinaldo")	Kirby Lunn	2-053075	13
Lasciati amar	Caruso	7-52042	9
Lass of Killiecrankie	Lauder	02165	55

Song	Artist	Record No.	Page
Lass with the delicate air, The	Alma Gluck	2-3014	21
Lass with the delicate air, The	Olive Kline	B 667	66
Last Call, The	Topliss Green	C 775	61
Last rose of summer ("Marta")	Patti	03062	16
Last rose of summer	Tetrazzini	03241	18
Last Watch, The	Ruby Helder	C 449	65
Last Year	Percy Whitehead	B 351	63
Laugh and Sing	Evelyn Harding	B 750	64
Laughter's Song, The	Agnes Nicholls	03473	37
Laughing Song	H. Klauser	B 460	79
Laughing Song	Burt Shephard	B 468	82
Laughing Song	Henry Lytton	B 453	81
Laughing Song ("Manon Lescaut")	Amelita Galli-Curci	7-33017	12
Laughteri.is	Charles Penrose	B 459	81
Lead, kindly Light	Evan Williams	02267	24
Leaves and the wind	Clara Butt	03150	8
Legend of Kleinsack	Walter Hyde	02256	22
Less than the dust	Stewart Gardner	02221	34
Let me gaze ("Faust")	Matthews and Harrison	04147	40
Let me introduce you to my father	Berry and Dare	C 032	85
Let the bright Seraphim	Flora Woodman	03416	39
Let the great big world keep turning ("The Bing Girls are There")	Violet Loraine	03552	56
Let's all go raving mad ("Tails Up!")	L. Leigh, Courtland and Jefferies	B 967	89
Lift up your heads	Perceval Allen and Choir	B 382	63
Light in darkness	Phyllis Lett	03509	36
Lighterman Tom	Harry Dearth	02331	33
Like a ghost his vigil keeping ("Yeoman of the Guard")	Sullivan Operatic Party	B 410	91
Like stars above	John McCormack	02402	23
Lilac Domino, The—Operetta	—	B 903	89, 90
Lilac Domino, The ("Lilac Domino")	Louise Leigh	C 848	80
Lilac time	Ruth Vincent	03350	24
Lily of Laguna	Eugene Stratton	C 556	82
Lily, my Water Lily	Courtland and Jefferies	B 913	84
Listen to the Mocking Bird	Alma Gluck	03532	21
Little bit of Heaven, A	Denis O'Neil	C 661	62
Little bit of Heaven, A	Walter Jefferies	B 549	78
Little Brown Jug	Cecilian Quartet	B 361	65
Little Dutch Heaven for two, A	E. Courtland	B 762	76
Little girl, little girl	George Grossmith	—	75
Little grey home in the west	Evelyn Harding and Charles Nelson	B 729	67
Little grey home in the west	Alma Gluck	2-3030	21
Little grey home in the west	Reinald Werrenrath	B 318	63
Little grey home in the west	C. W. Harrison	B 511	61
Little home with you, A	Hubert Eisdell	B 850	60
Little Irish Girl	Denis O'Neil	B 559	62
Little Love, a little kiss, A	John McCormack	4-2373	23
Little Love, a little kiss, A	C .W. Harrison	B 512	61

Song	Artist	Record No.	Page
Manager of the Splitz Hotel, The	George Robey	C 551	82
Mandalay	Stewart Gardner	02362	34
Mandolinata	Gogorza	7-52020	11
Mandoline	—	2-033042	15
Manella Mia	Caruso	2-052091	9
M'appari tutt' amor ("Marta")	Caruso	052121	9
March on to Berlin	George Carvey	B 449	76
March of the Men of Harlech	Stewart Gardner and Ernest Pike	2-4213	39
Marechiare	Ruffo	052383	16
Marguerite	Herbert Teale	B 839	63
Marseillaise, La	Chaliapin	032261	10
Marseillaise, La	Journet	032038	13
Marseillaise, La (in English) (Rouget de l'Isle)	Robert Radford	02738	24
Mary	John Harrison	3-2390	34
Mary	Hugh Friel	B 970	61
Mary Morrison	Alexander Macgregor	B 976	62
Mary of Allandale	Herbert Teale	C 838	63
Massa's in de cold, cold ground	Violet Oppenshaw	B 607	66
Massa's in de cold, cold ground	Minster Singers	B 368	69
Mattinata ('Tis the Day) (Leoncavallo)	Martinelli	7-52087	14
Mattinata	Melba	053107	15
Mavis	John McCormack	4-2601	23
May morning, A	Evan Williams	4-2206	24
Mayor of Mudcomdyke	George Robey	C 551	82
Meet me round the corner	Moya Mannering and Leslie Henson	B 484	88
Megan	Hubert Eisdell	B 740	60
Melanie	Hubert Eisdell	B 741	61
Melisande	Herbert Teale	B 525	62
Melisande in the Wood	Palgrave Turner	B 338	67
Memory, A	Kirkby Lunn	2-3192	22
Memory, A	Renée Mayer	B 624	66
Mentra Gwen	Evan Williams	4-2115	24
Merce, dilette amiche ("I Vespri Siciliani")	Tetrazzini	2-053118	18
Meriggiata	Titta Ruffo	2-52685	16
Merrie England—Opera	—	—	44 / 45
Merry Farewell, A ("Carminetta")	Mdlle. Delysia	03589	54
Message, The	Ruby Helder	C 758	65
Message Boy	Lauder	02300	55
Messiah—Oratorio	—	—	70
Messmates	Thorpe Bates	B 559	59
Messmates, Ahoy! ("H.M.S. Pinafore")	Sullivan Operatic Party	C 514	89
Meynell Hunt	Robert Radford	3-2859	37
Mi chiamano Mimi	Melba	2-053025 / 03071	14 / 15
Mi chiamino Mimi ("La Bohême")	Lucrezia Bori	2-053103	7
Mi chiamano Mimi	Donalda	053104	11
Mia canzone, La	Caruso	7-52068	9
Mia madre ("Carmen")	De Lucia and Huguet	054172	9
Micaela's Air ("Carmen")	Tetrazzini	2-053118	18
Midshipmite, The	Thorpe Bates	C 433	59
Mifanwy	Carmen Hill	2-3117	35
Mighty like a rose	Violet Oppenshaw	C 709	66

Song	Artist	Record No.	Page
Mignon, Gems from	Grand Opera Company	04537	45
Mikado, The—Opera	—	—{	90 / 91
Milagro de la Virgen, El	Caruso	2-062002	10
Military Stamp, The ("Soldier Boy")	L. Leigh and W. Jefferies	B 968	87
Mimi io son ("Bohême")	Farrar and Scotti	054203	5
Minaccie, Le ("Forza del Destino")	Caruso and Amato	2-054028	3
Minor objections ("Theodore & Co.")	George Grossmith	02693	54
Minstrel Boy, The	John McCormack	4-2071	23
Minstrel Parade, The	Ethel Levey	C 611	88
Mio dolce pastorale ("Pique Dame")	Destinn and Duchene	2-034020	4
Mirror Song ("Tales of Hoffmann")	William Samuell	02614	37
Miserere Scene ("Trovatore")	Caruso and Alda	2-054007	3
Miserere ("Il Trovatore")	Martinelli and Destinn	2-054063	4
Misérére	Jones-Hudson and Pike	B 340	68
Mississippi Days	Courtland and Jefferies	B 817	84
Mister Bear	Renee Mayer	B 541	66
Mistletoe Bough, The	P. Allen, E. Thornton, J. Harrison and S. Gardner	04122	41
Molly Bawn	John McCormack	02286	23
Molly Brannigan	John McCormack	4-2379	23
Molly Brannigan	Plunket Greene	4-2017	34
Mon cœur est pénétré d'épouvante ("Faust")	Caruso and Farrar	2-034005	3
Mon cœur s'ouvre à ta voix	Mdlle. Brohly	033064	32
Mon cœur s'ouvre à ta voix ("Samson and Delilah")	Kirkby Lunn	2-033033	13
Month o' May, The ("Merrie England")	Edna Thornton and Chorus	D 25	44
Moon hath raised her lamp above, The ("The Lily of Killarney")	John McCormack and Reinald Werrenrath	2-4205	25
Moon hath raised her Lamp above, The	John Harrison and Robert Radford	04014	40
Moonstruck	Gertie Millar	C 530	81
More humane Mikado never did in Japan exist, A	Robert Radford	D 10	91
More in sorrow than in anger	George Robey	C 548	82
Mormon's Song, The	George Robey	B 466	82
Morning Hymn	Gervase Elwes	B 322	61
Morning in the Highlands ("Three Cheers")	Blanche Tomlin	03546	56
Morning Prayer, Church of England	Rev. Canon Fleming	—	47
Morte d'Otello	Tamagno	52674 / 052068	18 / 18
Morte di Valentine	Scotti	2-032001	17
Mother ("Soldier Boy")	E. Courtland and Joseph Reed	C 866	85
Mother Machree	John McCormack	4-2142	23
Mother Machree	C. W. Harrison	B 666	61

Song	Artist	Record No.	Page
Wandering Minstrel I, A	John Harrison	02073 / D 3	35 / 90
Wandern, Das	Sir G. Henschel	7-42006	22
Watchman, The	Peter Dawson	C 756 {	60 / 77
Watchman, what of the night ?	John Harrison and Robert Radford	04058	40
Watch your step— Revue	—	—{	104 / 105
Wayfarer's Night Song	Dearth	4-2554	33
We are four men of Windsor ("Merrie England")	E. Thornton, B. Jones, G. Baker, E. Holland, John Harrison, E. Pike and Chorus	D 24	44
We are two proper men ("Merrie England")	G. Baker and E. Holland	D 19	44
We all go home the same way	Lauder	02781	55
We'd better bide a wee	Lizzie Hunter	B 787	65
We don't want a lot of flags a-flying	Courtland and Jefferies	B 817	84
We parted on the shore	Lauder	02224	55
We parted the best of friends	George Robey	C 571	82
We three Kings of Orient are	Westminster Cathedral Choir	04800	47
Wearin' o' the green	John McCormack	4-2213	23
Wedding Day Song ("Carminetta")	Marie Blanche	03587	54
Wedding of Lauchie McGraw	Lauder	02138	55
Wedding of Sandy McNab	Lauder	02132	55
Wee Deoch an' Doris, A	Lauder	02371	55
Wee hoose 'mang the heather	Lauder	02446	55
Wee Jean McGregor	Lauder	4-2146	55
Weep ye no more, sad fountains	Carmen Hill and Marcus Thompson	3-4015	33
We'll ne'er let the old flag fall	Edward Hamilton	B 855	61
Wells of Sleep, The	Hubert Eisdell and Bessie Jones	B 873	67
Were you not to Koko plighted ("Mikado")	V. Essex and John Harrison	D 6	91
Were I thy bride ("Yeomen of the Guard")	Jones-Hudson	B 407	91
We're all crazy ("Some") Musical Comedy	W. Jefferies	B 689	78
We've been married just one year	B. Jones and M. Johnson	B 473	86
What a duke should be ("Theodore & Co.")	Davy Burnaby and Chorus	B 753	76
What a naughty old Gentleman ("My Lady Frayle")	Gretchen Yates	C 679	83
What do you want to make those eyes at me for ?	W. Jefferies	B 842	79
What have I to do with Thee ? ("Elijah")	Jones-Hudson and P. Dawson		70
What ho! Mr. Watteau ("As you were")	Blanche Dare	B 987	77
What if I were young again ("The Boatswain's Mate")	Rosina Buckman	03527	21

Song	Artist	Record No.	Page
What is life without love ("High Jinks")	W. H. Berry	02679	53
What is done, you never can undo ("Lilac Domino")	Louise Leign and Randell Jackson	C 850	87
What kind of an American are you ?	Peerless Quartet	B 855	68
What's it got to do with you ?	Margaret Cooper	03380	33
When a foeman bares his steel ("Pirates of Penzance")	Sullivan Operatic Party	B 401	90
When all was young	Edna Thornton	03419	38
When all was young	Kirkby Lunn	03257	13
When a merry maiden marries ("Gondoliers")	Sullivan Operatic Party	B 398	90
When a pullet is plump ("Chu Chin Chow")	Courtice Pounds	4-2812	56
When a wooer ("Yeomen of the Guard")	Sullivan Operatic Party	B 411	91
When Cupid first this old world trod ("Merrie England")	C. Mott, E. Thornton, B. Jones and C. Pike	D 28	45
When hands meet	P. Allen, E. Thornton, J. Harrison and R. Radford	04096	41
When I come back to you	W. Jefferies	B 760	78
When I get back to Bonnie Scotland	Lauder	02135	55
When Irish eyes are smiling	Gerald Orme	B 449	81
When it's apple blossom time	Dunlap and MacDonough	B 343	67
When I leave the world behind	Cobbett and Walker	B 711	83
When Johnny comes marching home	Cecilian Quartet	B 363	68
When love calls	E. Crampton	B 504	59
When love is but tender and sweet	Walter Hyde	02257	22
When love is calling	Herbert Teale	B 911	63
When love is kind	Gluck	3987	21
When maiden loves	Carrie Tubb	B 404	91
When Myra sings	Flora Woodman	03407	39
When my ships come sailing home	John McCormack	02610	23
When other lips	Ruby Helder	B 299	65
When our gallant Norman foes	Florence Venning	B404	91
When Paderevski plays that baby grand	Cobbett & Walker	B 654	83
When Richard the First sat on the Throne	Ada Reeve	2-3184	56
When Richard the First sat on the Throne	Nelson Jackson	B 445	78
When rocked on the billows	Courtice Pounds	02697	37
When shadows gather	John McCormack	4-2070	23
When shadows gather	Herbert Cave	4-2860	32
When the Angelus is ringing	Mixed Quartet	B 370	68
When the Autumn leaves are falling ("Zig-Zag")	L. Leigh and F. Berens	C 793	87
When the Bells of Peace are ringing	Courtland and Jefferies	B 877	84
When the crimson sun has set	Westminster Abbey Choir	04798	47

Celebrity Section

ABRIDGED LIST

For Complete List see Celebrity Catalogue

□ □ □

INDEX OF OPERAS

OPERAS—*continued.*

OPERAS—*continued.*

OPERAS—*continued.*

Index: 'His Master's Voice' Operatic Records—*cont.*

OPERAS—*continued.*

OPERAS—*continued.*

OPERAS—*continued.*

CELEBRITY RECORDS

SEXTETS

CARUSO, GALLI-CURCI, EGENER, JOURNET, DE LUCA and BADA

12-inch record 30s.

2—054067 Chi mi frena (" Lucia di Lammermoor ")   *(Donizetti)* **(79)**

CARUSO, SCOTTI, JOURNET, SEMBRICH, SEVERINA and DADDI

12-inch record 30s.

054205 Chi mi frena (" Lucia di Lammermoor ")   *(Donizetti)* **(78)**

QUINTET

CARUSO, HEMPEL, DUCHÊNE, ROTHIER and DE SEGUROLA

12-inch record 25s.

2—054050 E scherzo, od è folia (" Un Ballo in Maschera," Act I.)   *(Verdi)* **(80)**

QUARTETS

BATTISTINI, COLAZZA, SILLICH, E. CORSI and Chorus

12-inch record 12s. 6d.

054107 O sommo Carlo (" Ernani ")   *(Verdi)* **(78)**

CARUSO, ALDA, JACOBY and JOURNET

12-inch records 20s.

2—054031 Che vuol dir ciò (" Marta ")   *(Flotow)* **(80)**

CARUSO, FARRAR, GILIBERT and JOURNET

12-inch records 20s.

2—034003 " Seigneur Dieu " (" Faust "—Garden Scene, Part I.) *(Gounod)* **(80)**
2—034004 " Eh quoi, toujours seule" (" Faust "—Garden Scene Part II.) *(Gounod)* **(80)**

CARUSO, GALLI-CURCI, PERINI and DE LUCA

12-inch record 16s. 6d.

2—054066 Un dì, se ben rammentomi (" Rigoletto ")   *(Verdi)* **(79)**

CARUSO, HEMPEL, ROTHIER, DE SEGUROLA and Chorus

12-inch record 20s.

2—054052 La rivedrà nell' estasi (" Un Ballo in Maschera," Act I.)   *(Verdi)* **(80)**

These records should be played with " His Master's Voice " needles, sold only in boxes bearing our copyright picture, " His Master's Voice," on the lid

CELEBRITY RECORDS

QUARTETS—*continued.*

CARUSO, SCOTTI, ABOTT, HOMER and Chorus
12-inch record 25s.
054117   Bella figlia dell' amore (" Rigoletto ")   *(Verdi)* **(80)**

CARUSO, SCOTTI, FARRAR and VIAFORA
12-inch record 25s.
054204   Quartet from " La Bohême "   *(Puccini)* **(80)**

HUGUET, PAOLI, CIGADA and PINI CORSI
10-inch record 6s.
54339   Versa il filtro nella tazza sua (" Pagliacci ")   *(Leoncavallo)* **(76)**

TRIOS

CARUSO, FARRAR and JOURNET
12-inch record 20s.
2—034002   Alerte ! ou vous êtes perdus.   Prison Scene, Part III (" Faust ")
       (Gounod) **(80)**

CARUSO, JOURNET and SCOTTI
12-inch record 20s.
2—034001   The Duel, Act III (" Faust ")   *(Gounod)* **(80)**

TITTA RUFFO, ISCHIERDO and TITTA FOSCA
10-inch record 8s.
54359   Di geloso amor (" Il Trovatore ")   *(Verdi)* **(78)**

DUETS

BATTISTINI and EMILIA CORSI
12-inch record 12s. 6d.
054104   La ci darem la mano (" Don Giovanni ")   *(Mozart)* **(78)**

BONINSEGNA and BOLIS
12-inch record 9s.
2—054071   M'ami, m'ami (Duet, Act II) (" Un Ballo in Maschera ")   *(Verdi)* **(79)**

CALVÉ and DALMORES
12-inch record 16s. 6d.
034023   Là-bas dans la montagne (" Carmen ")   *(Bizet)* **(79)**

The figures in brackets at end of selections indicate the speed at which the records · · · · should be played · · · ·

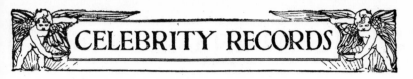

DUETS—*continued*

CARUSO and ALDA

12-inch record 20s.

2—054007   Miserere Scene (with Chorus of the Metropolitan Opera, New
York)   (" Il Trovatore ")   *(Verdi)* **(82)**

CARUSO and AMATO

12-inch records 20s.

2—054027   " Invano, Alvaro " (" La Forza del Destino," Part I.)   *(Verdi)* **(81)**
2—054028   " Le minaccie, i fieri accenti " (" La Forza del Destino," Part II.) *(Verdi)* **(81)**

CARUSO and ANCONA

12-inch record 20s.

054134   Del tempio al limitar (" Pescatori di Perle ")   *(Bizet)* **(78)**

CARUSO and DESTINN

12-inch record 20s.

2—054053   Sento una forza indomita (" Il Guarany ")   *(Gomez)* **(79)**

CARUSO and FARRAR

12-inch records 20s.

2—034005   Mon cœur est pénétré d'épouvante, Prison Scene, Part I (" Faust ")
     (Gounod) **(81)**
2—034006   Attends ! voici la rue.   Prison Scene, Part II (" Faust ")   *(Gounod)* **(81)**
2—034011   Il se fait tard (" Faust ")   *(Gounod)* **(81)**
2—034012   O nuit d'amour (" Faust ")   *(Gounod)* **(80)**
2—034018   On l'appelle Manon (" Manon ")   *(Massenet)* **(79)**
054201   O quanti occhi fisi (" Madama Butterfly ")   *(Puccini)* **(79)**

CARUSO and GADSKI

12-inch records 20s.

2—054005   Final Duet, Part I (" Aïda ")   *(Verdi)* **(81)**
2—054006   Final Duet, Part II (" Aïda ")   *(Verdi)* **(81)**

CARUSO and GLUCK

WITH METROPOLITAN OPERA CHORUS

10-inch record 12s. 6d.

7—54006   Brindisi (" Traviata ")   *(Verdi)* **(79)**

CARUSO and HOMER

12-inch records 20s.

054198   Ai nostri monti (" Il Trovatore ")   *(Verdi)* **(82)**
2—054017   Mal reggendo all' aspro assalto (" Il Trovatore ")   *(Verdi)* **(81)**

CARUSO and JOURNET

12-inch records 20s.

2—034013   Crucifix   *(Faure)* **(81)**
2—034000   O merveille (" Faust ")   *(Gounod)* **(81)**

**These records should be played with " His Master's
Voice " needles, sold only in boxes bearing our
copyright picture, " His Master's Voice," on the lid**

CELEBRITY RECORDS

DUETS—*continued*

CARUSO and RUFFO
12-inch record 20s.

2—054049 Si pel ciel, Act II, Scene V (" Otello ")   (*Verdi*) (79)

CARUSO and SCOTTI
12-inch records 20s.

054127	Ah Mimi, tu più (" La Bohême ")	(*Puccini*) (82)
2—054014	Duet, Act I (" Madama Butterfly ")	(*Puccini*) (80)
2—054013	Duet, Act II (" Madama Butterfly ")	(*Puccini*) (80)
054070	Solenne in quest'ora (" Forza del Destino ")	(82)

CLARA BUTT and KENNERLEY RUMFORD
12-inch records 12s. 6d.

04046	Night Hymn at Sea	(*Goring Thomas*) (Key C)
04045	Snowdrops	(*Lehmann*) (Key E)
04060	The Keys of Heaven	(*L. Broadwood*) (81)

(It is important that these records should be played in the keys indicated)

DE LUCIA and HUGUET
12-inch record 9s.

054172 Mia Madre (" Carmen ")   (*Bizet*) (78)

DESTINN and DINH GILLY
12-inch record 16s. 6d.

2—054062 Good-night (Folk Song)   (78)

DESTINN and DUCHÈNE
12-inch record 16s. 6d.

2—034020 Mio dolce pastorale (" Pique Dame," Act II)   (*Tschaikowsky*) (79)

DESTINN and KIRKBY LUNN
12-inch record 16s. 6d.
ORCHESTRA CONDUCTED BY MR. PERCY PITT

2—054023 Ebben qual nuovo fremito (" Aïda ")   (*Verdi*) (78)

DESTINN and MARTINELLI
WITH METROPOLITAN OPERA CHORUS
12-inch record 16s. 6d.

2—054063 Miserere (" Il Trovatore ")   (*Verdi*) (79)

DE TURA, CIGADA and Chorus
12-inch record 9s.

054144 A voi tutti salute (" Cavalleria Rusticana ")   (*Mascagni*) (77)

**The figures in brackets at end of selections
indicate the speed at which the records
. . . . should be played . . . .**

DUETS—*continued*

EAMES and DE GOGORZA
12-inch record 16s. 6d.
054071   La ci darem la mano (" Don Giovanni ")   *(Mozart)* **(78)**

FARRAR and AMATO
WITH METROPOLITAN OPERA CHORUS
12-inch record 16s. 6d.
2—034021   Si tu m'aimes (" Carmen ")   *(Bizet)* **(79)**

FARRAR and CLEMENT
10-inch record 8s.
7—34002   Au clair de la lune   *(Lully)* **(79)**

FARRAR and HOMER
12-inch record 16s. 6d.
054126   Duet of the Flowers (" Madama Butterfly ")   *Puccini* **(81)**

FARRAR and JOURNET
12-inch records 16s. 6d
2—034009   Scène de l'Eglise, Part I (" Faust ")   *(Gounod)* **(81)**
2—034008   Scène de l'Eglise, Part II (" Faust ")   *(Gounod)* **(81)**

FARRAR and SCOTTI
12-inch records 16s. 6d.
054203   Mimi, io son (" La Bohême ")   *(Puccini)* **(80)**
054202   Ora a noi ! (" Madama Butterfly ")   *(Puccini)* **(80)**
10-inch record 12s. 6d.
7—34000   Barcarolle (" Contes d'Hoffmann ")   *(Offenbach)* **(81)**

KNÜPFER and YADLOVKER
12-inch records 9s.
044252   Charfreitagszauber (Good Friday Spell), Part I (" Parsifal ")   *(Wagner)* **(80)**
044253   Charfreitagszauber, Part II (" Parsifal ")   *(Wagner)* **(80)**

LUCREZIA BORI and DE SEGUROLA
10-inch record 8s.
7—64000   El puñao de rosas—Romanza   *(Chapí)* **(79)**

McCORMACK and KIRKBY LUNN
12-inch record 16s. 6d.
2—054040   T'eri un giorno ammalato (" I Giojelli della Madonna ")   *(Wolf-Ferrari)* **(80)**

These records should be played with " His Master's Voice " needles, sold only in boxes bearing our copyright picture, " His Master's Voice," on the lid

CELEBRITY RECORDS

DUETS—*continued*

McCORMACK and LUCREZIA BORI
12-inch record 16s. 6d.
2—054055 Parigi, o cara (" Traviata," Act III)   *(Verdi)* **(78)**
10-inch record 12s. 6d.
7—54003 O soave fanciulla (" La Bohême ")   *(Puccini)* **(79)**

McCORMACK and LUCY MARSH
12-inch records 9s.
2—054059 O terra, addio (" Aïda ")   *(Verdi)* **(80)**
2—034019 Parle-moi de ma mère (" Carmen ")   *(Bizet)* **(78)**

McCORMACK and SAMMARCO
12-inch record 16s. 6d.
2—054011 Ah Mimi, tu più (" La Bohême ")   *(Puccini)* **(80)**

MELBA and CARUSO
12-inch records 20s.
054129 O soave fanciulla (" La Bohême ")   *(Puccini)* **(82)**

MELBA and GILIBERT (the late)
12-inch record 20s.
034014 Un ange est venu   *(Bemberg)* **(80)**

SEMBRICH and SCOTTI
12-inch record 16s. 6d.
054074 Pronta io son (" Don Pasquale ")   *(Donizetti)* **(78)**

TITTA RUFFO and DE SEGUROLA
10-inch record 8s.
54360 Suoni la tromba (" I Puritani ")   *(Bellini)* **(78)**

TITTA RUFFO and GRAZIELLA PARETO
12-inch record 12s. 6d.
054229 La ci darem la mano (" Don Giovanni ")   *(Mozart)* **(80)**

ALMA GLUCK and ZIMBALIST
12-inch records 9s.
03349 Angels' Serenade (Serenata)   *(Braga)* **(78)**
2—033038 Le Nil (The Nile)   *(Leroux)* **(79)**
10-inch records 6s.
7—33005 Elégie (Song of Mourning)   *(Massenet)* **(78)**
7—33011 Le bonheur est chose légère (" Timbre d'Argent ")   *(Saint-Saëns)* **(78)**
2—3107 Old folks at home (Swanee River) (violin obb. of Dvořák's " Humoreske ")   *(Foster)* **(78)**

The figures in brackets at end of selections indicate the speed at which the records . . . . should be played . . . .

6

CELEBRITY RECORDS

AMATO, PASQUALE (baritone)

12-inch records 12s. 6d.

2—052053 Di Provenza il mar (" Traviata ")   *(Verdi)* **(78)**
2—052079 O vecchio cor che batti—Scena and Romanza (" I due Foscari ") *(Verdi)* **(79)**

10-inch record 8s.

7—52057 Torna a Surriento   *(G. B. & E. di Curtis)* **(79)**

(On page 3 are given some superb duets by Amato and Caruso)

BATTISTINI, MATTIA (Baritone)

12-inch records 12s. 6d.
WITH PIANOFORTE ACCOMPANIMENT

052303—Allor che tu coll' estro (" Tannhäuser ")   *(Wagner)* **(81)**
052144 A tanto amor (" La Favorita ")   *(Donizetti)* **(76)**
052315 Bella e di sol vestita (" Maria di Rohan ")   *(Donizetti)* **(81)**
052302 Brindisi (" Amleto ")   *(Ambroise Thomas)* **(81)**
052146 Eri tu che macchiavi quell' anima (" Un Ballo in Maschera ")   *(Verdi)* **(76)**
052403 Malia (The Spell)   *(Tosti)* **(79)**
052321 O ma charmante   *(Quaranta)* **(80)**
052313 Recit. " O santa medaglia," Aria " Dio possente " (" Faust ")   *(Gounod)* **(79)**
052148 Perchè tremar (" Zampa ")   *(Herold)* **(76)**
052312 Te Deum (" Tosca," Act I) (with Chorus)   *(Puccini)* **(76)**

BONINSEGNA, CELESTINA, (Soprano)

12-inch record 9s.

053089 Madre pietosa (" La Forza del Destino ") (with Chorus of La Scala Theatre, Milan)   *(Verdi)* **(76)**

BORI, LUCREZIA (Soprano)

12-inch records 12s. 6d.

2—033046 Depuis le jour (" Louise ")   *(Charpentier)* **(78)**
2—053103 Mi chiamano Mimi (" La Bohême ")   *(Puccini)* **(78)**
2—033051 Romance—Elle a fui (" Contes d'Hoffmann ")   *(Offenbach)* **(78)**

BUTT, CLARA (Contralto)

12-inch records 12s. 6d.

03179 Abide with me   *(Liddle)* (Key C)
03223 A Summer Night (with 'cello obbligato played by Mr. W. H. Squire) *(Goring Thomas)*
03368 (a) A youth once loved a maiden   *(M. V. White)*
     (b) The tears that night   *(M. V. White)*
03186 Barbara Allan   (Key D)
03155 Believe me, if all those endearing young charms (accompanied by the composer)   *(Landon Ronald)* (Key E flat)
03399 God shall wipe away all tears (" The Light of the World ") *(Sullivan)*
03176 He shall feed His flock (" Messiah "   *(Handel)* (Key F)
03152 Husheen   *(Needham)* (Key B flat)
2—033010 Il segreto   *(Donizetti)* (Key B flat)
03178 Kathleen Mavourneen   *(Crouch)* (Key C)
03239 Land of Hope and Glory (accompanied by Band of H.M. Coldstream Guards, conducted by Major J. Mackenzie Rogan, M.V.O., Mus.Doc.) *(Elgar)*

These records should be played with " His Master's Voice " needles, sold only in boxes bearing our copyright picture, " His Master's Voice," on the lid

CELEBRITY RECORDS

Butt, Clara—*continued*

12-inch records 12s. 6d.

03510	Land of Hope and Glory (orchestra conducted by Mr. Arthur Godfrey)		*(Elgar)*
03283	My ain folk (accompanied by Mr. Harold Craxton)		*(Laura Lemon)*
03154	Ombra mai tu	*(Handel)*	(Key E flat)
03425	O Divine Redeemer		*(Gounod)*
03177	O rest in the Lord (" Elijah ")	*(Mendelssohn)*	(Key C)
2—053088	Rendi'l sereno al ciglio—Aria (" Sosarme ")		*(Handel)*
03150	The leaves and the wind		*(Leoni)* (Key C)
03156	The little silver ring	*(Chaminade)*	(Key D flat)
03151	The Lost Chord	*(Sullivan)*	(Key E flat)
03157	The Promise of Life		*(Cowen)* (Key D)
03222	Three fishers went sailing		*(Hullah)*
03220	Time's garden (with 'cello obbligato, played by Mr. W. H. Squire)		*(Goring Thomas)*
03299	Where corals lie (" Sea Pictures ")		*(Elgar)*
03224	Will he come		*(Sullivan)*
03305	Women of Inver (accompanied by Mr. Harold Craxton) *(Loughborough)*		

(It is important that these records should be played in the keys indicated)

(The approximate speed is **81***)*

(For Duet Records by Madame Clara Butt and Mr. Kennerley Rumford see page 4)

CALVÉ (Mezzo-Soprano)

12-inch records 12s. 6d.

033060	Charmant oiseau (" La Perle du Brésil ")	*(David)*	(80)
033059	Habañera (" Carmen ")	*(Bizet)*	(79)
033058	Les tringles des sistres (" Carmen ")	*(Bizet)*	(80)
03092	The old folks a home	*(Foster)*	(79)
053183	Voi lo sapete (" Cavalleria Rusticana ")	*(Mascagni)*	(79)

CARUSO (Tenor)

WITH ORCHESTRAL ACCOMPANIMENT

12-inch records 12s. 6d.

2—052083	Addio alla madre (" Cavalleria Rusticana ")	*(Mascagni)*	(78)
02470	Agnus Dei	*(Bizet)*	(79)
052210	Ah si ben mio (" Il Trovatore ")	*(Verdi)*	(82)
2—032000	Air de la fleur (" Carmen ")	*(Bizet)*	(81)
2—052101	Angelo casto e bel—Romanza (" Il Duca d'Alba ")	*(Donizetti)*	(78)
052224	Celeste Aïda (" Aïda ")	*(Verdi)*	(82)
2—052032	Cielo e mar (" Gioconda ")	*(Ponchielli)*	(81)
2—052060	Core 'ngrato (Neapolitan Song)	*(Carolli)*	(81)
2—052086	Cujus animam (" Stabat Mater ")	*(Rossini)*	(80)
02396	Dreams of long ago (in English)	*(Caruso)*	(78)
2—052077	Fenesta che lucive (Neapolitan Song)	*(Bellini)*	(79)
2—052058	For all Eternity (Eternamente)	*(Mascheroni)*	(81)
2—052065	Forse la soglia—Scène : Ma se m'e forza perderti—Romanza (" Un Ballo in Maschera ")	*(Verdi)*	(80)
2—052035	Good-bye (" Addio ")	*(Tosti)*	(81)
2—032008	Hosanna	*(Granier)*	(81)
052154	Ideale	*(F. Paolo Tosti)*	(80)
2—052007	Il fior che avevi a me (" Carmen ")	*(Bizet)*	(81)
02585	Ingemiso—" Requiem Mass "	*(Verdi)*	(78)

The figures in brackets at end of selections indicate the speed at which the records . . . . should be played . . . .

CELEBRITY RECORDS

Caruso—*continued*

WITH ORCHESTRAL ACCOMPANIMENT
12-inch records 12s. 6d.

052209	In terra solo (" Don Sebastien ")	(*Donizetti*)	(82)
2—052061	Io non ho che una povera stanzetta (" La Boheme ")	(*Leoncavallo*)	(81)
2—032005	Je suis seul--Récit. ; Ah ! fuyez, douce image—Air (" Manon ")		
		(*Massenet*)	(80)
2—052068	La Danza—Tarantella Napolitana	(*Rossini*)	(81)
2—032012	Les rameaux (The Palms)	(*Fauré*)	(78)
2—052005	Mamma mia che vo sape	(*Nutile*)	(82)
2—052091	Manella mia (Neapolitan Song)	(*Valente*)	(79)
052121	M'appari tutt' amor (" Marta ")	(*Flotow*)	(79)
2—052034	No, Pagliacci, non son (" Pagliacci ")	(*Leoncavallo*)	(81)
2—032022	Noël (Cantique de Noël) (Christmas Hymn)	(*Adolphe Adam*)	(77)
2—052006	Oh tu che segno agl' angeli (" Forza del Destino ")	(*Verdi*)	(81)
052157	O Paradiso (" L'Africana ")	(*Meyerbeer*)	(82)
2—052076	Parmi veder le lagrime (" Rigoletto ")	(*Verdi*)	(80)
2—052098	Perche ? (Why ?)	(*Pennino*)	(78)
2—052008	Più bianca (" Gli Ugonotti ")	(*Meyerbeer*)	(82)
2—032021	Prête-moi ton aide (Lend me your aid) (" La Reine de Saba ")	(*Gounod*)	(78)
032030	Salut, demeure (" Faust ")	(*Gounod*)	(78)
2—052107	Santa Lucia (Neapolitan Folk Song)		(79)
062005	Spanish Serenade (" Lolita ")	(*Buzzi—Pecchia*)	(81)
052120	Spirito gentil (" La Favorita ")	*Donizetti*	(78)
2—052067	Tarantella sincera (Humorous Neapolitan Song)		
		(*Vincenzo de Crescenzo*)	(81)
2—052059	Testa adorata (" La Bohême ")	(*Leoncavallo*)	(81)
02397	The Lost Chord (in English)	(*Sullivan*)	(81)
2—052108	Tiempo antico (Olden Times)	(*Caruso*)	(79)
2—052064	Una furtiva lagrima (" L'Elisir d'Amore ")	(*Donizetti*)	(78)
032070	Valse lente (" Adorables Tourments ")	(*Caruso—Barthelemy*)	(82)
052159	Vesti la giubba (" Pagliacci ")	(*Leoncavallo*)	(82)

10-inch records 8s.
WITH HARP ACCOMPANIMENT

7—52018	La Siciliana (" Cavalleria Rusticana ")		(82)

WITH ORCHESTRAL ACCOMPANIMENT

7—52055	Amor mio (My Love)—Vocal Waltz	(*Ricciardi*)	(79)
7—32004	Because (sung in French)	(*Guy d'Hardelot*)	(78)
7—52026	Canta pe'me (Neapolitan Song)	(*de Curtis*)	(78)
7—52073	Cielo turchino (Neapolitan Song)	(*Coiciano*)	(78)
2—52489	Di quella pira (" Il Trovatore ")	(*Verdi*)	(78)
7—52025	Di' tu se fidele (" Ballo in Maschera ")	(*Verdi*)	(78)
7—52039	Donna non vidi mai (Act I, " Manon Lescaut ") (harp accompaniment by		
	Mme. Regis-Rossini)	(*Puccini*)	(78)
7—52002	E lucevan le stelle (" Tosca ")	(*Puccini*)	(80)
4—2122	For you alone (in English)	(*Geehl*)	(81)
7—52043	Guardann'a luna (Lovely Moon)	(*Crescenzo*)	(78)
7—32009	Hantise d'amour (Love's Haunting)	(*Szulc*)	(78)
2—52641	La donna è mobile (" Rigoletto ")	(*Verdi*)	(82)
7—52068	La mia canzone	(*Tosti*)	(78)
7—52042	Lasciati amar (Let me love thee)	*Leoncàvallo*	(79)
4—2205	Love is mine (in English)	(*Gartner*)	(81)
7—52080	Luna d'estate (Summer Moon)	(*Tosti*)	(79)
7—52003	Magiche note (" La Regina di Saba ")	(*Goldmark*)	(32)
7—52017	Ora e per sempre addio (" Otello ")	(*Verdi*)	(81)

These records should be played with " His Master's Voice " needles, sold only in boxes bearing our copyright picture, " His Master's Voice," on the lid

CELEBRITY RECORDS

Caruso—*continued*

10-inch records 8s.
WITH ORCHESTRAL ACCOMPANIMENT

7—32000	Pour un baiser	(*Tosti*)	**(82)**
2—52642	Questa o quella (" Rigoletto ")	(*Verdi*)	**(80)**
7—52004	Recondita armonia (" Tosca ")	(*Puccini*)	**(81)**
7—32006	Sérénade de Don Juan	(*Tschaikovsky*)	**(78)**
7—32008	Sérénade espagnole	(*Landon Ronald*)	**(78)**
4—2480	Trusting eyes (in English)	(*Gartner*)	**(79)**
4—2375	Your eyes have told me what I did not know (in English)	(*O'Hara*)	**(78)**

12-inch records 12s. 6d.
WITH PIANOFORTE ACCOMPANIMENT

052074	Celeste Aïda (" Aïda ")	(*Verdi*)	**(78)**
2—062002	El milagro de la Virgen	(*Chapi*)	**(79)**
2—062003	La partida (" Canción española ")	(*Alvarez*)	**(78)**
052086	Serenata (" Don Pasquale ")	(*Donizetti*)	**(78)**

10-inch record 8s.

7—52038	Pimpinella (Florentine Song)	(*Tschaikovsky*)	**(80)**

(Many concerted numbers with Caruso are given on pages 1 and 4)

CARUSO and ELMAN (Violin)

12-inch records 16s. 6d.

02472	Ave Maria (" Hail Mary ")	(*Percy B. Kahn*)	**(78)**
2—032010	Elégie—Mélodie	(*Massenet*)	**(78)**
2—032018	Si vous l'aviez compris—Mélodie	(*Denza*)	**(78)**
2—032017	Les deux sérénades	(*Leoncavallo*)	**(78)**

CHALIAPIN (Russian Bass)

12-inch records 12s. 6d.

022187	Arise, red sun (Russian Folk Song) sung in Russian		**(78)**
022222	Farewell of Boris, Finale, Part I (" Boris Godounóv ") sung in Russian		
		(*Moussorgsky*)	**(78)**
022223	Death of Boris, Finale, Part II (" Boris Godounóv ") sung in Russian		
		(*Moussorgsky*)	**(79)**
022225	Do not weep, child (" The Demon ") sung in Russian	(*Rubinstein*)	**(79)**
022093	How the King went to war	(*Kenneman*)	**(78)**
022208	In the town of Kasan (" Boris Godounóv ") sung in Russian		
		(*Moussorgsky*)	**(78)**
052353	Ite sul colle, o Druidi (" Norma ")	(*Bellini*)	**(80)**
052354	La calunnia e un venticello (" Il Barbiere di Siviglia ")	(*Rossini*)	**(81)**
032261	La Marseillaise	(*De L'Isle*)	**(79)**
022226	Now let us depart (Church Hymn) (with Chorus) sung in Russian		
		(*Strokin*)	**(79)**
032260	Pourquoi donc se taisent les voix	(*Glazounoff*)	**(79)**
052387	Recit.: " Le rovine son pueste " · Evocazione " Donne, che riposate "		
	(" Roberto il Diavolo ")	(*Meyerbeer*)	**(79)**
022095	Sérénade, Mephisto (" Faust ")	(*Gounod*)	**(78)**
022224	Song of Galitzky (" Prince Igor ") sung in Russian	(*Borodin*)	**(80)**
052356	Vi ravisso, o luoghi ameni (" La Sonnambula ")	(*Bellini*)	**(80)**
052388	Vien, la mia vendetta (" Lucrezia Borgia ")	(*Donizetti*)	**(80)**

The figures in brackets at end of selections
indicate the speed at which the records
. . . . should be played . . . .

CELEBRITY RECORDS

CICCOLINI, GUIDO (Tenor)
12-inch record 9s.
2—052082 Che gelida manina (" La Bohême ") *(Puccini)* **(80)**

DALMORES (Tenor)
10-inch record 8s.
3—32989 C'est elle (" Contes d'Hoffmann ") *(Offenbach)* **(81)**

DE GOGORZA (Baritone)
12-inch record 9s.
02628 The Pipes of Pan *(Elgar)* **(79)**
10-inch records 6s.
7—52020 Mandolinata *(Paladilhe)* **(81)**
7—52015 O sole mio *(Di Capua)* **(80)**

DE LUCA (Baritone)
10-inch record 6s.
7—52095 Il balen (" Il Trovatore ") *(Verdi)* **(79)**

DE LUCIA, FERNANDO (Tenor)
12-inch record 9s.
052111 Addio, Mignon (" Mignon ") *(Thomas)* **(77)**

DE MURO (Tenor)
12-inch record 9s.
2—052119 Esultate (" Otello ") *(Verdi)* **(79)**

DESTINN, EMMY (Soprano)
12-inch records 12s. 6d.
2—053054 Ritorna vincitor (" Aïda ") *(Verdi)* **(81)**
2—053104 Suicidio ! Act IV (" Gioconda ") *(Ponchielli)* **(78)**
2—053052 Un bel dì vedremo (" Madama Butterfly ") *(Puccini)* **(81)**
2—053053 Vissi d' arte (" La Tosca ") *(Puccini)* **(80)**

DE TURA (Tenor) (with chorus)
10-inch record 6s.
2—52594 Brindisi (" Cavalleria Rusticana ") *(Mascagni)* **(77)**

DONALDA, PAULINE (Soprano)
12-inch record 9s.
053104 Mi chiamano Mimi (" La Bohême ") *(Puccini)* **(77)**

These records should be played with " His Master's Voice " needles, sold only in boxes bearing our copyright picture, " His Master's Voice," on the lid

CELEBRITY RECORDS

EAMES, EMMA (Soprano)

12-inch record 12s. 6d.

033019 Chanson d'amour ('cello obbligato played by Joseph Hollman) *(Hollman)* **(77)**

FARRAR, GERALDINE (Soprano)

12-inch records 12s. 6d.

2—033012	Air des bijoux (" Faust ")	*(Gounod)* **(81)**
2—033021	Le Roi de Thulé (" Faust ")	*(Gounod)* **(79)**
053176	Un bel dì vedremo (" Madama Butterfly ")	*(Puccini)* **(81)**

10-inch record 8s.

7—53002 Entrance of Butterfly (" Madama Butterfly ") *(Puccini)* **(80)**

FRANZ, PAUL (Tenor)

12-inch records 12s. 6d.

032239	Air de la fleur (" Carmen ")	*(Bizet)* **(81)**
032238	O celeste Aïda (" Aïda ")	*(Verdi)* **(80)**
032212	Récit du Graal (" Lohengrin ")	*(Wagner)* **(80)**
032227	Salut ! Tombeau ! (" Romeo et Juliette ")	*(Gounod)* **(80)**

10-inch record 8s.

4—32274 Arrêtez, ô mes frères (" Samson et Dalila ") *(Saint-Saëns)* **(80)**

GADSKI, JOHANNA (Soprano)

12-inch record 12s. 6d.

043077 Isolde's Liebestod (" Tristan und Isolde ") *Wagner* **(80)**

GALLI-CURCI, AMELITA (Soprano)

10-inch record 6s.

7—33017 Laughing Song (Bourbonnaise) (" Manon Lescaut ") (sung in French— L'Eclat de rire) *(Auber)* **(79)**

12-inch records 9s.

2—053128 Il dolce suono (Mad Scene, Act III, " Lucia di Lammermoor ") *(Donizetti)* **(78)**
2—063006 La partida (" Canción española ") *(Alvarez)* **(78)**

GALVANY, MARIA (Soprano)

12-inch records 9s.

053165	L'Incantatrice (Walzer)	*(Arditi)* **(80)**
053200	Spargi d'amaro pianto (" Lucia di Lammermoor ")	*(Donizetti)* **(80)**

GAY, MARIA (Mezzo-Soprano)

10-inch record 8s.

53516 Seguidilla (" Carmen ") *(Bizet)* **(79)**

The figures in brackets at end of selections indicate the speed at which the records . . . . should be played . . . .

CELEBRITY RECORDS

HEMPEL, FRIEDA (Soprano)

12-inch records 12s. 6d.

053265	Cavatina (" Ernani ")	*(Verdi)*	**81**
033127	La Villanelle	*(dell' Acqua)*	**(79)**
053290	Oh, d'amore (" Mirella ")	*(Gounod)*	**(81)**

JOURNET, MARCEL (Bass)

12-inch records 9s.

2—032009	Bénédiction des poignards (" Les Huguenots ") (with chorus)	*(Meyerbeer)*	**(79)**
032038	La Marseillaise	*(De l'Isle)*	**(77)**
042130	O du mein holder Abendstern (" Tannhäuser ")	*(Wagner)*	**(76)**
032036	Serenade Mephistofele (" Faust ")	*(Gounod)*	**(77)**

10-inch records 6s.

7—32002	Invocation (" Faust ")	*(Gounod)*	**(80)**
3—42550	King's Song (" Lohengrin ")	*(Wagner)*	**(76)**
7—32001	Le veau d'or (" Faust ")	*(Gounod)*	**(80)**

KURZ, SELMA (Soprano)

12-inch records 9s.

043180	Czardas (" Die Fledermaus ") (Nightbirds)	*(Strauss)*	**(80)**
053275	Saper vorreste (" Un Ballo in Maschera ")	*(Verdi)*	**(81)**

LIPKOVSKAYA, LYDIA (Russian Soprano)

12-inch records 9s.

023140	Pizzicato (" Sylvia Ballet ")	*(Délibes)*	**(79)**
023135	Valse (" Coppelia Ballet ")	*(Délibes)*	**(79)**

LUNN, KIRKBY (Contralto)

12-inch records 12s. 6d.

2—033032	Amour, viens (" Samson et Dalila ")	*(Saint-Saëns)*	**(81)**
2—033030	Card Song (" Carmen ")	*(Bizet)*	**(80)**
2—053121	Che farò (" Orfeo ")	*(Gluck)*	**(78)**
2—033029	Habanera (" Carmen ")	*(Bizet)*	**(81)**
2—053075	Lascia ch'io pianga (" Rinaldo ")	*(Handel)*	**(81)**
2—033033	Mon cœur s'ouvre à ta voix (" Samson et Dalila ")	*(Saint-Saëns)*	**(30)**
2—053068	Non più di fiori (clarinet obbligato by Mr. Manuel Gomez) (" La Clemenza ")	*(Mozart)*	**(80)**
2—053000	O don fatale (" Don Carlos ")	*(Verdi)*	**(80)**
03440	O righteous God (Gerechter Gott) (" Rienzi ")	*(Wagner)*	**(79)**
2—033031	Printemps qui commence (" Samson et Dalila ")	*(Saint-Saëns)*	**(81)**
2—033028	Seguidilla (" Carmen ")	*(Bizet)*	**(80)**
2—053067	Stride la vampa (" Il Trovatore ")	*(Verdi)*	**(80)**
2—053074	Voce di donna o d'angelo (" La Gioconda ")	*(Ponchielli)*	**(81)**
03257	When all was young (" Faust ")	*(Gounod)*	**(80)**

10-inch records 8s.

7—33012	Habañera (" Carmen ")	*(Bizet)*	**(78)**
7—33013	Seguidilla (" Carmen ")	*(Bizet)*	**(78)**

(For Kirkby Lunn's Ballad Records see pages 22 and 23)

CELEBRITY RECORDS

MARTINELLI (Tenor)

10-inch records 6s.

7—52076	Come rugiada al cespite (" Ernani ")	*(Verdi)*	**(77)**
7—52056	Donna non vidi mai (" Manon Lescaut ") **(Act I)**	*(Puccini)*	**(79)**
7—52051	E lucevan le stelle (" Tosca ")	*(Puccini)*	**(79)**
7—52067	Ideale—Melodia	*(Tosti)*	**(80)**
7—52053	La donna è mobile (Act III) (" Rigoletto ")	*(Verdi)*	**(78)**
7—52087	Mattinata (" 'Tis the Day ") (composed expressly for the Gramophone Co., Ltd.)	*(Leoncavallo)*	**(78)**
7—52060	Recondita armonia (" Tosca ")	*(Puccini)*	**(79)**

12-inch records 9s.

2—052100	Celeste Aïda (" Aïda ")	*(Verdi)*	**(78)**
2—052099	Serenata	*(Mascagni)*	**(78)**

McCORMACK, JOHN (Tenor)

12-inch records 9s.

2—052023	Fra poco a me ricovero (" Lucia di Lammermoor ")	*(Donizetti)*	**(82)**
2—052027	Il fior che avevi a me (" Carmen ")	*(Bizet)*	**(80)**
2—052111	Non è ver	*(Mattei)*	**(78)**
2—052026	Per viver vicino (" La Figlia del Reggimento ")	*(Donizetti)*	**(80)**
2—052021	Racconto di Rodolfo (" La Bohême ")	*(Puccini)*	**(82)**
2—052028	Salve, dimora (" Faust ")	*(Gounod)*	**(80)**
2—052024	Tu che a Dio spiegasti (" Lucia di Lammermoor ")	*(Donizetti)*	**(80)**
2—052022	Una furtiva lagrima (" L'Elisir d'Amore ")	*(Donizetti)*	**(81)**

10-inch record 6s.

7—52061	Funiculi, Funicula (with chorus)	*(Denza)*	**(79)**

(For McCormack's ballad records see page 23).

McCORMACK, JOHN, and KREISLER

12-inch record 9s.

02540	Angels' Serenade	*(Braga)*	**(78)**

10-inch record 6s.

4—2700	Serenata	*(Moszkovski)*	**(78)**

MELBA (Soprano)

12-inch records 12s. 6d.

WITH ORCHESTRAL ACCOMPANIMENT

2—053028	Addio (" La Bohême ")	*(Puccini)*	**(80)**
053108	Ah! fors è lui (" Traviata ")	*(Verdi)*	**(78)**
2—033002	Air des bijoux (" Faust ")	*(Gounod)*	**(81)**
03523	Annie Laurie	*(Scott)*	**(78)**
2—053021	Ave Maria (" Otello ")	*(Verdi)*	**(80)**
053110	Caro nome (" Rigoletto ")	*(Verdi)*	**(78)**
2—053019	Elsa's dream ("Lohengrin")	*(Wagner)*	**(80)**
03206	Good-bye	*(Tosti)*	**(80)**
03203	Lo ! here the gentle lark (with flute)	*(Bishop)*	**(81)**
053112	Mad scene (" Lucia di Lammermoor ")	*(Donizetti)*	**(78)**
033028	Mad scene (Part I) (" Hamlet ")	*(Thomas)*	**(78)**
033027	Mad scene (Part II) (" Hamlet ")	*(Thomas)*	**(78)**
2—053025	Mi chiamano Mimi (" La Bohême ")	*(Puccini)*	**(80)**

The figures in brackets at end of selections indicate the speed at which the records . . . . should be played . . . .

CELEBRITY RECORDS

Melba—*continued*

12-inch records 12s. 6d.
WITH ORCHESTRAL ACCOMPANIMENT

03363	Old Folks at Home (in English)	*(Foster)*	**(80)**
03204	O lovely night	*(Landon Ronald)*	**(80)**
033062	On m'appelle Mimi (" La Bohême ")	*(Puccini)*	**(79)**
2—033020	Pleurez, mes yeux (" Le Cid ")	*(Massenet)*	**(80)**
053211	Salce (Willow Song) (" Otello ")	*(Verdi)*	**(78)**
2—053023	Se saran rose	*(Arditi)*	**(81)**
2—033023	Sevillana (" Don César de Bazan ")	*(Massenet)*	**(80)**
03089	Sweet bird (with flute)	*(Handel)*	**(78)**
2—053020	Vissi d'arte (" La Tosca ")	*(Puccini)*	**(80)**
2—053027	Voi che sapete (" Nozze di Figaro ")	*(Mozart)*	**(80)**

10-inch records 12s. 6d.

3615	Auld lang syne (acc. by Coldstream Guards)		**(76)**
3616	Come back to Erin (acc. by Coldstream Guards)		**(76)**

12-inch records 12s. 6d.

03072	Aubade (" Le Roi d'Ys ") (with piano)	*(Lalo)*	**(76)**
03069	Ave Maria (with piano and 'cello)	*(Gounod)*	**(76)**
03188	Bid me discourse	*(Bishop)*	**(80)**
03036	Chant Hindu (acc. by composer)	*(Bemberg)*	**(76)**
03369	Comin' thro' the rye (with piano)		**(80)**
03049	Home, sweet home (piano accompaniment)		**(76)**
03371	John Anderson, my Jo	*(White)*	**(79)**
053114	La Serenata (harp accompaniment)	*(Tosti)*	**(78)**
2—033037	Le temps de lilas (with piano)	*(Chausson)*	**(78)**
03047	Lo, here the gentle lark	*(Bishop)*	**(76)**
03370	Magdalen at Michael's Gate (with piano)	*(Lehmann)*	**(78)**
053107	Mattinata (accompaniment by Melba)	*(Tosti)*	**(78)**
03071	Mi chiamano Mimi (" La Bohème ")	*(Puccini)*	**(76)**
03016	Nymphes et Sylvains (with piano)	*(Bemberg)*	**(76)**
03199	O, for the wings of a dove	*(Mendelssohn)*	**(81)**
03070	Pastorale (piano accompaniment)	*(Bizet)*	**(78)**
03028	Porgi amor (piano accompaniment)	*(Mozart)*	**(78)**
2—033042	(a) Romance (*Bourget*), (b) Mandoline (*Debussy*) (piano by Prof. Lapierre)		**(79)**
033026	Si mes vers avaient des ailes (harp accompaniment)	*(Hahn)*	**(78)**
03328	Spring (piano by Landon Ronald)	*(Henschel)*	**(81)**
03046	Sur le lac (piano accompaniment by composer)	*(Bemberg)*	**(76)**
03027	Three Green Bonnets (piano accompaniment)	*(d'Hardelot)*	**(78)**
03035	Valse Aria (" Romeo and Juliette ") (with piano)		**(76)**

10-inch records 12s. 6d.

3619	Away on the hill there runs a stream (accompanied by the composer)	*(Landon Ronald)*	**(76)**
7—33004	Chanson triste (accompanied by Prof. Lapierre)	*(Duparc)*	**(80)**
3575	Chant vénétien (piano accompaniment by composer)	*(Bemberg)*	**(76)**
3576	Les anges pleurent (with piano)	*(Bemberg)*	**(73)**

MELBA and KUBELIK

12-inch records 16s. 6d.

03333	Ave Maria (piano by Lapierre)	*(Gounod)*	**(80)**
2—053083	L'amerò, sarò costante (" Il Rè Pastore ") (piano by Prof. Lapierre)	*(Mozart)*	**(78)**

These records should be played with " His Master's Voice " needles, sold only in boxes bearing our copyright picture, " His Master's Voice," on the lid

CELEBRITY RECORDS

PAOLI, ANTONIO (Tenor)

12-inch records 9s.

052167	No, Pagliacci, non son (" Pagliacci ")	*(Leoncavallo)*	**(79)**
052166—	Vesti la giubba (" Pagliacci ")	*(Leoncavallo)*	**(79)**

PATTI, ADELINA (Soprano)

12-inch records 12s. 6d.

03055	Batti, batti (" Don Giovanni ")	*(Mozart)*	**(78)**
03061	Comin' thro' the rye		**(76)**
03083	Connais-tu le pays (" Mignon ")	*(Thomas)*	**(76)**
03053	Home, sweet Home	*(Sir H. Bishop)*	**(76)**
03056	Jewel Song (" Faust ")	*(Gounod)*	**(75)**
03079	La Serenata	*(Tosti)*	**(76)**
03054	Old folks at home		**(76)**
03052	Pur dices'i	*(Lotti)*	**(76)**
03059	Robin Adair		**(77)**
03062	The last rose of summer	*(Thomas Moore)*	**(76)**
03051	Voi che sapete (" Nozze di Figaro ")	*(Mozart*	**(75)**
03064	Within a mile o' Edinboro' Town		**(77)**

PLANÇON, POL (Bass), The late

12-inch records 12s. 6d.

052217	Berceuse (" Mignon ")	*(Thomas)*	**(81)**
032023	Le cor	*(A. Flegier)*	**(79)**
032027	Nazareth	*(Gounod)*	**(78)**
032032	Noël	*(Adam)*	**(76)**
032077	Nonnes qui reposez (" Robert le Diable ")	*(Meyerbeer)*	**(80)**
052117	Qui sdegno (" Il Flauto Magico ")	*(Mozart)*	**(78)**

ROSING, M. VLADIMIR (Russian Tenor)

12-inch records 9s.

2—022000	Forgive Me, Oh Divinity (" La Dame de Pique," Act I, Scene II)		
		(Tchaikovsky)	**(80)**
2—022001	If you ever knew (" La Dame de Pique ")	*(Tchaikovsky)*	**(79)**

RUFFO, TITTA (Baritone)

12-inch records 12s. 6d.

052188	Brindisi (" Amleto ")	*(Thomas)*	**(78)**
2—052090	Credo (" Otello ")	*(Verdi)*	**(79)**
2—052104	Dio possente (" Faust ")	*(Gounod)*	**(79)**
2—052103	I due Granatieri (Two Grenadiers)	*(Schumann)*	**(79)**
052383	Marechaire—(Neapolitan Song)	*(Tosti)*	**(79)**

10-inch records 8s.

7—52048	Aimé! fanciullo ancora (" Thais ")	*(Massenet)*	**(78)**
7—52035	Buona Zaza, del mio buon tempo (" Zaza," Act II)	*(Leoncavallo)*	**(78)**
2—52624	Disse il saggio (" Malena ")	*(E. Titta Ruffo)*	**(78)**
7—62013	El guitarrico	*(A. Peres Soriano)*	**(79)**
7—52049	E suonan le campane	*(Ettore Titta Ruffo)*	**(78)**
2—52623	Ma tu sfiorata (" Malena ")	*(E. Titta Ruffo)*	**(78)**
2—52685	Meriggiata (composed expressly for The Gramophone Co., Ltd.)		
		(Leoncavallo)	**(80)**

The figures in brackets at end of selections indicate the speed at which the records . . . . should be played . . . .

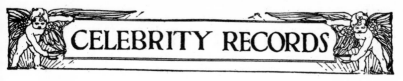
Ruffo, Titta—*continued*

10-inch records 8s.

7—52040	Non penso a lei (I think not of you)	*(Ferradini)*	(78)
7—52062	Oh che m'importa ?	*(Ettore Titta-Ruffo)*	(80)
7—52070	Rammenta i lieti dì (" Faust ")	*(Gounod)*	(79)
2—52621	Spettro santo (" Amleto ")	*(Thomas)*	(78)
7—52029	Suono e fantasia	*(Capolongo)*	(80)
7—52031	Zaza piccola Zingara (" Zaza ")	*(Leoncavallo)*	(79)

SAMMARCO, G. MARIO (Baritone)

12-inch records 12s. 6d.

2—052073	Aprila, bella, la fenestrella (" I Giojelli della Madonna ") (with Chorus)	*(Wolf-Ferrari)*	(81)
2—052044	Cruda funesta (" Lucia di Lammermoor ")	*(Donizetti)*	(81)
2—052009	Il sogno (" Otello ")	*(Verdi)*	(80)
2—052042	Non più andrai (" Nozze di Figaro ")	*(Mozart)*	(81)

SCHUMANN-HEINK, ERNESTINE (Mezzo-Soprano)

12-inch record 12s. 6d.

043111	Stille Nacht, heilige Nacht (Still night, holy night)	*(Gruber)*	(81)

SCOTTI, ANTONIO (Baritone)

12-inch records 12s. 6d.

052225	Cantabile Scarpia (" Tosca ")	*(Puccini)*	(81)
2—052003	Dio possente (" Faust ")	*(Gounod)*	(81)
052091	Eri tu (" Un Ballo in Maschera ")	*(Verdi)*	(77)
2—032001	Morte di Valentine (" Faust ") (with Chorus)	*(Gounod)*	(81)
052113	{ (a) Serenata (" Don Giovanni ")	*(Mozart)*	(76)
	{ (b) Quand ero paggio (" Falstaff ")	*(Verdi)*	(76)

10-inch record 8s.

7—52019	Scétate—Serenade (Awake !)	*(T. Mario Costa)*	(78)

SEMBRICH, MARCELLA (Soprano)

12-inch record 12s. 6d.

053054	Ah ! fors' è lui (" La Traviata ")	*(Verdi)*	(77)

SMIRNOFF (Russian Tenor)

12-inch record 12s. 6d.

052410	Se il mio nome (" Barbiere di Siviglia ") (sung in Italian)	*(Rossini)*	(79)

TAMAGNO, FRANCESCO (Tenor), The late

The price of these special Tamagno Records is £1 each.

10-inch records

52688	Corriam, corriamo (" William Tell ")	*(Rossini)*	(75)
52678	Di quella pira (" Il Trovatore ")	*(Verdi)*	(75)
52673	Esultate (" Otello ")	*(Verdi)*	(74)
52681	Figli miei v'arrestante (" Samson and Delilah ")	*(Saint-Saëns)*	(75)
52676	Improvviso (" Andrea Chenier ")	*(Giordano)*	(75)

These records should be played with " His Master's Voice " needles, sold only in boxes bearing our copyright picture, " His Master's Voice," on the lid

CELEBRITY RECORDS

Tamagno, Francesco—*continued*

10-inch records

52677	Inno (" Il Profeta ")	(*Meyerbeer*)	(**74**)
52674	Morte d'Otello (" Otello ")	(*Verdi*)	(**74**)
52682	O muto asil (" William Tell ")	(*Rossini*)	(**75**)
52675	Ora e per sempre (" Otello ")	(*Verdi*)	(**75**)
52684	Quand nos jours s'éteindront comme une chaste flamme (" Herodiade ")	(*Massenet*)	**75**
52679	Sopra, Berta. l'amor mio (" Il Profeta ")		(**75**)

12-inch records

052101	Esultate (" Otello ")	(*Verdi*)	(**75**)
052100	Improvviso (" Andrea Chenier ")	(*Giordano*)	(**74**)
052068	Morte d'Otello (" Otello ")	(*Verdi*)	(**74**)
052103	O muto asil (" William Tell ")	(*Rossini*)	(**74**)
052102	Ora e per sempre (" Otello ")	(*Verdi*)	(**75**)

TETRAZZINI (Soprano)

12-inch records 12s. 6d.

2—053063	Ballata d'Ofelia (Mad Scene) (" Hamlet ")	(*Ambroise Thomas*)	(**78**)
2—053034	Bel raggio (" Semiramide ")	(*Rossini*)	(**80**)
2—053033	Bolero (" I Vesperi Siciliani ")	(*Verdi*)	(**80**)
2—053085	D'amor sull'ali rosee (" Il Trovatore ")	(*Verdi*)	(**79**)
2—053087	Grande Valse, Op. 10	(*Venzano*)	(**79**)
03286	Home, sweet Home (in English)	(*Bishop*)	(**80**)
2—053040	L'Eco (The Echo)	(*Carl Eckert*)	(**79**)
2—053118	Mercè, dilette amiche ("I Vesperi Siciliani ")	(*Verdi*)	(**79**)
2—053113	Micaela's Air (" Carmen ")	(*Bizet*)	(**80**)
2—053115	O luce di quest' anima (" Linda di Chamounix ")	(*Donisetti*)	(**79**)
2—053114	Pace, mio Dio ! (" La Forza del Destino ")	(*Verdi*)	(**77**)
2—053092	Pastoral from " R salinda "	(*Veracini*)	(**79**)
2—053058	Polonaise (" Mignon ")	(*Thomas*)	(**79**)
2—053055	Prayer—Entrance Scene (with Chorus) (" Lakmé ")	(*Délibes*)	(**80**)
2—053064	Ritcrna vincitor (" Aïda ")	(*Verdi*)	(**81**)
2—053116	Solveig's Song, Op. 23, No. 1 (" Peer Gynt ")	(*Grieg*)	(**80**)
2—03034	Tacea la notte placida ("Il Trovatore ")	(*Verdi*)	(**78**)
03241	The last rose of summer (in English)	(*Moore*)	(**80**)
03280	The Swallows (in English)	(*Cowen*)	(**81**)
2—053065	Variations	(*Proch*)	(**81**)
2—053072	Vien, diletto (" I Puritani ")	(*Bellini*)	(**79**)
2—053013	Waltz (" Mirella ")	(*Gounod*)	(**80**)

YADLOVKER (Tenor)

12-inch records 9s.

042375	Grälserzählung (" Lohengrin ")	(*Wagner*)	(**80**)
042376	Preislied (" Meistersinger ")	(*Wagner*)	(**80**)

10-inch record 6s.

4—42519	Am stillen Herd (" Meistersinger ")	(*Wagner*)	(**81**)

The figures in brackets at end of selections indicate the speed at which the records . . . . should be played . . . .

CELEBRITY RECORDS

INSTRUMENTAL

□ □ □ □ □

PIANOFORTE

PADEREVSKI

12-inch records 12s. 6d.

2—045506	Aufschwung	*(Schumann)* **(80)**
045560	Hark ! Hark ! the lark—Serenade	*(Schubert-Liszt)* **(80)**
05567	La Bandoline—Rondeau	*(Couperin)* **(79)**
05565	Le Carillon de Cythère (The Chimes of Cythera)	*(Couperin)* **(80)**
045530	Minuet in G Major	*(Paderevski)* **(80)**

(For other piano records by famous pianists see pages 26, 49)

VIOLIN

ELMAN STRING QUARTET (Mischa Elman and Messrs. Bak, Rissland, and Nagel of the Boston Symphony Orchestra)

12-inch record 9s.

08056	Quartet in G Major—Andante	*(C. von Dittersdorf)* **(78)**

10-inch record 6s.

8195	Quartet in E Flat—Allegro (Finale)	*(C. von Dittersdorf)* **(79)**

(For other violin records by famous violinists see pages 26, 27, 50, 127, 128)

KUBELIK

12-inch records 9s.

07952	Dudziarz Mazurka	*(Wieniavski)* **(78)**
07978	Mélodie de Gluck	(arr. by *A. Wilhelmj*) **(78)**
07954	Perpetuum Mobile	*(Ries)* **(78)**
07951	Pierrot Serenade	*(Alberto Randegger, Jr.)* **(78)**
07988	Spanish Dance, No. 8, op. 26	*(Sarasate)* **(80)**
07953	Zapateado	*(Pablo de Sarasate)* **(78)**

These records should be played with " His Master's Voice " needles, sold only in boxes bearing our copyright picture, " His Master's Voice," on the lid

FAUST (GOUNOD)

🔲 🔲 🔲 🔲 🔲

PART I

12-in.	2—034000	" O merveille "	.. .. ..	Caruso and Journet
10-in.	7— 32001	" Le veau d'or "	.. .. ..	Journet
12-in.	2—052003	" Dio possente "	.. .. ..	Scotti
12-in.	2—034001	" Que voulez-vous, messieurs "—Duel—Act III.		Caruso, Journet, and Scotti
12-in.	2—033021	" Le Roi de Thulé "	.. .. ..	Geraldine Farrar
12-in.	2—033012	" Air des bijoux "	.. .. ..	Geraldine Farrar

PART II

12-in.	2—034003	" Seigneur Dieu "—Garden Scene, Part I		Caruso, Geraldine Farrar, Mdme. Gilibert, and Journet
12-in.	2—034004	" Eh quoi, toujours seule "—Garden Scene, Part II	.. .. ..	Caruso, Geraldine Farrar, Mdme. Gilibert, and Journet
12-in.	2—034011	" Il se fait tard "	.. .. ..	Caruso and Farrar
12-in.	2—052028	" Salve, dimora "	.. .. ..	McCormack
12-in.	2—034012	" O nuit d'amour "	.. .. ..	Caruso and Farrar

PART III

10-in.	7—32002	" Invocation "	.. .. ..	Journet
12-in.	2—034009	" Scène de l'Eglise," Part I ..	..	Geraldine Farrar and Journet
12-in.	2—034008	" Scène de l'Eglise," Part II	..	Geraldine Farrar and Journet
12-in.	2—034005	" Mon cœur est pénétré d'épouvante "—Prison Scene, Part I		Caruso and Geraldine Farrar
12-in.	2—034006	" Attends ! voici la rue "—Prison Scene, Part II		Caruso and Geraldine Farrar
12-in.	2—034002	" Alerte ! ou vous êtes perdus "—Prison Scene, Part III		Caruso, Geraldine Farrar, and Journet

The figures in brackets at end of selections indicate the speed at which the records . . . . should be played . . . .

VIOLET LABEL RECORDS

BUCKMAN, ROSINA (Soprano)

10-inch Record 5s.

2-3308 Waiata Poi (A Maori love song)—*Hill*

12-inch records 7s.

03527 (a) Contrariness (" The Boatswain's Mate "—*Dr. Ethel Smyth*) (79)
(b) What if I were young again (" The Boatswain's Mate"—*Dr. Ethel Smyth*) (79)

03610 It was a dream (*Cowen*) (79)
03591 Tacea la notte placida (in English) (The night calm and serene) (" Il Trovatore "—*Verdi*) (78)

BUTT, CLARA (Contralto)

(*For Madame Clara Butt's other Records see Special Celebrity Section*)

12-inch record (Special Label) 7s.

03240 God Save the King (accompanied by the Band of the Coldstream Guards, conducted by Major J. Mackenzie Rogan, M.V.O., Mus. Doc.) (80

CULP, JULIA (Mezzo-Soprano)

10-inch record 5s.

2-3027 All through the night (Old Welsh Air) (78)

DAVIES, BEN (Tenor)

12-inch records 7s.

02514 To Mary (*M. V. White*) (79)
02498 The Star of Bethlehem (*Adams*) (78)

GLUCK, ALMA (Soprano)

10-inch records 5s.

2-3015 Carmena (Vocal Waltz) (*H. Lane Wilson*) (79)
2-3036 Comin' thro' the rye (Scotch Air) (78)
3983 From the land of the sky blue water (*Cadman*) (78)
2-3198 I'se gwine back to Dixie (Old Plantation Song) (with chorus) (*C. A. White*) (78)
2-3030 Little grey home in the west (with 'cello obbligato and orchestra) (*Löhr*) (80)

GLUCK, ALMA—*continued.*

3978 Lo! here the gentle lark (with flute obbligato and orchestra) (*Sir H. Bishop*) (80)
3964 Red, red rose (*Cottenet*) (78)
3995 Song of the Chimes (Cradle Song) (*Worrell*) (78)
2-3119 The braes o' Balquhidder (Scotch Air) (79)
3963 The Brook (*Dolores*) (79)
2-3014 The lass with the delicate air (*Arne* arr *A. L.*) (80)
2-3016 The Swallows (*Sir F. H. Cowen*) (78)
3987 When love is kind (*Moore*) (79)
3980 Will o'' the Wisp (*Spross*) (79)

12-inch records 7s.

2-053066 Balatella (Bird Song) (" Pagliacci ") (80)
2-033045 Berceuse de Jocelyn (Angels guard thee) (*Godard*) (79)
03415 Carry me back to Old Virginny (*Bland*) (with Male Chorus) (78)
03532 Listen to the Mocking Bird (with bird voices by Charles Kellogg) (*A. Hawthorne*), arr. by *S. Winner* (78)
03533 My Old Kentucky Home (*Stephen C. Foster*) (with male chorus) (79)
03467 Old Black Joe (*Foster*) (with Male Chorus) (79)
2-033034 Rossignols amoureux (Nightingale s Passion Song) (*Rameau*) (80)

(*For Records of Gluck with Zimbalist see page 6*)

HALEY, OLGA (Mezzo-Soprano)

(with pianoforte accompaniment played by Mrs. Edward Haley)

10-inch record 5s.

2-3295 Song of love and June (*Guy d'Hardelot*) (79)

12-inch records 7s.

03622 Annie Laurie (*Lady J. W. Scott*) (79)
03620 Hush'd is my lute (*Montague Phillips*) (79)
03621 In the silent night (*Rachmaninoff*) (79)
03619 (a) Oh, tell me nightingale (*Liza Lehmann*)
(b) Good morning, brother sunshine (*Liza Lehmann*) (79)

These records should be played with " His Master's Voice " needles, sold only in boxes bearing our copyright picture, " His Master's Voice," on the lid

HENSCHEL, SIR GEORGE (Bass)

10-inch record 5s.

7–42006 Das Wandern (*Schubert*) **(78)**

12-inch records 7s.

02527 By the Waters of Babylon (*Dvořák*) (piano accompaniment by himself) **(78)**
2–042012 Der Erlkönig (The Erl-King) (*Loewe*) (piano accompaniment by himself) **(78)**
2–042011 Die beiden Grenadiere (The Two Grenadiers *Schumann*) (piano accompaniment by himself) **(78)**

HYDE, WALTER (Tenor)

10-inch records 5s.

4–2702 Little red house on the hill (*E. La Touche*) **(77)**
4–2745 Sweet evenings come and go, love (*Coleridge-Taylor*) **(78)**

12-inch records 7s.

02292 Eleänore (*Coleridge-Taylor*) **(81)**
02650 I think (*Guy d'Hardelot*) **(77)**
02256 Legend of Kleinsack (with Chorus) ("Tales of Hoffmann"—*Offenbach*) **(80)**
02626 Once again (*Sullivan*) **(77)**
02378 Sympathy (*Marshall*) **(80)**
02257 When love is but tender and sweet (with Chorus) ("Tales of Hoffmann") **(80)**

LAZARO, IPPOLITO (Tenor)

12-inch record 7s.

2–052047 O Paradiso ("L'Africaine"—*Meyerbeer*) **(78)**

LICETTE, MIRIAM (Soprano)

12-inch records 7s.

2–053122 Ah! fors è lui—Part I. ("La Traviata"—*Verdi*) **(79)**
2–053123 Ah! fors è lui—Part II. ("La Traviata"—*Verdi*) **(79)**
03514 Ah! I know it—Pamina's Aria ("The Magic Flute"—*Mozart*) **(77)**
2–033055 Polonaise ("Mignon"—*Thomas*) **(78)**
03596 Porgi amor qualche ristoro ("Nozze di Figaro"—*Mozart*) (sung in English) (Love, I pray, on me take pity) **(79)**
03482 Waltz Song ("Romeo and Juliet"—*Gounod*) **(79)**

LLOYD, EDWARD (Tenor)

10-inch record 5s.

3–2938 Bonnie Mary of Argyle **(81)**

LUNN, KIRKBY (Contralto)

(*For Mdme. Kirkby Lunn's* OPERATIC *Records see Special Celebrity Section*)

10-inch records 5s.

2–3192 A Memory (*Goring-Thomas*) (pianoforte accompaniment by Mr. Percy Pitt) **(79)**
2–3054 A Psalm of Love (*Dorothy Forster*) (organ by Mr. E. Stanley Roper, and piano by Mr. Percy Pitt) **(79)**
3903 A Song of Sleep (*Somerset*) **(80)**
2–3042 Harvest (*del Riego*) **(79)**
2–3138 Jock o' Hazeldean (*Scott*) (pianoforte accompaniment by Mr. Percy Pitt) **(79)**
3997 My Treasure (*Joan Trevalsa*) **(78)**
2–3139 O that we two were maying (*Nevin*) (pianoforte accompaniment by Mr. Percy Pitt) **(78)**
2–3063 Soul of mine (*Ethel Barns*) (pianoforte accompaniment by Mr. Percy Pitt and organ by Mr. E. Stanley Roper) **(80)**
3875 The pretty creature (arr. by *Lane Wilson*) **(81)**

12-inch records 7s.

03255 A Summer Night (*Goring Thomas*) ('cello obbligato by Mr. W. H. Squire) **(81)**
03217 As once in May (*Lassen*) **(81)**
03499 Daddy (*Behrend*) **(79)**
03395 Entreat me not to leave thee (*Gounod*) (arr. by Percy Pitt) (orchestra conducted by Mr. Percy Pitt and piano played by Mr. E. Stanley Roper) **(78)**
03572 Have you news of my boy Jack? (*Kipling-German*) (accompanied by the Symphony Orchestra, conducted by Edward German) **(79)**
03210 He shall feed His flock ("Messiah"—*Handel*) **(80)**
03287 In sweet September (*Hope Temple*) **(79)**
03272 Largo—"Rest" (Ombra mai fù) (*Handel*) (organ by Mr. E. Stanley Roper and orchestra conducted by Mr. Percy Pitt) **(81)**
03259 O lovely night (*Ronald*) ('cello obbligato by Mr. W. H. Squire) **(80)**

The figures in brackets at end of selections indicate the speed at which the records . . . . should be played . . . .

VIOLET LABEL RECORDS

12-inch records 7s.

03269 O rest in the Lord (' Elijah "—*Mendelssohn*) (81)
03448 On the banks of Allan Water (old Scottish melody) (pianoforte accompaniment by Mr. Percy Pitt) (78)
03295 { (a) Rose in the bud (*Forster*) ; (b) It is not because.your heart is mine (*Löhr*) (81)
03556 Rule Britannia (*Arne*) (accompanied by the Band of H.M. Coldstream Guards, conducted by Major J. Mackenzie Rogan, M.V.O., Mus.Doc., Hon. R.A.M.) (79)
03537 She wore a wreath of roses (*Knight*) (pianoforte accompaniment by Mr. Percy Pitt) (79)
03447 The Land o' the Leal (old Scottish melody) (pianoforte accompaniment by Mr. Percy Pitt) (78)
03584 There's a land (*Ailitsen*) (accompanied by the Band of H.M. Coldstream Guards, conducted by Major J. Mackenzie Rogan, M.V.O., Mus.Doc., Hon. R.A.M.) (79)
03142 Three Fishers (*Hullah*) (pianoforte accompaniment by Mr. Percy Pitt). (80)

McCORMACK, JOHN (Tenor)

(For John McCormack's Celebrity Records see Special Celebrity Section)

10-inch records 5s.

4-2218 A Farewell (*Liddle*) (79)
4-2373 A little love, a little kiss (Un peu d'amour) (*Silèsu*) (78)
4-2072 Annie Laurie (81)
4-2326 At dawning (*Cadman*) (80)
4-2579 Because (*Guy d'Hardelot*) (79)
4-2482 Bonnie Wee Thing (*Lehmann*) (79)
4-2472 Come where my love lies dreaming (*Foster*) (80)
4-2396 Dear Love, remember me (*Marshall*) (80)
4-2378 Geneviève (*Tucker*) (77)
4-2370 I hear a thrush at eve (*Cadman*) (78)
4-2076 I hear you calling me (*Marshall*) (80)
4-2513 It's a long, long way to Tipperary (with Chorus) (78)
4-2601 Mavis (*Craxton*) (78)
4-2379 Molly Brannigan (Old Irish Melody) (79)

10-inch records 5s.

4-2142 Mother Machree (*Olcott*) (80)
4-2368 Mother o' mine (*Tours*) (77)
4-2382 Sav au revoir, but not good-bye (*Kennedy*) (79)
4-2215 Silver threads among the gold (*Danks*) (81)
4-2074 The dear little shamrock (*Jackson*) (80)
4-2216 The harp that once thro' Tara's Halls (*Balfe*) (81)
4-2366 The low-backed car (*Samuel Lover*) (79)
4-2071 The Minstrel Boy (*Moore*) (82)
4-2221 The Rosary (*Nevin*) (80)
4-2886 The Star-Spangled Banner (*Key*) (78)
4-2328 There is a flower that bloometh (" Maritana "—*Wallace*) (78)
4-2645 Until (*Sanderson*) (78)
4-2213 Wearin' o' the green (*Hall*) (80)
4-2070 When shadows gather (*Marshall*) (82)
4-2473 Who knows ? (*Ball*) (77)
4-2380 Within the garden of my heart (*Scott*) (79)

12-inch records 7s.

02323 An Evening Song (*Blumenthal*) (80)
02401 Asthore (*Trotère*) (80)
02244 Come back to Erin (*Claribel*) (82)
02245 Drink to me only with thine eyes (81)
02481 Good-bye (*Tosti*) (79)
02306 Has sorrow thy young days shaded (*Moore*) (980)
02327 " In a Persian Garden "—Ah ! Moon of my delight (*Lehmann*) (81)
02325 Kathleen Mavourneen (*Crouch*) (81)
02246 Killarney (*Balfe*) (82)
02402 Like stars above (*W. H. Squire*) (80)
02286 Molly Bawn (arr. by *Dermot MacMurrough*) (80)
02324 She is far from land (*Lambert*) (81)
02326 The Irish Emigrant (*Barker*) (81)
02247 The snowy-breasted pearl (*Robinson*) (81)
02630 The Trumpeter (*Airlie Dix*) (77)
02610 When my ships come sailing home (*F. Dorel*) (79)

MURRAY-DAVEY, M. (Bass)

12-inch records 7s.

2-032030 Don Juan's Serenade, Op. 38, No. 1 (*Tchaikovsky*) (78)
2-052114 Possenti numi (" Il Flauto Magico "—*Mozart*) (79)

These records should be played with " His Master's Voice " needles, sold only in boxes bearing our copyright picture, " His Master's Voice," on the lid

VIOLET LABEL RECORDS

RADFORD, ROBERT (Bass)

12-inch records 7s.

02738 La Marseillaise (in English) (*Rouget de l'Isle*) (accompanied by the Band of H.M. Coldstream Guards, conducted by Major J. Mackenzie-Rogan, M.V.O., Mus. Doc., Hon. R.A.M.) (79)

02792 My power is absolute("Boris Godounov" —*Moussorgsky*) (79)

02761 Scots, wha hae wi' Wallace bled (accompanied by the Band of H.M. Coldstream Guards, conducted by Major J. Mackenzie-Rogan, M.V.O., Mus. Doc., Hon. R.A.M.) (78)

RANALOW, FREDERICK (Baritone)

12-inch record 7s.

04183 (a) A friend and I were on the pier
(b) When the sun is setting (*Rosina Buckman and Frederick Ranalow*) (" The Boatswain's Mate "—*Dr. Ethel Smyth*) (79)

VINCENT, RUTH (Soprano)

10-inch records 5s.

2–3004 A Birthday (*F. H. Cowen*) (79)

2–3289 I bring you joy (*Haydn Wood*) (79)

2–3269 I heard a sweet song (*Dorothy Forster*) (77)

2–3044 I wonder if Love is a dream (*Dorothy Forster*) (79)

2–3290 In my garden (*Liddle*) (79)

2–3049 The stars tha light my garden (*Kennedy Russell*) (pianoforte accompaniment played by the composer) (79)

2–3069 Waltz Song (" Tom Jones "—*Edward German*) (80)

12-inch records 7s.

2–053124 Il bacio (" The Kiss ") (sung in Italian) (*Arditi*) (78)

03350 Lilac time (*Willeby*) (79)

03566 The smile of spring (Vocal Waltz) (*Percy E. Fletcher*) (79)

WHITEHILL, CLARENCE (Bass)

10-inch records 5s.

4–2234 Is not His word like a fire ? (" Elijah " —*Mendelssohn*) (79)

4–2235 The Calf of Gold (" Faust "—*Gounod*) (78)

12-inch records 7s.

02416 Pater Noster (*L. Niedermeyer*) (with Westminster Cathedral Choir, under the direction of Dr. R. R. Terry) (80)

02418 Toreador Song (" Carmen "—*Bizet*) (78)

02425 Vulcan's Song (" Philémon et Baucis " —*Gounod*) (78)

02422 Why do the nations ? (" Messiah "— *Handel*) (81)

WILLIAMS, EVAN (the late) (Tenor)

10-inch records 5s.

3–2763 Acushla Machree (*Julian Edwards*) (76)

4–2206 A May morning (*Denza*) (81)

4–2181 A per ect day (*Jacobs Bond*) (81)

4–2060 Auld Lang Syne (83)

4–2456 Beautiful Isle of somewhere (*Fearis*) (80)

3–2425 Jean (*Burleigh*) (77)

4–2115 Mentra Gwen (Old Welsh Song) (81)

4–2009 Serenade (*Schubert*) (81)

3–2986 The Bay of Biscay (80)

12-inch records 7s.

02565 Beloved, it is morn (*Aylward*) (79)

02278 Crossing the bar (*Willeby*) (81)

02274 Cujus animam (" Stabat Mater "— *Rossini*) (81)

02267 Lead, kindly Light (*Rev. J. B. Dykes*) (80)

02241 Lohengrin's Narrative (" Lohengrin " —*Wagner*) (81)

02276 Murmuring Zephyr (*Jensen*) (80)

02612 My ain Folk (*Lemon*) (78)

02299 O ! Na Byddai'n Haf O Hyd (*Davies*) (81)

02238 O Paradise (" L'Africaine "—*Meyerbeer*) (81)

02304 Open the Gates (*Crosby-Knapp*) (80)

02529 The Holy City (*Stephen Adams*) (78)

02164 Walther's Prize Song (" Meistersinger "—*Wagner*) (79)

02183 Your tiny hand is frozen (Rudolph's Narrative) (" Bohême "—*Puccini*) (81)

The figures in brackets at end of selections indicate the speed at which the records . . . . should be played . . . .

VIOLET LABEL RECORDS

DUETS

BUCKMAN, ROSINA, and WALTER HYDE

12-inch records 7s.

04187 Far from gay Paris (Parigi, o cara) ("La Traviata"—*Verdi*) (79)
04195 O shrine of beauty ("Romeo and Juliet"—*Gounod*) (78)
04217 Oh, Maritana ("Maritana"—*Wallace*) (79)

BUCKMAN, ROSINA and FREDERICK RANALOW

12-inch records 7s.

04185 ⎰ (a) Oh, dear, if I had known ("The Boatswain's Mate"—*Dr.Ethel Smyth*) (79)
    ⎱ (b) The Keeper (piccolo duet) (GILBERT BARTON and W. GORDON WALKER) "The Boatswain's Mate"—*Dr. Ethel Smyth*) (79)

04183 ⎰ (a) A friend and I were on the pier (FREDERICK RANALOW) ("The Boatswain's Mate"—*Dr. Ethel Smyth*) (79)
    ⎱ (b) When the sun is setting ("The Boatswain's Mate"—*Dr.Ethel Smyth*) (79)

McCORMACK, JOHN and REINALD WERRENRATH

10-inch record 5s.

2-4205 The Moon hath raised her lamp above ("The Lily of Killarney"—*Benedict*) (78)

WILLIAMS, EVAN and ROBERT RADFORD

12-inch records 7s.

04073 Flow gently, Deva (*Parry*) (80)
04070 It is of the Lord's great mercies("Abraham"—*Molique*) (80)
04075 The Crucifix (*Faure*) (81)

TRIO

BUCKMAN, ROSINA COURTICE POUNDS and FREDERICK RANALOW

12-inch record 7s.

04184 The first thing to do is to get rid of the body ("The Boatswain's Mate"—*Dr. Ethel Smyth*) (79)

⊡ ⊡ ⊡

CHURCH CHOIR

WESTMINSTER ABBEY CHOIR

(Conducted by Sir Frederick Bridge, C.V.O., M.A., Mus.Doc., Organist of Westminster Abbey, and Director of Music at the Coronation.)

12-inch record 7s.

04792 Rejoice in the Lord (Homage Anthem) (*Sir F. Bridge*) (Solo by Mr. Edward Lloyd) (81)

Sung at the Coronation of Their Majesties King George V. and Queen Mary.

⊡ ⊡ ⊡

ORCHESTRA

THE ROYAL ALBERT HALL ORCHESTRA

(late New Symphony Orchestra)
(conducted by LANDON RONALD)

12-inch records 7s.

2-0660 1812 Overture, Op. 49—Part I. (*Tchaikovsky*) (79)
2-0664 1812 Overture, Op. 49—Part II. (*Tchaikovsky*) (79)
2-0674 1812 Overture, Op. 49—Part III. (*Tchaikovsky*) (78)
2-0639 "Casse-noisette" Suite—
    (a) Marche (*Tchaikovsky*) (78)
    (b) Danse Russe (Trepak) (*Tchaikovsky*) (78)
0846 "Casse-noisette" Suite—Valse des Fleurs (*Tchaikovsky*) (78)
2-0653 "Casse-noisette" Suite—
    (a) Dance of the Sugar Plum Fairy (*Tchaikovsky*) (78)
    (b) Danse Chinoise (*Tchaikovsky*) (78)

VIOLET LABEL RECORDS

ROYAL ALBERT HALL ORCHESTRA—
continued

2-0720	"Casse-noisette" Suite—Danse Arabe *(Tchaikovsky)* **(79)**
2-0749	"Casse-noisette" Suite—Danse des Mirlitons *(Tchaikovsky)* **(79)**
2-0740	"Casse-noisette", Suite — Miniature Overture *(Tchaikovsky)* **(79)**
2-0761	"Flying Dutchman," Overture, Part I. *(Wagner)* **(79)**
2-0762	"Flying Dutchman," Overture, Part II. *(Wagner)* **(79)**
2-0771	"Lohengrin," Prelude, Part I. *(Wagner)* **(78)**
2-0782	"Lohengrin," Prelude, Part II. *(Wagner)* **(78)**
2-0774	Mazurka (" Coppelia ") *(Délibes)* **(79)**
2-0792	Marche Militaire Française (Suite Algérienne, Op. 60, No. 4) *(Saint-Saëns)* **(79)**

ROYAL ALBERT HALL ORCHESTRA—
continued

0722	" Prélude à l'après-midi d'un Faune," Part I. *(Debussy)* **(79)**
0723	" Prélude à l'après-midi d'un Faune," Part II. *(Debussy)* **(79)**
2-0834	Slav March, Op. 31 *(Tchaikovsky)* **(79)**
2-0698	" Sylvia Ballet "—Prélude des Chasseresses *(Délibes)* **(79)**
2-0702	Rouet d'Omphale. Op. 31 (Poème symphonique) (The Spinning Wheel of Omphale) *(Saint-Saëns)* **(79)**
2-0802	Scheherazade, Op. 35 (Suite Symphonique) Part I. *(Rimsky-Korsakoff)* **(78)**
2-0678	" Tannhäuser "—Overture, Part I. *(Wagner)* **(78)**
0866	" Tannhäuser "—Overture, Part II *(Wagner)* **(80)**

(See pages 28 and 29 for Black Label records of Royal Albert Hall Orchestra)

▣ ▣ ▣ ▣ ▣

INSTRUMENTAL

PIANO

BACKHAUS, WILHELM

(See also page 49)

12-inch records 7s.

05550	(a) Moment musical *(Schubert)*; (b) Hark, hark the lark *(Schubert)* **(79)**
05553	(a) Etude, Op. 10, No. 7 *(Chopin)*; (b) Waltz in D flat *(Chopin)* **(79)**

(For Backhaus' Black Label records and records by other great pianists see page 49)

MOISEIVITCH, BENNO

10-inch record 5s.

5597	Le Coucou (The Cuckoo) from " Pièce de Clavecin " *(Daquin)* **(78)**

12-inch records 7s.

05590	Berceuse *(Chopin)* **(79)**
05612	Chant polonais *(Chopin-Liszt)* **(78)**
05613	Capriccio in B minor, Op. 76, No. 2 *(Brahms)*
05624	Clair de lune *(Debussy)* **(79)**
055^2	Jardins sous la pluie (Rain in the Garden) *(Debussy)* **(78)**
05581	Jeux d'eau (Water play) *(Ravel)* **(78)**
05598	Nocturne (for the left hand only) *(Scriabine)* **(78)**

VIOLIN

ELMAN, MISCHA

10-inch records 5s.

3-7924	Fantasia from Garden Scene (" Faust " —*Gounod)* **(79)**
3-7923	Minuet *(Haydn)* **(81)**
3-7921	Minuet in G, No. 2 *(Beethoven)* **(79)**
4-7930	Souvenir *(Drdla)* **(79)**
3-7976	Vogel als Prophet (Op. 82, No. 7) *(Schumann)* **(78)**

12-inch records 7s.

07995	Ave Maria *(Schubert-Wilhelmj)* **(80)**
07934	(a) Gavotte *(Gossec)* ; (b) Deutscher Tanz *(Dittersdorf)* **(81)**
07932	Introduction Rondo Capriccioso *(Saint-Saëns)* **(78)**
07929	Mélodie *(Tschaikovsky)* **(76)**
07928	Nocturne *(Chopin)* **(76)**
07927	Serenade *(Schubert)* **(91)**
07933	Souvenir de Moscou *(Wieniavski)* **(74)**
07996	" Thaïs " Méditation *(Massenet)* **(79)**

KREISLER, FRITZ

10-inch records 5s.

3-7956	Berceuse *(Townsend)* **(77)**
3-7942	La Chasse *(Cartier-Kreisler)* **(80)**
3-7953	Schön Rosmarin (Fair Rosmarin) *(Kreisler)* **(78)**
3-7927	Variations *(Tartini-Kreisler)* **(80)**

The figures in brackets at end of selections indicate the speed at which the records . . . . should be played . . . .

VIOLET LABEL RECORDS

KREISLER, FRITZ—continued

12-inch records 7s.

07960 Caprice viennois (*Kreisler*) (78)
07967 Chanson, Louis XIII and Pavane (*Couperin-Kreisler*) (78)
07964 Chanson Méditation (*R. Cottenet*) (81)
07965 Chant sans paroles (*Tchaikovsky*) (78)
07968 E major Gavotte (*Bach*) (81)
07939 Humoreske (*Dvořák*) (80)
07966 Hungarian Dance, G minor (*Brahms-Joachim*) (80)
07963 Liebesfreud (*Kreisler*) (78)
07962 Liebesleid (*Kreisler*) (78)
07985 Praeludium (*Bach*) (78)
07958 Scherzo (*Dittersdorf-Kreisler*) (81)

POWELL, MAUD

10-inch records 5s.

3–7979 Gavotte ("Mignon"—*Thomas*) (78)
3–7965 Serenata (*Moszkovski*) (77)
3–7964 Souvenir (Morceau) (*Drdla*) (78)

12-inch record 7s.

2–07900 Thaïs—Intermezzo (Méditation religieuse) (*Massenet*) (78)

ZIMBALIST, EFREM.

10-inch record 5s.

4–7905 Chant d'automne, Op. 37, No. 10 (*Tchaikovsky*) (78)

12-inch record 7s.

2–07928 The Broken Melody (*Van Biene*) (77)

\ (For other violin records see pages 26, 27, 50)

TRIO

**MARK HAMBOURG,
MARJORIE HAYWARD and
C. WARWICK EVANS.**

12-inch record 7s.

08055 Scherzo from Trio in D minor, Op. 49 (*Mendelssohn*) (79)

QUARTET

**MARK HAMBOURG,
MARJORIE HAYWARD,
C. WARWICK EVANS and
FRANK BRIDGE**

12-inch record 7s.

08054 Scherzo from Quartet, Op. 41, in B flat (*Saint-Saëns*) (79)

QUINTET

**MARK HAMBOURG,
MARJORIE HAYWARD,
C. WARWICK EVANS,
HERBERT KINZE and
FRANK BRIDGE**

12-inch record 7s.

08053 Scherzo from Quintet, Op. 44, in E flat (*Schumann*) (79)

▣ ▣ ▣ ▣ ▣

ORCHESTRAL RECORDS

Ten- and Twelve-inch Single-sided and Double-sided Records

10-inch records 4s. each ; 12-inch records 6s. each (excepting when otherwise marked). 12-inch double-sided records 7s.

ORCHESTRAS

THE ROYAL ALBERT HALL ORCHESTRA

(late New Symphony Orchestra)

CONDUCTED BY

LANDON RONALD

12-inch records 6s.

0863	" Carmen "—Prelude (*Bizet*) (80)
0739	" Cavalleria Rusticana "—Intermezzo (*Mascagni*) (81)
2–0513	Danse Macabre (*Saint-Saëns*) (79)
0835	" Die Meistersinger "—Dance of the Apprentices (*Wagner*) (80)
0836	" Die Meistersinger "—Procession of the Mastersingers (*Wagner*) (81)
0817	" Die Meistersinger" Overture, Part I. (*Wagner*) (31)
0818	" Die Meistersinger" Overture, Part II. (*Wagner*) (81)
0734	" Egmont " Overture (*Beethoven*) (81)
0692	" Figaro " Overture (*Mozart*) (80)
0683	Finlandia—Symphonic Poem (*Sibelius*) (81)
0848	Funeral March of a Marionette (*Gounod*) (80)
2–0553	Gopak (*Moussorgsky*) (78)
2–0586	Henry VIII. Dances—Shepherd's Dance (*Edward German*) (78)
2–0587	Henry VIII. Dances—Morris Dance and Torch Dance (*Edward German*) (78)
0726	Hungarian Rhapsody (*Liszt*) (81)
2–0518	Invitation to the Waltz (*Weber*) (79)
0701	" Leonora " Overture (No. 3), Part I. (*Beethoven*) (81)
0702	" Leonora " Overture (No. 3), Part II. (*Beethoven*) (81)
0703	" Leonora " Overture (No. 3), Part III. (*Beethoven*) (81)
0828	" L'Arlésienne Suite "—Prelude and Minuet (2nd Movement) (*Bizet*) (78)
0837	" L'Arlésienne Suite "—Adagietto for Strings (*Bizet*) (77)

0834	" L'Arlésienne Suite " — Farandole (*Bizet-Ronald*) (81)
0799	" Lyrische Suite," No. 1—Shepherd's Boy (*Grieg*) (80)
0800	" Lyrische Suite," No. 2—Norwegian Rustic March (*Grieg*) (80)
0887	" Lyrische Suite," No. 3—Notturno (*Grieg*) (80)
0888	" Lyrische Suite," No. 4, March of the Dwarfs (*Grieg*) (81)
0746	Marche hongroise (*Berlioz*) (81)
0864	Marche militaire (*Schubert*) (81)
0735	" Merry Wives of Windsor " Overture (*Nicolai*) (81)
0681	" Midsummer Night's Dream," Scherzo (*Mendelssohn*) (80)
0756	" MidsummerNight'sDream," Nocturne (80)
0853	" Midsummer Night's Dream " Overture (80)
2–0561	" Mors et Vita "—Judex (*Gounod*) (80)
0724	" Oberon " Overture (*Weber*) (81)
0717	" Peer Gynt " Suite—Morning (*Grieg*) (81)
0718	" Peer Gynt " Suite—Death of Ase (*Grieg*) (80)
0719	" Peer Gynt " Suite—Anitra's Dance (*Grieg*) (80)
0720	" Peer Gynt " Suite—In the Hall of the Mountain King (*Grieg*) (82)
2–0609	" Philémon et Baucis "—Danse des Bacchantes (*Gounod*) (79)
2–0551	Præludium (*Järnefeldt*) (79)
0725	" Ruy Blas " Overture (*Mendelssohn*) (81)
0838	" Samson et Dalila "—Danse des Prêtresses de Dagon (*Saint-Saëns*) (78)
2–0580	" Scènes pittoresques "—Fête Bohême (*Massenet*) (79)
2–0599	" Scènes pittoresques "—Angelus (*Massenet*) (78)
0765	" Shepherd Fennel's Dance " (*Balfour-Gardiner*) (80)
2–0615	Shepherd's Hey (*Percy Grainger*) (78)

The figures in brackets at end of selections indicate the speed at which the records . . . . should be played . . . .

28

ORCHESTRAL RECORDS

ROYAL ALBERT HALL ORCHESTRA—
continued **12-inch records 6s.**

- **0738** Spring Song and Bees' Wedding (*Mendelssohn*) (80)
- **0852** "Sylvia"—Pizzicato (*Délibes*) **78)**
- **0849** Sylvia Ballet—Intermezzo and Valse lente (*Délibes*) (78)
- **0845** Sylvia Ballet—Cortège de Bacchus (*Delibes*) (78)
- **0757** Symphonie pathétique—Third Movement (*Tchaikovsky*) (30)
- **0792** Theme and Variations, Suite No. 3 in G, Op. 5, Variations 1, 2, 3 (*Tchaikovsky*) (81)
- **0793** Theme and Variations, Suite No. 3 in G, Op. 55, Variations 4, 5, 6 (*Tchaikovsky*) (81)
- **0794** Theme and Variations, Suite No. 3 in G, Op. 55, Variations 8, 9, 10 (*Tchaikovsky*) (81)
- **0731** Unfinished Symphony—1st part of First Movement (*Schubert*) (81)
- **0732** Unfinished Symphony—2nd part of First Movement (*Schubert*) (81)
- **0733** Unfinished Symphony—Second Movement (*Schubert*) (80)
- **0755** Wedding March (*Mendelssohn*) (80)
- **0753** "William Tell" Overture—Andante Pastorale (*Rossini*) (81)
- **0754** "William Tell"—Allegro (*Rossini*) (81)
- **0850** "William Tell" Overture—Opening Andante (*Rossini*) (78)
- **2-0560** "William Tell"—Storm (*Rossini*) (80)
- **2-0571** Zampa Overture, Part I. (*Herold*) (79)
- **2-0572** Zampa Overture, Part II. (*Herold*) (79)
- **0831** Zanetta Overture (*Auber*) (78)

NEW QUEEN'S HALL LIGHT ORCHESTRA

**Proprietors :
Messrs. Chappell & Co., Ltd.**

CONDUCTED BY
MR. ALICK MACLEAN

12-inch double-sided records 7s.

- **D. 16** { "Ballet Egyptien "—Suite, Part I. (*Luigini*) (79)
  "Ballet Egyptien "—Suite, Part II. (*Luigini*) (79)
- **D. 17** { "Ballet Egyptien " Suite, Part III. (*Luigini*) (79)
  "Ballet Egyptien "—Suite, Part IV. (*Luigini*) (79)
- **D. 29** { "Miniature Suite "—No. 1, Children's Dance (*Eric Coates*) (79)
  "Miniature Suite "—No. II., Intermezzo (*Eric Coates*) (79)

BERLIN PHILHARMONIC ORCHESTRA

CONDUCTED BY
NIKISCH.

12-inch records 6s.

- **040786** Fifth Symphony—Andante—Part I. (*Beethoven*) (78)
- **040787** Fifth Symphony—Andante—Part II. (*Beethoven*) (78)
- **040784** Fifth Symphony—1st Movement— Part I. (*Beethoven*) (78)
- **040785** Fifth Symphony—1st Movement— Part II. (*Beethoven*) (78)
- **040788** Fifth Symphony—Scherzo and Part I., Finale (*Beethoven*) (78)
- **040789** Fifth Symphony—Finale. Part II. (*Beethoven*) (78)
- **040790** Fifth Symphony—Finale, Part III. (*Beethoven*) (78)
- **040791** Fifth Symphony—Finale, Part IV. (*Beethoven*) (78)

CONDUCTED BY
Dr. ALFRED HERTZ.

12-inch records 6s.

- **040772** "Parsifal"—Vorspiel (Prelude), Part I., Act I. (*Wagner*) (78)
- **040773** "Parsifal"—Vorspiel (Prelude), Part II., Act I. (*Wagner*) (78)
- **040774** "Parsifal"—Vorspiel (Prelude), Part III., Act I. (*Wagner*) (78)
- **040778** "Parsifal"—Verwandlungsmusik (Transformation Music), Part I., Act I. (*Wagner*) (78)
- **040779** "Parsifal" — Verwandlungsmusik (Transformation Music), Part II., Act I. (*Wagner*) (78)
- **040775** "Parsifal" — Verwandlungsmusik (Transformation Music), Act III. (*Wagner*) (78)
- **040776** "Parsifal"—Charfreitagszauber (Good Friday Music), Part I. (*Wagner*) (78)
- **040777** "Parsifal"—Charfreitagszauber (Good Friday Music), Part II. (*Wagner*) (78)

LONDON SYMPHONY ORCHESTRA

CONDUCTED BY
NIKISCH.

12-inch record 6s.

- **2-0502** "Nozze di Figaro"—Overture (*Mozart*) (79)

ORCHESTRAL RECORDS

THE SYMPHONY ORCHESTRA

CONDUCTED BY

Sir EDWARD ELGAR, O.M.

12-inch records 6s.

2–0824	Bavarian Dances, No. I., Op. 27 (*Elgar*) (78)
2–0519	Bavarian Dances, No. 2 (*Elgar*) (78)
2–0530	Bavarian Dances, No. 3 (*Elgar*) (78)
2–0522	Carillon, Part I., Sing, Belgians, sing (Chantons, Belges, chantons) (Cammaerts' verses delivered in English by Mr. Henry Ainley) (*Elgar*) (78)
2–0523	Carillon, Part II. (78)
0967	Carissima (*Elgar*) (73)
2–0728	"Cockaigne Concert" — Overture (*Elgar*) (78)
2–0511	Pomp and Circumstance March, Op. 29 (introducing "Land of Hope and Glory") (*Elgar*) (79)
2–0517	Pomp and Circumstance March (No. 4 in G), Op. 39 (*Elgar*) (80)
2–0775	Prelude and Angel's Farewell ("The Dream of Gerontius"—*Elgar*) (78)
2–0512	Salut d'amour (*Elgar*) (78)
2–0729	"Wand of Youth" (*a*) The Tame Bear (*b*) The Wild Bear (music to a Child's Play) Second Suite—Nos. 5 and 6 (*Elgar*) (78)

CONDUCTED BY

Sir FREDERIC H. COWEN.

10-inch record 4s.

2–572	Intermezzo ("Monica's Blue Boy") (*Cowen*) (79)

12-inch records 6s.

2–0750	Rustic Dance "Old English Dances"—1st Set (*Cowen*) (79)
2–0703	The Butterfly's Ball—Overture (*Cowen*) (78)
2–0714	"The Language of Flowers"—1st Set Gavotte—Yellow Jasmine (*Cowen*) (79)
2–0715	"The Language of Flowers"—2nd Set—Waltz Viscaria (*Cowen*) (79)

CONDUCTED BY

EDWARD GERMAN.

12-inch records 6s.

2–0661	Masque from "As You Like It" (*German*) (78) Nos. 1 and 2 { Woodland Dance { Children's Dance
2–0665	Masque from "As You Like It," No. 3 Rustic Dance (*German*) (78)
2–0716	"Much Ado about Nothing"—No. I.—Bourrée (*German*) (78)
2–0717	"Much Ado about Nothing"—No. II.—Gigue (*German*) (78)
2–0743	Three Dances—Henry VIII., Morris Dance and Torch Dance (*German*) (77)
2–0742	Three Dances—Henry VIII, Shepherds' Dance (*German*) (77)
2–0675	Three Dances—"Nell Gwyn," No. 1 Country Dance (*German*) (78)
2–0741	Three Dances—"Nell Gwyn," No. 2 Pastoral Dance (*German*) (78)
2–0803	"Tom Jones," Dances—No. 1, Morris Dance No. 2, Gavotte (*German*) (78)

CONDUCTED BY

Dr. ETHEL SMYTH.

12-inch records 6s.

2–0696	"The Boatswain's Mate"—Overture, Part I. (*Smyth*) (79)
2–0697	"The Boatswain's Mate"—Overture, Part II. (*Smyth*) (79)

CONDUCTED BY

Sir ALEXANDER C. MACKENZIE.

12-inch records 6s.

2–0679	"London Day by Day"—Suite, No. 1 Under the Clock (Humoresque) (*Mackenzie*) (79)
2–0721	Saltarello—Ballet Music from "Colomba" (*Mackenzie*) (78)
2–0719	"The Cricket on the Hearth"—Overture (*Mackenzie*) (78)

CONDUCTED BY

Sir CHARLES V. STANFORD.

12-inch records 6s.

2–0763	Irish Rhapsody, No. 1 (*Stanford*) (79)
2–0793	Masque from "The Critic," Part I. (*Stanford*) (79)
2–0699	"Shamus O'Brien"—Overture (*Stanford*) (79)
2–0718	"Suite of Ancient Dances" (*a*) Sarabande (*b*) Morris Dance (*Stanford*) (79)

IMPERIAL RUSSIAN BALALAIKA COURT ORCHESTRA

CONDUCTED BY

W. W. ANDREEFF

12-inch record 6s.

028500	{ (1) Molodka (Comic Folk Song) (80) { (2) Sun in the sky, stop shining (Folk Dance) (80)

The figures in brackets at end of selections indicate the speed at which the records
. . . . should be played . . . .

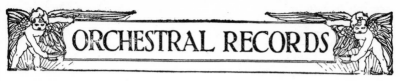

ORCHESTRAL RECORDS

LIGHT OPERA ORCHESTRA

12-inch double-sided record 7s.

D. 2
{ "The Mikado"—Overture, Part I. (*Gilbert and Sullivan*) (79)
"The Mikado"—Overture, Part II. (*Gilbert and Sullivan*) (79) }

D. 18
{ "Merrie England." Introduction—Rustic Dance and Jig (*German*) FULL CHORUS
"Sing a-down, a-down. Opening Chorus, Act I. ("Merrie England" (*German*) }

IMPERIAL PHILHARMONIC ORCHESTRA

CONDUCTED BY

Mr. PERCY PITT.

12-inch records 6s.

0758 "The Jewels of the Madonna"—Intermezzo after Act I. (*Wolf-Ferrari*) (81)

0759 "The Jewels of the Madonna"—Intermezzo after Act II. (*Wolf-Ferrari*) (81)

⊡ ⊡ ⊡ ⊡ ⊡

THE ALBUM OF EIGHT ORCHESTRAL RECORDS

of Works of our

GREAT BRITISH COMPOSERS

conducted by themselves

⊡ ⊡ ⊡

THE SYMPHONY ORCHESTRA

CONDUCTED BY

Sir EDWARD ELGAR, O.M.

12-inch records 6s.

2–0728 "Cockaigne Concert" — Overture (*Elgar*) (78)

2–0729 "Wand of Youth" (*a*) The Tame Bear (*b*) The Wild Bear (music to a child's play) Second Suite—Nos. 5 and 6 (*Elgar*) (78)

CONDUCTED BY

Sir FREDERIC H. COWEN.

12-inch records 6s.

2–0714 "The Language of Flowers"—1st Set, Yellow Jasmine (*Cowen*) (79)

2–0715 "The Language of Flowers"—2nd Set, Waltz Viscaria (*Cowen*) (79)

CONDUCTED BY

Sir CHARLES V. STANFORD.

12-inch record 6s.

2–0718 "Suite of Ancient Dances "—(*a*) Sarabande (*b*) Morris Dance (*Stanford*) (79)

CONDUCTED BY

EDWARD GERMAN.

12-inch records 6s.

2–0716 "Much Ado about Nothing "—No. 1 —Bourrée (*German*) (78)

2–0717 "Much Ado about Nothing "—No. 2 Gigue (*German*) (78)

CONDUCTED BY

Sir ALEXANDER C. MACKENZIE.

12-inch record 6s.

2–0719 "The Cricket on the Hearth "—Overture (*Mackenzie*) (78)

Complete £2 8s. 0d.

These records should be played with " His Master's Voice " needles, sold only in boxes bearing our copyright picture, " His Master's Voice," on the lid

BALLAD RECORDS

BALLADS AND OTHER CONCERT MUSIC

10-inch, 4s. each ; 12-inch, 6s. each

(Excepting where otherwise marked.)

BAKER, GEORGE (Baritone)

10-inch records 4s.

4–2767 Myself when young (" In a Persian Garden ") (*Liza Lehmann*) (79)
4–2917 Joggin' along the highway (*H. Samuel*) (79)

12-inch record 6s.

04171 (a) As then the Tulip (" In a Persian Garden ") (*Liza Lehmann*) (79)
(b) Alas! that Spring should vanish with the Rose (AGNES NICHOLLS, EDNA THORNTON, HUBERT EISDELL and GEORGE BAKER) (79)

BROHLY, (Contralto)

12-inch record 6s.

033064 Mon cœur s'ouvre à ta voix (" Samson et Dalila "—*Saint-Saëns*) (80)

BROLA, JEANNE (Soprano)

12-inch records 6s.

03586 Dear Heart (*Mattei*) (78)
03464 They call me Mimi (" La Bohême "—*Puccini*) (78)
03449 The Prayer (Vissi d'arte) (" Tosca "—*Puccini*) (78)
03603 Voi che sapete (" Nozze di Figaro "—*Mozart*) (sung in English—Twilight) (78)

BROWN, HERBERT (Baritone)

10-inch record 4s.

4–2747 The Song of the Waggoner (*Breville-Smith*) (79)

BURKE, EDMUND (Baritone)

12-inch record 6s.

02491 My dark Rosaleen (*Needham*) (78)

BUTCHER, ERNEST (Baritone)

10-inch records 4s.

4–2932 Derry Down Dale (Old English Song) (78)
4–2985 O good ale, thou art my darling (Old English Song) (79)
4–2899 The lad with the carrotty poll (*Butcher*) (79)

12-inch record 6s.

02731 The Bulls won't bellow (*Hetty Hocking*) (79)

BUTTERWORTH, CLARA (Soprano)

12-inch record 6s.

03543 O now my heart—Waltz Song (*Clutsam*) (" Young England ") (78)

CAVE, HERBERT (Tenor)

10-inch records 4s.

4–2830 The April of my heart (*Clutsam*) (" Young England ") (78)
4–2934 The Dream Cottage (*Sparrow*) (78)
4–2329 The Steersman's Song (*Clutsam*) (" Young England ") (78)
4–2860 When shadows gather (*Marshall*) (79)

COATES, JOHN (Tenor)

10-inch records 4s.

4–2552 Ninetta (*Brewer*) (79)
4–2614 O may my dreams come true (*Fothergill*) (79)

COFFIN, HAYDEN (Baritone)

10-inch record 4s.

4–2834 When travelling days are over (*Bath*) (" Young England ") (81)

12-inch record 6s.

02714 Who sings of England ? (with chorus) (*Clutsam*) (" Young England ") (78)

The figures in brackets at end of selections indicate the speed at which the records . . . . should be played . . . .

BALLAD RECORDS

COOPER, MARGARET
at the piano

Miss Margaret Cooper plays her own accompaniments on a Chappell Concert Grand Piano

10-inch records 4s.

2–3134	Bonjour, Marie (*Brunell*) (78)
3831	Dingle, Dongle, Dell (81)
2–3073	Inquisitive Ann (*Sterndale Bennett*) (79)
3820	Love is meant to make us glad (*German*) (80)
3811	Ma dusky Maid (*Vere Smith*) (78)

12-inch records 6s.

03228	Agatha Green (*Margaret Cooper*) (81)
03209	Catch Me! (*Margaret Cooper*) (81)
03432	Come down to Brighton (*Sterndale Bennett*) (77)
03281	Come to Town, Miss Brown (*Sterndale Bennett*) (81)
03264	Dreamland (*Garstin*) (81)
03164	Hullo, Too-Too (*Scott-Gatty*) (81)
03628	I am only seven (*Gray*) (79)
03396	I don't seem to want you when you're with me (*Rubens*) (78)
03567	Liza Brown (*Harrison*) (79)
03612	Lonely (*Foulde*) (79)
03218	Peter (*Scott-Gatty*) (81)
03263	Plumstones (*Worlock*) (81)
03452	The Fox Trot Hop (*Kingston-Stewart*) (77)
03582	Tou-Tou was a dainty doll (*L. Wright*) (79)
03380	What's it got to do with you? (*Tennent*) (74)

D'ARGEL, NORA (Soprano)

10-inch record 4s.

2–3118	Antonia's Song (" Tales of Hoffmann "—*Offenbach*) (Act III.) (80)

12-inch records 6s.

03580	Rosebuds—Valse Song (*Arditi*) (79)
03404	The Doll's Song (" Tales of Hoffmann "—*Offenbach*) (78)
03409	Valse Song (" Romeo and Juliet "—*Gounod*) (78)

DEARTH, HARRY (Bass)

10-inch records 4s.

4–2187	A chip of the old block (*Squire*) (81)
4–2833	Almighty Strength (The Prayer) (with chorus) (*Bath*) (" Young England ") (78)

4–2639	Captain Mac (*Sanderson*) (77)
4–2228	Drinking Song (" Rose of Persia "—*Sullivan*) (80)
4–2078	Ho! Jolly Jenkin (" Ivanhoe "—*Sullivan*) (80)
4–2831	I love a maid (*Clutsam*) (" Young England ") (78)
4–2058	Stone Cracker John (*Eric Coates*) (80)
4–2962	The Company Sergeant Major (*Sanderson*) (79)
4–2186	The Corporal's Ditty (*Squire*) (81)
4–2551	The Crown of the Year (" Songs of Open Country "—*Easthope Martin*) (with pianoforte accompaniment by the composer and orchestra) (78)
4–2861	The Widow of Penzance (*Eric Coates*) (79)
4–2083	Tommy, Lad (*Margetson*) (81)
4–2554	Wayfarer's Night Songs (" Song of Open Country ")—*Easthope Martin*) (with pianoforte accompaniment by the composer and orchestra) (78)
4–2832	Who'll venture with me (with chorus) (*Bath*) (" Young England ") (78)

12-inch records 6s.

02441	A Dinder Courtship (*Eric Coates*) (81)
02230	A Sergeant of the Line (*Squire*) (82)
02486	Bashful Tom (*Kemp*) (80)
02561	Cloze-Props (*Wolseley Charles*) (79)
02331	Lighterman Tom (*Squire*) (81)
02291	My Old Shako (*Trotère*) (81)
02250	Onaway, awake! (*Cowen*) (81)
02384	Reuben Ranzo (*Eric Coates*) (81)
02762	Speed the plough (*Easthope Martin*) (79)
02260	The Lowland Sea (*Eric Coates*) (81)
02313	The Ringers (*Löhr*) (81)
02534	(*a*) The Sandwichman; (*b*) The Fortune Hunter (Song Cycle, " Bow Bells "—*Willeby*) (79)
02413	The Sentry Song (" Iolanthe "—*Sullivan*) (81)
02673	The Two Grenadiers (*Schumann*) (78)

EISDELL, HUBERT (Tenor)

12-inch records 6s.

02674	Ah! moon of my delight (" In a Persian Garden "—*Liza Lehmann*) (79)
04170	(*a*) Alas! that Spring should vanish with the Rose (" In a Persian Garden " —*Liza Lehmann*) (79) (*b*) The worldly hope men set their hearts upon (EDNA THORNTON) (79)

These records should be played with " His Master's Voice " needles, sold only in boxes bearing our copyright picture, " His Master's Voice," on the lid

BALLAD RECORDS

ESSEX, VIOLET (Soprano)

10-inch record 4s.

2-3075 Musetta's Song ("La Bohême"—*Puccini*) **(79)**

12-inch records 6s.

03418 Ah, was it he! ("Ah! fors è lui")—Part I. ("Traviata"—*Verdi*) **(78)**
03424 Ah, was it he! ("Ah! fors è lui")—Part II. ("Traviata"—*Verdi*) **(79)**
03436 Jewel Song ("Faust"—*Gounod*) **(79)**
03531 Oh! come my heart's delight ("Nozze di Figaro"—*Mozart*) **(79)**
03398 The Kiss (Il Bacio) (*Arditi*) **(78)**

EVANS, EDITH (Soprano)

12-inch records 6s.

03508 Breeze of the night (" Il Trovatore "—*Verdi*) **(78)**
03515 Lord of our chosen race (" Ivanhoe "—*Sullivan*) **(79)**

GANGE, FRASER (Baritone)

10-inch records 4s.

4-2990 Border Ballad (*Cowen*) **(79)**
5-2003 To Mary (*M. V. White*) **(79)**

12-inch record 6s.

02793 Beauty's Eyes (*Tosti*) (violin obbligato played by Marjorie Hayward) **(79)**

GARDNER, STEWART (Baritone)

10-inch records 4s.

4-2530 Clieveden Woods—(" The Call of the River "—*Breville-Smith*) **(80)**
4-2063 Rolling down to Rio (*German*) **(81)**
4-2067 Son o' mine (*Wallace*) **(81)**
4-2532 Sussex by the Sea (Marching Song) (*Ward Higgs*) **(79)**
4-2443 The Carnival (*Molloy*) **(79)**

12-inch records 6s.

02348 An Old Garden (*Hope Temple*) **(81)**
02458 Chorus, Gentlemen (*Löhr*) **(81)**
02284 Danny Deever (*Damrosch*) **(81)**
02779 Even bravest hearts may swell (" Faust "—*Gounod*) **(78)**
02687 Friend o' mine (*Sanderson*) **(80)**
02220 Kashmiri Song (Pale hand. I loved) (*Amy Woodforde-Finden*) **(81)**
02475 { (a) Lady mine (*La Touche*) **(78)**
{ (b) There are no roses (*La Touche*) **(78)**

02362 Mandalay (*Willeby*) **(80)**
02618 O Star of Eve (" Tannhäuser "—*Wagner*) **(78)**
02405 Ora pro nobis (Pray for us) (*Piccolomini*) **(81)**
02604 Prologue (" Pagliacci "—*Leoncavallo*) **(78)**
02520 The Devout Lover (*M. V. White*) **(78)**
02551 The Garden of Sleep (*de Lara*) **(79)**
02410 The Lute Player (*Allitsen*) **(81)**
02221 { (a) The Temple Bells
{ (b) Less than the dust (*Amy Woodforde-Finden*) **(78)**

GREENE, PLUNKET (Baritone)

10-inch records 4s.

3-2335 Little Red Fox (arr. by *Somervell*) **(78)**
4-2017 Molly Brannigan (*Stanford*) **(82)**

12-inch record 6s.

02174 Off to Philadelphia (*Haynes*) **(81)**

GUILBERT, YVETTE

10-inch record 4s.

3737 The Keys of Heaven **(79)**

HARRISON, JOHN (Tenor)

10-inch records 4s.

4-2425 All Souls' Day. Op. 10, No. 8 (*Richard Strauss*) **(79)**
4-2019 Annie Laurie **(80)**
4-2103 Beautiful Garden of Roses (*Schmid*) **(80)**
4-2077 Because (*Guy d'Hardelot*) **(82)**
4-2397 Bonnie Mary of Argyle **(79)**)
3-2437 But Thou didst not leave (" Messiah "—*Handel*) **(77)**
4-2126 For you alone (*Geehl*) **(81)**
3-2854 { I know a lovely garden (*Guy d'Hardelot*) **(77)**
{ A Love Song (*Kaiser*) **(77)**
3-2902 I know of two bright eyes (*Clutsam*) **(80)**
3-2390 Mary (*Richardson*) **(77)**
4-2848 My Lady Fair (*Gregh*) **(78)**
3-2280 Nirvana (*Stephen Adams*) (with orchestra) **(76)**
4-2027 O flower of all the world (*Woodforde-Finden*) **(81)**
3-2800 Roses (*Stephen Adams*) **(80)**
4-2086 Take a pair of sparkling eyes (" Gondoliers "—*Sullivan*) **(81)**
4-2113 The Rosary (*Nevin*) **(81)**

The figures in brackets at end of selections indicate the speed at which the records . . . . should be played . . . .

BALLAD RECORDS

HARRISON, JOHN—*continued*

10-inch records 4s.

4–2196	The sweetest flower that blows (*Hawley*) (81)
4–2510	The Yeomen of England (" Merrie England "—*German*) (79)
3–2427	There is a flower that bloometh (" Maritana "—*Wallace*) (with orchestra) (77)
3–2484	Thou shalt break them (" Messiah " —*Handel*) (77)
3–2213	'Tis the day (*Leoncavallo*) (with orchestra) (78). Specially composed for the Gramophone Co., Ltd.
4–2447	Tom Bowling (*Dibdin*) (78)
3–2941	Two Eyes of Grey (*McGeogh*) (78)

12-inch records 6s.

02223	A Song of Sleep (with violin obbligato) (*Lord H. Somerset*) (81)
02073	A wandering minstrel I (with chorus) (78)
02254	Ailsa mine (*Newton*) (81)
02332	An Evening Song (*Blumenthal*) (81)
02617	Beloved, it is morn (*Aylward*) (79)
02468	Beyond the Dawn (*Sanderson*) (with piano and organ accompaniment) (80)
02333	Come into the garden, Maud (*Balfe*) (81)
02075	Comfort ye (Recit.) (" Messiah "—*Handel*) (77)
02074	Every valley (" Messiah"—*Handel*) (76)
02780	I'll sing thee songs of Araby (*Clay*) (79)
02152	Kathleen Mavourneen (*Crouch*) (79)
02147	My Dreams (*Tosti*) (81)
02764	My pretty Jane (The Bloom is on the Rye) (*Bishop*) (78)
02342	My sweetheart when a boy (*Morgan*) (81)
02179	O, vision entrancing (*Goring Thomas*) (81)
02794	Oft in the stilly night (*Moore*) (79)
02214	Star of Bethlehem (*Stephen Adams*) (with piano and organ) (81)
02322	Tell her I love her so (*P. de Faye*) (81)
02651	The Children's Home (with piano and organ) (*Cowen*) (81)
02375	The Holy City (*Adams*) (81)
02249	{ (*a*) The night has a thousand eyes (*Lambert*) (*b*) Across the blue sea (*Lord Henry Somerset*) (80)
02499	The Rosary (*Nevin*) (with chorus, organ and bells) (78)
02225	The Sailor's Grave (*Sullivan*) (81)
02125	There is a green hill (*Gounod*) (with organ and piano accompaniment) (78)

02122	Thora (*Stephen Adams*) (78)
02070	Waft her, angels (Aria) (with orchestra) (" Jephtha "—*Handel*) (77)

HILL, CARMEN (Mezzo-Soprano)

10-inch records 4s.

2–3266	If I might only come to you (*Squire*) (79)
2–3237	John Anderson, my Jo ! (Old Scotch Air) (79)
2–3117	Mifanwy (*Dorothy Forster*) (80)
2–3270	Rose in the bud (*Dorothy Forster*) (79)
2–3055	Roses of Forgiveness (*Guy d'Hardelot*) (79)
2–3287	When the dream is there (*Guy d'Hardelot*) (79)

12-inch records 6s.

03618	Flow down, cold rivulet (*Graham Peel*) (79)
03538	The Green Hills o' Somerset (*Eric Coates*) (79)

HINKLE, FLORENCE (Soprano)

12-inch record 6s.

2–033035	Depuis le jour (" Louise "—*Charpentier*) (80)

JAMES, LEWYS (Baritone)

10-inch record 7s.

4–2754	The Vicar of Bray (Old English Melody) (78)

JAY, DOROTHY

10-inch record 4s.

2–3224	He's a Man (*Clutsam*) (" Young England ") (78)

KENNERLEY RUMFORD, R. (Baritone)

12-inch records 6s.

02200	Four Jolly Sailormen (*German*) (80)
02197	King Charles (*M. V. White*) (Key G)
02201	{ (*a*) Myrra (*Clutsam*) (Key A Minor) (*b*) Border Ballad (*Cowen*) (Key A Minor)
02199	The Devout Lover (*M. V. White*) (Key E Flat)
02198	Three for Jack (*Squire*) (Key G)

It is important that these records should be played in the keys indicated

These records should be played with " His Master's Voice " needles, sold only in boxes bearing our copyright picture, " His Master's Voice," on the lid

BALLAD RECORDS

KORSOFF, LUCETTE (Soprano)
10-inch record 4s.

33696　Il Bacio—Valse (*Arditi*) (78)

LABBETTE, DORA (Soprano)
12-inch record 6s.

03592　Rose softly blooming (*Spohr*) (78)

LAUDER, HARRY (Baritone)
10-inch records 4s.

4–2840　Bonnie Mary of Argyle (*Traditional*) (79)
4–2821　Loch Lomond (78)

LETT, PHYLLIS (Contralto)
10-inch record 4s.

2–3281　Your heart will call me home (*Tate*) (78)

12-inch records 6s.

03557　Caller Herrin' (Old Scotch Air) (79)
03509　Light in darkness (*F. H. Cowen*) (organ played by Mr. E. Stanley Roper) (78)
03494　Sink, red sun (organ played by Mr. E. Stanley Roper) (*Teresa del Riego*) (79)
03581　The Glory of the Sea (*Sanderson*) (79)
03462　The Hills of Donegal (*Sanderson*) (79)
03521　The Arrow and the Song (*Balfe*) (79)
03611　The Pearl Cross (*Marshall*) (79)

MARINI, ALBERTO (Tenor)
10-inch record 4s.

4–2779　For you alone (*Geehl*) (79)

MARSH, LUCY (Soprano)
10-inch record 4s.

2–3011　Twickenham Ferry (*Marzials*) (78)

12-inch record 6s.

03337　Oh, for the wings of a dove (" Hear my prayer "—*Mendelssohn*) (80)

MICHAILOVA, M. A. (Soprano)
10-inch records 4s.

Sung in Russian.

23476　Angels guard thee (Berceuse—*Godard*) (with violin obbligato) (75)
23477　Ave Maria (*Gounod*) (with violin obbligato) (76)

MILLETT, BEN (Alto Vocalist)
12-inch record 6s.

02787　Pie Jesu (*Niedermeyer*) (79)

MOTT, CHARLES (the late) (Baritone)
10-inch records 4s.

4–2849　Curate's Song (" The Sorcerer") (*Gilbert and Sullivan*) (78)
4–2924　For ever and for ever (*Tosti*) (79)
4–2933　Inside the bar (*Elgar*) (words by Sir Gilbert Parker) (assisted by Messrs. FREDERICK HENRY, FREDERICK STEWART and HARRY BARRATT) (78)
4–2898　It's up to a man (*W. H. Squire*) (79

12-inch records 6s.

02706　Can't you hear me callin' (Caroline) (*Roma*) (80)
02615　Simon the Cellarer (*Hatton*) (79)
02684　The Friar of Orders Grey (*W. Reeve*) (78)
02642　" Curfew Song " (Orion) (" The Starlight Express "—*Elgar*) (78)
02643　{ (a) Song—" Come Little Winds " (" The Starlight Express "—*Elgar*) (78) (b) Wind Dance (Orchestra) (78)
02734　" The Fringes of the Fleet," No. 1. The Lowestoft Boat (*Kipling-Elgar*), assisted by Messrs. FREDERICK HENRY, FREDERICK STEWART and HARRY BARRATT, accompanied by the Symphony Orchestra, conducted by Sir EDWARD ELGAR, O.M. (79)
02735　" The Fringes of the Fleet," No. 2. Fate's Discourtesy (*Kipling-Elgar*),
02736　" The Fringes of the Fleet," No. 3. Submarines (*Kipling-Elgar*),
02737　" The Fringes of the Fleet," No. 4. The Sweepers (*Kipling-Elgar*) (79)
02639　The Organ Grinder's Songs, No. 1, " To the Children " (" The Starlight Express "—*Elgar*) (78)
02640　The Organ Grinder's Songs, No 2, " The Blue Eyes Fairy " (" The Starlight Express "—*Elgar*) (78)
02641　The Organ Grinder's Songs, No. 3, " My Old Tunes " (" The Starlight Express "—*Elgar*) (78)
02676　Thou'rt passing hence (*Sullivan*) (79)

The figures in brackets at end of selections indicate the speed at which the records . . . . should be played . . . .

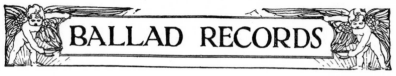

BALLAD RECORDS

NICHOLLS, AGNES (Soprano)

12-inch records 6s.

03505   I sent my soul through the invisible ("In a Persian Garden"—*Liza Lehmann*) (79)

03472   (a) Tears and Laughter ("The Starlight Express"—*Elgar*) (78)
(b) Sunrise Song ("The Starlight Express"—*Elgar*) (78)

03473   The Laugher's Song ("The Starlight Express"—*Elgar*) (78)

POUNDS, COURTICE

12-inch records 6s.

02668   Come into the garden, Maud (*Balfe*) (78)
02697   When rocked on the billows ("The Boatswain's Mate'—*Smyth*) (79)

RADFORD, ROBERT (Bass)

10-inch records 4s.

4-2028   A Chip of the Old Block (*Squire*) (82)
4-2319   Drake goes West (*Sanderson*) (82)
3-2798   D'ye ken John Peel (with chorus) (77)
4-2694   Father O'Flynn (Old Irish Melody) (arr. by *Stanford*) (78)
3-2803   For the mountains shall depart ("Elijah"—*Mendelssohn*) (80)
3-2894   Glorious Devon (*German*) (79)
3-2907   In cellar cool (79)
3-2804   Is not His word like a fire ("Elijah"—*Mendelssohn*) (80)
4-2781   O Isis ("Magic Flute"—*Mozart*) (78)
3-2788   Rocked in the cradle of the deep (*Knight*) (77)
4-2494   Shipmates o' mine (*Sanderson*) (88)
3-2934   Simon the Cellarer (*Hatton*) (79)
3-2859   The Meynell Hunt (with chorus) (*Cotton*) (78)
4-2502   The Old Brigade (*Barri*) (80)
3-2887   Wrap me up in my old stable jacket (with chorus) (77)

12-inch records 6s.

02231   Arm, arm ye brave ("Judas Maccabæus"—*Handel*) (78)
02437   Blow, blow, thou winter wind (*Sarjeant*) (80)
02339   Erl King (*Schubert*) (82)
02560   Hear me, gentle Maritana ("Maritana"—*Wallace*) (79)
02589   He who treads the path of duty ("The Magic Flute"—*Mozart*) (79)

02209   Honour and Arms (*Handel*) (82)
02102   I'm a roamer (*Mendelssohn*) (78)
02084   It is enough ("Elijah"—*Mendelssohn*) (78)
02083   Lord God of Abraham ("Elijah"—*Mendelssohn*) (80)
02280   Love, could I only tell thee (*Capel*) (80)
02117   Nazareth (*Gounod*) (79)
02490   Oh, oh, hear the wild wind blow (*Mattei*) (78)
02128   Recit. and Aria ("Acis and Galatea") I rage, I melt, I burn—O ruddier than the cherry (*Handel*) (80)
02294   She alone charmeth my sadness ("La Reine de Saba"—*Gounod*) (82)
02216   The Diver (*Loder*) (82)
02451   The Palms (*Faure*) (and Westminster Cathedral Choir) (81)
02454   The Song of the Flea (*Moussorgsky*) (82)
02085   The Village Blacksmith (*Weiss*) (with orchestral accompaniment) (78)
02343   The Wanderer (*Schubert*) (82)
02616   The Windmill (*Nelson*) (79)
02552   Thy Sentinel am I (*Watson*) (78)
02399   When the King went forth to war (*Koenemann*) (82)

SAMUELL, WILLIAM (the late) Baritone)

10-inch records 4s.

4-2695   The Yeomen of England ("Merry England"—*German*) (79)
4-2633   There's a hill by the sea (*Löhr*) (78)

12-inch records 6s.

02614   Mirror Song ("Tales of Hoffmann"—*Offenbach*) (79)
02631   Queen Mab ("Romeo and Juliet"—*Gounod*) (79)
2-032019   Vision Fugitive ("Herodiade"—*Massenet*) (76)

SANTLEY, SIR CHARLES (Baritone)

10-inch records 4s.

2-2862   Simon the Cellarer (*J. L. Hatton*) (73)
2-2863   The Vicar of Bray (73)
2-2864   To Anthea (*J. L. Hatton*) (73)

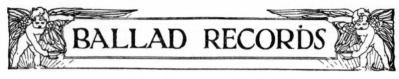

BALLAD RECORDS

THORNTON, EDNA (Contralto)

10-inch records 4s.

2–3181	A land of roses (*Teresa del Riego*) (with pianoforte accompaniment. and organ by Mr. E. Stanley Roper) **(79)**
2–3188	Because (*Guy d'Hardelot*) **(78)**
2–3052	Danny boy (Old Irish Air) **(79)**
2–3286	Dashing White Sergeant (*Bishop*) **(79)**
2–3155	Fierce Flames (Stride la vampa) (" Il Trovatore "—*Verdi*) **(79)**
3915	God's Garden (*Lambert*) **(80)**
2–3086	Habanera (" Carmen "—*Bizet*) **(79)**
3936	My ain folk (*Lemon*) **(79)**
3901	The birds go north again (*Willeby*) **(81)**
3912	The Rosary (*Nevin*) **(80)**
2–3074	The Secret (Il Segreto) (" Lucrezia Borgia "—*Donizetti*) **(79)**
2–3226	Time's Garden (*Goring Thomas*) **(79)**

12-inch records 6s.

03322	Abide with me (*Liddle*) **(80)**
03265	Angus MacDonald (*Roeckel*) **(81)**
03180	Entreat me not to leave thee (*Gounod*) **(81)**
04169	{ (*a*) I sometimes think (" In a Persian Garden "—*Liza Lehmann*) **(79)** (*b*) A book of verses underneath the bough (AGNES NICHOLLS AND HUBERT EISDELL) **(79)** }
2–053051	Largo (Ombra mai fu) (*Handel*) **(80)**
03247	Love's Coronation (*Aylward*) **(81)**
03122	My heart is weary (*Goring Thomas*) **(80)**
03351	Nearer, my God to Thee (*Carey*) (with piano and organ accompaniment) **(79)**
03253	O dry those tears (*del Riego*) **(81)**
03408	Softly awakes my heart (" Samson and Delilah "—*Saint-Saëns*) **(79)**
03271	Song of Thanksgiving (*Allitsen*) **(81)**
03573	The Better Land (*Cowen*) (piano and organ accompaniment, organ by Mr. E. Stanley Roper) **(79)**
03627	The Children's home (*Cowen*) **(79)**
03166	The Enchantress (*Hatton*) **(80)**
04170	{ (*b*) The worldly hope men set their hearts upon (" In a Persian Garden "—*Liza Lehmann*) **(79)** (*a*) Alas! that Spring should vanish with the rose (HUBERT EISDELL) **(79)** }
03585	There is a green hill far away (*Gounod*) **(78)**
03419	When all was young (" Faust "—*Gounod*) **(79)**

TREE, CHARLES (Baritone)

10-inch records 4s.

4–2337	A fat li'l' feller wid his Mammy's eyes (*S. Gordon*) **(79)**
4–2227	A Frivolous Ballad (*Slater*) **(81)**
4–2330	Kitty! (what a pity) (*Fletcher*) **(80)**
4–2099	No, John, No (*Sharp*) **(80)**
4–2197	Phil the Fluter's Ball (*Percy French*) **(80)**
4–2376	Richard of Taunton Deane (arr. by *Molloy*) **(79)**
4–2268	Tavvystock Goozey Vair (*Trythall*) **(81)**
4–2607	The Admiral's Broom (brought up to date) (*Bevan*) **(80)**
4–2231	The Drum Major (*Newton*) **(80)**
4–2544	The Somerset Farmer (*Lane Wilson*) **(79)**
4–2839	Uncle Tom Cobbley at War (Devonshire Folk Song) (*Masland*) **(79)**
4–2123	Widdicombe Fair (*Heath*) **(81)**
4–2121	Young Tom o' Devon (*Kennedy Russell*) **(80)**

12-inch records 6s.

02680	Ould John Braddleum (" Three Northern County Folk Songs "—*Johnston*) **(80)**
02677	The fly be on the turmuts (with chorus) (*Millington*) **(79)**
02502	The Kerry Dance (*Molloy*) **(79)**
02590	The Longshoreman (*Chesham*) **(78)**
02739	The Song of the Flea (*Moussorgsky*) **(79)**
02507	Up from Somerset (*Sanderson*) **(79)**
02444	Will-o'-the-Wisp (*Cherry*) **(80)**

WARRENDER, LADY MAUD (Contralto)

The royalty payable on these records is handed over by Lady Maud Warrender to Naval Charities to be selected by her.

10-inch records 4s.

3796	O that we two were maying (*Nevin*) **(81)**
3795	Three fishers went sailing (*Hullah*) **(83)**

WILNA, ALICE

10-inch record 4s.

2–3309	A little twilight song (*Clarke*) **(79)**

The figures in brackets at end of selections indicate the speed at which the records
. . . . should be played . . . .

DUET RECORDS

WOODMAN, FLORA (Soprano)

10-inch records 4s.

2-3288 A Pastoral (*Carey*, arr. *Lane Wilson*) (79)
2-3062 Oh! tell me, Nightingale (*Liza Lehmann*) (79)
2-3124 Shepherd, thy demeanour vary (*Brown arr. by Lane Wilson*) (79)

12-inch records 6s.

03522 April Morn (*Batten*) (77)
03463 Come to the dance (*Oliver*) (78)

03574 L'Echo (Swiss Echo Song) (*Eckert*) (Orchestra conducted by Mr. Percy Pitt) (79)
03416 Let the bright seraphim (with trumpet obbligato) (" Samson"—*Handel*) (78)
03451 One morning, very early (*Sanderson*) (79)
03423 Spring's Awakening (*Sanderson*) (78)
03407 When Myra sings (*A. L.*) (79)

◫ ◫ ◫ ◫ ◫

MISCELLANEOUS DUETS
(Male and Female Voices)

ALLEN, PERCEVAL, and JOHN HARRISON

12-inch records 6s.

04006 Love Divine (" Daughter of Jairus "—*Stainer*) (78)
04050 O that we two were maying (*Smith*) (80)

ALLEN, PERCEVAL, and ROBERT RADFORD

10-inch record 4s.

2-4008 In Springtime (*Newton*) (81)

ALLEN, PERCEVAL, and EDNA THORNTON

10-inch record 4s.

2-4013 Barcarolle, Lovely Night (" Tales of Hoffmann "—*Offenbach*) (81)

12-inch record 6s.

04061 I know a bank whereon the wild thyme blows (*C. Horn*) (80)

BUTCHER, ERNEST, and MURIEL GEORGE

10-inch record 4s.

2-4474 My Boy Billy (*Butcher*) (79)

BUTTERWORTH, CLARA, HERBERT CAVE, and Chorus

10-inch record 4s.

2-4382 I love a man (*Clutsam*) (" Young England ") (78)

BUTTERWORTH, CLARA, and HARRY DEARTH

10-inch records 4s.

2-4383 Jollity (*Clutsam*) (" Young England ") (78)
2-4384 Traveller's Duet (*Clutsam*) (" Young England ") (78)

BUTTERWORTH, CLARA, and DOROTHY JAY

10-inch record 4s.

2-4381 Tell Nobody (*Clutsam*) (" Young England ") (78)

D'ARGEL, NORA, and WILLIAM SAMUELL (the late)

Orchestra conducted by Mr. Percy Pitt

10-inch record 4s.

2-4337 Friendship (*Marzials*) (78)

12-inch records 6s.

04140 Dear child, recall not to my mind (Deh non parlare al misero)—Act I. (" Rigoletto "—*Verdi*) (80)
04141 Gilda, Gilda, my daughter (Piangi, fanciulla)—Act II. (" Rigoletto "—*Verdi*) (79)
04139 Sincerity (*Emile Clarke*) (78)

GARDNER, STEWART, and ERNEST PIKE

10-inch record 4s.

2-4213 March of the Men of Harlech (79)

DUET RECORDS

HARRISON, JOHN and JOSEPH

12-inch records 6s.

04244 All's well (*Braham*) **(79)**
04179 The Two Beggars (*Lane Wilson*) **(79)**

HARRISON, JOHN, and ROBERT RADFORD

10-inch records 4s.

4453 Larboard Watch (*Williams*) **(79)**
4483 The Gendarmes' Duet (*Offenbach*) **(80)**

12-inch records 6s.

04019 Be mine the delight (Scene from Act I. "Faust") **(79)**
04022 Excelsior (*Balfe*) **(79)**
04014 The moon hath raised her lamp above (*Benedict*) **(79)**
04058 Watchman, what of the night? (*Sargeant*) **(81)**

HILL, CARMEN, and MARCUS THOMSON

10-inch record 4s.

2-4431 Sweet and Low (*A. Hollins*) **(78)**
3-4015 Weep ye no more, sad fountains (*Cooke*) **(79)**

12-inch records 6s.

04167 A summer night (*Goring Thomas*) **(78)**
04127 The Swing Song ("Véronique"—*Messager*) **(79)**
04164 Venetian Song (*Tosti*) **(79)**

MARSH, LUCY, and MARGUERITE DUNLAP

10-inch record 4s.

2-4169 Barcarolle ("Tales of Hoffmann"—*Offenbach*) **(78)**

MATTHEWS, EVELINE, and JOHN HARRISON

12-inch records 6s.

04147 Let me gaze ("Faust"—*Gounod*) **(79)**
04174 Speak to me of Mother ("Carmen"—*Bizet*) **(80)**

MURPHY, LAMBERT, and REINALD WERRENRATH

10-inch record 4s.

7-54004 Ah Mimi, tu più non torni ("Bohême"—*Puccini*) **(80)**

12-inch record 6s.

2-054051 Solenne in quest'ora (Swear in this hour) ("Forza del Des ino"—*Verdi*) **(78)**

NICHOLLS, AGNES, and HUBERT EISDELL

12-inch record 6s.

04169 { (a) I sometimes think (EDNA THORNTON) **(79)**
{ (b) A book of verses underneath the bough ("In a Persian Garden"—*Liza Lehmann*) **(79)**

NICHOLLS, AGNES, and CHARLES MOTT (the late)

12-inch record 6s.

04151 Finale—"Hearts must be soft-shiny dressed" ("The Starlight Express"—*Elgar*) **(78)**

REEVES, SYDNEY, and BERNARD MOSS.

10-inch records 4s.

2-4475 Forty Years on ("Harrow School Song") (*Farmer*) **(79)**
2-4386 The Eton Boating Song (*A. D. E. W.*) **(79)**

SALTZMANN-STEVENS, and PETER CORNELIUS

12-inch records 6s.

044111 Duet, last Act, Brunnhilde and Siegfried ("Siegfried"—*Wagner*) **(81)**

THORNTON, EDNA, and ROBERT RADFORD.

10-inch record 4s.

2-4134 Where are you going to, my pretty maid? (*S. Smith*) **(79)**

The figures in brackets at end of selections indicate the speed at which the records . . . . should be played . . . .

CONCERTED RECORDS

TRIOS

**PERCEVAL ALLEN,
ALICE LAKIN and
JOHN HARRISON.**

12-inch record 6s.

04057 O Memory (*Leslie*) (82)

**EDNA THORNTON,
PERCEVAL ALLEN and
ROBERT RADFORD**

12-inch record 6s.

04131 Queen of the Night (*Smart*) (79)

QUARTETS, etc.

**PERCEVAL ALLEN,
EDNA THORNTON,
JOHN HARRISON and
STEWART GARDNER.**

10-inch records 4s.

2–4217 Good King Wenceslas (78)
2–4218 While Shepherds watched their flocks (78)

12-inch records 6s.

04121 Hark ! the Herald Angels sing (78)
04122 The Mistletoe Bough (arr. by *Kennedy Russell*) (78)

**PERCEVAL ALLEN,
EDNA THORNTON,
JOHN HARRISON and
ROBERT RADFORD.**

10-inch record 4s.

2–4011 O, who will o'er the downs so free (*Pearsall*) (81)

12-inch records 6s.

04090 { (a) God so loved the world (" Crucifixion "—*Stainer*)
       { (b) Sevenfold Amen (*Stainer*) (80)
04008 O gladsome Light (*Sullivan*) (77)
04088 O hush thee my babie (*Sullivan*) (81)

04059 Quando Corpus (" Stabat Mater "—*Rossini*) (81)
04010 Sweet and low (76)
04064 The long day closes (*Sullivan*) (80)
04096 When hands meet (*Pinsuti*) (80)

**PERCEVAL ALLEN,
ALICE LAKIN,
JOHN HARRISON and
ROBERT RADFORD**

12-inch records 6s.

04056 Believe me, if all those endearing young charms (82)
04025 God is a Spirit (*Bennett*) (81)
04047 In England, Merrie England (*German*) (80)
04028 In this hour of softened splendour (*Pinsuti*) (81)

**NORA D'ARGEL,
EDNA THORNTON,
WALTER HYDE and
ROBERT RADFORD**

12-inch records 6s.

04145 " Elijah " Memories, Part I. (*Mendelssohn*) (arr. by Hubert Bath) (79)
04146 " Elijah " Memories, Part II (*Mendelssohn*) (arr. by Hubert Bath) (79)
04148 " Elijah " Memories, Part III. (*Mendelssohn*) (arr. by Hubert Bath) (79)
04149 " Elijah " Memories, Part IV. (*Mendelssohn*) (arr. by Hubert Bath) (79)

**AGNES NICHOLLS,
EDNA THORNTON,
HUBERT EISDELL and
GEORGE BAKER.**

12-inch records 6s.

04171 { (a) As then the tulip (GEORGE BAKER) (79)
      { (b) Alas ! that spring should vanish with the rose (" In a Persian Garden "—*Liza Lehmann*) (79)
04172 They say the lion and the lizard keep (" In a Persian Garden "—*Liza Lehmann*) (79)
04168 Wake, for the sun, etc. (" In a Persian Garden "—*Liza Lehmann*) (79)

These records should be played with " His Master's Voice " needles, sold only in boxes bearing our copyright picture, " His Master's Voice," on the lid

COMPLETE OPERAS

CLARA BUTTERWORTH, DOROTHY JAY, VIOLET OPPENSHAW, HERBERT CAVE, HARRY DEARTH, HAYDEN COFFIN, ERNEST PIKE, and EDWARD HALLAND

10-inch record 4s.

2–4385   Young fresh- England (*Hubert Bath*) " Young England ") (78)

THE GRESHAM SINGERS

10-inch records 4s.

2–4451   Down in a flow'ry vale (*Festa*) (78)
2–4406   In absence (*D. Buck*) (79)
2–4482   The Mulligan Musketeers (*Atkinson*) (79)

12-inch record 6s.

04189   D'ye ken John Peel (78)

OLDE LUDGATE SINGERS (Unaccompanied)

10-inch records 4s.

2–4341   Drink to me only with thine eyes (**arr.** by *Elliot-Button*) (78)
2–4356   Pickaninny Lullaby (*Macy*) (80)
2–4344   The Goslings (*Sir F. Bridge*) (77)

THE ST. GEORGE'S GLEE SINGERS.

Gentlemen of St. George's Chapel and H.M. Private Chapel, Windsor Castle.

10-inch records 4s.

4401   On the banks of Allan Water (77)
4395   Simple Simon (77)

ST. PETERSBURG QUARTET

10-inch record 4s.

7–24000   Volga Boatmen's Song (unaccompanied) (78)

▫ ▫ ▫ ▫ ▫

COMPLETE OPERAS

" CARMEN " (Bizet)

54682   Sulla piazza si schiamazza (In the Square) (La Scala Chorus) (77)
053149   Entrata di Micaela(Entrance of Micaela) (Gilda Butti and La Scala Chorus) (77)
54681   Coro di ragazzi (Chorus of Boys) (La Scala Chorus) (78)
54677   Suona la campana (" 'Tis the noon-day bell ") (La Scala Chorus) (79)
54679   Coro delle sigaraie (Cigarette Chorus) (La Scala Chorus) (79)
054172   Mia madre veggo ancor (Duet) (" My Mother I behold ") (F. de Lucia and G. Huguet) (9s.) (77)
53516   Seguidilla (Near to the walls of Seville) (Maria Gay) (8s.) (78)
54356   Canzone del toreador (Toreador's Song) (F. Cigada, G. Huguet, Inez Salvador and La Scala Chorus)(78)

54353   Lassù, lassù (" Away, away to yonder mountains ") (Inez Salvador and E. Ischierdo) (78)
50519   Intermezzo (La Scala Orchestra) (78)
54680   Ascolta, ascolta (Chorus of Smugglers) (La Scala Chorus) (78)
54362   E nostro affar (" They like to please ") (Butti, Passeri and La Scala Chorus) (78)
053136   Aria di Micaela (G. Huguet) (78)
54355   Ho nome Escamillo (" I am Escamillo ") (F. Cigada, E. Ischierdo) (80)
54676   Chi ne vuole (Orange Chorus) (La Scala Chorus) (78)
054509   Marcia (March and Chorus) (La Scala Chorus) (78)
54354   Se tu m'ami (" If you love me ") (Inez Salvador and F. Cigada) (78)
54361   Terzetto (Trio) (Butti, Alexina, and Passeri) (78)

Unless otherwise marked, all numbers commencing with 0 are 6s. each, and the remainder 4s. each

All numbers commencing with **0** *are 12-inch records*

The figures in brackets at end of selections indicate the speed at which the records . . . . should be played . . . .

42

COMPLETE OPERAS

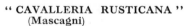

" CAVALLERIA RUSTICANA " (Mascagni)

054506   Coro d'introduzione (La Scala Chorus) (77)
2–52592   Il cavallo scalpita (Minolfi and Renzo) (77)
054144   A voi tutti salute (De Tura, Cigada and Chorus) (9s.) (77)
054145   Regina coeli (Minolfi, Rumbelli and Chorus) (78)
053183   Voi lo sapete (Calvé) (12s. 6d.) (79)
54334   Fior giaggiolo (Joanna, Salvador and De Tura) (77)
54335   Turiddu mi tolsi l'onore (Joanna—Minolfi) (78)
₵4336   Ad essi non perdona (Joanno--Minolfi) (77)
2–52594   Brindisi (De Tura and Chorus) (6s.) (77)
54337   Finale (La Scala Chorus) (78)

" DER ROSENKAVALIER " (Richard Strauss)

10-inch record 4s.

3–44102   Nein, nein !, Ich trink kein Wein (Elisabeth Boehm van Endert and Paul Knüpfer) (80)

12-inch record 6s.

044183   Ist ein Traum, kann nicht wirklich sein (Eva Plaschke von der Osten and Minnie Nast) (80)

" FAUST " (Gounod)

2–52522   La vaga pupilla (Lanzirotti and Chorus) (77)
54352   Io voglio il piacere (Pini-Corsi and Sillich) (77)
054503   Kermesse (La Scala Chorus) (77)
052181   Dío possente (F. Cigada) (77)
2–52567   Dio dell' or (Segurola and Chorus) (77)
54675   Waltzer (La Scala Chorus) (78)
54320   Permettereste a me (Brambilla, Codolini, Acerbi, Sillich and Chorus) (77)
53414   Le parlate d'amor (E. Zaccaria) (77)
2–033021   Le Roi de Thulé (Geraldine Farrar) (12s. 6d.) (79)
053081   Aria dei gioielli (G. Huguet) (78)
2–52570   Invocazione (A. Sillich) (77)
53424   Ei m'ama (G. Piccoletti) (78)
054087   Scena della chiesa (I.) (Huguet, De Luna and Chorus) (78)
054088   Scena della chiesa (II.) (Huguet, De Luna and Chorus) (78)

54664   Coro de i soldati (La Scala Chorus) (77)
2–52568   Serenata (Segurola) (77)
54287   Che fate qui, signor ? (Martinez-Patti, Pignataro, Preve) (78)
052150   Morte di Valentino (Minolfi and Chorus) (76)
054113   Dueto finale (Corsi, Acerbi) (78)
054114   Preludio e terzetto finale (Brambilla Acerbi, Sillich) (78)
54298   O del ciel angeli immortali (Huguet, Lara, De Luna) (78)

GRAND OPERA TRIO

10-inch record 4s.

2–4159   " Faust "—Trio from Prison Scene, Act V. (78)

" IL TROVATORE " (Verdi)

2–52412   Abbietta Zingari (De Luna and Chorus) (76)
2–52429   Sull' orlo déi tetti (De Luna and Chorus) (76)
53410   Tacea la notte placida (Lucia Crestani) (76)
54553   La Zingarella (Chorus) (76)
53420   Stride la vampa (Madame Lina Mileri) (76)
053064   Condotta ell'era in ceppi (Madame Lina Mileri) (76)
2–52467   Il balen del suo sorriso (Francesco Cigada) (76)
2–52431   Per me ora fatale (E. Caronna and La Scala Chorus) (76)
054500   Coro dei soldati (Chorus) (77)
054061   Giorni poveri vivea (Mameli, Minolfi, Preve and Chorus) (76)
52158   Ah ! si ben mio (Giorgio Malesci) (76)
2–52476   Di quella pira (Giovanni Valls and La Scala Chorus) (76)
53411   D'amor sull, ali rosee (Lucia Crestani) (76)
054054   Miserere (Giacomella, Martinez-Patti and La Scala Chorus) (76)
54063   Mira d'acerbe lagrime (Bernacchi and Caronna) (76)
54265   Vivrà ! contende il giubilo (De Angelis and F. Cigada) (76)
54259   Ai nostri monti ritorneremo (Esposito and Colazza) (76)
054055   Ha quest' infame (Giacomelli, Mileri and Martinez-Patti) (76)

COMPLETE OPERAS

Song-Cycle—

" IN A PERSIAN GARDEN "
(Liza Lehmann)

The Selection and Performance under the direction of the Composer.

12-inch records 6s.

04168 I. Quartet " Wake, for the sun, e'c," (Agnes Nicholls, Edna Thornton, Hubert Eisdell, George Baker) (**79**)

04169 II. (a) Contralto Recit. and Solo " I sometimes think " (Edna Thornton) (**79**)
(b) Duet " A book of verses underneath the bough " (Agnes Nicholls and Hubert Eisdell) (**79**)

10-inch record 4s.

4-2767 III. Bass solo, " Myself when young " (George Baker) (**79**)

12-inch records 6s.

03505 IV. Soprano Recit. and Solo " I sent my soul through the invisible " (Agnes Nicholls) (**79**)

04170 V. (a) Tenor solo, " Alas ! that spring should vanish with the rose " (Hubert Eisdell) (**79**)
(b) Contralto solo, " The worldly hope men set their hearts upon " (Edna Thornton) (**79**)

04172 VI. Quartet, " They say the Lion and the Lizard keep " (Agnes Nicholls, Edna Thornton, Hubert Eisdell and George Baker) (**79**)

02674 VII. Tenor Recit. and solo, " Ah ! moon of my delight "(Hubert Eisdell) (**79**

04171 VIII. (a) Bass solo, " As then the tulip " (George Baker) (**79**)
(b) Quartet, " Alas ! that spring should vanish with the rose ' (Agnes Nicholls, Edna Thornton, Hubert Eisdell and George Baker) (**79**)

A beautifully illustrated Album will be given free to every purchaser of the Complete Set of " In a Persian Garden.")

" MERRIE ENGLAND "
(Edward German)

Recorded under direction of and orchestra conducted by the composer.

12-inch double-sided records 7s.

Act I.

D. 18 Introduction—Rustic Dance and Jig (Light Opera Orchestra)
Opening chorus, Act I., Part I.—Sing a-down, a-down (Full Chorus)

D. 19 (a) Opening chorus, Act I., Part II.—Now choose me two men (Bessie Jones with Chorus)
(b) Duet and chorus—We are two proper men (George Baker and Edward Halland)
(a) Song and chorus—O, where the deer do lie (Edna Thornton)
(b) Song and chorus—That every Jack (John Harrison)

D. 20 Song and chorus—I do counsel that your playtime (George Baker)
Quintet—Love is meant to make us glad (Edna Thornton, Bessie Jones, Charles Mott (the late), Ernest Pike and Edward Halland)

D. 21 She had a letter from her love (Bessie Jones)
Duet—Come to Arcadie (Bessie Jones and John Harrison)

D. 22 Song and chorus—The Yeomen of England (Charles Mott, the late)
Long live Elizabeth (Full Chorus)

D. 23 Song and chorus—O, peaceful England (Edna Thornton)
Song and chorus—King Neptune (George Baker)

D. 24 Finale, Act I., Part I.—It is a tale of Robin Hood (Edna Thornton, Bessie Jones, George Baker, Edward Halland, Soloists, and Full Chorus)
Finale, Act I., Part II.—We are four men of Windsor (Edna Thornton, Bessie Jones, John Harrison, George Baker, Ernest Pike, Edward Halland, Soloists and Full Chorus)

D. 25 Finale, Act I., Part III.—My troth is plighted(Edna Thornton, John Harrison, Bessie Jones, Soloists, and Full Chorus)
Opening chorus, Act II.—The month o' May (Edna Thornton, Soloist, and Full Chorus)

The figures in brackets at end of selections indicate the speed at which the records · · · · should be played · · · ·

44

COMPLETE OPERAS

" MERRIE ENGLAND "—*continued*

12-inch double-sided records 7s.

D. 26
- (a) Quartet—In England, merrie England (Edna Thornton, Bessie Jones, Charles Mott (the late), and Ernest Pike)
- (b) Quartet and Male Chorus—The Sun in the Heavens Duet—It is the merry month of May (Edna Thornton and John Harrison)

D. 27
- The English Rose (John Harrison) Duet and chorus—Two merry men a-drinking (Charles Mott (the late), and Ernest Pike)

D. 28
- Waltz song—O, who shall say that love is cruel (Bessie Jones)
- (a) Song and Trio—When Cupid first this old world trod (Charles Mott (the late), and trio : Edna Thornton, Bessie Jones and Ernest Pike)
- (b) Finale, Act II.—Robin Hood's Wedding (Edna Thornton, Bessie Jones, Charles Mott (the late), Ernest Pike and Chorus)

Complete Opera in a beautifully decorated album £3 17s. 0d.

" PAGLIACCI " (Leoncavallo)

ACT I.

052163	Prologue. Part I., Si può? (Francesco Cigada) (77)
052162	Prologue, Part II., Un nido di memorie (Cigada) (77)
54673	Opening Chorus (La Scala Chorus) (77)
054507	Coro delle campane (La Scala Chorus) (77)
053130	Aria degli uccelli (Madame G. Huguet) (77)
054150	So ben che deforme (Huguet and Cigada) (77)
054148	E allor perchè (Huguet and Badini) (76)
054149	Nulla scordai (Huguet, Cigada, Badini) (76)
052166	Vesti la giubba (A. Paoli) (9s.) (79)

ACT II.

50544	Intermezzo (La Scala Symphony Orchestra) (77)
054146	Opening Chorus (Cigada, Huguet, Badini and Chorus) (77)
054151	Commedia (Part I.) (G. Huguet and Pini-Corsi) (77)
054152	Commedia (Part II.) (Huguet, Cigada and Pini-Corsi) (77)

54338	Arlecchin ! Colombina ! (Huguet, Cigada and Pini-Corsi) (77)
54339	Versa il filtro nella tazza sua (Paoli, Huguet, Cigada, Pini-Corsi) (6s.) (73)
052167	No ! Pagliaccio non son (A. Paoli) (9s.) (77)

" THE FRINGES OF THE FLEET "

(Kipling-Elgar)

**Accompanied by
THE SYMPHONY ORCHESTRA,
conducted by Sir EDWARD ELGAR, O.M.**

12-inch records 6s.

02734	I.—The Lowestoft Boat (Mr. Charles Mott, assisted by Messrs. Frederick Henry, Frederick Stewart and Harry Barratt) (79)
02735	II.—Fate's Discourtesy (79)
02736	III.—Submarines. (79)
02737	IV.—The Sweepers (79)

THE GRAND OPERA COMPANY

10-inch record 4s.

4626	Anvil Chorus ("Il Trovatore"—*Verdi*) (79)

12-inch records 6s.

04617	Gems from " Aïda," Part I. (*Verdi*) (80)
04618	Gems from " Aïda," Part II. (*Verdi*) (80)
04568	Gems from " Carmen " (*Bizet*) (80)
04539	Gems from " Cavalleria Rusticana " (*Mascagni*) (80)
04562	Gems from " Faust " (*Gounod*) (79)
2-054024	Sextet (" Lucia di Lammermoor"—*Donizetti*) (81)
04527	The Bridal Chorus from " Lohengrin " (*Wagner*) (81)
04575	Gems from " Il Trovatore " (*Verdi*) (78)
04537	Gems from " Mignon " (*Thomas*) (80)
04553	Gems from " Pagliacci " (*Leoncavallo*) (80)
04573	Gems from " Rigoletto " (*Verdi*) (79)
04572	Gems from " Tales of Hoffmann " (*Offenbach*) (80)
04619	Gems from " Traviata," Part I. (*Verdi*) (79)
04620	Gems from " Traviata," Part II. (*Verdi*) (79)

COMPLETE OPERAS

" THE BOATSWAIN'S MATE "
(Dr. Ethel Smyth)

Accompanied by
THE SYMPHONY ORCHESTRA,
conducted by the Composer

12-inch records 6s.

02697 When rocked on the billows (Courtice Pounds) (79)
2–0696 Overture—Part I. (The Symphony Orchestra) (79)
2–0697 Overture—Part II. (The Symphony Orchestra) (79)

12-inch records 7s.

04183 { (a) A friend and I were on the pier (Frederick Ranalow) (79)
(b) When the sun is setting (Rosina Buckman and Frederick Ranalow) (79)

04184 The first thing to do is to get rid of the body (Rosina Buckman, Courtice Pounds and Frederick Ranalow) (79)

04185 { (a) Oh dear, if I had known (Rosina Buckman and Frederick Ranalow) (79)
(b) The Keeper (piccolo duet) (Gilbert Barton and W. Gordon Walker) (79)

03527 { (a) Contrariness (Rosina Buckman) (79)
(b) What if I were young again (Rosina Buckman) (79)

(A beautifully illustrated Album will be given free to every purchaser of the Complete Set of " The Boatswain's Mate.")

" THE STARLIGHT EXPRESS "
(Sir Edward Elgar, O.M.)

(Orchestra personally conducted by the composer.

12-inch records 6s.

02639 The Organ Grinder's Songs. No. 1. " To the Children " (Charles Mott) (78)
02640 The Organ Grinder's Songs. No. 2. " The Blue-Eyes Fairy " (Charles Mott) (78)
02641 The Organ Grinder's Songs. No. 3. " My Old Tunes " (Charles Mott) (78)
02642 " Curlew Song " (Orion) (Charles Mott) (78)

02643 { (a) Song—" Come little winds " (Charles Mott)
(b) Wind Dance (Orchestra)

03472 { (a) Tears and Laughter (Agnes Nicholls) (78)
(b) Sunrise Song (Agnes Nicholls) (78)

03473 The Laugher's Song (Agnes Nicholls) (78)

04151 Finale—" Hearts must be soft-shiny dressed " (Agnes Nicholls and Charles Mott) (78)

" YOUNG ENGLAND "

10-inch records 4s.

4–2829 The Steersman's Song (Herbert Cave and Chorus) (78)
4–2830 The April of my heart (Herbert Cave) (78)
4–2831 I love a maid (Harry Dearth) (78)
4–2832 Who'll venture with me (Harry Dearth and Chorus) (78)
4–2833 Almighty Strength (The Prayer) (Harry Dearth and Chorus) (78)
4–2834 When travelling days are over (Hayden Coffin) (81)
2–3224 He's a man (Dorothy Jay) (78)
2–4382 I love a man (Clara Butterworth, Herbert Cave and Chorus) (78)
2–4381 Tell Nobody (Clara Butterworth and Dorothy Jay) (78)
2–4383 Jollity (Clara Butterworth and Harry Dearth) (78)
2–4384 Traveller's Duet (Clara Butterworth and Harry Dearth) (78)
2–4385 Young fresh England (Clara Butterworth, Dorothy Jay, Violet Oppenshaw, Herbert Cave, Harry Dearth, Hayden Coffin, Ernest Pike and Edward Halland) (78)

12-inch records 6s.

02714 Who sings of England ? (Hayden Coffin and Chorus) (78)
03543 O now my heart—Waltz Song (Clara Butterworth) (78)

12-inch record 5s. 6d.

C. 781 { " Young England "—Selection I. (Mayfair Orchestra) (79)
" Young England "—Selection II. (Mayfair Orchestra) (79)

The figures in brackets at end of selections indicate the speed at which the records . . . . should be played . . . .

CHOIR RECORDS

CHOIR RECORDS

MORNING PRAYER, CHURCH OF ENGLAND

By the Rev. Canon Fleming (the late), the Rev. J. R. Parkyn and the Choir of St. Andrew's, Wells Street, W.

The Complete Service, 2 10-inch and 6 12-inch, in Special Albums, £2 4s.

PART 1

04764 Opening Sentences—A General Confession—The Absolution (The Rev. J. R. PARKYN and Choir of St. Andrew's, Wells Street) (78)

PART 2

04765 The Lord's Prayer—Responses—Venite (The Rev. J. R. PARK N and Choir of St. Andrew's, Wells Street) (78)

PART 3

04766 Special Psalms—
23rd, The Lord is my Shepherd
42nd, Like as the hart
(The Choir of St. Andrew's, Wells Street) (78)

PART 3A

4878 Special Psalms—
148th, O Praise the Lord of Heaven
150th, O Praise God in His Holiness
(The Choir of St. Andrew's, Wells Street) (78)

PART 4

04767 Te Deum laudamus
(The Choir of St. Andrew's, Wells Street) (78)

PART 5

04768 Jubilate Deo—The Apostles' Creed—Prayers and Responses (The Rev. J. R. PARKYN and Choir of St Andrew's, Wells Street) (78)

PART 6

4879 The Second Collect for Peace—The Third Collect for Grace—A Prayer for the King's Majesty—A Prayer for the Royal Family (The Rev. J. R. PARKYN and Choir of St. Andrew's, Wells Street) (78)

PART 7

04769 A Prayer for the Clergy and People
A Prayer for all sorts and conditions of men
A General Thanksgiving
A Prayer of St. Chrysostom
The Grace
(The Rev. Canon FLEMING, B.D. (the late), and Choir of St. Andrew's, Wells Street) (78)

WESTMINSTER ABBEY CHOIR

(Conducted by Sir Frederick Bridge, C.V.O., M.A., Mus. Doc., Organist,Westminster Abbey)

10-inch record 4s.

4911 Ring out with jocund chime (*Sir F. Bridge*) (80)

12-inch records 6s.

04797 In sorrow and in want (*Sir F. Bridge*) (80)

04798 When the crimson sun has set (arr. by *Greathead*) (80)

WESTMINSTER CATHEDRAL CHOIR

(Under the direction of Dr. R. R. Terry, Musical Director, Westminster Cathedral

10-inch records 4s.

4876 Arise, shine (Anthem) (*Elvey*) (78)
4884 Come to the Manger (80)
4925 Good people all—Carol (arr. by *Dr. Terry*) (with Organ and Bells) (78)
4912 Nearer my God to Thee (80)
4875 Old French Carol (78)
4923 To us a Child is born (arr. by *Dr. Terry*) (with Organ and Bells) (78)
4874 Vespers and Compline (78)

12-inch records 6s.

04770 Adeste Fideles, Part I. (80)
04771 Adeste Fideles, Part II. (80)
04781 Kyrie and Gloria from Mass, Æterna Christi (*Palestrina*) (80)
04796 Motet—Ave Verum Corpus (*Mozart*) (80)
04762 Nazareth (harmonised) (*Gounod*) (78)
04795 O Salutaris Hostia (*Elgar*) (80)
04784 Responses and Agnus Dei from Mass, Æterna Christi (*Palestrina*) (80)
04783 Responses and Preface with Sanctus from Mass, Æterna Christi (*Palestrina*) (80)
04799 Sanctus from "St. Cecilia" Messe Solennelle (*Gounod*) (80)
04778 See amid the winter snow (80)
04806 Te Deum—Part I. (*Francesco Anerio*) (79)
04807 Te Deum—Part II. (*Francesco Anerio*) (79)
04800 { (a) We three Kings of Orient are (80)
{ (b) Good Christian men (*Hopkins*) (80)

These records should be played with "His Master's Voice" needles, sold only in boxes bearing our copyright picture, "His Master's Voice," on the lid

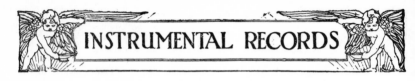

INSTRUMENTAL RECORDS

INSTRUMENTAL RECORDS

VIOLONCELLO

EVANS, C. WARWICK

10-inch records 4s.

2-7854 Mon cœur s'ouvre à ta voix (" Samson et Dalila "—*Saint-Saëns*) (78)
2-7853 When you're away (*Victor Herbert*) (" The Only Girl ") (79)

12-inch records 6s.

07889 A Keltic Lament (*J. H. Foulds*) (78)
07894 Murmuring breezes (*A. Jensen*) (79)
07886 Solemn Melody (*Walford Davies*) (78)
07891 Sonata—Part I. (*Eccles*) (79)
07895 Sonata—Part II. (*Eccles*) (79)

HAMBOURG, BORIS

10-inch record 4s.

7893 From the land of the sky-blue water (*Cadman*, arr. by *Hambourg*) (78)

12-inch record 6s.

07860 Chant sans paroles (*Tchaikovsky*) (80)

HARRISON, BEATRICE

10-inch records 4s.

2-7852 Orientale (Kaléidoscope, Op. 50, No. 9) (*César Cui*) (78)
2-7850 Slumber Song (*Rimsky-Korsakoff*) (78)

12-inch record 6s.

07893 Ave Maria (Op. 52, No. 4) (*Schubert*) (78)
07897 Gigue in C major (unaccompanied) (*Bach*) (79)

HOLLMAN, JACQUES

10-inch record 4s.

37851 Ave Maria (*Schubert*) (74)

RENARD, JACQUES

10-inch record 4s.

7884 Mélodie (*Massenet*) (with organ acc.) (80)

12-inch record 6s.

07864 Ave Maria (*Schubert*) (81)

SHARPE, CEDRIC

10-inch records 4s.

2-7857 A Memory (*Goring Thomas* arr. *Squire*) (79)
2-7851 Prière (*W. H. Squire*) (77)
7898 Serenade (*Pierne*) (78)
2-7856 Slumber Song (*Schubert*, arr. *Squire*) (79)

12-inch records 4s.

07890 Largo in G, " Serse " (*Handel*) (78)
07896 Romanze (G) Op. 26 (*Svendsen*) (79)
07884 The Broken Melody (*Van Biene*) (79)

SQUIRE, W. H.

10-inch records 4s.

7885 Barcarolle (*Offenbach*) (80)
7881 Gavotte No. 2 (*Popper*) (76)
7887 La Cinquantaine (*Gabriel-Marie*) (80)
7895 La Danza (Tarantella Napolitana) (*Rossini*, arr. by *Piatti*) (78)
7890 Mazurka (*Chopin*) (80)
7879 Melody in F (*Rubinstein*) (76)
7886 O Star of eve (" Tannhäuser "— *Wagner*) (81)
7883 Simple aveu (*Thome*) (76)

12-inch records 6s.

07877 Air (*Bach*, arr. by *Squire*) (78)
07871 Angels guard thee (*Godard*) (80)
07874 Ave Maria (*Gounod*) (78)
07869 Drink to me only with thine eyes (*Jonson*) (81)
07872 Le Cygne (*Saint Saëns*) (81)
07868 Serenade (*Squire*) (80)
07879 Silver threads among the gold (*Danks*, arr. by *Squire*) (78)
07878 Si mes vers avaient des ailes (*Hahn*) (78)
07876 Valse Apache (*Van Biene*) (80)

FLUTE

LEMMONE, JOHN

12-inch records 6s.

09154 Scherzo capriccio (*Sabathil*) (80)
09153 Wind among the trees (*Briccialdi*) (81)

The figures in brackets at end of selections indicate the speed at which the records · · · · should be played · · · ·

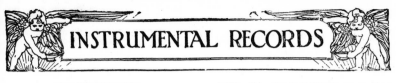

INSTRUMENTAL RECORDS

PIANOFORTE

BACKHAUS, WILHELM

(Played on a Chappell Concert Grand Piano)

12-inch records 6s.

05534 Bohemian Dance (*Smetana*) (**80**)
05533 Waltz in A flat, Op. 42 (*Chopin*) (**81**)
For Backhaus's violet label records, see page 26)

DE GREEF, ARTHUR

12-inch record 6s.

05623 Melody in F (*Rubinstein*) (**79**)

DE PACHMANN, VLADIMIR

12-inch record 6s.

05593 { (a) Prelude, Op. 28, No. 24 (*Chopin*)
{ (b) Étude, Op. 10, No. 5 (*Chopin*) (**78**)

GRAINGER, PERCY

Played on a Chappell Concert Grand Piano)

'10-inch record 4s.

5581 Shepherd's Hey (*Grainger*) (**80**)

12-inch records 6s.

05558 Mock Morris Dances (*Grainger*) (**79**)
05554 Toccata (*Debussy*) (**79**)

HAMBOURG, MARK

(Played on a Chappell Concert Grand Piano)

10-inch records 4s.

5573 Étude—A major (*Poldini*) (**79**)
5594 Humoreske, Op. 101, No. 7 (*Dvořák*) (**78**)
5634 Humoreske (*Tchaikovsky*) (**79**)
5572 Scherzo from Sonata, Op. 31, E flat (*Beethoven*) (**81**)

12-inch records 6s.

05530 Étude in G flat (*Moszkovski*) (**81**)
05548 Kiss Waltz (*Johann Strauss*) (**78**)
05579 La Campanella (*Liszt*) (**79**)
05580 Liebestraüme (*Liszt*) (**78**)
05544 Moonlight Sonata, Part I. (*Beethoven*) (**81**)
05520 Moonlight Sonata, Part II. (*Beethoven*) (**81**)
05562 Nocturne, No. 18, in E major (*Chopin*) (**79**)

05578 Norwegian Bridal March, Op. 19, No. 2 (*Grieg*) (**80**)
05528 { (a) Pastoral
{ (b) Capriccio (*Scarlatti*) (**81**)
05547 Polonaise in B flat (*Chopin*) (**79**)
05574 Prelude in C sharp minor, Op. 3, No. 2 (*Rachmaninoff*) (**78**)
05592 { (a) Prelude in G flat (*Rachmaninoff*)(**78**)
{ (b) Étude in C sharp major (*Scriabine*) (**78**)
05599 Sonata in C major, Op. 2, No. 3 (last movement) (*Beethoven*) (**78**)
05561 The Harmonious Blacksmith (*Handel*) (**78**)
05575 { (a) Waltz in D flat (*Chopin*) (**78**)
{ (b) Étude in G flat (*Chopin*)
05611 Waltz in A flat, Op. 42 (*Chopin*) (**79**)

RONALD, LANDON

(Played on a Chappell Concert Grand Piano)

10-inch records 4s.

5593 " L'Enfant Prodigue "—Pierrot's Love Declaration to Phrynette (*Wormser*) (**78**)

12-inch record 6s.

05577 " L'Enfant Prodigue "—Selection (*Wormser*) (**78**)

SCHARRER, IRENE

(Played on a Chappell Concert Grand Piano)

12-inch records 6s.

05573 Allegro scherzando, from Pianoforte Concerto in G minor, Op. 22 (*Saint-Saëns*) (**79**)
05542 { (a) Étude in A flat, No. 1, Op. 25 (*Chopin*) (**81**)
{ (b) Étude in F minor, No. 2, Op. 25 (*Chopin*) (**81**)
05541 { (a) Étude in G flat, No. 9, Op. 25 .. (*Chopin*) (**80**)
{ (b) Valse in D flat, No. 1, Op. 64 (*Chopin*) (**80**)
05571 { (a) Étude in G sharp minor, Op. 25, No. 6 (*Chopin*) (**79**)
{ (b) Danse Nègre (*Scott*) (**79**)
05610 Étude in E flat major (*Chopin*) (**79**)
05625 { (a) Étude in G flat (*Chopin*)
{ (b) Bee's Wedding (*Mendelssohn*) (**79**)
05583 Fantaisie Impromptu (*Chopin*) (**78**)
05622 Funeral March (*Chopin*) (**79**)
05591 Intermezzo in E flat (*Schumann*) (**79**)
05526 Rhapsody (*Liszt*) (**81**)
05539 Rondo Capriccioso (*Mendelssohn*) (**81**)
05576 " Tipperary "—Five Variations (*Goodhart*) (**79**)

These records should be played with " His Master's Voice " needles, sold only in boxes bearing our copyright picture, " His Master's Voice," on the lid

49

INSTRUMENTAL RECORDS

VIOLIN

HALL, MARIE

10-inch records 4s.

3–7974	Canzonetta, Op. 6 (*d'Ambrosio*) **(78)**
3–7971	Gavotte (*Bach*) **(78)**
4–7924	Humoreske (*Tor Aulin*) **(78)**
4–7931	Humoreske (*Dvořák*) **(78)**
3–7973	La Précieuse (*Kreisler*) **(78)**
3–7972	Le Cygne (The Swan) (*Saint-Saëns*) **(79)**
3–7945	Menuett (*Beethoven*) **(81)**

12-inch records 6s.

07974	{ (a) Bourrée (*Handel*) **(80)** { (b) L'Abeille (*Schubert*) **(81)**
07972	Cavatina (*Raff*) **(80)**
2–07916	Moto perpetuo (*Paganini*) **(78)**
2–07953	Sarabande et Tambourin (*Leclaire*) **(79)**
2–07938	Romance, Op. 9 (*d'Ambrosio*) **(78)**
2–07942	Violin Concerto in B minor, Op. 61— Allegro (*E gar*) accompanied by the Symphony Orchestra, conducted by Sir EDWARD ELGAR, O.M. **(79)**
2–07943	Violin Concerto in B minor, Op. 61— Andante (*Elgar*) accompanied by the Symphony Orchestra, conducted by Sir EDWARD ELGAR, O.M. **(79)**
2–07945	Violin Concerto in B minor, Op. 61— Allegro Molto (*Elgar*), accompanied by the Symphony Orchestra, conducted by Sir EDWARD ELGAR, O.M. **(79)**
2–07944	Violin Concerto in B minor, Op. 61— Cadenza (Lento) (*Elgar*), accompanied by the Symphony Orchestra, conducted by Sir EDWARD ELGAR, O.M. **(79)**

JOACHIM, PROF. JOSEPH (the late)

12-inch record 6s.

047905	Hungarian Dance, D minor, No. 2 (*Brahms*) **(75)**

MACMILLEN, FRANCIS

10-inch records 4s.

3–7944	Minuet (*Mozart*) **(81)**
3–7935	Sérénade à la Colombine (*Pierné*) **(81)**

MENGES, ISOLDE

10-inch record 4s.

3–7999	Hungarian Dance, No. 7 (*Brahms*) **(80)**

12-inch records 6s.

2–07939	Benedictus, No. 3 (*A. C. Mackenzie*) **(79)**
2–07935	Hungarian Dance in A, No. 2 (*Brahms*) **(79)**
2–07933	Nocturne in E minor (*Chopin*) **(78)**
2–07923	Polonaise in D, Op. 4 (*Wieniawski*) **(79)**

SZIGETI, JOSKA

12-inch records 6s.

07948	Andante and Variations (" Kreutzer Sonata ") (*Beethoven*) **(81)**
07971	Valse triste (*Sibelius*) **(76)**

THOMAS, TESSIE

12-inch records 6s.

2–07950	" Carmen," Selection I. (*Bizet*) **(78)**
2–07951	" Carmen," Selection II. (*Bizet*) **(78)**
2–07952	Polonaise (*Vieuxtemps*) **(79)**

VIOLIN, 'CELLO and PIANO

RENARD TRIO

10-inch records 4s.

8070	Barcarolle (" Tales of Hoffmann "—*Offenbach*) **(80)**
8068	Berceuse (*Järnefeldt*) **(80)**

12-inch records 6s.

08008	Adagio from Trio 4, Op. 2 (*Beethoven*) **(78)**
08031	Andante religioso (*Thomé*) **(80)**
08036	Familiengemälde, Op. 34, No. 4 (*Schumann*) **(80)**
08027	Lied (*Schumann*) **(81)**
08011	Love's Garden (*Schumann*) **(80)**
08030	Sérénade (*Widor*) **(81)**
08029	Slavonic Dance in C (*Dvořák*) **(80)**
08014	Song without words (*Mendelssohn*) **(81)**

VIOLIN, 'CELLO, PIANO and FLUTE

RENARD QUARTET

12-inch records 6s.

08024	Chant sans paroles (*Tchaikovsky*) **(81)**
08017	Humoreske (*Dvořák*) **(80)**
08021	Sérénade d'amour (*Von Blon*) **(80)**
08019	Sizilietta (*Von Blon*) **(81)**
08025	Slavische Tänze, No. 8 (*Dvořák*) **(80)**
08015	Spinning Song (*Mendelssohn*) **(81)**

**The figures in brackets at end of selections
indicate the speed at which the records
. . . . should be played . . . .**

TALKING RECORDS

STRING QUARTET

PHILHARMONIC STRING QUARTET

10-inch records 4s.

8112	Canzonetta in E flat (*Mendelssohn*) (79)
8130	Gavotte (" Mignon "—*Thomas*) (79)
8101	Minuet (*Boccherini*) (78)
8104	Slow movement from Quartet in D major (*Tchaikovsky*) (79)
8121	Spring Song (*Mendelssohn*) (78)

12-inch record 6s.

08043	Death and the Maiden (Variations in D minor) (*Schubert*) (79)

10-inch double-sided record 5s.

E. 1 { Cherry Ripe arr. *Frank Bridge*) (79) / Marche Militaire, Op. 51 (*Schubert*) (79)

12-inch double-sided records 7s.

D. 13 { Quartet in A major, Op. 41, No. 3, Part I. (*Schumann*) (79) / Quartet in A major, Op. 41, No. 3, Part II. (*Schumann*) (79)

D. 14 { Sally in our alley (arr. *Frank Bridge* (79) / Londonderry Air (arr. *Frank Bridge*) (79)

D. 15 { Scotch Reels (*Holbrooke*) (79) / Quartet (3rd and 4th Movements) (*Ravel*) (79)

☐ ☐ ☐ ☐ ☐

RECITATIONS, TALKING, etc.

HIS EMINENCE THE CARDINAL ARCHBISHOP OF WESTMINSTER

10-inch record 4s.

1311	Speech on Education (74)

F.M. LORD ROBERTS, V.C., K.G. (the late)

12-inch records 6s.

01083	Speech on National Service, Part I. (78)
01084	Ditto, Part II. (78)
01085	Ditto, Part III. (78)
01086	Ditto, Part IV. (78)
01087	Ditto, Part V. (78)
01088	Ditto, Part VI. (78)

THE RT. HON. THE EARL OF MEATH, P.C., K.P.

12-inch records 6s.

01041	A Message to the Boys and Girls of the Empire (80)
01042	Address on the Empire Movement (80)
01040	Speech on the Empire Movement (80)

AINLEY, HENRY

(with The Symphony Orchestra conducted by Sir EDWARD ELGAR, O.M.)

12-inch records 6s.

2-0522	Carillon—Part I., Sing, Belgians, sing (" Chantons, Belges, chantons ") (*Elgar-Cammaerts*) (78)
2-0523	Carillon—Part II., Sing, Belgians, sing (" Chantons, Belges, chantons ") (*Elgar-Cammaerts*) (78)

BOURCHIER, ARTHUR

12-inch record 6s.

01039	The Dagger Speech, " Macbeth " (78)

CHEVALIER, ALBERT

10-inch record 4s.

4-2204	Wot's the good of hanyfink ? (*Ingle*) (81)

12-inch records 6s.

02398	'E can't take a roise out of Oi (*West*) (81)
02361	Future Mrs. 'Awkins (*Chevalier*) (81)
02368	My old Dutch (*Ingle*) (81)
02351	Our little Nipper (*Ingle*) (81)
01103	The Fallen Star (*Chevalier-West*) (78)
02355	Wot vur do ee luv oi ? (*West*) (81)

These records should be played with " His Master's Voice " needles, sold only in boxes bearing our copyright picture, " His Master's Voice," on the lid

TALKING RECORDS

COLERIDGE, THE HON. STEPHEN

12-inch record 6s.

01062 Speech on " Mercy to Animals " (80)

FLEMING, REV. CANON (the late)

10-inch records 4s.

1356 The Bells, I., II., III. verses (*E. A. Poe*) (78)
1357 The Bells, IV. verse (*E. A. Poe*) (78)
1353 The Charge of the Light Brigade (*Tennyson*) (78)

GALWAY, THE RT. HON. VISCOUNT M.F.H.

12-inch record 6s.

09274 Hunting Calls (78)

GRENFELL, DR., C.M.G.

10-inch record 4s.

1382 A Gramophone on the Labrador Coast (78)

12-inch record 6s.

01044 Adrift on an Ice-floe (80)

HALE, ROBERT, and TOM WALLS

12-inch record 6s.

01133 The Wireless Scene (*Wimperis and Carrick*) (" Follow the Crowd ") (78)

MAUDE, CYRIL

12-inch record 6s.

01023 Speech (78)

A Puzzle Record

12-inch record 6s.

09255 The Conundrum (A Paradox) (78)

PEARY, COMMANDER ROBERT E.

12-inch record 6s.

01035 The Discovery of the North Pole (80)

SHACKLETON, SIR E., M.V.O.

12-inch record 6s.

01028 The Dash for the South Pole (80)

TERRY, FRED, and JULIA NEILSON

(assisted by Alfred Kendrick and Malcolm Cherry)

10-inch record 4s.

1317 Scene from " The Scarlet Pimpernel " (76)

TOLSTOI, COUNT (the late)

10-inch record 4s.

1412 Thoughts from the Book " For Every Day " (85)

TREE, SIR H. BEERBOHM (the late)

10-inch records 4s.

1314 Antony's Lament over the body of Julius Cæsar (" Julius Cæsar," Act III., Scene I.) (74)
1316 Falstaff's Speech on Honour (" Henry IV.," Part I., Act V., Scene I.) (74)
1312 Hamlet's Soliloquy on Death (" Hamlet," Act. III., Scene I.) (75)
1315 Soliloquy on the Death of Kings (77)
1313 Svengali mesmerises Trilby (75)

WALLER, LEWIS (the late)

10-inch records 4s.

1443 Charge of the Light Brigade (*Tennyson*) (81)
1442 Henry V. at Harfleur (*Shakespeare*) (81)

The figures in brackets at end of selections indicate the speed at which the records . . . . should be played . . . .

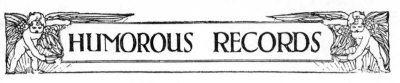

HUMOROUS RECORDS

POLITICAL RECORDS

◨ ◨ ◨

SPEECHES

RT. HON. H. H. ASQUITH, M.P.

12-inch record 6s.

01026　Speech on the Budget (80)

RT. HON. WINSTON CHURCHILL, M.P.

12-inch record 6s.

01025　Speech on the Budget (80)

RT. HON. D. LLOYD GEORGE, M.P.

12-inch record 6s.

01027　Speech on the Budget (80)

HON. ARTHUR LEE, M.P.

10-inch record 4s.

1390　On the Navy (78)

12-inch record 6s.

01024　On the Navy (78)

RT. HON. WALTER LONG, P.C., M.P.

10-inch record 4s.

1388　On Home Rule (78)

CAPT. PRETYMAN

12-inch record 6s.

01006　On the Navy (78)

HIS EXCELLENCY MONSIEUR VENIZELOS, THE GREEK PREMIER

10-inch record 4s.

1473　Speech delivered at the Mansion House on November 16th, 1917 (78)

MR. JOSIAH C. WEDGWOOD, M.P.

12-inch record 6s.

01046　Land and Labour (80)

MR. ARTHUR BOURCHIER

12-inch records 6s.

01108　Mr. Lloyd George's Speech at the Queen's Hall on September 19, 1914, entitled, "The Empire's Honour," Part I. (79)
01109　Ditto, Ditto, Part II. (79)
01110　Mr. Asquith's Speech on "Causes of the War" (78)

◨ ◨ ◨ ◨ ◨

HUMOROUS AND MUSICAL COMEDY, etc.

ADAMS, IDA (and Chorus)

12-inch record 6s.

03542　Oh, how she could Yacki, Hacki, Wicki Wacki Woo (*Von Tilzer*) ("Houp-la!") (79)

BARNES, WINIFRED

12-inch records 6s.

03594　It's just a memory (*Ivor Novello*) ("Arlette") (78
03593　The Fairy Ring (*Le Feuvre*) ("Arlette") (78)

BERRY, W. H.

10-inch records 4s.

4-2785　I could love a nice little girl (with chorus) (*Paul Rubens*) ("High Jinks") (78)
4-2784　It's wonderful how trouble clings to me (*Tate*) ("High Jinks") (78)
4-2944　When the heart is young (*Talbot*) ("The Boy") (79)

12-inch records 6s.

02679　What is life without love? (*Talbot and Greenbank*) ("High Jinks") (78)
02776　I want to go to bye-bye (with chorus) (*L. Monckton*) ("The Boy") (79)

These records should be played with "His Master's Voice" needles, sold only in boxes bearing our copyright picture, "His Master's Voice," on the lid

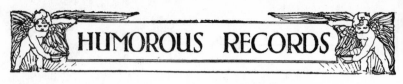

HUMOROUS RECORDS

BLANCHE, MARIE

12-inch record 6s.

03587 Wedding Day Song (*Finck*) (" Car-minetta ") **(79)**

CHOISEUILLE, MADELEINE (and Chorus)

10-inch record 4s.

7–33015 L'amour est bon (*Marcel Labbé*) (" Houp-La ! ") **(79)**

CLARE, TOM

10-inch record 4s.

4–2967 The Hindenburg Trot (*Clare*) **(79)**

12-inch records 6s.

02678 Drake is going to sea (*T. C. Sterndale Bennett*) **(80)**

02799 Exemptions and otherwise (*Lee, Weston and Hastings*) **(79)**

02757 Fritz (*Gilbert and Pether*) **(79)**

02782 Rumours (*Lee and Weston*) **(79)**

02707 Somewhere in London Town (*Clare*) **(77)**

02726 The Gay River (*Braham*) **(78)**

02770 Women's Work (*Clare and Pearson*) **(79)**

DELYSIA, ALICE

12-inch records 6s.

03589 A merry Farewell (Waltz Song) (*H. Darewski and Lassailly*) (" Car-minetta ") **(78)**

03588 Clicquot (with chorus) (*H. Darewski*) (" Carminetta ") **(79)**

03590 Habanera (Come laugh · at love) (*Lassailly*) (" Carminetta ") **(79)**

DESLYS, GABY

12-inch record 6s.

2–033039 Tout en rose (*Vincent Scotto*) **(78)**

ELSIE, LILY

12-inch records 6s.

03601 Cupid, Cupid (*Norton*) (" Pamela ") **(79)**

03602 I loved you so (*Norton*) (" Pamela ") **(79)**

ESSEX, VIOLET

10-inch records 4s.

2–3178 Bohemia (*Paul Rubens*) (" The Happy Day ") **(78)**

2–3208 Cleopatra's Nile (with chorus) (*Norton*) (" Chu Chin Chow ") **(79)**

2–3177 The Seasons (*Paul Rubens*) (" The Happy Day ") **(78)**

12-inch record 6s.

03528 I love you so (*Norton*) (" Chu Chin Chow ") **(79)**

FLORY, REGINE

12-inch record 6s.

03539 A little love, a little kiss (*Kern*) (" Vanity Fair ") **(79)**

GERARD, TEDDIE

10-inch record 4s.

2–3218 The Kirchner Girl (*Finck*) (" Vanity Fair ") **(79)**

GORDON, MARJORIE

12-inch records 6s.

03613 The touch of a woman's hand (with chorus) (*Hirsch*) (" Going Up ") **(79)**

03614 The Tickle Toe (with chorus) (Dialogue-FRANKLYN BELLAMY) (*Hirsch*) (" Going Up ") **(79)**

GRIFFIN, NORMAN

10-inch record 4s.

4–2965 Carry on the good work (with chorus) (*Nat D. Ayer*) (" Yes, Uncle ! ") **(79)**

12-inch record 6s.

02790 Ninny, Nonny, no (*Nat D. Ayer*) (" Yes, Uncle ! ") **(79)**

GROSSMITH, GEORGE

12-inch records 6s.

02692 Every little girl can teach me some-thing new (with chorus) (*Ivor Novello*) (" Theodore & Co.") **(78)**

02693 Minor objections (*Paul Rubens*) (" Theo-dore & Co.") **(78)**

The figures in brackets at end of selections indicate the speed at which the records · · · · should be played · · · ·

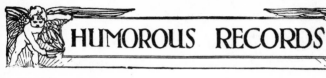

HUMOROUS RECORDS

HENSON, LESLIE
12-inch record 6s.
02691 My friend John (*Ivor Novello*) (" Theodore & Co.") (78)

HITCHCOCK, RAYMOND
12-inch record 6s.
02660 When you're all dressed up and no place to go (*Silvio Hein*) (" Mr. Manhattan ") (78)

JAMES, JULIA
12-inch record 6s.
03609 Widows are wonderful (*Nat D. Ayer*) (" Yes, Uncle! ") (79)

JANIS, ELSIE
12-inch records 6s.
03526 I'm not prepared (*Irving Berlin*) (79)
03516 When you're in Louisville (call on me) (*Bert Grant*) (79)
03511 Yaaka Hula Hickey Dula (*Goetz, Young and Wendling*) (79)

LAUDER, HARRY
10-inch records 4s.
4-2124 Good-bye till we meet again (*Lauder*) (81)
4-2104 Hey, Donal' (80)
3-2473 I wish I had some one to love me (77)
4-2105 Queen among the heather (80)
4-2146 Wee Jean Macgregor (80)
12-inch records 6s.
02371 A wee Deoch an' Doris (*Lauder*) (81)
02446 A wee hoose 'mang the heather (*Lauder and Elton*) (80)
02756 Back, back to where the heather grows (*Lauder*) (79)
02186 Bonnie Leezie Lindsay (81)
02588 Bonnie Maggie Tamson (*Lauder*) (79)
02282 Breakfast in Bed (*Lauder*) (81)
02601 Doughie the Baker (*Lauder*) (79)
02287 Every lassie loves a laddie (81)
02765 I think I'll get wed in the summer (*Lauder*) (78)
02116 I love a lassie (79)
02685 I love to be a sailor (*Lauder*) (79)
02681 I'm going to marry-arry (*Lauder*) (79)
02303 It's just like being at hame (81)
02390 It's nice when you love a wee lassie (*Lauder*) (81)
02484 It's nicer to be in bed (*Lauder*) (79)

02189 I've loved her ever since she was a baby (81)
01003 I've something in the bottle for the morning (79)
02572 Jean (*Lauder*) (78)
02170 Mr. John Mackay (81)
02704 Nanny (I never loved another lass but you) (*Lauder*) (78)
02763 O, sing to me the auld Scotch sangs (*J. F Leeson*) (78)
02320 Roaming in the gloaming (*Lauder*) (81)
02227 Saftest o' the family (81)
01004 She is my daisy (81)
02689 She is my rosie (*Lauder*) (79)
02435 She's the lass for me (*Lauder*) (80)
02089 Stop yer tickling, Jock (78)
02478 Ta-ta, my bonnie Maggie darling (*Lauder and Grafton*) (80)
02142 That's the reason noo' I wear a kilt (80)
02571 The British Bulldog's watching at the door (*Lauder*) (78)
02428 The Kilty Lads (*Lauder*) (80)
02688 The lads who fought and won (*Lauder*) (79)
02165 The Lass of Killiecrankie (81)
02300 The Message Boy (*Lauder*) (81)
02488 The Portobello Lass (*Lauder*) (80)
02395 The same as his father did before him (*Lauder*) (81)
02740 The waggle o' the kilt (*Lauder*) (79)
02138 The Wedding of Lauchie McGraw (80)
02132 The Wedding of Sandy McNab (77)
02217 Ticklie Geordie (81)
02146 Tobermory (80)
02781 We all go hame the same way (*Lauder*) (79)
02224 We parted on the shore (81)
02135 When I get back to Bonnie Scotland (81)

12-inch double-sided record 7s.
D. 1 {Appeal for £1,000,000 for maimed Scottish Soldiers and Sailors (78) Shouther to Shouther (Shoulder to Shoulder) (*Lauder*) (78)

LEVEY, ETHEL
12-inch records 6s.
03476 I love a piano (*Irving Berlin*) (" Follow the Crowd ") (78)
03477 That Hula Hula (*Irving Berlin*) ("Follow the Crowd ") (78)
03544 The Ragtime - Bagpipe Band (with chorus) (*Melville Gideon*) (" Three Cheers ") (79)
03478 Where did Robinson Crusoe go with Friday on Saturday night ? (*Meyer*) (" Follow the Crowd ") (78)

These records should be played with " His Master's Voice " needles, sold only in boxes bearing our copyright picture, " His Master's Voice," on the lid

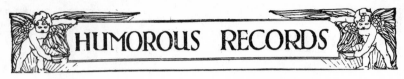

LORAINE, VIOLET

12-inch records 6s.

03605 College days (*Nat D. Ayer*) ("The Bing Boys on Broadway") **(79)**

03606 Hello! New York (*Nat D. Ayer*) ("The Bing Boys on Broadway") **(79)**

03575 Here comes Tootsie (with chorus) (*Finck*) ("Round the Map") **(78)**

03552 Let the great big world keep turning (with chorus) (*Nat D. Ayer*) ("The Bing Girls are There") **(79)**

03553 So he followed me (*Headley*) ("The Bing Girls are There") **(79)**

03576 Some girl has got to darn his socks (*Finck*) ("Round the Map") **(78)**

03577 Some day I'll make you love me (*Nat D. Ayer*) ("Round the Map") **(78)**

03604 Something Oriental (*Nat D. Ayer*) ("The Bing Boys on Broadway") **(79)**

LUPINO, STANLEY

12-inch record 6s.

02773 On the staff (with chorus) (*Ivor Novello*) ("Arlette") **(78)**

MILLAR, GERTIE

10-inch record 4s.

2-3223 The Fool of the Family (*Nat D. Ayer*) ("Houp-La!") **(79)**

12-inch records 6s.

03540 Houp-La! (*Nat D. Ayer*) ("Houp-La!") **(79)**

03541 Pretty Baby (*Jackson*) ("Houp-La!") **(79)**

03578 Pussy Cat in love (with chorus) (*Monckton*) ("Airs and Graces") **(78)**

NARES, OWEN

10-inch record 4s.

4-2957 Piccadilly, London, West (*Norton*) ("Pamela") **(79)**

POUNDS, COURTICE

10-inch record 4s.

4-2812 When a pullet is plump (*Norton*) ("Chu Chin Chow") **(79)**

12-inch record 6s.

02659 Song of the Bowl (*Finck*) ("My Lady Frayle") **(78)**

REEVE, ADA

10-inch record 4s.

2-3184 When Richard the First sat on the Throne (*Manning*) **(79)**

SMITH, CLAY

10-inch record 4s.

02732 My Lily of Killarney (*Smith, Weston and Lee*) ("Cheep!") **(78)**

TOMLIN, BLANCHE

12-inch records 6s.

03545 Just my love (*H. Darewski*) "(Three Cheers") **(79)**

03546 Morning in the Highlands (with chorus) (*H. Darewski*) ("Three Cheers") **(79)**

WHITE, LEE

10-inch record 4s.

2-3271 America answers the call (Just to help you see this through) (*Smith, Weston and Lee*) **(78)**

12-inch records 6s.

03559 Good-bye, Madame Fashion (*Smith, Weston and Lee*) ("Cheep!") **(78)**

03558 I shall see you to-night (*Smith, Weston and Lee*) ("Cheep!") **(78)**

03560 Somebody's coming to tea (*Smith, Weston and Lee*) ("Cheep!") **(78)**

03561 Where did that one go to? (*Smith, Weston and Lee*) ("Cheep!") **(78)**

The figures in brackets at end of selections indicate the speed at which the records . . . . should be played . . . .

HUMOROUS RECORDS

DUETS, etc.

**BARNES, WINIFRED, and
JOSEPH COYNE**

12-inch records 6s.

04213 Didn't know the way to (*Ivor Novello*)
("Arlette") (**78**)

04212 Love in my heart is ringing (Telephone
duet) (*Le Feuvre*) ("Arlette") (**78**)

**BERRY, W. H., and
MARIE BLANCHE**

12-inch record 6s.

04176 It isn't my fault (*Kern*) ("High
Jinks") (**78**)

**BLANCHE, MARIE, and
DENNIS NEILSON TERRY**

12-inch record 6s.

04210 Won't you kiss me! (*Lassailly*)
("Carminetta") (**78**)

**COYNE, JOSEPH, and
MARJORIE GORDON**

12-inch record 6s.

04232 First act, second act, third act
(*Hirsch*) ("Going Up") (**79**)

**DELYSIA and
DENNIS NEILSON TERRY**

12-inch record 6s.

04211 Love Duet—Finale, Act I. (*Lassailly*)
("Carminetta") (**78**)

**DORMEUIL, EDMEE, and
LUCIENNE DERVYLE**

10-inch record 4s.

3-4020 Rintintin and Nénette (with chorus)
(*Braham*) ("Telling the Tale") (**79**)

ELSIE, LILY, and OWEN NARES

12-inch records 6s.

04223 Waltz Theme and Cupid—Finale, Act II.
(*Norton*) ("Pamela") (**79**)

04224 I'm so very glad I met you (*Norton*)
("Pamela") (**79**)

04225 It's not the things you've got (*Norton*)
("Pamela") (**79**)

**ESSEX, VIOLET, and
COURTICE POUNDS**

12-inch record 6s.

04186 Any time's kissing time (*Norton*)
("Chu Chin Chow") (**79**)

**FLORY, REGINE, and
NELSON KEYS**

12-inch record 6s.

04190 Some Sort of Somebody (*Kern*)
("Vanity Fair") (**79**)

**GORDON, MARJORIE, and
H. DE BRAY**

12-inch record 6s.

04234 Kiss me! (*Hirsch*) ("Going Up") (**79**)

**GORDON, MARJORIE, and
EVELYN LAYE**

12-inch record 6s.

04233 If you look in her eyes (*Hirsch*)
("Going Up") (**79**)

**GRIFFIN, NORMAN, and
DAVY BURNABY**

12-inch record 6s.

04231 Would you believe it? (*Nat D. Ayer*)
("Yes. Uncle!") (**79**)

**GROSSMITH, GEORGE, and
MADGE SAUNDERS.**

12-inch record 6s.

04182 All I want is somebody to love me
(*Kern*) ("Theodore & Co.") (**78**)

**HENSON, LESLIE, and
DAVY BURNABY**

12-inch record 6s.

04181 Three hundred and sixty-five days
(*Kern*) ("Theodore & Co.") (**78**)

57

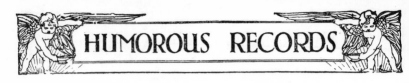

HUMOROUS RECORDS

DUETS, etc.—*continued*

LEVEY, ETHEL, and WALTER WILLIAMS

12-inch record 6s.

04194 Hold me in your loving arms (*Hirsch*) ("Three Cheers") (**79**)

LORAINE, VIOLET, and JOSEPH COYNE

12-inch records 6s.

04197 Do you like me? (*Darnley*) ("The Bing Girls are There") (**79**)

04196 That dear old home of mine (with (chorus) (*Nat D. Ayer*) ("The Bing Girls are There") (**79**)

LORAINE, VIOLET, and WALTER JEFFERIES

12-inch records 6s.

04226 First love, last love, best love (*Nat D. Ayer*) ("The Bing Boys on Broadway") (**79**)

04227 Day after day (*Nat D. Ayer*) ("The Bing Boys on Broadway") (**79**)

MILLAR, GERTIE, and NAT D. AYER

12-inch records 6s.

04191 I've saved all my loving for you (*Stamper*) ("Houp-La!") (**79**)

04192 You can't love as I do (*Paul Rubens*) ("Houp-La!") (**79**)

MILLAR, GERTIE, and ERNEST PIKE

12-inch record 6s.

04208 Whisper to me (*Monckton*) ("Airs and Graces") (**78**)

WHITE, LEE, and CLAY SMITH

12-inch records 6s.

04199 At the Calico Ball (*Smith, Weston and Lee*) ("Cheep") (**78**)

04200 Don't blame me (*Smith Weston and Lee*) ("Cheep") (**78**)

ADAMS, IDA, GERTIE MILLAR and NAT D. AYER

12-inch record 6s.

04193 Wonderful girl, wonderful boy, wonderful time (*Nat D. Ayer*) ("Houp-La!") (**79**)

LORAINE, VIOLET ALFRED LESTER and NELSON KEYS

12-inch record 6s.

04207 D.S.O. and V.A.D. (*Rice and Burnaby*) ("Round the Map") (**78**)

COYNE, JOSEPH AUSTIN MELFORD, ROY BYFORD and FRANKLYN BELLAMY.

12-inch record 6s.

04235 Down! Up! Left! Right (Finale, Act II) (*Hirsch*) ("Going Up") (**79**)

The figures in brackets at end of selections
indicate the speed at which the records
. . . . should be played . . . .

58

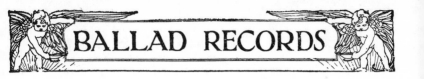

BALLAD RECORDS

" His Master's Voice "

DOUBLE-SIDED

Ten- and Twelve-inch Plum Label Records

10-inch, 3s. 6d. each ; 12-inch, 5s. 6d. each
(excepting where otherwise marked)

▣ ▣ ▣

BALLAD MUSIC, etc.

BATES, THORPE (Baritone)

10-inch records 3s. 6d.

B. 312 { Stars may forget (*Groome*) (81)
The Admiral's Broom (*Bevan*) (80)

B. 313 { The Vagabond (*Molloy*) (80)
The Yeoman's Wedding Song (*Poniatovski*) (80)

B. 314 { Four Jolly Sailormen (*German*) (78)
Long ago in Alcala (*Messager*) (81)

B. 315 { The Arrow and the Song (*Balfe*) (81)
Because (*Cowen*) (81)

B. 559 { Messmates (*Löhr*) (79)
    DENIS O'NEIL (Tenor)
Little Irish Girl (*Löhr*) (79)

12-inch records 5s. 6d.

C. 433 { The Deathless Army (*Trotère*) (80)
The Midshipmite (*Adams*) (81)

C. 434 { (a) Jock the Fiddler ; (b) The Balladmonger ("Songs of the Fair"—*Easthope Martin*) (78)
(a) Langley Fair ; (b) Fairings ("Songs of the Fair"—*Easthope Martin*) (80)

C. 441 { The dear Homeland (*Slaughter*) (81)
    PETER DAWSON
The Floral Dance (*Katie Moss*) (81)

BENSON, MAURICE (Baritone)

10-inch records 3s. 6d.

B. 687 { Ben the Bo'sun (*Stephen Adams*) (78)
The old grey Fox (*M. V. White*) (78)

B. 693 { An old Salt's Yarn (*Manville Brooke*) (79)
The Veteran's Song (*Stephen Adams*) (79)

12-inch record 5s. 6d.

C. 790 { The Bo'sun, the Gunner and me (*Trotère*) (79)
    PETER DAWSON
I'm a Roamer (*Mendelssohn*) (79)

BURNETT, ROBERT (Baritone)

10-inch record 3s. 6d.

B. 319 { Loch Lomond (Traditional) (80)
    PETER DAWSON
Love and Wine (" Gipsy Love "—*Lehar*) (81)

CRAMPTON, ERNEST (Baritone)
of the Crampton Concert Parties

10-inch records 3s. 6d.

B. 504 { When Love calls (*Crampton*) (80)
    DENIS O'NEIL
Phil the Fluter's Ball (*French*) (80)

B. 776 { Persian Prayer Rug " Curios," No. 3 (Seven Impressions) (*Crampton*) (78)
Oriental Embroidery " Curios," No. 4 (Seven Impressions) (*Crampton*) (78)

12-inch record 5s. 6d.

C. 618 { The Old Belfry (*Crampton*) (80)
    DENIS O'NEIL
The Mountains of Mourne (*French*) (78)

(For Crampton duets see page 67)

These records should be played with " His Master's Voice " needles, sold only in boxes bearing our copyright picture, " His Master's Voice," on the lid

BALLAD RECORDS

DAWSON, PETER (Baritone)

10-inch records 3s.-6d.

B. 318
- The Blue Dragoons (*Kennedy Russell*) (80)
  REINALD WERRENRATH
- Little grey home in the west (*Löhr*) (80)

B. 319
- Love and Wine (" Gipsy Love "—*Lehar*) (81)
  ROBERT BURNETT
- Loch Lomond (Traditional) (80)

B. 777
- The blind Ploughman (*Clarke*) (78)
- The Call (*Herbert Oliver*) (78)

B. 785
- The old Sexton (*Russell*) (79)
- The Armourer's Song (" Robin Hood "—*de Koven*) (79)

B. 805
- A Bachelor Gay (*Tate*) (" The Maid of the Mountains ") (78)
  LOUISE LEIGH and PETER DAWSON
- A Paradise for two (The Key to your Heart) (*Tate*) (" The Maid of the Mountains ") (78)

B. 841
- Australia (*F. Matson*) (79)
- O Canada, March on ! (*Wakefield*) (79)

B. 851
- Down among the dead men (*Macfarren*) (79)
- O Mistress mine (*Sullivan*)(79)

B. 874
- The Green Hills o' Somerset (*Eric Coates*) (79)
- The Soul of England (*Lewis Barnes*) (78)

B. 910
- Your England and mine (*Simpson*) (79)
- Home ! Canada ! Home ! (*Hennessy*) (79)

12-inch records 5s. 6d.

C. 423
- Asleep in the Deep (*Petrie*) (78)
- Bedouin Love Song (*Pinsuti*) (78)

C. 437
- Anchored (*Watson*) (81)
- At Santa Barbara (*Kennedy Russell*) (80)

C. 438
- Hybrias the Cretan (*Elliott*) (80)
- I fear no foe (*Pinsuti*) (81)

C. 439
- Thou'rt passing hence (*Sullivan*) (78)
- Sincerity (*Emile Clarke*) (81)

C. 441
- The Floral Dance (*Katie Moss*) (81)
  THORPE BATES
- The dear Homeland (*Slaughter*) (81)

C. 459
- The Bandolero (*Leslie Stuart*) (78)
  GERVASE ELWES
- So we'll go no more a-roving (*White*) (78)

C. 756
- The Watchman (*Squire*) (79)
- The Cobbler's Song (*Norton*) (" Chu Chin Chow ") (79)

C. 790
- I'm a Roamer (*Mendelssohn*) (79)
  MAURICE BENSON
- The Bo'sun, the Gunner and me (*Trotère*) (79)

DIXON, RAYMOND (Tenor)

10-inch record 3s. 6d.

B. 856
- My Own United States (with chorus) (*Julian Edwards*) (78)
  LAMBERT MURPHY
- Columbia, the Gem of the Ocean (with chorus) (The Red, White and Blue) (*Shaw*) (78)

EISDELL, HUBERT (Tenor)

10-inch records 3s. 6d.

B. 732
- A little world of love (*Kennedy Russell*) (77)
- A wild, wild rose (*Dorothy Forster*) (79)

B. 733
- Bird of love divine (*Haydn Wood*) (80)
- A Lullaby (with celeste) (*Gould*) (78)

B. 734
- Blue eyes I love (*Clarke*) (78)
- Dream o' Nights (" The Mill of Dreams "—*Eric Coates*) (78)

B. 735
- Down in the Forest (*Landon Ronald*) (78)
- Come to me (*Wadham*) (77)

B. 736
- Farewell to Summer (*Noel Johnson*) (79)
- Love Lily (*Thomson*) (78)

B. 737
- Flow'r of Brittany (*Löhr*) (79)
- Galway by the Sea (*Barclay*) (79)

B. 738
- I don't suppose (*Trotère*) (79)
- Mother mine (*Lewis Barnes*) (79)

B. 739
- If thou wert blind (*Noel Johnson*) (79)
- My message (*Guy d'Hardelot*) (80)

B. 740
- Love Ships (*Kitty Parker*)·(79)
- Megan (*Ivor Novello*) (79)

B. 741
- O Flower divine (*Haydn Wood*) (79)
- Red Devon by the Sea (*Clarke*) (80)

B. 742
- The Land of long ago (*Lilian Ray*) (78)
- The little white town (*Guy d'Hardelot*) (78)

B. 743
- Thank God for a garden (*Teresa del Riego*) (78)
- The road to love (*Kitty Parker*) (79)

B. 744
- Where my caravan has rested (*Löhr*) (81)
- Madrigal (*Chaminade*) (78)

B. 745
- Offerings (with celeste) (*Gould*) (81)
- My memories (with celeste and violin) (*Tosti*) (79)

B. 775
- Wait (*Guy d'Hardelot*) (79)
- In an old fashioned town (*Squire*) (79)

B. 799
- Until (*Sanderson*) (78)
- So fair a flower (*Löhr*) (78)

B. 831
- Dear hands that gave me violets (*Haydn Wood*) (79)
- The Joy Bird (*Lewis Barnes*) (79)

B. 850
- Do you remember ? (*Haydn Wood*) (78)
- A little home with you (*Dorothy Forster*) (78)

B. 876
- Speak of love again (*Kitty Parker*) (78)
- Steppin' down along the road (*Wilson*) (79)

B. 900
- Roses of a summer day (*Elliott*) (79)
- Roses of memory (*Dorothy Forster*) (79)

The figures in brackets at end of selections indicate the speed at which the records . . . . should be played . . . .

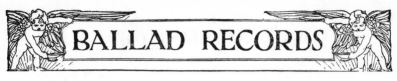

BALLAD RECORDS

EISDELL, HUBERT—*continued*

12-inch records 5s. 6d.

C. 738 { Angels guard thee (with 'cello) (*Godard*) (78)
I arise from dreams of thee (*Salaman*) (78)

C. 739 { Come sing to me (*Jack Thompson*) (80)
Awake! (*Pelissier*) (81)

C. 740 { Land of delight (*Sanderson*) (76)
Love's garden of roses (*Haydn Wood*) (78)

C. 741 { Melanie (*Weatherley-Coates*) (79)
Ninette (*Pedro de Zulueta*) (80)

C. 742 { Parted (*Tosti*) (80)
Speak (with violin) (*Tosti*) (78)

C. 743 { Somewhere a voice is calling (*Tate*) (81)
Sweet early violets (*Sherrington*) (78)

ELWES, GERVASE (Tenor)

10-inch records 3s. 6d.

B. 320 { Phyllis has such charming graces (arr. by *Lane Wilson*) (81)
Sigh no more, ladies (*Aiken*) (80)

B. 321 { (a) To Daisies (*Quilter*) ; (b) Song of the Blackbird (*Quilter*) (81)
Absent, yet present (*M. V. White*) (81)

B. 322 { Ich liebe dich (*Grieg*) (78)
Morning Hymn (*Henschel*) (81)

12-inch record 5s. 6d.

C. 459 { So we'll go no more a-roving (*M. V. White*) (78)
PETER DAWSON
The Bandolero (*Leslie Stuart*) (78)

FRIEL, HUGH (Tenor)

10-inch records 3s. 6d.

B. 969 { My ain wee house (*Munro*))79)
Ae fond iss (*Scott Gatty*) (79)

B. 970 { Mary (*Richardson*) (79)
The Scottish emigrant's farewell (*Hume*) (79)

GREEN, TOPLISS (Baritone)

10-inch records 3s. 6d.

B. 564 { A short cut (*Trotère*) (78)
Kitty, what a pity (*Fletcher*) (78)

B. 609 { The Love of my heart (*Nutting*) (79)
Barnicombe Fair (*Kennedy Russell*) (79)

B. 650 { In an old-fashioned town (*Squire*) (78)
HERBERT TEALE
Jean upon the Uplands (*Robertson*) (78)

12-inch record 5s. 6d.

C. 775 { The last call (*Sanderson*) (79)
Queen of my heart (" Dorothy "—*Cellier*) (79)

HAMILTON, EDWARD (Baritone)

10-inch record 3s. 6d.

B. 855 { We'll never let the old flag fall (with chorus) (*MacNutt and Kelly*) (78)
THE PEERLESS QUARTET
What kind of an American are you ? (*Von Tilzer*) (78)

HARRISON, CHARLES W. (Tenor)

10-inch records 3s. 6d.

B. 351 { Where my caravan has rested (*Löhr*) (78)
PERCY WHITEHEAD
Last Year (*White*) (78)

B. 352 { Macushla (*MacMurrough*) (78)
PERCY WHITEHEAD
Back to Ireland (*Stanford*) (78)

B. 511 { A Dream (*Bartlett*) (79)
Little grey home in the west (*Löhr*) (79)

B. 512 { I hear you calling me (*Marshall*) (79)
A little love, a little kiss (*Silesu*) (79)

B. 666 { Mother Machree (*Olcott and Ball*) (79)
Alice, where art thou ? (*Ascher*) (79)

12-inch record 5s. 6d.

C. 442 { A furtive tear (" Elixir of Love "— *Donizetti*) (78)
All hail, thou dwelling pure and lowly (78)

KNOWLES, CHARLES (Baritone)

10-inch records 3s. 6d.

B. 380 { For behold darkness (Recit.) (" Messiah " —*Handel*) (77)
Thus saith the Lord (Recit.) (" Messiah " —*Handel*) (77)

B. 383 { Why do the nations (Air) (" Messiah "— *Handel*) (77)
Madame JONES-HUDSON and PETER DAWSON
What have I to do with Thee (" Elijah " —*Mendelssohn*) (77)

12-inch records 5s. 6d.

C. 476 { But who may abide (Air) (" Messiah "— *Handel*) (77)
The people that walked (Air) (" Messiah " —*Handel*) (77)

C. 479 { The trumpet shall sound (Air) (" Messiah " —*Handel*) (77)
Hallelujah Chorus (" Messiah "—*Handel*) (Choir) (80)

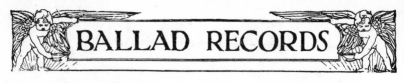

BALLAD RECORDS

MACLEOD, RODERICK
(Tenor and choir)
10-inch records 3s. 6d.

B. 973
{ Psalm 118, verses 1 and 2 (" Kilmarnock")
(Sung in Gaelic) **(79)**
Psalm 103, verses 1 and 2 (" Coleshill ")
(Sung in Gaelic) **(79)**

B. 979
{ Psalm 34, verses 1 and 2 (" St. David ")
(Sung in Gaelic) **(79)**
Stornoway (Paraphrase 18, verse 4) (Sung in Gaelic) **(79)**

MACGREGGOR, ALEXANDER
(Baritone)
10-inch records 3s. 6d.

B. 975
{ The nameless lassie (*Mackenzie*) **(79)**
There's a wee bit land (*Grieve*) **(79)**

B. 976
{ Rolling home to Bonnie Scotland (arr. by *Rene Farban*) **(79)**
Mary Morrison (*Sullivan*) **(79)**

MURPHY, LAMBERT (Tenor)
10-inch record 3s. 6d.

B. 856
{ Columbia, the Gem of the Ocean (with chorus) (The Red, White, and Blue) (*Shaw*) **(79)**
RAYMOND DIXON
My own United States (with chorus) (*Julian Edwards*) **(79)**

O'NEIL, DENIS (Tenor)
10-inch records 3s. 6d.

B. 504
{ Phil the Fluter's Ball (*French*) **(80)**
ERNEST CRAMPTON
When love calls (*Crampton*) **(80)**

B. 559
{ Little Irish Girl (*Löhr*) **(79)**
THORPE BATES
Messmates (*Löhr*) **(79)**

B. 708
{ Sometimes you'll remember (*Head*) **(79)**
Dreamtime and you (*Nicholls*) **(79)**

12-inch records 5s. 6d.

C. 618
{ The Mountains of Mourne (*French*) **(78)**
ERNEST CRAMPTON
The old Belfry (*Crampton*) **(80)**

C. 661
{ A little bit of heaven (*Ball*) **(79)**
Irish home of mine (*Dene*) **(78)**

PIKE, ERNEST (Tenor)
10-inch record 3s. 6d.

B. 964
{ The heart of a rose (*Nicholls*) **(79)**
RUBY HEYL
One little hour (*Sharpe*) **(79)**

12-inch record 5s. 6d.

C. 793
{ Roses of Picardy (*Haydn Wood*) **(78)**
LOUISE LEIGH and FLORENCE BERENS (*Whistler*)
When the autumn leaves are falling (*Stamper*) (" Zig-Zag ") **(78)**

RATCLIFFE, STAFF-CAPTAIN H.
(Baritone)
12-inch record 5s. 6d.

C. 656
{ Rose in the bud (*Dorothy Forster*) (acc. by de Groot and the Piccadilly Orchestra) **(78)**
AIMEE MAXWELL
Can it be love (*Rubens*) (" Betty ") **(78)**

TALBOT, HARRY (Baritone)
10-inch record 3s. 6d.

B. 728
{ Giles (*Loughborough*) **(78)**
Down Zummerzet way (*T. C. Sterndale Bennett*) **(78)**

12-inch record 5s. 6d.

C. 872
{ The bellringer (*Wallace*) **(79)**
A farmer's Boy (Old English Song)

TEALE, HERBERT (Tenor)
10-inch records 3s. 6d.

B. 525
{ Love's devotion (*Tate*) **(79)**
Melisande (*Ashleigh*) **(79)**

B. 540
{ The Lovelight in your eyes (*Dunkley*) **(78)**
Of the North I sing (" Songs of the Northern Hills "—*Oliver*) **(79)**

B. 573
{ Friend and Lover (*Landon Ronald*) **(80)**
The little rose clad window (*Dorothy Forster*) **(80)**

B. 634
{ Maire, my girl (*Aitken*) **(78)**
Come, gentle sleep ("Ivanhoe"—*Sullivan*) **(77)**

B. 650
{ Jean upon the uplands (*Robertson*) **(78)**
TOPLISS GREEN
In an old-fashioned town (*Squire*) **(78)**

B. 686
{ Until (*Sanderson*) **(79)**
A Request (*Amy Woodforde-Finden*) **(79)**

The figures in brackets at end of selections indicate the speed at which the records . . . . should be played . . . .

BALLAD RECORDS

TEALE, HERBERT—*continued*

10-inch records 3s. 6d.

B. 698 { Love's garden of roses (*Haydn Wood*) (78)
Love's sorrow (*Shelley*) (78)

B. 755 { God made thee mine (*Haydn Wood*) (78)
The siesta (*Squire*) (78)

B. 839 { Who is Sylvia ? Op. 106, No. 4 (*Schubert*) (79)
Marguerite (*C. A. White*) (78)

B. 864 { The song that reached my heart (*Jordan*) (78)
If you were the op'ning rose (*Hewitt*) (78)

B. 911 { She's the daughter of Mother Machree (*Ball*) (79)
When love is calling (*Brewer*) (79)

12-inch records 5s. 6d.

C. 763 { Non è ver (Never more) (*Mattei*) (78)
Death of Nelson (*Braham*) (78)

C. 789 { Love is waiting (*Squire*) (77)
Bantry Bay (*Molloy*) (77)

C. 838 { Whisper and I shall hear (*Piccolomini*) (78)
Mary of Allandale (*Hook*, arr. by Lane Wilson) (78)

VALLO, ALESSANDRO (Tenor)

10-inch record 3s. 6d.

B. 364 { A Trieste (" Salve, O terra irredenta "—*Carosio*) (Italian Patriotic Hymn) (75)
CECILIAN QUARTETTE
Russian National Anthem sung in English (78)

WERRENRATH, REINALD (Baritone)

10-inch records 3s. 6d.

B. 305 { Three for Jack (*Squire*) (78)
The Ringers (*Lohr*) (78)

B. 318 { Little grey home in the west (*Lohr*) (80)
PETER DAWSON
The blue Dragoons (*Kennedy Russell*) (80)

WHITEHEAD, PERCY (Baritone)

10-inch records 3s. 6d.

B. 323 { Eldorado (*Walthew*) (80)
The gentle maiden (*Somervell*) (80)

B. 351 { Last Year (*White*) (78)
CHARLES W. HARRISON
Where my caravan has rested (*Lohr*) (78)

B. 352 { Back to Ireland (*Stanford*) (78)
CHARLES W. HARRISON
Macushla (*MacMurrough*) (78)

ALLEN, PERCEVAL (Soprano)

10-inch records 3s. 6d.

B. 381 { Come unto Him (Air) " Messiah "—*Handel* (76)
How beautiful are the feet (" Messiah "—*Handel*) (76)

B. 382 { Rejoice greatly (Air) (" Messiah "—*Handel*) (76)
Lift up your heads (" Messiah "—*Handel*) (Choir) (77)

12-inch records 5s. 6d.

C. 443 { Scenes that are brightest " Maritana "—*Wallace*) (80)
I dreamt that I dwelt (" Bohemian Girl" —*Balfe*) (82)

C. 444 { Ave Maria (*Gounod*) (violin by ERNEST LAWRENCE) (78)
O rejoice in the Lord (" Cavalleria Rusticana"—*Mascagni*) (with Westminster Cathedral Choir) (80)

C. 478 { I know that my Redeemer (Air) (" Messiah "—*Handel*) (78)
Madame DEWS
O thou that tellest (Air) (" Messiah "—*Handel*) (78)

BAKER, ELSIE (Contralto)

10-inch records 3s. 6d.

B. 544 { A perfect day (*Bond*) (79)
I love you truly (*Bond*) (79)

B. 616 { Voices of the woods (Melody in F) (*Rubinstein*) (78)
OLIVE KLINE
Spring (Printemps) Valse chantée (*Leo Stern*) (78)

B. 784 { Two Roses (*Hallett Gilberte*) (79)
RUBY HEYL
Wait (*Guy d'Hardelot*) (79)

12-inch record 5s. 6d.

C. 422 { Old Folks at Home (*Foster*) (78)
Home, sweet Home (*Bishop*) (78)

BEELEY, MARION (Contralto)

12-inch records 5s. 6d.

C. 445 { Songs my mother sang (*Grimshaw*) (80)
My ships (*Barratt*) (81)

C. 446 { The call of the homeland (*Teschemacher*) (78)
OLGA, ELGAR and ELI HUDSON
The sunshine of your smile (*Ray*) (78)

BALLAD RECORDS

BLACK, JENNY (Contralto)

10-inch records 3s. 6d.

B. 871 { Afton Water (*Hume*) (**79**)
Lochnagar (Traditional) (**79**)

972 { O, sing to me the auld Scotch songs (Traditional) (**79**)
Jock o' Hazeldean (Traditional))**79**)

CAROL, STELLA (Soprano)

12-inch record 5s. 6d.

C. 605 { The Swallows (*Cowen*) (**79**)
Lo, here the gentle lark (*Sir H. Bishop*) (**79**)

CASTLES, AMY (Soprano)

10-inch record 3s. 6d.

B. 325 { Angels guard thee ('cello obbligato) (*Godard*) (**75**)
La Serenata (*Braga*) ('cello by W. H. Squire) (**75**)

CROSS, JEAN (Soprano)

10-inch record 3s. 6d.

B. 977 { Castles in the air (*Ballantine*) (**79**)
Rothesay Bay (*Scott Gatty*) (**79**)

DESMOND, VERA (Soprano)

10-inch records 3s. 6d.

B. 832 { Take me to flowerland with you (*Dorothy Forster*) (**79**)
Where the bee sucks (*Arne*) (**79**)

B. 875 { Good Luck (*Lewis Barnes*) (**78**)
Fairy Revel (*Oliver*) (**78**)

12-inch record 5s. 6d.

C. 776 { Orpheus with his lute (*Sullivan*) (**78**)
LOUISE LEIGH
Any place is heaven if you are near me (*Löhr*) (**78**)

DEWS, MDME. (Contralto)

10-inch records 3s. 6d.

B. 326 { Abide with me (*Liddle*) (**75**)
Caller Herrin' (**75**)

B. 327 { The Promise of life (*Cowen*) (**74**)
Love's old sweet song (*Molloy*) (**73**)

12-inch records 5s. 6d.

C. 477 { He shall feed His flock (Air) (" Messiah " —*Handel*) (**76**)
He was despised (Air) (" Messiah "—*Handel*) (**75**)

C. 478 { O Thou that tellest (Air) (" Messiah "—*Handel*) (**78**)
PERCEVAL ALLEN
I know that my Redeemer (Air) (" Messiah "—*Handel*) (**78**)

C. 485 { O rest in the Lord (" Elijah "—*Mendelssohn*) (**77**)
Madame JONES-HUDSON
Hear ye, Israel (" Elijah "—*Mendelssohn*) (**78**)

DICKESON, GERTIE (Soprano)

10-inch record 3s. 6d.

B. 302 { In an old-fashioned town (*Squire*) (**78**)
My ships (*Barratt*) (**78**)

ESSEX, VIOLET (Soprano)

12-inch record 5s. 6d.

C. 871 { Songs my mother used to sing (**79**)
Three wonderful letters from home (*Hanley*) (**78**)

HARDING, EVELYN (Soprano)

10-inch records 3s. 6d.

B. 330 { Dearest, I bring you daffodils (*Dorothy Forster*) (**81**)
Madame JONES-HUDSON
Rose in the bud (*Dorothy Forster*)(**81**)

B. 495 { Down Vauxhall way (" Songs of Old London "—*Oliver*) (**80**)
Gretna Green(" Songs of Merry England " —*Oliver*) (**80**)

B. 750 { Laugh and sing (*Drummond*) (**78**)
Break o' day (*Sanderson*) (**78**)

12-inch records 5s. 6d.

C. 447 { Spring's awakening (*Sanderson*) (**79**)
CARRIE TUBB
The valley of laughter (*Sanderson*) (**80**)

C. 702 { The dancing lesson (*Oliver*) (**79**)
Love the Pedlar (*German*) (**79**)

The figures in brackets at end of selections indicate the speed at which the records . . . . should be played . . . .

HELDER, RUBY (Lady Tenor)

10-inch records 3s. 6d.

B. 298 { Tell me you care (*Elliott*) (78) / Have you forgotten ? (*Geehl*) (78)

B. 299 { To be near you (*Coote*) (78) / When other lips (" Bohemian Girl"—*Balfe*) (78)

B. 332 { I'll sing thee songs of Araby (*Clay*) (80) / Courage (*Van den Heuvel*) (79)

12-inch records 5s. 6d.

C. 419 { If with all your hearts (" Elijah "—*Mendelssohn*) (78) / You are all the world to me (*Squire*) (78)

C. 420 { My Queen (*Blumenthal*) (78) / For all Eternity (*Mascheroni*) (78)

C. 449 { The last Watch (*Pinsuti*) (81) / My dreams (*Tosti*) (81)

C. 450 { Th ra (*Stephen Adams*) (80) / Mountain Lovers (*Squire*) (81)

C. 453 { Be thou faithful (" St. Paul"—*Mendelssohn*) (78) / ELEANOR JONES-HUDSON / Ave Maria (" Cavalleria Rusticana "—*Mascagni*) (79)

C. 563 { Green Isle of Erin (*Roeckel*) (78) / Beauty's Eyes (*Tosti*) (78)

C. 758 { The Message (*Blumenthal*) (78) / LOUISE LEIGH / God bring you home again (*Trelawny*) (78)

HEYL, RUBY (Contralto)

10-inch records 3s. 6d.

B. 756 { God send you back to me (*Adams*) (78) / Coming home (*Willeby*) (79)

B. 784 { Wait (*Guy d'Hardelot*) (79) / ELSIE BAKER / Two Roses (*Hallett Gilberte*) (79)

B. 816 { You gave me comfort (*Wakley*) (80) / Humility (*Grant*) (80)

B. 838 { One lone star (*MacCunn*) (79) / My heart's with the old folks (*Trelawny*) (79)

B. 868 { When the great red dawn is shining (*Sharpe*) (79) / Until we meet again (*Shirley*) (79)

B. 894 { Till you come Home again (*Gayne*) (79) / Before you came (*Lane Wilson*) (78)

B. 964 { One little hour (*Sharpe*) (79) / ERNEST PIKE / The heart of a rose (*Nicholls*) (79)

12-inch record 5s. 6d.

C. 785 { The Bells of St. Mary's (*Adams*) (78) / NAT D. AYER and OLIVE BURTON / Who taught you all those things that you taught me ? (*Nat D. Ayer*) (78)

HORSBURGH, NINA (Contralto

10-inch record 3s. 6d.

B. 333 { Will ye no come back again ? (Traditional) (JENNY TAGGART) (81) / Gin a body (Comin' thro' the rye, (80)

HUNTER, LIZZIE (Contralto)

10-inch record 3s. 6d.

B. 787 { We'd better bide a wee (*Claribel*) (79) / Lang, lang syne (79)

12-inch record 5s. 6d.

C. 803 { Lochnagar (Traditional) (79) / Fair ta' the gloamin' (Traditional) (79)

JONES-HUDSON, ELEANOR (Soprano)

10-inch records 3s. 6d.

B. 330 { Rose in the bud (*Dorothy Forster*) (81) / EVELYN HARDING / Dearest, I bring you daffodils (*Dorothy Forster*) (78)

B. 334 { Vilja's song (" The Merry Widow "—*Lehar*) (78) / Musetta's song (" La Bohême "—*Puccini*) (78)

B. 335 { Lo, here the gentle lark (with flute obligato) (*Bishop*) (79) / De sun is a-sinkin' (with harp and flute) (80)

12-inch records 5s. 6d.

C. 451 { Home, sweet home (*Bishop*) (80) / La Serenata (*Braga*) (with flute by ELI HUDSON) (80)

C. 452 { Angels ever bright and fair (*Handel*) (79) / Serenade (*Gounod*) (flute by ELI HUDSON) (80)

C. 453 { Ave Maria (" Cavalleria Rusticana "—*Mascagni*) (79) / RUBY HELDER / Be thou faithful (" St. Paul "—*Mendelssohn*) (78)

C. 485 { Hear ye, Israel (" Elijah "—*Mendelssohn*) (78) / Madame DEWS / O rest in the Lord (" Elijah "—*Mendelssohn*) (77)

BALLAD RECORDS

KLINE, OLIVE (Soprano)

10-inch records 3s. 6d.

B. 616 { Spring (Printemps) Valse chantée (*Leo Stern*) (78) ELSIE BAKER
Voices of the woods (Melody in F) (*Rubinstein*) (78)

B. 667 { The Wren: from "Bird Songs" (*Liza Lehmann*) (78)
The lass with the delicate air (*Arne*) (78)

B. 800 { Charme d'amour (Love's Spell) (*Kendall*) (78) VIOLET OPPENSHAW
Down here (*May Brahe*) (78)

LAKIN, ALICE (Contralto)

10-inch record 3s. 6d.

B. 494 { Little Silver Ring (*Chaminade*) (79)
Irish Love song (*Lang*) (79)

12-inch records 5s. 6d.

C. 454 { Promise of Life (*Cowen*) (79)
Husheen (*Needham*) (78)

LEIGH, LOUISE (Soprano)

10-inch record 3s. 6d.

B. 697 { Love, here is my heart (*Leo Silesu*) (79) VERA DESMOND (Soprano)
Some night, some waltz, some girl (*Bennett Scott*) (79)

12-inch records 5s. 6d.

C. 758 { God bring you home again (*Trelawny*) (78) RUBY HELDER
The Message (*Blumenthal*) (78)

C. 776 { Any place is Heaven if you are near me (*Löhr*) (78) VERA DESMOND
Orpheus with his lute (*Sullivan*) (78)

LONSDALE, GERTRUDE (Contralto)

10-inch record 3s. 6d.

B. 348 { Absent (*Tirindelli*) (78) PALGRAVE TURNER
My dear Soul (*Sanderson*) (78)

MARQUIS, PHEMIE (Soprano)

10-inch records 3s. 6d.

B. 973 { The boatman (" Fear a Bhata ") (Sung in Gaelic) (*Lawson*) (79)
Hebridean sea reivers song (" Na Reubairean) " (Sung in Gaelic) (79)

B. 974 { The land of the mountains (" An teid thm leam arighinn og ") (Sung in Gaelic) (79)
A fairy's love song (" Tha mi sgith ") (Sung in Gaelic) (79)

MAXWELL, AIMEE (Soprano)

12-inch records 5s. 6d.

C. 672 { When you come home (*Squire*) (78)
A Broken Doll (*Tate*) (" Samples " Revue) (78)

MAYER, RENEE (Soprano)

10-inch records 3s. 6d.

B. 541 { Mister Bear (*Blaney*) (79)
Laddie in khaki (*Ivor Novello*) (79)

B. 624 { Till the boys come home (*Ivor Novello*) (with chorus) (79)
A Memory (*Edna Park*) (78)

OPPENSHAW, VIOLET (Contralto)

10-inch records 3s. 6d.

B. 607 { Shepherd's Cradle Song (*Somervell*) (79)
Massa's in de cold, cold ground (*Foster*) (79)

B. 688 { Winds in the trees (*Goring Thomas*) (78)
Big Lady Moon (" Five Fairy Ballads "— *Coleridge-Taylor*) (78)

B. 800 { Down here (*May Brahe*) (78) OLIVE KLINE
Charme d'amour (Love's Spell) (*Kendall*) (78)

12-inch records 5s. 6d.

C. 655 { An old Garden (*Hope Temple*) (79)
Sabbath morning at Sea (" Sea Pictures "— *Elgar*) (79)

C. 709 { Mighty like a rose (*Nevin*) (79)
Where corals lie (" Sea Pictures "— *Elgar*) (79)

The figures in brackets at end of selections indicate the speed at which the records · · · · should be played · · · ·

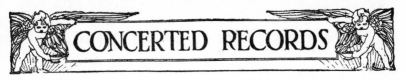

CONCERTED RECORDS

SMITHSON, FLORENCE (Soprano)

12-inch record 5s. 6d.

C. 532 {
My Boy (*Kennedy Russell*) (78)
The vale of Dreams (*Baer and Schmid*) (80)
}

TUBB, CARRIE (Soprano)

12-inch record 5s. 6d.

C. 447 {
The Valley of Laughter (*Sanderson*) (80)
EVELYN HARDING
Spring's Awakening (*Sanderson*) (79)
}

TAGGART, JENNY (Soprano)

10-inch record 3s. 6d.

B. 333 {
Gin a body (Comin' thro' the rye) (80)
NINA HORSBURGH
Will ye no come back again ? (Traditional) (81)
}

TURNER, PALGRAVE (Contralto)

10-inch records 3s. 6d.

B. 338 {
Melisande in the wood (*Goetz*) (81)
Time's roses (*Barry*) (81)
}

B. 348 {
My dear soul (*Sanderson*) (78)
GERTRUDE LONSDALE
Absent (*Tirindelli*) (78)
}

▣ ▣ ▣

DUETS, QUARTETS, etc.

ALLEN, PERCEVAL, and CARRIE TUBB

12-inch record 5s. 6d.

C. 458 {
I waited for the Lord (" Hymn of Praise") *Mendelssohn*) (78)
DESCRIPTIVE RECORD
Divine Service in Camp (arr. by VIVIAN BENNETTS) (Prayer and Exhortation by the Rev. J. R. Parkyn) (78)
}

CRAMPTON, ERNEST, and MARJORIE VERNON
of the Crampton Concert Parties

12-inch record 5s. 6d.

C. 457 {
An old-world Garden (*Crampton*) (78)
Lack-a-day (*Crampton*) (78)
}

DUNLAP, MARGUERITE, and HARRY MacDONOUGH

10-inch record 3s. 6d.

B. 343 {
When it's apple blossom time in Normandy (*Trevor*) (78)
MAURICE FARKOA (the late)
Two dirty little hands (*Cobb and Edwards*) (81)
}

EISDELL, HUBERT, and BESSIE JONES

10-inch record 3s. 6d.

B. 873 {
The Wells of sleep (*Norton*) (78)
Miss RUBY HEYL and Mr. ERNEST PIKE
Down Zummerzet way (We don't do things like that in Zummerzet) (*T. C. Sterndale Bennett*) (78)
}

HARDING, EVELYN, and CHARLES NELSON

10-inch records 3s. 6d.

B. 729 {
Somewhere a voice is calling (*A. Tate*) (78)
Little grey home in the West (*Löhr*) (78)
}

B. 751 {
Where my caravan has rested (*Löhr*) (77)
EVELYN HARDING and HARRY TALBOT
Down the Vale (*Moir*) (77)
}

HARDING, EVELYN, and HARRY TALBOT

10-inch record 3s. 6d.

B. 751 {
Down the Vale (*Moir*) (77)
EVELYN HARDING and CHARLES NELSON
Where my caravan has rested (*Löhr*) (77)
}

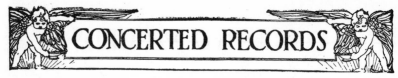

CONCERTED RECORDS

HEYL, RUBY, and ERNEST PIKE

10-inch record 3s. 6d.

B. 873
{ Down Zummerzet way (We don't do things like that in Zummerzet) (*T. C. Sterndale Bennett*) (78)
HUBERT EISDELL and BESSIE JONES
The wells of sleep (*Norton*) (78) }

JONES-HUDSON, MDME., and ERNEST PIKE

10-inch records 3s. 6d.

B. 340
{ Miserere (" Il Trovatore "—*Verdi*) (77)
ERNEST PIKE and ALAN TURNER
The Waltz Duet (" A Waltz Dream "—*Oscar Straus*) (80) }

B. 341
{ O that we two were maying (*Smith*) (79)
The Keys of Heaven (79) }

KLINE, OLIVE, and ELSIE BAKER

10-inch record 3s. 6d.

B. 522
{ Abide with me (*Monk*) (79)
Whispering hope (*Hawthorne*) (79) }

PIKE, ERNEST, and ALAN TURNER

10-inch record 3s. 6d.

B. 340
{ The Waltz Duet (" A Waltz Dream "—*Oscar Straus*) (80)
MADAME JONES-HUDSON and ERNEST PIKE
Miserere (" Il Trovatore "—*Verdi*) (77) }

AMERICAN QUARTET

10-inch records 3s. 6d.

B. 344
{ On the Mississippi (*MacDonough-Carroll-Fields*) (80)
Pucker up your lips, Miss Lindy (*Von Tilzer*) (80) }

B. 345
{ That Mysterious Rag (*Berlin-Snyder*) (80)
Waiting for the Robert E. Lee (*Gilbert-Muir*) (80) }

B. 514
{ The Red, White and Blue (*Hirsch*) (80)
Tip Top Tipperary Mary (*Carroll*) (80) }

CECILIAN QUARTET

10-inch records 3s. 6d.

B. 347
{ It's a long, long way to Tipperary (*Judge and Williams*) (78)
Hearts of Oak (*Boyce*) (78) }

B. 361
{ Who killed Cock Robin ? (78)
Little Brown Jug (78) }

B. 363
{ When Johnny comes marching home (78)
The Girl I left behind me (78) }

B. 364
{ Russian National Anthem (sung in English) (78)
ALESSANDRO VALLO
A Trieste (" Salve, o terra irredenta "—*Carosio*) (Italian Patriotic Hymn) (75) }

HAYDN QUARTET

10-inch record 3s. 6d.

B. 365
{ The Holy City (*Stephen Adams*) (79)
MEISTER GLEE SINGERS
Dinah Doe (76) }

MIXED QUARTET

10-inch record 3s. 6d.

B. 370
{ When the Angelus is ringing (*Grant*) (78)
AMERICAN RAGTIME OCTET
Oh, you beautiful doll (*Brown and Ayer*) (80) }

THE PEERLESS QUARTET

10-inch record 3s. 6d.

B. 855
{ What kind of an American are you ? (*Von Tilzer*) (78)
EDWARD HAMILTON
We'll never let the old flag fall (with chorus) (*MacNutt and Kelly*) (78) }

THE AMERICAN RAGTIME OCTET

(accompanied by MELVILLE GIDEON)

10-inch record 3s. 6d.

B. 370
{ Oh, you beautiful doll (*Brown and Ayer*) (80)
MIXED QUARTET
When the Angelus is ringing (*Grant*) (78) }

The figures in brackets at end of selections indicate the speed at which the records . . . . should be played . . . .

CHOIR RECORDS

MINSTER SINGERS

10-inch records 3s. 6d.

B. 366 { Click, Clack (*Scott-Gatty*) (**81**)
De ole banjo (*Scott-Gatty*) (**81**)

B. 367 { Oh, dem golden slippers (**81**)
The old folks at home (with banjo accompaniment) (**76**)

B. 368 { Good-night (*Scott-Gatty*) (**81**)
Massa's in de cold, cold ground (with banjo) (**76**)

12-inch record 5s. 6d.

C. 512 { Sea Songs (**78**)
SULLIVAN OPERATIC PARTY
Entrance and March of the Peers (" Iolanthe "—*Sullivan*) (**78**)

MEISTER GLEE SINGERS

10-inch record 3s. 6d.

B. 365 { Dinah Doe (**76**)
HAYDN QUARTET
The Holy City (*Stephen Adams*) (**79**)

田 田 田

CHURCH CHOIRS, ORATORIOS, etc.

THE MINSTER CHOIR
(conducted by Mr. VIVIAN BENNETTS)
10-inch records 3s. 6d.

B. 699 { When the crimson sun has set (*Greathead*) (**78**)
The First Noel (**78**)

B. 700 { Ring out with jocund chime (*Bridge*) (**78**)
CHARLES HOPKINS (Celeste)
Lead, Kindly Light (*Rev. J. B. Dykes*) (**78**)

B. 862 { Sweet Christmas Bells (*Stainer*) (**78**)
Christmas Bells (*Bridge*) (**78**)

12-inch records 5s. 6d.

C. 712 { Bethlehem (*Gounod*) (**78**)
O Holy Night (*Adolphe Adam*, arr. by *West*) (**78**)

C. 822 { Glory to God in the Highest (*Pergolesi*) (**78**)
Nazareth (*Gounod*) (**78**)

CHURCH CHOIR (Mixed)
10-inch records 3s. 6d.

B. 371 { Crown Him with many crowns (**80**)
Days and moments quickly flying (**80**)

B. 372 { For ever with the Lord (**80**)
Hark, hark my soul (**81**)

B. 373 { Holy, Holy, Holy (**80**)
Jesus Christ is risen to-day (**80**)

B. 374 { Nearer, my God, to Thee (**80**)
Now the labourer's task is o'er (**80**)

B. 375 { O Jesus, I have promised (**81**)
Onward, Christian Soldiers (**80**)

B. 376 { Christian, dost thou see them ? (**80**)
O come, all ye faithful (**81**)

B. 377 { There is a green hill (**80**)
The National Anthem (solo by THORPE BATES) (**79**)

B. 378 { Christ the Lord is risen to-day (*Elvey*) (**81**)
CHOIR OF ST. ANDREW'S, Wells Street, W.
O God our Help (**81**)

B. 379 { All hail the Power (**81**)
Come unto Me, ye weary (**80**)

12-inch records 5s. 6d.

C. 471 { Bow down and hear me (Et incarnatus est) (" Twelfth Mass "—*Mozart*) (**78**)
Glorious is Th·· Name (Gloria in Excelsis) (" Twelfth Mass "—*Mozart*) (**78**)

C. 472 { Praise the Lord (Quoniam Tu Solus Sanctus) (" Twelfth Mass "—*Mozart*) (**78**)
Thou, Lord, art God alone (Cum Sancto Spiritu) (" Twelfth Mass "—*Mozart*) (**78**)

C. 473 { He is blessed (Benedictus) (" Twelfth Mass "—*Mozart*) (**78**)
They have taken away my Lord (Anthem) (*Stainer*) (**81**)

C. 474 { Worthy is the Lamb (" Messiah "—*Handel*) (**76**)
LEEDS FESTIVAL CHOIR, 1907
And the Glory of the Lord (" Messiah "—*Handel*) (**80**)

CHOIR OF ST. ANDREW'S CHURCH,
Wells Street, W.
10-inch record 3s. 6d.

B. 378 { O God our Help (**81**)
CHURCH CHOIR (Mixed)
Christ the Lord is risen to-day (*Elvey*) (**81**)

These records should be played with " His Master's Voice " needles, sold only in boxes bearing our copyright picture, " His Master's Voice," on the lid

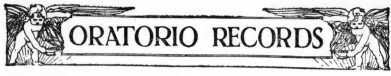

ORATORIO RECORDS

THE LEEDS FESTIVAL CHOIR, 1907

(60 selected voices, conducted by Mr. H. A. FRICKER, Mus. Bac., F.R.C.O.)

12-inch records 5s. 6d.

C. 474 { And the Glory of the Lord (" Messiah "—*Handel*) (80)
CHURCH CHOIR (Mixed)
Worthy is the Lamb (" Messiah "—*Handel*) (76)

C. 481 { Hallelujah Chorus (" Messiah "—*Handel*) (80)
Introduction (PETER DAWSON); Overture (ORCHESTRA) (" Elijah ") (77)

THE TRINITY ORATORIO CHOIR

12-inch record 5s. 6d.

C. 586 { It came upon the midnight clear (*Willis*) (78)
The BELLS o' BOURNVILLE
Evening bells, ½ to 6 o'clock, introducing The Day Thou gavest, Lord, is ended (*Scholefield*) (78)

MAYFAIR ORCHESTRA with AIMÉE MAXWELL and GEORGE BAKER

12-inch records 5s. 6d.

C. 619 { Intercessory Hymns, including "Lead, kindly Light" and "Abide with me" (arr. by *Crudge*) (79)
A Sabbath Evening Scene, introducing Jude's "A Sabbath Evening Hymn" (arr. by *Crudge*) (79)

C. 620 { Sacred Selection—Grant us Thy Peace—Part I. (arr. by *Crudge*) (80)
MAYFAIR ORCHESTRA and GEORGE BAKER
Sacred Selection—Grant us Thy Peace—Part II. (arr. by *Crudge*) (80)
MAYFAIR ORCHESTRA and AIMÉE MAXWELL

▣ ▣ ▣

ORATORIO—" THE MESSIAH " (Handel)

10-inch records 3s. 6d.

B. 380 { For behold darkness (Recit.) (CHAS. KNOWLES) (77)
Thus saith the Lord (Recit.) (CHAS. KNOWLES) (77)

B. 381 { Come unto Him (Air) (PERCEVAL ALLEN) (76)
How beautiful are the feet (PERCEVAL ALLEN) (77)

B. 382 { Rejoice greatly (Air) (PERCEVAL ALLEN) (76)
Lift up your heads (Chorus) (CHOIR) (77)

B. 383 { Why do the Nations (Air) (CHARLES KNOWLES) (77)
What have I to do with thee ? (" Elijah ") (Duet) (E. JONES-HUDSON and PETER DAWSON) (77)

12-inch records 5s. 6d.

C. 474 { And the Glory of the Lord (Chorus) (*Choir*) (80)
Worthy is the Lamb (Chorus) (CHOIR) (76)

C. 475 { Overture (ORCHESTRA) (80)
Pastoral Symphony (ORCHESTRA) (75)

C. 476 { But who may abide (Air) (CHARLES KNOWLES) (77)
The people that walked (Air) (CHARLES KNOWLES) (76)

C. 477 { He shall feed His flock (Air) (Madame DEWS) (76)
He was despised (Air) (Madame DEWS) (75)

C. 478 { O thou that tellest (Air) (Madame DEWS) (76)
I know that my Redeemer (Air) (PERCEVAL ALLEN) (78)

C. 479 { Hallelujah Chorus (CHOIR) (80)
The trumpet shall sound (Air) (CHARLES KNOWLES) (76)

(For other records of " Messiah " see John Harrison, pages 34 and 35)

ORATORIO—" ELIJAH " (Mendelssohn)

10-inch records 3s. 6d.

B. 383 { What have I to do with Thee ? (Duet) (Madame JONES-HUDSON and PETER DAWSON) (77)
Why do the Nations (" Messiah ") (Mr. CHARLES KNOWLES) (77)

B. 384 { Blessed are the Men who fear Him (Chorus) (CHOIR) (77)
Call Him louder (PETER DAWSON and CHOIR) (76)

B. 385 { Cast thy burden upon the Lord (Quartette) (77)
Lift thine eyes (E. JONES-HUDSON, FLORENCE VENNING, CARRIE TUBB and ERNEST PIKE) (77)

B. 386 { He, watching over Israel (Chorus) (CHOIR) (77)
Then did Elijah (Chorus) (CHOIR) (76)

The figures in brackets at end of selections indicate the speed at which the records • • • • should be played • • • •

" ELIJAH "——*continued*

12-inch records 5s. 6d.

C. 480 { Help, Lord (Chorus) (CHOIR) (76)
Yet doth the Lord see it not (Chorus) (CHOIR) (77)

C. 481 { Introduction ; (PETER DAWSON) Overture (ORCHESTRA) (77)
Hallelujah Chorus (" Messiah ") (LEEDS FESTIVAL CHOIR) (80)

C. 482 { Thanks be to God (Chorus) (CHOIR) (77)
Have ye not heard (Chorus) (FLORENCE VENNING and CHOIR) (77)

C. 483 { Be not afraid (Chorus) (CHOIR) (77)
Behold ! God the Lord passeth by (Chorus) (CHOIR) (78)

C. 484 { O Lord, Thou has overthrown (Chorus) (PETER DAWSON, CARRIE TUBB and CHOIR) (76)
What have I to do with Thee ? (Duet) (E. JONES-HUDSON and PETER DAWSON) (77)

C. 485 { O rest in the Lord (Air) (Madame DEWS) (77)
Hear ye, Israel (E. JONES-HUDSON) (78)

C. 436 { O come everyone that thirsteth (Quartette) (78)
And then shall your light break forth (Chorus) (CHOIR) (77)

(For other records of " Elijah " see Robert Radford, page 37)

□ □ □ □ □

RECITATIONS, TALKING, etc.

AINLEY, HENRY

10-inch record 3s. 6d.

B. 393 { The Charge of the Light Brigade (*Tennyson*) (78)
The Day (*Chappell*) (78)

COLLIER, CONSTANCE

12-inch record 5s. 6d.

C. 606 { The Hellgate of Soissons, Part I. (*Kaufman*) (77)
The Hellgate of Soissons, Part II. (*Kaufman*) (77)

EMNEY, FRED (the late), and SYDNEY FAIRBROTHER

12-inch record 5s. 6d.

C. 492 { A sister to assist 'er (Episode) (*Le Breton*) (80)
Mrs. Le Browning (sequel to " A sister to assist 'er ") (*Le Breton*) (80)

HARVEY, MORRIS, and ERIC ROPER

12-inch record 5s. 6d.

C. 510 { Wilkinson, the ledger clerk (78) MARK SHERIDAN (the late)
The Three Trees : or There, there, there (*Dudley Powell*) (81)

HAZELL, RUPERT

10-inch records 3s. 6d.

B. 639 { The 'Oxton 'ero (*Hazell*) (79)
Speech Day (*Graham Squiers*) (78)

B. 683 { Oh, no ! (*Hazell*) (79)
My face (*Hazell*) (79)

HEMUS, PERCY

12-inch record 5s. 6d.

C. 493 { The Raven—Part I. (*Poe*) (77)
The Raven—Part II. (*Poe*) (77)

HUNTLEY, G. P.

10-inch record 3s. 6d.

B. 394 { Presence of mind (78)
Rabbits (" Mr. Porple "—*Rubens*) (78)

12-inch record 5s. 6d.

C. 494 { An Ode (*Huntley*) (78)
Oh ! Lor ! (*Winifred O'Connor*) (78)

HUNTLEY, G. P., and GEORGE CARROLL

10-inch record 3s. 6d.

B. 402 { The Golf Scene (" Three Little Maids ") (74)
THE SULLIVAN OPERATIC PARTY
The Judge's Song (" Trial by Jury "—*Sullivan*) (76)

LESTER, ALFRED

(assisted by the author, FRANK LEO)

12-inch record 5s. 6d.

C. 495 { Higgins on the river (*Frank Leo*) (79)
Higgins, the Quack (*Frank Leo*) (78)

(assisted by Miss BUENA BENT)

12-inch records 5s. 6d.

C. 496 { A Restaurant Episode (81)
The Hairdresser (*Fred Rome*) (81)

C. 497 { The Village Fire Brigade (78)
The Scene-shifter's Lament (81)

POTTER, PAULINE

12-inch records 5s. 6d.

C. 502 { Beauty and the Beast (80)
Cinderella (80)

C. 503 { Dick Whittington and his Cat (80)
Jack and the Beanstalk (80)

C. 504 { Red Riding Hood (80)
The Three Bears (80)

C. 505 { The Frog Prince (*Sutcliffe*) (78)
The Wolf and the Kids (*Sutcliffe*) (78)

C. 506 { The Witch and the Lake (*Sutcliffe*) (78)
The Golden Key (*Sutcliffe*) (78)

C. 507 { The Life of our Lord (78)
The Life of David (78)

C. 508 { The Life of Moses (78)
The Life of Joseph (78)

C. 509 { The Life of Abraham (78)
Daniel in the Lions' Den (78)

ROBERTS, ARTHUR

10-inch record 3s. 6d.

B. 395 { Trial by Jury (" Where's the Count ")
(with supers and effects) (76)
G. H. SNAZELLE (the late)
How Bill Adams won the Battle of
Waterloo (77)

SHERIDAN, MARK (the late)

12-inch record 5s. 6d.

C. 510 { The Three Trees : or There, there, there
(*Powell*) (81)
MORRIS HARVEY and ERIC ROPER
Wilkinson, the ledger clerk (78)

SNAZELLE, G. H. (the late)

10-inch record 3s. 6d.

B. 395 { How Bill Adams won the Battle of
Waterloo (77)
ARTHUR ROBERTS
Trial by Jury (" Where's the Count ")
(with supers and effects) (76)

WILLIAMS, BRANSBY

12-inch records 5s. 6d.

C. 499 { Scrooge—Before the Dream (" A Christ-
mas Carol "—*Dickens*) (80)
Scrooge—The Dream (" A Christmas
Carol "—*Dickens*) (80)

C. 500 { Scrooge—The Awakening (" A Christmas
Carol ") (80)
Sidney Carton's Farewell (" Tale of Two
Cities ") (80)

C. 501 { Micawber and Uriah Heep (" David
Copperfield ") (78)
Devil-may-care (82)

🔲 🔲 🔲

DESCRIPTIVE

10-inch records 3s. 6d.

B. 696 { Flannigan as a Special Constable (78)
Flannigan as Referee at a Prize Fight (78)

B. 476 { British Troops passing through Boulogne
(78)
BLACK DIAMONDS BAND
New Year's Eve (with Chorus) (80)

B. 782 { On the Plantation (Characteristic Piece)
(*Puerner*) (COLDSTREAM GUARDS) (79)
The Irish Patrol (*Puerner*) (COLDSTREAM
GUARDS) (79)

12-inch records 5s. 6d.

C. 458 { Divine Service in Camp (arr. by *Vivian
Bennetts*) (Prayer and Exhortation by
the Rev. J. R. PARKYN) (78)
PERCEVAL ALLEN and CARRIE TUBB
I waited for the Lord (" Hymn of Praise "
—*Mendelssohn*) (80)

C. 561 { Divine Service on a Battlefield (arr. by
Vivian Bennetts) (Prayer and Exhorta-
tion by the Rev. J. R. PARKYN) (78)
Divine Service on a Battleship (arr. by
Vivian Bennetts) (Prayer and Exhorta-
tion by the Rev. J. R. PARKYN) (78)

C. 772 { Military Tattoo—Part I. (Soloist, ED-
WARD HALLAND) (arr. by *Mackenzie-
Rogan*) (COLDSTREAM GUARDS) (79)
Military Tattoo—Part II. (Soloists, ER-
NEST PIKE and EDWARD HALLAND)
(arr. by *Mackenzie - Rogan*) (COLD-
STREAM GUARDS) (79)

**The figures in brackets at end of selections
indicate the speed at which the records
· · · · should be played · · · ·**

DESCRIPTIVE—*continued*

C. 786 ⎰ Church Parade—Part I. (Soloist, PETER DAWSON) (arr. by *Mackenzie - Rogan*) (COLDSTREAM GUARDS) (78)
Church Parade—Part II. (Soloists, ERNEST PIKE and PETER DAWSON) (arr. by *Mackenzie - Rogan*) (COLDSTREAM GUARDS) (78)

C. 825 ⎰ American Fantasia—Happy Days in Dixie, or Life in the Old Plantation (*T. Bidgood*) (78)
A Comical Contest—Burlesque (*C. Godfrey*) (78)

◨ ◨ ◨

RUSSIAN TEACHING RECORDS

from " First Russian Book " (Forbes)

spoken by
NEVILLE FORBES, M.A.
Reader in Russian to Oxford University

After the war, the commercial link with our Russian Allies will surely be strengthened, and many people are now preparing for the Anglo-Russian trade boom by mastering the Russian language. These admirable records enable the student to master the difficulties of pronunciation, emphasis, etc., while facilitating the learning of the grammar. The complete first Russian Book can be obtained of the publishers, the Clarendon Press, Oxford. (Price 2s. 6d.) ⌡

10-inch records 3s. 6d.

B. 657 ⎰ Chapters 1 and 2—The alphabet, and single words illustrating pronunciation
Chapter 3—Useful indeclinable words, words of greeting, etc.

B. 658 ⎰ Chapters 29 and 30—Useful phrases illustrating the use of the genitive, names of authors, etc.
Chapter 33—Asking for food and drink, etc.

B. 659 ⎰ Chapter 34—Use of the numbers
Chapters 35 and 36—Expression of time, the date, etc.

B. 660 ⎰ Chapter 40 (from page 36)—How to say " I have," etc.
Chapter 43—Useful phrases containing prepositions followed by the genitive.

B. 661 ⎰ Chapter 47 (to page 156)—Useful phrases with the dative ; feeling hot, cold, well, ill, etc.
Chapter 47 (pages 156 and 158) and Chapter 49—Wants and requests ; how old are you ?

B. 662 ⎰ Chapters 52 and 53—Useful phrases with the accusative, direction, time of day, etc.
Chapter 57 (middle of page 180 to Chapter 58)—Useful phrases with the instrumental ; the seasons, etc.

◨ ◨ ◨

PROFESSOR RIPMAN'S
French Dialogue Records
FRENCH LIFE AND WAYS

A set of thirty-one records of conversational French, produced under the direction of Professor Walter Ripman, M.A. The book (price 1s. 6d. net) accompanying these records contains the French text by Monsieur S. Barlet and an idiomatic English rendering by Professor Ripman. The titles of the dialogues show that the subjects treated are of special interest to those who visit France, while for educational purposes the records have the valuable object of affording models of good conversational French speech.

10-inch records 3s. 6d.

B. 491 ⎰ Introduction
I. On Board

B. 412 ⎰ II. On Board
III. At Dieppe ; The Customs ; Refreshments

B. 413 ⎰ IV. In the train
V. At the Western Station, Paris

B. 414 ⎰ VI. At the hotel ; dinner
VII. Breakfast ; letters ; cabs ; omnibus ; underground railway ; Seine steamers

B. 415 ⎰ VIII. The same continued
IX. The same continued

B. 416 ⎰ X. Post Office ; telegraph ; telephone
XI. A business call

B. 417 ⎰ XII. Losing one's way ; an appetiser
XIII. Looking about for lunch

TALKING RECORDS

FRENCH LIFE
AND WAYS—*continued*

B. 418 { XIV. After lunch : at the Zoological Gardens
XV. Dinner

B. 419 { XVI. After dinner : ways of spending the evening
XVII. After dinner ; ways of spending the evening

B. 420 { XVIII. The streets of Paris
XIX. The streets of Paris

B. 421 { XX. A visit to the theatre
XXI. At the Opera

B. 422 { XXII. At tea
XXIII. Sightseeing

B. 423 { XXIV. The same
XXV. At the barber's

B. 424 { XXVI. The markets
XXVII. A visit to the doctor

B. 425 { XXVIII. A visit to the dentist
XXIX. At the watchmaker's

B. 426 { XXX. The environs of Paris
XXXI. General impressions

◻ ◻ ◻

WHISTLING

CAPPER, CHAS.

10-inch records 3s. 6d.

B. 151 { Carmena (*Lane Wilson*) (**80**)
Cherry Ripe (*Horn*) (**80**)

B. 152 { Bid me discourse (*Bishop*) (**78**)
Nymphs and Shepherds (*Purcell*) (**79**)

B. 153 { Il Bacio (*Arditi*) (**78**)
Piccolo, Piccolo, Tsin, Tsin, Tsin (*Oscar Strauss*) (**78**)

MARCONI OFFICIAL TRAINING SIGNALS

prepared by

THE WIRELESS PRESS, Ltd.,

Marconi House, London

———

10-inch records 3s. 6d.

COURSE No. I.

B. 625 { International Morse Code Signals
Practice in difficult letters, etc.

B 626 { Press (slow)
Press (medium)

B. 627 { Messages (slow)
Assorted Messages (medium)

B. 628 { Commercial messages (medium)
Code and Cypher

B. 629 { Assorted Messages (fast)
Foreign Messages (fast)

B. 630 { Press and Press Jamming
Messages and Press Jamming

COURSE No. II.

B. 789 { Sounder Record (Morse Code)
Sounder Record (Press)

B. 790 { French Press
Italian Press

B. 791 { Spanish Press
Portuguese Press

B. 792 { Press with Interruptions
Figures and Fractions

B. 793 { Calling-up Procedure (Time-rush, etc.)
Distress Working

B. 794 { Messages and French Jamming—No. I.
Messages and French Jamming—No. II.

◻ ◻ ◻ ◻ ◻

The figures in brackets at end of selections indicate the speed at which the records . . . . should be played . . . .

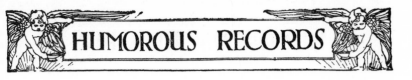

HUMOROUS RECORDS

MUSICAL COMEDY, VARIETY ARTISTS AND COMEDIANS

AGAR, DAN

12-inch record 5s. 6d.

C. 846
{
The fact is— (*Ayer*) (" The Bing Boys on Broadway ") (79)
Shurr-up! (*Ayer*) (" The Bing Boys on Broadway ") (79)
}

AYER, NAT D.

10-inch records 3s. 6d.

B. 640
{
In other words (*Ayer*) (" The Bing Boys are here ") (78)
Dear Old Shepherd's Bush (*Ayer*) (" The Bing Boys are here ") (78)
}

B. 641
{
The clock song (*Ayer*) (" The Bing Boys are here ") (78)
Come round London with me (*Ayer*) (" The Bing Boys are here ") (78)
}

B. 642
{
Another little drink wouldn't do us any harm (with chorus) (*Ayer*) (" The Bing Boys are here ") (78)
ALHAMBRA ORCHESTRA
The Whistler (*Ayer*) (" The Bing Boys are here ") (78)
}

B. 807
{
I bring my own girls along (*Ayer*) (" The Bing Girls are There ") (78)
When you're dancing with me—Fox Trot (*Ayer*) (" The Bing Girls are There ") (78)
}

B. 860
{
Sullivan will be there (*Ayer*) (79)
I'm on my way to Dixieland (*Ayer*) (79)
}

B. 866
{
Never let your right hand know what your left hand's going to do (*Ayer*) (79)
My Baby Soldier Boy (*Ayer*) (79)
}

12-inch records 5s. 6d.

C. 677
{
I stopped, I looked, and I listened (*Ayer*) (" The Bing Boys are here ") (78)
The Kipling Walk (*Ayer*) (" The Bing Boys are here ") (78)
}

C. 768
{
I like the place where the peaches grow (with chorus) (*Ayer*) (" Houp-La ! ") (79)
Any girl means ev'rything to me (*Ayer*) (" Houp-La ! ") (79)
}

C. 779
{
Yula Hicki Wicki Yacki Dula (with chorus) (*Ayer*) (" The Bing Girls are There ") (79)
O yes ! I remember (*Ayer*) (" The Bing Girls are There ") (79)
}

BARD, WILKIE

12-inch record 5s. 6d.

C. 533
{
The wriggly Rag (*David and Arthurs*) (80)
You've got to sing in Ragtime (*David and Arthurs*) (81)
}

BECK, CLARA

10-inch record 3s. 6d.

B. 766
{
You were the first one to teach me to love (*Godfrey, Wakley and Scott*) (78)
OLIVE BURTON
There's a ship that's bound for Blighty (*Shirley*) (78)
}

BERRY, W. H.

10-inch record 3s. 6d.

B. 445
{
The Bassoon (*Ashlyn*) (81)
NELSON JACKSON
When Richard the First sat on the Throne (81)
}

12-inch record 5s. 6d.

C. 644
{
Timbuctoo (*Rubens*) (" Tina ") (78)
I'm a self-made man (*Rubens*) (" Tina ") (78)
}

BLANCHE, MARIE

12-inch record 5s. 6d.

C. 720
{
The Bubble (" High Jinks ") (78)
PETER GAWTHORNE and CHORUS
Something seems tingle-ingleing (" High Jinks ") (78)
}

BROGDEN, GWENDOLINE

10-inch record 3s. 6d.

B. 481
{
I'll make a man of you (*Finck*) (" The Passing Show ") (78)
BASIL HALLAM (the late)
Gilbert the Filbert (*Finck*) (" The Passing Show ") (78)
}

12-inch records 5s. 6d.

C. 678
{
Heart of mine, come back to me (*Finck*) (" The Passing Show of 1915 ") (78)
ALHAMBRA ORCHESTRA
Ragging the Dog and the Shoeblack (*Ayer*) (" The Bing Boys are here ") (78)
}

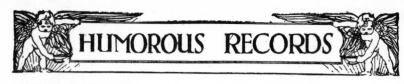

HUMOROUS RECORDS

BROGDEN, GWENDOLINE—*continued.*

12-inch record 5s. 6d.

C. 760
{ Sunlight and Shadow—Waltz Song (*Finck*)
(" Vanity Fair ") (79)
The Rainbow Song (with chorus) (*Finck*)
(" Vanity Fair ") (79)

BURNABY, DAVY

10-inch records 3s. 6d.

B. 753
{ What a duke should be (with chorus) (*Ivor Novello*) (" Theodore and Co.") (78)
HENRI LEONI
Oh! how I want to marry all the little candy girls (*Ivor Novello*) (" Theodore and Co.") (78)

B. 848
{ Reckless Reggie (*Braham*) (" Bubbly ")
(78)
COURTLAND and JEFFERIES
Raggin' thro' the rye (*Adams*)
(" Bubbly") (78)

B. 965
{ Gnee-ah! (*Braham*) (" Tails Up ") (79)
DAVY BURNABY and LOUISE LEIGH
Any little thing (*Ivor Novello*) (" Tails Up ") (79)

12-inch record 5s. 6d.

C. 851
{ The dear old days (with chorus) (*Ayer*)
(" Yes, Uncle! ") (79)
DE GROOT and the PICCADILLY ORCH.
Some day I'll make you love me (*Grey and Ayer*, arr. *Stoddon*) (" Round the Map ")
(79)

BURTON, OLIVE

10-inch records 3s. 6d.

B. 766
{ There's a ship that's bound for Blighty (*Shirley*) (78)
CLARA BECK
You were the first one to teach me to love (*Godfrey, Wakley and Scott*) (78)

B. 808
{ New Moon (*Morgan*) (" The Maid of the Mountains ") (78)
LOUISE LEIGH
Farewell (*H. Fraser-Simson*) (" The Maid of the Mountains ") (78)

CARLTON, HARRY

10-inch record 3s. 6d.

B. 446
{ Just like Father used to do (*Monckton*)
(" Quaker Girl") (80)
My Motter (*Monckton and Talbot*) (" The Arcadians ") (80)

CARVEY, GEORGE

10-inch record 3s. 6d.

B. 449
{ March on to Berlin (*Staunton and Meyer*)
(79) GERALD ORME
When Irish eyes are smiling (*Ball*) (78)

CLARE, TOM (at the piano)

10-inch records 3s. 6d.

B. 450
{ A Fishy Fishing Story (*Hanray*) (81)
Beautiful Girlie Girls (*Tom Clare*) (81)

B 451
{ My beastly eyeglass (*Montague*) (81)
Just a plain Girl (*Tennent*) (78)

12-inch records 5s. 6d.

C. 425
{ The Kaiser on the Telephone (*Clare*) (78)
Silly Ass (*Leigh*) (78)

C. 538
{ Tom Clare's version of the Telephone (81)
Winkelheimer's motor ride (*Marsh*) (78)

C. 540
{ Once the Kaiser's Army (arr. by *Clare*)
(78)
It's refined (*Lipton*) (78)

C. 617
{ Cohen rings up his tailor (*Bluff*) (78)
GEORGE ROBEY
—and that's that! (*Robey*) (80)

C. 668
{ Who bashed Bill Kaiser (*Clare*) (79)
My Hymn of Hate (*Sterndale Bennett*)
(79)

COURTLAND, ERIC

10-inch records 3s. 6d.

B. 676
{ Underneath the stars— A Romance (*Spencer*) (78)
MURRAY JOHNSON
The song the kettle is singing (*David and Wright*) (78)

B. 689
{ Every little while (*Tate*) (" Some ") (78)
WALTER JEFFERIES
We're all crazy (*Tate*) (" Some ") (78)

B. 762
{ A little Dutch Heaven for two (*Mills, Scott and Godfrey*) (78)
The roses have made me remember (*Darewski*) (" Samples ") (78)

B. 765
{ The Tanks that broke the ranks out in Picardy (*Castling and Carlton*) (78)
COURTLAND and JEFFERIES
I love my Motherland (*Mills, Scott and Godfrey*) (78)

B. 840
{ Star of the Night (*Lilian Ray*) (79)
My little cottage home in sweet Killarney (*Thompson*) (79)

B. 842
{ Poor Butterfly! (*R. Hubbell*) (79)
WALTER JEFFERIES
What do you want to make those eyes at me for? (*McCarthy, Johnson and Monaco*) (79)

The figures in brackets at end of selections
indicate the speed at which the records
. . . . should be played . . . .

COURTLAND, ERIC—*continued*

10-inch records 3s. 6d.

B. 869
- Ireland must be Heaven, for Mother came from there (*McCarthy, Johnson and Fischer*) (78) — LOUISE LEIGH and WALTER JEFFERIES
- Give me the key to your heart (The Gateway to Paradise) (*Knight and Scott*) (78)

B. 888
- Hong Kong (*Von Holstein and Sanders*) ("Any Old Thing") (79) — PETER GAWTHORNE
- I'm sick to death of women (*Talbot*) ("The Boy") (79)

B. 889
- On the other side of the big black cloud (*Arnold Blake*) (78)
- You taught me all I know (*Bernard and Rice*) (78)

B. 906
- Carnival night (with Chorus) (*Carr*) ("The Lilac Domino") (79) — RANDELL JACKSON
- Consolation (*Cuvillier*) ("The Lilac Domino") (79)

B. 987
- If you could care (*Darewski*) ("As you were") (79) — BLANCHE DARE.
- What ho! Mr. Watteau (with chorus) (*Darewski*) ("As you Were") (79)

CROFTS, ANNIE

12-inch record 5s. 6d.

C. 679
- Day by Day (*Talbot*) "My Lady Frayle") (78) — GRETCHEN YATES (with Chorus)
- What a naughty old gentleman (*Finck*) ("My Lady Frayle") (78)

DARE, BLANCHE

10-inch record 3s. 6d.

B. 987
- What ho! Mr. Watteau (with chorus) (*Darewski*) ("As you Were") (79) — ERIC COURTLAND
- If you could care (*Darewski*) ("As you were") (79)

DARE, PHYLLIS

12-inch record 5s. 6d.

C. 633
- The Violin Song (*Rubens*) ("Tina") (78) — PHYLLIS DARE and PAUL RUBENS
- Something in the atmosphere (*Rubens*) ("Tina") (78)

DAWSON, PETER

12-inch record 5s. 6d.

C. 756
- The Cobbler's Song (*Norton*) ("Chu Chin Chow") (79)
- The Watchman (*Squire*) (79)

DESMOND, VERA

10-inch records 3s. 6d.

B. 727
- A dream of delight (*Nicholls*) (80)
- I want to be loved that way (*Melville Gideon*) (80)

B. 697
- Some night, some waltz, some girl (*Bennett Scott*) (79) — LOUISE LEIGH (Soprano)
- Love, here is my heart (*Leo Silesu*) (79)

ELEN, GUS

10-inch record 3s. 6d.

B. 466
- Wait till the work comes round (75) — GEORGE ROBEY
- The Mormon's Song (*Robey*) (78)

EVELYN, CLARA

10-inch record 3s. 6d.

B. 480
- I can't refrain from laughing (*Lambelet*) ("Geisha") (80) — MARION JEROME
- The Pipes of Pan ("The Arcadians") (80)

FARKOA, MAURICE (the late)

10-inch records 3s. 6d.

B. 343
- Two dirty little hands (*Cobb and Edwards*) (81) — MARGUERITE DUNLAP and HARRY MACDONOUGH
- When it's apple blossom time in Normandy (*Trevor*) (78)

B. 453
- I like you in velvet (*Rubens*) ("Lady Madcap") (81) — HENRY LYTTON
- Laughing Song (*Lytton*) (81)

GAWTHORNE, PETER

10-inch record 3s. 6d.

B. 888
- I'm sick to death of women (*Talbot*) ("The Boy") (79) — ERIC COURTLAND
- Hong Kong (*Von Holstein and Sanders*) ("Any Old Thing") (79)

HUMOROUS RECORDS

GAWTHORNE, PETER—*continued*

12-inch record 5s. 6d.

C. 720 {
Something seems tingle-ingleing (with Chorus) (" High Jinks ") (78)
MARIE BLANCHE
The Bubble (" High Jinks ") (78)
}

GERARD, TEDDIE

10-inch record 3s. 6d.

B. 520 {
Glad to see you're back (*Lionel Monckton*) (" Bric-a-Brac ") (78)
Naughty, Naughty, one Gerrard (*Finck*) (" Bric-a-Brac ") (78)
}

GROSSMITH, GEORGE

12-inch records 5s. 6d.

C. 574 {
Murders (*Henty*) (" To-night's the Night ") (79)
Any old night is a wonderful night (*Kern*) (" To-night's the Night ") (79)
}

C. 577 {
The Only Way (*Rubens*) (" To-night's the Night ") (78)
Little girl, little girl (" The Sunshine Girl ") (78)
}

HALLAM, BASIL (the late)

10-inch records 3s. 6d.

B. 481 {
Gilbert the Filbert (*Finck*) (" The Passing Show ") (78)
GWENDOLINE BROGDEN
I'll make a man of you (*Finck*) (" The Passing Show ") (78)
}

B. 485 {
Keep smiling (*Irving Berlin*, arr. by *Finck*) (" The Passing Show of 1915 ") (78)
ELSIE JANIS and BASIL HALLAM
Ballin' the Jack Foxtrot ("Passing Show of 1915 ") (79)
}

12-inch record 5s. 6d.

C. 565 {
The Constant Lover (*Finck*) ("The Passing Show of 1915 ") (79)
Good-bye, Girls, I'm through (*Caryll*) (" The Passing Show of 1915 ") (78)
}

JACKSON, NELSON

10-inch record 3s. 6d.

B. 445 {
When Richard the First sat on the Throne (*Manning*) (81)
W. H. BERRY
The Bassoon (*Quentin Ashlyn*) (81)
}

JACKSON, RANDELL

10-inch record 3s. 6d.

B. 906 {
Consolation (*Cuvillier*) (" The Lilac Domino ") (79)
ERIC COURTLAND
Carnival night (with Chorus) (*Carr*) ("The Lilac Domino ") (79)
}

JAMES, JULIA

12-inch record 5s. 6d.

C. 748 {
That " come hither " look (*Kern*) (" Theodore & Co.") (78)
MADGE SAUNDERS and CHORUS
I'm getting such a big girl now (*Braham*) (" Theodore & Co.") (78)
}

JANIS, ELSIE

10-inch record 3s. 6d.

B. 488 {
Florrie was a Flapper (*Finck*) (" The Passing Show ") (78)
ELSIE JANIS and BASIL HALLAM
You're here and I'm here (*Kern*) (" The Passing Show ") (78)
}

12-inch record 5s. 6d.

C. 566 {
Prudence (*Finck*) (" The Passing Show of 1915 ") (79)
ELSIE JANIS and BASIL HALLAM
Same old song (*Finck*) (" The Passing Show of 1915 ") (79)
}

JEFFERIES, WALTER

10-inch records 3s. 6d.

B. 545 {
Till the boys come home (*Ivor Novello*) (78)
When the war is over, mother dear (*Mills, Long and Scott*) (79)
}

B. 549 {
A little bit of Heaven (*Ball*) (78)
MURRAY JOHNSON
Blue Eyes (*Nicholls*) (78)
}

B. 567 {
Everybody's crazy on the Fox Trot (*Scott*) (78)
There's a long, long trail (*Elliott*) (78)
}

B. 674 {
When we gather round the old home fires again (*Sterndale-Bennett*) (78)
MAYFAIR ORCHESTRA
You'll always be the same sweet baby (*Seymour Brown*) (" Razzle-Dazzle ")(78)
}

B. 689 {
We're all crazy (*Tate*) (" Some ") (78)
ERIC COURTLAND and CHORUS
Every little while (*Tate*) (" Some ") (78)
}

B. 760 {
When I come back to you (*Summers*) (78)
COURTLAND and JEFFERIES
Take me back to dear old Blighty (*Mills, Scott and Godfrey*) (" Blighty ") (78)
}

The figures in brackets at end of selections indicate the speed at which the records · · · · should be played · · · ·

78

HUMOROUS RECORDS

JEFFERIES, WALTER—*continued*

10-inch records 3s. 6d.

B. 842
- What do you want to make those eyes at me for ? (*McCarthy, Johnson and Monaco*) (**79**)
  ERIC COURTLAND
- Poor Butterfly ! (*R. Hubbell*) (**79**)

B. 883
- In my dear old Hometown (*McCarthy*) (**79**)
  BLANCHE DARE and ERIC COURTLAND
- Swing me in the moonlight (*Mills and Scott*) (**79**)

B. 885
- Over there (The Great American War Song) (*G. M. Cohan*) (**79**)
  ERIC COURTLAND and WALTER JEFFERIES
- That dear old home of mine (*Nat D. Ayer*) ("The Bing Girls are There") (**79**)

B. 886
- Smoke Clouds (*H. Darewski*) ("Topsy Turvy") (**79**)
  COURTLAND and JEFFERIES
- Along the way to Waikiki (*Whiting*) (**79**)

12-inch record 5s. 6d.

C. 704
- Jingle Johnnie (with Chorus) (*Tate*) ("Some") (**78**)
  COURTLAND, JEFFERIES and CHORUS
- Have you seen the ducks go by? (*F. Powell*) ("Some") (**78**)

JEROME, MARION

10-inch record 3s. 6d.

B 480
- The Pipes of Pan (*Monckton and Talbot*) ("The Arcadians") (**80**)
  CLARA EVELYN
- I can't refrain from laughing (*Lambelet*) ("Geisha") (**80**)

JOHNSON, MURRAY

10-inch records 3s. 6d.

B. 459
- When we've wound up the watch on the Rhine (with Chorus) (*Darewski*) (**80**)
  CHARLES PENROSE
- Laughteritis (*Penrose*) (**79**)

B. 549
- Blue Eyes (*Nicholls*) (**78**)
  WALTER JEFFERIES
- A little bit of Heaven (*Ball*) (**78**)

B. 605
- Pack up your troubles in your old kit bag (*Powell*) (**79**)
- Auntie Skinner's Chicken Dinner (*Morse*) (**79**)

B. 618
- Oh, Mr. Rubinstein (*Braham*) (**78**)
- The boys of good old London (*H. Darewski*) (**78**)

B. 644
- Since Chumley came back from London Town (*Ayer*) ("Bric-a-Brac") (**78**)
  ARNOLD RICHARDSON
- Flappers (*Talbot*) ("My Lady Frayle") (**78**)

B. 676
- The song the kettle is singing (**78**)
  ERIC COURTLAND
- Underneath the Stars—A romance (*H. Spencer*) (**78**)

JONES, BESSIE

10-inch record 3s. 6d.

B. 442
- Wonderful Rose of Love (with Chorus) (*Bennett Scott*) (**79**)
  DENISE ORME
- The interfering parrot (*Jones*) ("The Geisha") (**76**)

KIRKBY, STANLEY

10-inch record 3s. 6d.

B 460
- My Sumurun Girl (*Hirsch*) (**80**)
  HENRY KLAUSER
- Laughing Song (**76**

KLAUSER, HENRY
(the celebrated Norwegian Actor)

10-inch record 3s. 6d.

B. 460
- Laughing Song (as sung by him in every European Court) (**76**)
  STANLEY KIRKBY
- My Sumurun Girl (*Hirsch*) (**80**)

LA RUE, GRACE

12-inch record 5s. 6d.

C. 575
- A Tango Dream (*Elsa Maxwell*) (**78**)
  ETHEL LEVEY
- Carry on (*Maxwell*) (**75**)

LAURIER, JAY

10-inch records 3s. 6d.

B .669
- Swim, Sam, Swim (*B. Lee*) (**78**)
- I've had a glass of ginger wine (*B. Lee*) (**78**)

B. 682
- Six short soldiers (*Darewski*) (**78**)
- Cut me off a little bit of roly-poly (*Long and Mills*) (**78**)

B. 819
- Pudden ! (*Blackmore and Gibson*) (**79**)
- Nobody loves me (*Lee*) (**79**)

B. 844
- I'm a flirt (*F. Leigh*) (**79**)
- I'm wasting away (*Worton, David and Lee*) (**79**)

HUMOROUS RECORDS

LAURIER, JAY—*continued*
10-inch records 3s. 6d.

B. 887 { Shall us ? Let's (*B. Lee*) **(78)**
{ Top Hole (*Lambert*) **(78)**

B. 912 { I'd like to marry (but I couldn't leave the girls) (*Nat D. Ayer*) **(79)**
{ Long Boy (*Barclay Walker*) **(79)**

12-inch record 5s. 6d.

C. 673 { It's lovely to be in love (*Clifford Harris and Tate*) **(80)**
{ I want something to practise on (*B. Lee*) **(80)**

LEIGH, LOUISE
10-inch records 3s. 6d.

B. 803 { Louana Lou (with Chorus) (*D. Stamper*) ("Zig-Zag") **(78)**
{ In Grandma's days they never did the Fox Trot (with Chorus) (*D. Stamper*) ("Zig-Zag") **(78)**

B. 808 { Farewell (*H. Fraser-Simson*) ("The Maid of the Mountains") **(78)**
{ OLIVE BURTON
{ New Moon (*Merlin Morgan*) ("The Maid of the Mountains") **(78)**

B. 966 { The twinkle in her eye (with chorus) (*Braham*) ("Tails Up !") **(79)**
{ The Apache Rag (with chorus) (*Braham*) ("Tails Up !") **(79)**

B. 967 { Peter Pan (with chorus) (*Joel and Coward*) ("Tails Up !") **(79)**
{ LOUISE LEIGH, COURTLAND and JEFFERIES
{ Let's all go raving mad (*Braham*) ("Tails Up !") **(79)**

12-inch records 5s. 6d.

C. 848 { For your love, I am waiting (with Chorus) (*Carr*) ("The Lilac Domino ") **(79)**
{ The Lilac Domino (with Chorus) (*Cuvillier*) (" The Lilac Domino ") **(79)**

C. 868 { The Lonely Princess (*Barrett*) ("Soldier Boy ") **(79)**
{ LOUISE LEIGH and ERIC COURTLAND
{ The kiss waltz (*Romberg*) ("Soldier Boy " **(79)**

LENO, DAN (the late)
10-inch records 3s. 6d.

B. 462 { Mrs. Kelly **(74)**
{ My wife's relations **(74)**

B. 463 { Poppies **(75)**
{ The Shopwalker **(74)**

B. 464 { The Tower of London **(74)**
{ The Huntsman **(74)**

12-inch record 5s. 6d.

C. 545 { Going to the Races **(74)**
{ The Huntsman **(74)**

LEONI, HENRI
10-inch records 3s. 6d.

B. 753 { Oh ! how I want to marry all the little candy girls (*Ivor Novello*) (" Theodore & Co.") **(78)**
{ DAVY BURNABY and CHORUS
{ What a Duke should be (*Ivor Novello*) (" Theodore & Co.") **(78)**

B. 909 { Play me that marching melody (with chorus) (*Le Feuvre*) (" Yes, Uncle !') **(79)**
{ DE GROOT and the PICCADILLY ORCHESTRA
{ Widows are wonderful (*Nat D. Ayer*) (" Yes, Uncle ! ") **(79)**

12-inch record 5s. 6d.

C. 749 { Any old where (*Ivor Novello*) (with Chorus) (" Theodore & Co.") **(78)**
{ GAIETY THEATRE ORCHESTRA
{ Overture (" Theodore & Co.") (*Ivor Novello*) **(78)**

LESTER, ALFRED
12-inch record 5s. 6d.

C. 811 { A Conscientious Objector (*Rice*) (" Round the Map ") **(78)**
{ Hurrah for the rolling sea (*Finck*) (" Round the Map ") **(78)**

LEVEY, ETHEL
12-inch records 5s. 6d.

C. 572 { Good-bye Summer, So-long Fall, Hello Wintertime ! (*Wenrich*) **(79)**
{ How do you do, Miss Ragtime (*Hirsch*) **(79)**

C. 573 { That haunting Melody (*George M. Cohan*) **(79)**
{ My Tango Girl (*Hirsch*) **(79)**

C. 575 { Carry on (*Maxwell*) **(75)**
{ GRACE LA RUE
{ A Tango Dream (*Elsa Maxwell*) **(78)**

LOGAN, STANLEY
12-inch record 5s. 6d.

C. 808 { When the right girl comes along (with Chorus) (*Finck*) (" Round the Map ") **(78)**
{ MAYFAIR ORCHESTRA
{ " Round the Map "—Fox Trot (*Herman Finck*) **(79)**

The figures in brackets at end of selections indicate the speed at which the records . . . . should be played . . . .

HUMOROUS RECORDS

LYTTON, HENRY
10-inch record 3s. 6d.
B. 453 { Laughing Song (*Lytton*) (81)
MAURICE FARKOA (the late)
I like you in velvet (*Rubens*) ("Lady Madcap") (81)

MAXWELL, AIMÉE
12-inch records 5s. 6d.
C. 656 { Can it be love (*Paul Rubens*) ("Betty") (with Chorus) (78)
Staff-Captain H. RATCLIFFE
Rose in the bud (*Dorothy Forster*) (78)

C. 672 { A Broken Doll (*Tate*) ("Samples") (78)
When you come home (*Squire*) (78)

MAYNE, CLARICE
(accompanied by "THAT")
12-inch records 5s. 6d.
C. 526 { Come over the garden wall (*Tate*) (80)
Mr. and Mrs. Smith (81)

C. 527 { Nursey, nursey (*Lee and David*) (81)
I've got my eye on you (*Arthurs and Leigh*) (80)

C. 528 { Jenny Macgregor (*James and Tate*) (80)
Joshu—ah (*Arthurs and Leigh*) (80)

McKAY, LEONARD
12-inch records 5s. 6d.
C. 830 { His Country first of all (The People's King) (*Ivor Novello*) ("Arlette") (78)
ADRAH FAIR, JOHNNIE FIELDS and LEONARD McKAY
Cousinly Love (*Novello*) ("Arlette") (78)

MELFORD, AUSTIN
12-inch record 5s. 6d.
C. 681 { Piccadilly (*Braham*) ("Mr. Manhattan") (78)
PEGGY PHILLIPS and ERIC COURTLAND
'Twas in September (*Silvio Hein*) ("Mr. Manhattan") (78)

MILLAR, GERTIE
12-inch records 5s. 6d.
C. 529 { A Quaker Girl (*Monckton*) ("The Quaker Girl") (80)
In Yorkshire (*Monckton*) ("Our Miss Gibbs") (80)

C. 530 { Moonstruck (*Monckton*) ("Our Miss Gibbs") (80)
Tony from America (*Monckton*) ("The Quaker Girl") (81)

C. 592 { Chalk Farm to Camberwell (*Lionel Monckton*) ("Bric-a-Brac") (78)
GERTIE MILLAR and Monsieur A. SIMON GIRARD
I'm simply crazy over you (*Schwartz*) ("Bric-a-Brac") (78)

C. 593 { Toy Town (*Lionel Monckton*) ("Bric-a-Brac") (78)
Neville was a devil (*Lionel Monckton*) ("Bric-a-Brac") (78)

O'FARRELL, TALBOT
10-inch record 3s. 6d.
B. 820 { Come back to Ireland and me (*R. Wakley*) ("Hanky-Panky") (78)
HARRY TALBOT and LOUISE LEIGH
One hour of love with you (*M. Darewski*) ("Hanky-Panky") (78)

ORME, DENISE
10-inch record 3s. 6d.
B. 442 { The interfering Parrot (*Jones*) ("The Geisha") (76)
BESSIE JONES and CHORUS
Wondeful Rose of Love (*Bennett Scott*) (79)

ORME, GERALD
10-inch record 3s. 6d.
B. 449 { When Irish eyes are smiling (*Ball*) (78)
GEORGE CARVEY
March on to Berlin (*Staunton and Meher*) (79)

PENROSE, CHARLES
10-inch record 3s. 6d.
B. 459 { Laughteritis (*Penrose*) (79)
MURRAY JOHNSON and CHORUS
When we've wound up the Watch on the Rhine (*Darewski*) (80)

REEVE, ADA
10-inch record 3s. 6d.
B. 523 { Father's little man (*Elton*) (80)
Foolish Questions (*Hone*) (80)

These records should be played with "His Master's Voice" needles, sold only in boxes bearing our copyright picture, "His Master's Voice," on the lid

HUMOROUS RECORDS

RICHARDSON, ARNOLD

10-inch record 3s. 6d.

B. 644 {
Flappers (*Talbot*) (" My Lady Frayle ") (78)
MURRAY JOHNSON
Since Chumley came back from London Town (*Nat D. Ayer*) (" Bric-a-Brac ") (78)
}

ROBEY, GEORGE

10-inch records 3s. 6d.

B. 465 {
The Prehistoric Man (74)
Not that I wish to say anything (74)
}

B. 466 {
The Mormon's Song (*Robey*) (78)
GUS ELEN
Wait till the work comes round (75)
}

12-inch records 5s. 6d.

C. 426 {
The Servants' Registry Office (*Edgar*) (78)
The Editress (*Robey*) (78)
}

C. 546 {
And very nice too ! (*Joe Tabra*) (78)
Archibald ! certainly not (*Alfred Glover*) (81)
}

C. 547 {
Bang went the chance of a lifetime (79)
Good Queen Bess (77)
}

C. 548 {
Hey, ho, what might have been ! (*Sullivan and Edgar*) (79)
More in sorrow than in anger (*Sax Rhomer*) (80)
}

C. 549 {
I think I shall sleep well to-night (77)
Mrs. B. (81)
}

C. 550 {
Tempt me not (81)
The Barrister (80)
}

C. 551 {
The Manager of the Splitz Hotel (*Rogers*) (80)
The Mayor of Mudcomdyke (76)
}

C. 552 {
The Pro's Landlady (*Pether*) (80)
President of the Republic (*Greene*) (79)
}

C. 553 {
The Witness (*Wick*) (78)
You've a very nice day for it too (*Sullivan and Edgar*) 80)
}

C. 570 {
Worse, much worse (*Ross*) (80)
Robin Hood (*Rogers*) (80)
}

C. 571 {
I don't think it matters (*Edgar*) (78)
We parted the best of friends (*Edgar*) (78)
}

C. 617 {
—and that's that ! (*Robey*) (80)
TOM CLARE
Cohen rings up his tailor (*Bluff*) (78)
}

SAUNDERS, MADGE and Chorus

12-inch record 5s. 6d.

C. 748 {
I'm getting such a big girl now (*Braham*) (" Theodore and Co.") (78)
JULIA JAMES
That, come hither ' look (*Kern*) " Theodore and Co.") (78)
}

SCOTT, MAIDIE

10-inch record 3s. 6d.

B. 568 {
I'm glad I took my Mother's advice (*Langley*) (79)
Father got the sack from the Water-works (*Collins and Terry Sullivan*) (79)
}

12-inch record 5s. 6d.

C. 616 {
The Bird on Nelly's Hat (*Solman*) (78)
The School Strike (We all came out on strike) (*Lambert*) (78)
}

SEALBY, MABEL

12-inch record 5s. 6d.

C. 632 {
I've been to the pictures (*Paul Rubens*) (" Tina ") (78)
W. H. BERRY and PHYLLIS DARE
Let me introduce you to my Father (*Paul Rubens*) (" Tina ") (78)
}

SHEPARD, BURT (the late)

10-inch record 3s. 6d.

B. 468 {
Laughing Song (76)
The Whistling Coon (76)
}

SHERIDAN, MARK (the late)

10-inch record 3s. 6d.

B 470 {
At the Football Match last Saturday (76)
One of the B'hoys (*Scott*) (81)
}

SMITHSON, FLORENCE

10-inch record 3s. 6d.

B. 444 {
I know nothing of life (" Mousmé ") (80)
Waltz Song (*German*) (" Tom Jones") (80)
}

12-inch record 5s. 6d.

C. 531 {
My Samisen ! (*Monckton and Talbot*) (" Mousmé ") (80)
The Temple Bell (*Monckton and Talbot*) (" Mousmé ") (80)
}

STRATTON, EUGENE (the late)

12-inch record 5s. 6d.

C. 556 {
I may be crazy (*Leslie Stuart*) (81)
Lily of Laguna (*Leslie Stuart*) (81)
}

The figures in brackets at end of selections
indicate the speed at which the records
. . . . should be played . . . .

DUET RECORDS

TAYLOR, NELLIE

12-inch records 5s. 6d.

C. 737 — Honolulu Isle (*Melville Gideon*) **(79)**
NELLIE TAYLOR and PETER GAW-THORNE
Love's own kiss—Waltz Song (" High Jinks ") **(79)**

C 833 — Little Miss Melody (*L. Monckton*) (" The Boy ") **(78)**
DE GROOT and THE PICCADILLY ORCHESTRA
Valse poudrée (*F. Popy*) **(78)**

WELDON, HARRY

10-inch record 3s. 6d.

B. 901 — 'Sno Use (*Foley*) **(79)**
Sleuthy, the dread of the heads (*Castling*) **(79)**

12-inch records 5s. 6d.

C. 764 — The White Hope—Part I (*Weldon*) **(78)**
The White Hope—Part II (*Weldon*) **(78)**

C. 777 — The Pastoral Song—Part I (*Tate and Harris*) **(78)**
The Pastoral Song—Part II (*Tate and Harris*) **(78)**

C. 805 — I get more like a Pro every day (*Wise and Bennett*) **(79)**
Down home in Tennessee—Burlesque (*Donaldson and Weldon*) **(79)**

C. 827 — Tyrolean Song (*Wise and Bennett*) **(78)**
Cowboy (Dawson City) (*Castling and Weldon*) **(78)**

C. 864 — Travesty on " What do you want to make those eyes at me for ? (*Foley*) **(79)**
Somebody's baby (*Castling*) **(79)**

WILLIAMS, WALTER, and Chorus

12-inch record 5s. 6d.

C. 770 — Don't all speak at once little girls (*H. Darewski*) (" Three Cheers ") **(79)**
SHAFTESBURY THEATRE ORCHESTRA
Overture—(" Three Cheers ") **(79)**

YATES, GRETCHEN

12-inch record 5s. 6d.

C. 679 — What a naughty old gentleman father must have been (*Finck*) (" My Lady Frayle ") **(78)**
ANNIE CROFTS
Day by Day (*Talbot*) (" My Lady Frayle ") **(78)**

DUETS, etc.

AYER, NAT D., and OLIVE BURTON

12-inch record 5s. 6d.

C. 785 — Who taught you all those things that you taught me (*Nat D. Ayer*) **(78)**
RUBY HEYL
The Bells of St. Mary's (*A. E. Adams*) **(78)**

AYER, NAT D., and PEGGY PHILLIPS

12-inch record 5s. 6d.

C. 676 — If you were the only girl in the world and I were the only boy (*Nat D. Ayer*) (" The Bing Boys are here ") **(78)**
ALHAMBRA ORCHESTRA
The Languid Melody (*Nat D. Ayer*) (" The Bing Boys are here ") **(78)**

BURNABY, DAVY, and LOUISE LEIGH

10-inch record 3s. 6d.

B. 965 — Any little thing (*Ivor Novello*) (" Tails Up !") **(79)**
DAVY BURNABY
Gnee-ah ! (*Braham*) (" Tails Up !") **(79)**

BURTON, OLIVE, and ERIC COURTLAND

10-inch records 3s. 6d.

B. 786 — Oh how she could Yacki Hacki, Wicki Wacki Woo (*Von Tilzer*) (" Houp-La !") **(78)**
Come on to Nashville Tennessee (*Donaldson*) **(78)**

B. 802 — Arizona (*Melville Gideon*) **(78)**
There's a little bit of bad in every good little girl (*Clarke and Darewski*) (" Three Cheers ") **(78)**

COBBETT and WALKER

10-inch records 3s. 6d.

B. 621 — When you wore a tulip and I wore a big red rose (*Wenrich*) **(79)**
She wants to marry me (*Weston and Lee*) **(79)**

B. 638 — Are you from Dixie ? (*Cobb*) **(79)**
Old Man Brown (*Weston and Lee*) **(79)**

B. 654 — Down home in Tennessee (*Donaldson*) **(78)**
When Paderevski plays that baby grand (*Weston and Lee and The Two Bobs*) **(79)**

B. 711 — When I leave the world behind (*Irving Berlin*) **(79)**
Four-and-nine (*David and Lee*) **(79)**

DUET RECORDS

COURTLAND and JEFFERIES

10-inch records 3s. 6d.

B. 759
It's a long, long way to my home in Kentucky (*Nat D. Ayer*) (78)
If I could only say in French (what I'm thinking about in English) (*Gifford*) (78)

B. 760
Take me back to dear old Blighty (*Mills, Scott and Godfrey*) (" Blighty ") (78)
WALTER JEFFERIES
When I come back to you (*Summers*) (78)

B. 765
I love my Motherland (*Mills, Scott and Godfrey*) (78)
ERIC COURTLAND
The Tanks that broke the ranks out in Picardy (*Castling and Carlton*) (78)

B. 780
She is the sunshine of Virginia (*H. Carroll*) (78)
ERIC COURTLAND and LLEWELLYN MORGAN
Blighty (*Weston and Lee*) (79)

B. 806
Fancy you fancying me (*Lee and Weston*) (78)
Down where the Swannee River flows (*Von Tilzer*) (78)

B. 817
Mississippi days (*Piantadosi*) (78)
We don't want a lot of flags a-flying (when we all come marching home) (*Penso*) (73)

B. 833
I want to be somebody's baby (*David and Wright*) (78)
WALTON and CARTER
I'm going way back home and have a wonderful time (*Schwartz*) (79)

B. 843
O'Brien is tryin' to learn to talk Hawaiian (*R. Cormack*) (79)
I can hear the Ukuleles calling me (*H. Paley*) (79)

B. 848
Raggin' thro' the rye (*A. E. Adams*) (" Bubbly ") (78)
DAVY BURNABY
Reckless Reggie (*Braham*) (" Bubbly ") (78)

B. 853
Hawaiian butterfly (*Baskeite and Santley*) (" Bubbly ") (79)
LOUISE LEIGH, ERIC COURTLAND and WALTER JEFFERIES
Dream boat (*Ivor Novello*) (78)

B. 854
I wanted to go back to my home in London Town (*The Two Bobs*) (79)
LOUISE LEIGH and WALTER JEFFERIES
Come and cuddle me (*J. W. Tate*) (79)

B. 865
There's a little lane without a turning on the way to Home, Sweet Home (*G. W. Meyer*) (78)
I was going back home till I met you (*Gifford, Mellor and Scott*) (78)

B. 870
Down Texas Way (*Godfrey, Mills and Scott*) (78)
BLANCHE DARE and ERIC COURTLAND
Hullo! my dearie (*Stamper*) (" Zig-Zag ") (78)

B. 877
Good-bye, Dixie (I'm off to France) (*Bernard and Swanstone*) (" Any Old Thing ") (79)
When the Bells of Peace are ringing (*Wilson*) (79)

B. 880
Where the black-eyed Susans grow (*Whiting*) (" Cheep ") (79)
Hezekiah Johnson's Jubilee (*Weston, Lee and The Two Bobs*) (79)

B. 881
Oh, Johnny! Oh, Johnny! Oh! (*Abe Olman*) (79)
You oughtn't to do it, when you don't belong to me (*Carlton and Whidden*) (79)

B. 882
All the world will be jealous of me (*E. R. Ball*) (79)
My home in U.S.A. (*H. Flynn*) (79)

B. 885
That dear old home of mine (*Nat D. Ayer*) (" The Bing Girls are There ") (79)
WALTER JEFFERIES
Over There (The Great American War Song) (*Cohan*) (79)

B. 886
Along the way to Waikiki (*Whiting*) (79)
WALTER JEFFERIES
Smoke Clouds (*H. Darewski*) (" Topsy Turvy ") (79)

B. 895
For me and my gal (*Meyer*) (" Here and There ") (79)
There's a girl for every soldier (*Long and Scott*) (79)

B. 898
Oh! Oh! Oh! it's a lovely War (*Long and Scott*) (79)
Oh, boy! when you're home on leave (*Ayer*, arr. by *Stoddon*) (79)

B. 902
Good-bye-ee! (*Weston and Lee*) (79)
Somewhere in France (*Howard*) (79)

B. 904
Samoa, Samoa, some more (*Weston and Lee*) (79)
Tommy over there (*Darewski*) (78)

B. 913
Lily, my water Lily (*Tate*) (79)
Honey, will you miss me? (*Wilbur and Rice*) (79)

B. 916
Southern Gals (*Gumble*) (79)
Where do we go from here? (*Johnson and Wenrich*) (79)

B. 961
On the road to home, sweet home (*van Alstyne*) (79)
Some Sunday morning (*Whiting*) (79)

B. 968
I've got the sweetest girl in Maryland (*Donaldson*) (" Tabs ") (79)
LOUISE LEIGH and WALTER JEFFERIES
The military stamp (with Chorus) (*Crawford*) (" Soldier Boy ")

The figures in brackets at end of selections indicate the speed at which the records · · · · should be played · · · ·

84

DUET RECORDS

COURTLAND and JEFFERIES——*continued*

10-inch records 3s. 6d.

B. 984 Indianapolis **(79)**
LOUISE LEIGH, COURTLAND AND JEFFERIES
Give me a Little Cosy Corner (*Tate*) **(79)**

B. 966 Back to Blighty (*Darewski*) " As you were " **(79)**
I'm the Great Big Pot of Potsdam (" As you were ") **(79)**

12-inch record 5s. 6d.

C. 704 Have you seen the ducks go by (*Powell*) (with Chorus) (" Some ") **(78)**
WALTER JEFFERIES and CHORUS
Jingle Johnnie (*Tate*) (" Some ")**(78)**

COURTLAND, ERIC, and LLEWELLYN MORGAN

10-inch record 3s. 6d.

B. 780 Blighty (*Weston and Lee*) **(79)**
ERIC COURTLAND and WALTER JEFFERIES
She is the sunshine of Virginia (*Carroll*) **(78)**

COURTLAND, ERIC, and JOSEPH REED

12-inch record 5s. 6d.

C. 866 Mother (*Romberg*) (" Soldier Boy ") **(79)**
DE GROOT and THE PICCADILLY ORCHESTRA
En relisant vos lettres (Valse Lente) (*Masson-Kiek*) **(79)**

COWAN, DORIS, and GEORGE BAKER

10-inch records 3s. 6d.

B. 486 There was a Time (" Gondoliers "—*Sullivan*) **(78)**
Things are seldom what they seem (" Pinafore ") **(78)**

B. 493 Boy and Girl (*Monckton*) (" The Country Girl ") **(79)**
Dance with me (*Rubens*) (" Betty ") **(79)**

B. 513 Prithee, pretty maiden (" Patience "—*Sullivan*) **(78)**
None shall part us (" Iolanthe"—*Sullivan*) **(80)**

DARE, PHYLLIS, and W. H. BERRY

12-inch record 5s. 6d.

C. 632 Let me introduce you to my father (*Rubens*) (" Tina ") **(78)**
MABEL SEALBY
I've been to the pictures (*Rubens*) (" Tina ") **(78)**

DARE, PHYLLIS, and PAUL RUBENS

12-inch record 5s. 6d.

C. 633 Something in the atmosphere (*Rubens*) (" Tina ") **(78)**
PHYLLIS DARE
The Violin Song (*Rubens*) (" Tina ") **(78)**

DARE, BLANCHE, and COURTLAND, ERIC

10-inch records 3s. 6d.

B. 870 Hullo ! my dearie (*Stamper*) (" Zig-Zag ") **(78)**
COURTLAND and JEFFERIES
Down Texas Way (*Godfrey, Mills and Scott*) **(78)**

B. 883 Swing me in the moonlight (*Mills and Scott*) **(78)**
WALTER JEFFERIES
In my dear old Hometown (*McCarthy*) **(79)**

B. 884 I want you to know I miss you (*Bennet Scott*) **(78)**
The kiss that made you mine (*Worton, David and Wright*) **(78)**

GAWTHORNE, PETER, and MURIEL GRAY

12-inch record 5s. 6d.

C. 721 Love's own kiss (Waltz Song) (" High Jinks ") **(78)**
MAISIE GAY and W. H. RAWLINS
She says it with her eyes (" High Jinks ") **(78)**

These records should be played with " His Master's Voice " needles, sold only in boxes bearing our copyright picture, " His Master's Voice," on the lid

DUET RECORDS

GAY, MAISIE, and W. H. RAWLINS
12-inch record 5s. 6d.

C. 721
- She says it with her eyes (" High Jinks ") (78)
  - PETER GAWTHORNE and MURIEL GRAY
- Love's own kiss (Waltz Song) ·· gh Jinks ") (78)

GRAVES, GEORGE, and WILL EVANS
12-inch record 5s. 6d.

C. 560
- Another good thing you've missed (Glover) (" Happy Days ") (78)
- Developing a photograph (Graves and Evans) (78)

GROSSMITH, GEORGE, and EDMUND PAYNE (the late)
12-inch record 5s. 6d.

C. 567
- I beg your pardon (Stuart) (" Peggy ") (80)
- The Two Obadiahs (Lyste) (81)

GROSSMITH, GEORGE, and HAIDEE DE RANCE
12-inch record 5s. 6d.

C. 578
- They didn't believe me (Kern) (" To-night's the Night ") (79)
  - GEORGE GROSSMITH
- Tommy, wont' you teach me how to tango? (Penso) (78)

JAMES, JULIA, and FRED LESLIE
10-inch record 3s. 6d.

B. 754
- I'll make myself at home, dear (Ivor Novello) (" Theodore & Co.") (78)
  - GAIETY THEATRE ORCHESTRA
- Valse Saracenne (Ivor Novello) (" Theodore & Co.") (78)

JANIS, ELSIE, and BASIL HALLAM (the late)
10-inch records 3s. 6d.

B. 485
- Ballin' the Jack Foxtrot (" The Passing Show of 1915 ") (78)
  - BASIL HALLAM (the late)
- Keep smiling (Irving Berlin, arr. by Finck) (" The Passing Show of 1915 ") (78)

B. 488
- You're here and I'm here (Kern) (" The Passing Show ") (78)
  - ELSIE JANIS
- Florrie was a Flapper (Finck) (" The Passing Show ") (79)

12-inch records 5s. 6d.

C. 566
- Same old Song (Finck) (" The Passing Show of 1915 ") (79)
  - ELSIE JANIS
- Prudence (Finck) (" The Passing Show of 1915 ") (79)

C. 597
- I've got everything I want but you (Marshall, arr. by Finck) (" The Passing Show ") (78)
  - DE GROOT and PICCADILLY ORCHESTRA
- Piccadilly Grill—Waltz (de Groot) (78)

JONES, BESSIE, and MURRAY JOHNSON
10-inch record 3s. 6d.

B. 473
- We've been married just one year (Muir) (79) MURRAY JOHNSON and CHARLES STEWART
- On the 5.15 (Marshall) (80)

JOHNSON, MURRAY and CHARLES STEWART
10-inch record 3s. 6d.

B. 473
- On the 5.15 (Marshall) (78)
  - BESSIE JONES and MURRAY JOHNSON
- We've been married just one year (Muir) (79)

KEYS, NELSON, and ARTHUR PLAYFAIR
12-inch record 5s. 6d.

C. 594
- The Optimist and the Pessimist (Finck) (" Bric-a-Brac ") (78)
  - THE LIGHT OPERA COMPANY
- Gems from " To-night's the Night " (Rubens) (78)

LAYE, EVELYN, and AUSTIN MELFORD
12-inch record 5s, 6d.

C. 860
- Do it for me (Hirsch) (" Going Up ") (79)
  - JOSEPH COYNE, MARJORIE GORDON, EVELYN LAYE, H. DE BRAY (solo), AUSTIN MELFORD and CLIFTON ALDERSON
- Finale, Act I. " Going Up " (Hirsch) (79)

The figures in brackets at end of selections indicate the speed at which the records · · · · should be played · · · ·

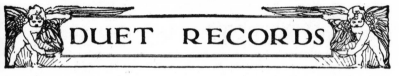

DUET RECORDS

LEIGH, LOUISE, and FLORENCE BERENS (Whistler)

12-inch record 5s. 6d.

C. 793
{ When the autumn leaves are falling (*Stamper*) ("Zig-Zag") (78)
ERNEST PIKE
Roses of Picardy (*Haydn Wood*) (78)

LEIGH, LOUISE, and ERIC COURTLAND

10-inch record 3s. 6d.

B. 852
{ Hoola Boola Lou (*Bernard and Rice*) (78)
Yaddie, Kaddie, Kiddie, Kaddie, Koo (*Meyer*) (78)

12-inch record 5s. 6d.

C. 868
{ The Kiss Waltz (*Romberg*) ("Soldier Boy") (79)
LOUISE LEIGH
The lonely princess (*Barrett*) ("Soldier Boy") (79)

LEIGH, LOUISE, and PETER DAWSON

10-inch record 3s. 6d.

B. 805
{ A Paradise for two (The key to your heart (*Tate*) ("The Maid of the Mountains") (78)
PETER DAWSON
A Bachelor Gay (*Tate*) ("The Maid of the Mountains") (78)

LEIGH, LOUISE, and RANDELL JACKSON

12-inch records 5s. 6d.

C. 848
{ Song of the chimes (*Cuvillier*) ("The Lilac Domino") (79)
Where love is waiting (*Cuvillier*) ("The Lilac Domino") (79)

C. 850
{ What is done you never can undo (with chorus) (Finale, Act II.) (*Cuvillier*) ("The Lilac Domino") (79)
DE GROOT and the PICCADILLY ORCHESTRA
The land of happy memories (*de Groot*) (79)

LEIGH, LOUISE, and WALTER JEFFERIES

10-inch records 3s. 6d.

B. 854
{ Come and cuddle me (*Tate*) (79)
COURTLAND and JEFFERIES
I wanted to go back to my home in London Town (*The Two Bobs*) (79)

B. 869
{ Give me the key to your heart (The Gateway to Paradise) (*C. Knight and B. Scott*) (78)
ERIC COURTLAND
Ireland must be Heaven, for Mother came from there (*McCarthy, Johnson and Fischer*) (78)

B. 968
{ The military stamp (with Chorus) (*Crawford*) ("Soldier Boy") (79)
COURTLAND and JEFFERIES
I've got the sweetest girl in Maryland (*Donaldson*) ("Tabs") (79)

LEIGH, LOUISE, and CHARLES NELSON

10-inch record 3s. 6d.

B. 709
{ Sympathy (Waltz Song) ("The Firefly") (78)
My heart is calling you (*H. Nicholls*) (78)

LEIGH, LOUISE, and HARRY TALBOT

10-inch record 3s. 6d.

B. 820
{ One hour of love with you (*M. Darewski*) ("Hanky-Panky") (78)
TALBOT O'FARRELL
Come back to Ireland and me (*Wakley*) ("Hanky-Panky") (78)

LEONI, HENRI, and MIMI CRAWFORD

10-inch record 3s. 6d.

B. 908
{ Think of me (with Chorus) (*Ayer*) ("Yes, Uncle!") (79)
You may take me round Paree (*Ayer*) ("Yes, Uncle!") (79)

These records should be played with "His Master's Voice" needles, sold only in boxes bearing our copyright picture, "His Master's Voice," on the lid

CONCERTED RECORDS

**LEVEY, ETHEL, and
BLANCHE TOMLIN**

12-inch record 5s. 6d.

C. 611 {
The Simple Melody (*Irving Berlin*)
(" Watch your Step ") **(78)**
ETHEL LEVEY (drums played by
JOSEPH COYNE)
The Minstrel Parade (*Irving Berlin*)
(" Watch your Step ") **(78)**

**MANNERING, MOYA, and
LESLIE HENSON**

10-inch record 3s. 6d.

B. 484 {
I'd like to bring my Mother (*Rubens*)
(" To-night's the Night ") **(78)**
Meet me round the corner (*Rubens*)
(" To-night's the Night ") **(78)**

**MILLAR, GERTIE, and
A. SIMON GIRARD**

12-inch record 5s. 6d.

C. 592 {
I'm simply crazy over you (*Schwartz*)
(" Bric-a-Brac ") **(78)**
GERTIE MILLAR
Chalk Farm to Camberwell (*Monckton*)
(" Bric-a-Brac ") **(78)**

**NELSON, CHARLES, and
HARRY TALBOT**

10-inch record 3s. 6d.

B. 710 {
Hello! Hawaii, how are you? (*Schwartz*)
(79)
When you're a long, long way from home
(*Meyer*) **(79)**

**PHILLIPS, PEGGY, and
ERIC COURTLAND**

12-inch record 5s. 6d.

C. 681 {
'Twas in September (*Hein*) (" Mr. Man-
hattan ") **(78)**
AUSTIN MELFORD
Piccadilly (*Hein*) (" Mr. Manhattan ")
(78)

**TAYLOR, NELLIE, and
PETER GAWTHORNE**

12-inch records 5s. 6d.

C. 737 {
Love's own kiss (Waltz Song) (" High-
Jinks ") **(79)**
NELLIE TAYLOR
Honolulu Isle (*Melville Gideon*) **(79)**

C. 834 {
I've always got time to talk to you (*H.
Talbot*) (" The Boy ") **(79)**
Have a heart (*Kern*) (" The Boy ") **(79)**

WALTON and CARTER

10-inch records 3s. 6d.

B. 731 {
They called it Dixieland (*Whiting*)
(" Some ") **(80)**
Put me to sleep with an old-fashioned
melody (*Jentes*) **(80)**

B. 833 {
I'm going way back home and have a
wonderful time (*Schwartz*) **(79)**
COURTLAND and JEFFERIES
I want to be somebody's baby (*David and
Wright*) **(79)**

**BURTON, OLIVE,
ERIC COURTLAND and
LLEWELLYN MORGAN**

10-inch record 3s. 6d.

B. 818 {
Down Honolulu way (*Burnett and Burke*)
(79)
Baby (You're the sweetest baby I know)
(*Ayer*) **(79)**

**FAIR, ADRAH,
JOHNNIE FIELDS and
LEONARD McKAY**

12-inch record 5s. 6d.

C 830 {
Cousinly Love (*Novello*) (" Arlette ")
(78)
LEONARD McKAY
His Country first of all (The People's
King) (*Novello*) (" Arlette ") **(78)**

The figures in brackets at end of selections
indicate the speed at which the records
· · · · should be played · · · ·

88

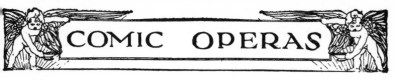

COMIC OPERAS

LEIGH, LOUISE
ERIC COURTLAND and
WALTER JEFFERIES

10-inch record 3s. 6d.

B. 853 {
Dream Boat (*Novello*) (78)
ERIC COURTLAND and WALTER JEFFERIES
Hawaiian Butterfly (*B. Baskette and J. Santley*) (" Bubbly ") (79)

B. 967 {
Let's all go raving mad (*Braham*) (" Tails Up ") (79)
LOUISE LEIGH
Peter Pan (with chorus) (*Joel and Coward*) (" Tails Up ") (79)

B. 984 {
Give me a little cosy corner (*Tate*) (79)
COURTLAND and JEFFERIES
Indianapolis (79)

COYNE, JOSEPH,
MARJORIE GORDON,
EVELYN LAYE,
H. DE BRAY (solo),
AUSTIN MELFORD and
CLIFTON ALDERSON

12-inch record 5s. 6d.

C. 860 {
Finale, Act I (" Going Up ") (with dialogue and chorus (*Hirsch*) (79)
EVELYN LAYE and AUSTIN MELFORD
Do it for me (*Hirsch*) (" Going Up ") (79)

COMIC OPERA

" H.M.S. PINAFORE "
(Gilbert and Sullivan)

10-inch records 3s. 6d.

B. 435 {
Sorry her lot (Mdme. JONES-HUDSON) (79)
Opening Chorus— Hail ! Men-o'-Warsmen (AMY AUGARDE and CHORUS) (79)

B. 436 {
The Captain's Song (THORPE BATES and CHORUS) (79)
Fair moon, to thee I sing (THORPE BATES) (79)

B. 437 {
Over the bright blue sea (CHORUS) (78)
Now give three cheers (ALAN TURNER and CHORUS) (79)

B. 438 {
A British tar is a soaring soul (CHORUS) (79)
Refrain, audacious tar (Mdme. JONES-HUDSON and ERNEST PIKE) (78)

B. 439 {
Things are seldom what they seem (AMY AUGARDE and THORPE BATES) (79)
Never mind the why and the wherefore (Mdme. JONES-HUDSON, THORPE BATES and ALAN TURNER) (79)

B. 440 {
Kind Captain (PETER DAWSON and THORPE BATES) (79)
In uttering a reprobation (ALAN TURNER and CHORUS) (78)

B. 441 {
Farewell my own (AMY AUGARDE and CHORUS) (79)
Oh, joy ! oh, rapture ! (AMY AUGARDE and CHORUS) (79)

B. 486 {
Things are seldom what they seem (*Sullivan*) (DORIS COWAN and GEORGE BAKER) (78)
There was a time (" Gondoliers ")— (*Sullivan*) (DORIS COWAN and GEORGE BAKER) (78)

12-inch records 5s. 6d.

C. 513 {
A maiden fair to see (ERNEST PIKE and CHORUS) (79)
The hours creep on apace (Mdme. JONES-HUDSON) (78)

C. 514 {
Messmates, ahoy ! (CHORUS) (78)
This very night (CHORUS) (78)

C. 517 {
Gems from " H.M.S. Pinafore," Part I. (THE LIGHT OPERA COMPANY) (81)
Gems from " H.M.S. Pinafore," Part II. (THE LIGHT OPERA COMPANY) (81)

C. 714 {
" H.M.S. Pinafore "—Selection I. (COLDSTREAM GUARDS) (79)
" H.M.S. Pinafore "—Selection II. (COLDSTREAM GUARDS) (79)

" THE LILAC DOMINO "
(Operetta)

10-inch records 3s. 6d.

B. 903 {
" The Lilac Domino "—Waltz (DE GROOT and the PICCADILLY ORCHESTRA) (79)
" Pamela "—Valse (*Norton*) (DE GROOT and the PICCADILLY ORCHESTRA) (79)

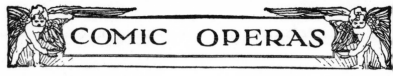

COMIC OPERAS

"THE LILAC DOMINO"—continued

10-inch records 3s. 6d.

B. 906 { Carnival night (with chorus) (ERIC COURTLAND) (79)
Consolation (RANDELL JACKSON) (79)

B. 907 { For your love I am waiting (DE GROOT and the PICCADILLY ORCHESTRA) (79)
First love, last love, best love (Nat D. Ayer) (" The Bing Boys on Broadway ") (DE GROOT and the PICCADILLY ORCHESTRA) (79)

12-inch records 5s. 6d.

C. 847 { "The Lilac Domino "—Selection I (MAYFAIR ORCHESTRA) (79)
"The Lilac Domino "—Selection II (MAYFAIR ORCHESTRA) (79)

C. 848 { For your love I am waiting (with chorus) (LOUISE LEIGH) (79)
The Lilac Domino (with chorus) (LOUISE LEIGH) (79)

C. 849 { Song of the Chimes (LOUISE LEIGH and RANDELL JACKSON) (79)
Where love is waiting (LOUISE LEIGH and RANDELL JACKSON) (79)

C. 850 { What is done, you never can undo (with chorus) (Finale, Act II) (LOUISE LEIGH and RANDELL JACKSON) (79)
The land of happy memories (De Groot) (DE GROOT and the PICCADILLY ORCHESRTA) (79)

THE SULLIVAN OPERATIC PARTY

10-inch records 3s. 6d.

B. 396 { A Regular Royal Queen ("The Gondoliers"—Gilbert and Sullivan) (78)
Dance à Cacucha)(" The Gondoliers ")) (78)

B. 397 { I am a Courtier, grave and serious (" Gondoliers ") (77)
In a contemplative fashion (" Gondoliers ") (76)

B 398 { In enterprise of martial kind (" Gondoliers ") (80)
When a merry maiden marries (" Gondoliers ") (77)

B. 399 { In friendship's name (" Iolanthe "—Sullivan) (78)
None but the brave deserve the fair (" Iolanthe ") (78)

B 400 { Where Britain rules the waves (" Iolanthe "—Sullivan) (80)
With cat-like tread (Chorus of Pirates) (" Pirates of Penzance "—Sullivan) (80)

B. 401 { Pour, O King, the Pirate Sherry (" Pirates of Penzance "—Sullivan) (80)
When a foeman bares his steel (" Pirates of Penzance ")—Sullivan (77)

B. 402 { The Judges Song (" Trial by Jury "—Sullivan) (76)
G. P. HUNTLEY and GEORGE CARROLL The Golf Scene (" Three Little Maids "—Rubens) (74)

12-inch record 5s. 6d.

C. 512 { Entrance and March of the Peers (" Iolanthe ") (78)
MINSTER SINGERS
Sea Songs (78)

"THE MIKADO"
(Gilbert and Sullivan)

Recorded under the direction of the D'OYLY CARTE OPERA COMPANY (Mr. Rupert D'Oyly Carte). Orchestral accompaniment conducted by Mr. Arthur Wood.

12-inch double-sided records 7s.

Act I.

D. 2 { "The Mikado," Overture Part I (LIGHT OPERA ORCHESTRA) (79)
"The Mikado " Overture Part II (LIGHT OPERA ORCHESTRA) (79)

D. 3 { Chorus of men—If you want to know who we are (JOHN HARRISON soloist, GEO. BAKER, E. PIKE and ED. HALLAND) (79)
A Wandering Minstrel I (with chorus) (JOHN HARRISON) (79)

D. 4 { (a) Our Great Mikado (with chorus) (GEORGE BAKER) (79)
(b) Young man, despair likewise to go (with chorus) (ROBERT RADFORD) (79)
(a) Recit. And have I journey'd for a month (JOHN HARRISON and ROBERT RADFORD) (79)
(b) Behold the Lord High Executioner (with chorus) (GEORGE BAKER) (79)

D. 5 { As some day it may happen (with Chorus of men) (GEORGE BAKER) (79)
(a) Chorus of Girls—Comes a train of little ladies (EDNA THORNTON, V. ESSEX, V. OPPENSHAW and Chorus of girls) (79)
(b) Trio—Three little maids from school (EDNA THORNTON, V. ESSEX, V. OPPENSHAW and Chorus of girls) (79)

The figures in brackets at end of selections indicate the speed at which the records . . . . should be played . . . .

COMIC OPERAS

" THE MIKADO "—*continued*

12-inch double-sided record 7s.

D. 6
- (a) Quintet—So please you, sir, we much regret (with a chorus) (EDNA THORNTON, VIOLET ESSEX, BESSIE JONES, ROBERT RADFORD and GEORGE BAKER) (79)
- (b) Duet — Were you not to Ko-Ko plighted· (VIOLET ESSEX and JOHN HARRISON) (79)

Trio—I am so proud (ROBERT RADFORD, GEORGE BAKER and ERNEST PIKE) (79)

D. 7
Finale Act I, Part I.—With aspect stern and gloomy stride (V. ESSEX, J. HARRISON, R. RADFORD, G. BAKER and Full Chorus) (79)

Finale, Act. I, Part II. (EDNA THORNTON soloist, and Full Chorus) (79)

D. 8
- Finale, Act I. Part III. (EDNA THORNTON soloist, and Full Chorus) (79)
- ACT II.
- Opening Chorus, Act II.—Braid the raven hair (VIOLET OPPENSHAW soloist, and chorus of girls) (79)

D. 9
- The sun whose rays are all ablaze (VIOLET ESSEX) (79)
- Madrigal—Brightly dawns our wedding day. (EDNA THORNTON, BESSIE JONES, ROBT. RADFORD and ERNEST PIKE) (79)

D. 10
- (a) Trio—Here's a how-de-do! (VIOLET ESSEX, JOHN HARRISON and GEORGE BAKER) (79)
- (b) Entrance of Mikado and Katisha (EDNA THORNTON, ROBERT RADFORD and Chorus of girls) (79)

A more humane Mikado never did in Japan exist (with chorus) (ROBERT RADFORD) (79)

D. 11
- Trio and chorus—The criminal cried as he dropped him down (EDNA THORNTON, ROBT. RADFORD and GEO. BAKERS) (79)
- (a) Glee—See now the Fates their gift allot (EDNA THORNTON, BESSIE JONES, J. HARRISON, R. RADFORD, and G. BAKER) (79)
- (b) Duet—The flowers that bloom in the Spring (JOHN HARRISON and GEORGE BAKER) (79)

D. 12
- (a) Alone and yet alive (EDNA THORNTON) (79)
- (b) Willow, tit-willow (GEO. BAKER) (79)
- (a) There is beauty in the bellow of the blast (EDNA THORNTON and GEORGE BAKER) (79)
- (b) Finale, Act II.—For he's gone and married Yum-Yum (FULL CHORUS) (79)

Complete Opera in a beautifully decorated album £3 17s. 0d.

" YEOMEN OF THE GUARD " (Gilbert and Sullivan)

10-inch records 3s. 6d.

B. 403
- Rapture, rapture (FLORENCE VENNING and PETER DAWSON) (77)
- Chorus of Men (" The Gondoliers "—*Gilbert and Sullivan*) (SULLIVAN OPERATIC PARTY) (77)

B. 404
- When maiden loves (CARRIE TUBB) (79)
- When our gallant Norman foes (FLORENCE VENNING) (77)

B. 405
- Here's a man of jollity (SULLIVAN OPERATIC PARTY) (78)
- Alas! I waver to and fro (FLORENCE VENNING, PIKE and DAWSON) (77)

B. 406
- I have a song to sing, O (Mdme. JONES-HUDSON and STANLEY KIRKBY) (77)
- How say you, maiden (Mdme. JONES-HUDSON and KIRKBY and DAWSON) (77)

B. 407
- 'Tis done! I am a bride (Mdme. JONES-HUDSON) (78)
- Were I thy bride (Mdme. JONES-HUDSON) (76)

B. 408
- To thy fraternal care (SULLIVAN OPERATIC PARTY) (78)
- Here upon we've both agreed (Messrs. KIRKBY and DAWSON) (80)

B. 409
- Freed from his fetters (ERNEST PIKE) (76)
- Is life a boon (ERNEST PIKE) (77)

B. 410
- Strange adventure (SULLIVAN OPERATIC PARTY) (77)
- Like a ghost his vigil keeping (SULLIVAN OPERATIC PARTY) (78)

B. 411
- A man who would woo a fair maid (SULLIVAN OPERATIC PARTY) (78)
- When a wooer goes a wooing (SULLIVAN OPERATIC PARTY) (76)

12-inch record 5s. 6d.

C. 511
- Overture (BOHEMIAN ORCHESTRA) (77)
- Finale (SULLIVAN OPERATIC PARTY) (77)

▣ ▣ ▣

MUSICAL COMEDIES

MUSICAL COMEDY, etc.

" THE ARCADIANS "

10-inch records 3s. 6d.

B. 446 { My Motter (HARRY CARLTON) (80)
Just like father used to do (Monckton) (" Quaker Girl ") (HARRY CARLTON) (80)

B. 480 { The Pipes of Pan (MARION JEROME) (80)
I can't refrain from laughing (Lambelot) (" Geisha ") (CLARA EVELYN) (80)

12-inch records 5s. 6d.

C. 124 { " The Arcadians," Selection I. (COLD-STREAM GUARDS BAND) (81)
" The Arcadians," Selection II. (COLD-STREAM GUARDS BAND) (81)

C. 143 { Gems from " The Arcadians " (with Chorus) (BOHEMIAN ORCHESTRA) (80)
Gems from " Our Miss Gibbs " (with Chorus) (Monckton and Caryll) (BOHEMIAN ORCHESTRA) (81)

" ARLETTE "

12-inch records 6s.

03593 The Fairy Ring (WINIFRED BARNES) (78)
03594 It's just a memory (WINIFRED BARNES) (78)
02773 On the Staff (with chorus) (STANLEY LUPINO) (78)
04212 Love in my heart is ringing (Telephone Duet) (WINIFRED BARNES and JOSEPH COYNE)
04213 Didn't know the way to (WINIFRED BARNES and JOSEPH COYNE) (78)

10-inch record 3s. 6d.

B. 893 { Didn't know the way to (DE GROOT and the PICCADILLY ORCHESTRA) (79)
Poor Butterfly ! (R. Hubbell) (DE GROOT and the PICCADILLY ORCHESTRA) (79)

12-inch records 5s. 6d.

C. 828 { " Arlette," Gems from, Part I. (78)
" Arlette," Gems from, Part II. (78)

C. 830 { Cousinly Love (ADRAH FAIR, JOHNNIE FIELDS and LEONARD McKAY) (78)
His Country first of all (The People's King) (LEONARD McKAY) (78)

C. 831 { " Arlette," Selection I. (MAYFAIR ORCHESTRA) (78)
" Arlette," Selection II. (MAYFAIR ORCHESTRA) (78)

" BETTY "

10-inch record 3s. 6d.

B. 493 { Dance with me (DORIS COWAN and GEORGE BAKER) (79)
Boy and Girl (" The Country Girl ") (DORIS COWAN and GEORGE BAKER) (79)

12-inch records 5s. 6d.

C. 413 { " Betty," Selection I. (MAYFAIR ORCHESTRA) (78)
" Betty," Selection II. (MAYFAIR ORCHESTRA) (78)

C. 414 { " Betty " Waltz (MAYFAIR ORCHESTRA) (78)
" For Valour "—Military Valse (Ancliffe) arr. by Lotter) (MAYFAIR ORCHESTRA) (78)

C. 596 { Gems from " Betty," Part I. (THE LIGHT OPERA COMPANY) (78)
Gems from " Betty," Part II. (THE LIGHT OPERA COMPANY) (78)

C. 656 { Can it be love (AIMEE MAXWELL) (78)
Rose in the bud (Dorothy Forster) (Staff-Captain H. RATCLIFFE) (78)

" THE BOY "

10-inch record 4s.

4-2944 When the heart is young (W. H. BERRY) (79)

12-inch record 6s.

02776 I want to go to bye-bye (with Chorus) (W. H. BERRY) (79)

10-inch records 3s. 6d.

B. 888 { I'm sick to death of women (PETER GAWTHORNE) (79)
Hong Kong (Von Holstein and Sanders) (" Any Old Thing ") (ERIC COURTLAND) (79)

B. 963 { Little Miss Melody (DE GROOT and the PICCADILLY ORCHESTRA) (79)
If you look in her eyes (Hirsch) (" Going Up ") (DE GROOT and the PICCADILLY ORCHESTRA) (79)

12-inch records 5s. 6d.

C. 833 { Little Miss Melody (NELLIE TAYLOR) (78)
Valse poudrée (F. Popy) (DE GROOT and the PICCADILLY ORCHESTRA) (78)

The figures in brackets at end of selections
indicate the speed at which the records
. . . . should be played . . . .

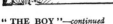

MUSICAL COMEDIES

" THE BOY "—*continued*

12-inch records 5s. 6d.

C. 834 { I've always got time to talk to you (NELLIE TAYLOR and PETER GAWTHORNE) (79)
Have a heart (NELLIE TAYLOR and PETER GAWTHORNE) (79)

C. 835 { "The Boy," Selection I. (MAYFAIR ORCHESTRA) (78)
"The Boy," Selection II. MAYFAIR ORCHESTRA) (78)

" CARMINETTA "

12-inch records 6s.

03589 A Merry Farewell (Waltz Song) (DELYSIA) (78)

03590 Habanera (Come laugh at love) (DELYSIA) (79)

03588 Clicquot (with Chorus) (DELYSIA) (79)

03587 Wedding Day Song (MARIE BLANCHE) (79)

04210 Won't you kiss me? (MARIE BLANCHE and DENNIS NEILSON TERRY) (78)

04211 Love Duet—Finale, Act I. (DELYSIA and DENNIS NEILSON TERRY) (78)

10-inch record 3s. 6d.

B. 892 { A Merry Farewell (Valse Song) (DE GROOT and the PICCADILLY ORCH.) (79)
Clicquot (DE GROOT and the PICCADILLY ORCHESTRA) (79)

12-inch records 5s. 6d.

C. 821 { "Carminetta" Valse (METROPOLITAN DANCE BAND) (79)
Waltz we love—Waltz (La Valse que nous aimons) (*Vecsey*) (79)

C. 823 { "Carminetta" Selection I. (MAYFAIR ORCHESTRA) (79)
"Carminetta" Selection II. (MAYFAIR ORCHESTRA) (79)

C. 824 { Musical Quartet (THE LIGHT OPERA Co.) (79)
Hypnotism Quintet (THE LIGHT OPERA Co.) (79)

" CHU CHIN CHOW "

10-inch records 4s.

2–3208 Cleopatra's Nile (VIOLET ESSEX and CHORUS) (79)

4–2812 When a pullet is plump (COURTICE POUNDS) (79)

12-inch records 6s.

04186 Any time's kissing time (VIOLET ESSEX and COURTICE POUNDS) (79)

03528 I love you so (VIOLET ESSEX) (79)

10-inch records 5s. 6d.

C. 755 { "Chu Chin Chow" Selection I. (MAYFAIR ORCHESTRA) (79)
"Chu Chin Chow," Selection II. (MAYFAIR ORCHESTRA) (79)

C. 756 { The Cobbler's Song (PETER DAWSON) (79)
The Watchman (*Squire*) (PETER DAWSON) (79)

C. 778 { Any time's kissing time (DE GROOT and the PICCADILLY ORCHESTRA) (78)
Some sort of somebody (*Kern*) ("Vanity Fair") (DE GROOT and the PICCADILLY ORCHESTRA) (78)

" THE GEISHA "

10-inch records 3s. 6d.

B. 442 { The interfering parrot (DENISE ORME) (79)
BESSIE JONES and CHORUS
Wonderful rose of love (*Bennett Scott*) (79)

B. 480 { I can't refrain from laughing (CLARA EVELYN) (80)
MARION JEROME
The Pipes of Pan (" The Arcadians ") (80)

12-inch record 5s. 6d.

C. 199 { "The Geisha," (Selection I. BAND OF H.M. COLDSTREAM GUARDS) (81)
"The Geisha," Selection II. (BAND OF H.M. COLDSTREAM GUARDS) (81)

" GOING UP."

12-inch records 6s.

04235 Down! Up! Left! Right! (Finale, Act II.) (JOSEPH COYNE, AUSTIN MELFORD, ROY BYFORD and FRANKLYN BELLAMY (79))

04232 First act, second act, third act (JOSEPH COYNE and MARJORIE GORDON) (79)

04233 If you look in her eyes (MARJORIE GORDON and EVELYN LAYE) (79)

04234 Kiss me! (MARJORIE GORDON and H. DE BRAY) (79)

03614 The tickle toe (with Chorus) (MARJORIE GORDON, Dialogue—FRANKLYN BELLAMY) (79)

03613 The touch of a woman's hand (with Chorus) (MARJORIE GORDON) (79)

MUSICAL COMEDIES

"GOING UP"—*continued*

10-inch records 3s. 6d.

B. 963
- If you look in her eyes (DE GROOT and the PICCADILLY ORCHESTRA) **(79)**
- Little Miss Melody (*Monckton*) ("The Boy") (DE GROOT and the PICCADILLY ORCHESTRA) **(79)**

B. 988
- (*a*) I'll bet you; (*b*) The touch of a woman's hand (GAIETY THEATRE ORCHESTRA) **(79)**
- Medley—Two-Step (GAIETY THEATRE ORCHESTRA) **(79)**

B. 982
- The tickle toe (DE GROOT and the PICCADILLY ORCHESTRA) **(79)**
- The Apache Rag (*Braham*) ("Tails up") (DE GROOT and the PICCADILLY ORCHESTRA) **(79)**

12-inch records 5s. 6d.

C. 860
- Do it for me (EVELYN LAYE and AUSTIN MELFORD) **(79)**
- Finale, Act I. (with dialogue and chorus (JOSEPH COYNE, MARJORIE GORDON, EVELYN LAYE, H. DE BRAY (solo), AUSTIN MELFORD and CLIFTON ALDERSON) **(79)**

C. 861
- "Going Up"—Selection I. (GAIETY THEATRE ORCHESTRA) **(79)**
- "Going Up," Selection II. (GAIETY THEATRE ORCHESTRA) **(79)**

"THE GONDOLIERS"

10-inch records 3s. 6d.

B. 486
- There was a time (DORIS COWAN and GEORGE BAKER) **(78)**
- Things are seldom what they seem ("H.M.S. Pinafore") (DORIS COWAN and GEORGE BAKER) **(78)**

12-inch records 5s. 6d.

C. 102
- "The Gondoliers," Selection I. (COLDSTREAM GUARDS BAND) **(81)**
- "The Gondoliers," Selection II. (COLDSTREAM GUARDS BAND) **(81)**

"THE HAPPY DAY"

10-inch records 4s.

2-3177 The Seasons (VIOLET ESSEX) **(78)**
2-3178 Bohemia (VIOLET ESSEX) **(78)**

10-inch record 3s. 6d.

B. 747
- Bohemia (DE GROOT and the PICCADILLY ORCHESTRA) **(79)**
- O Flower Divine (*Haydn Wood*) (LENSEN and the TROCADERO ORCHESTRA) **(79)**

12-inch records 5s. 6d.

C. 687
- "The Happy Day," Selection I. (MAYFAIR ORCHESTRA) **(78)**
- "The Happy Day," Selection II. (MAYFAIR ORCHESTRA) **(78)**

C. 718
- "The Happy Day," Gems from, Part I. (LIGHT OPERA COMPANY) **(79)**
- "The Happy Day," Gems from, Part II. (LIGHT OPERA COMPANY) **(79)**

C. 727
- "The Happy Day," Fox Trot (METROPOLITAN DANCE BAND) **(79)**
- "The Happy Day," Waltz (METROPOLITAN DANCE BAND) **(79)**

"HIGH JINKS"

10-inch records 4s.

4-2784 It's wonderful how trouble clings to me (W. H. BERRY) **(78)**
4-2785 I could love a nice little girl (with Chorus) (W. H. BERRY) **(78)**

12-inch records 6s.

02679 What is life without love? (W. H. BERRY) **(78)**
04176 It isn't my fault (W. H. BERRY and MARIE BLANCHE) **(78)**

10-inch record 3s. 6d.

B. 769
- Something seems tingle-ingleing (DE GROOT and the PICCADILLY ORCH.) **(79)**
- It's a long, long way to my home in Kentucky (*Ayer*) (DE GROOT and the PICCADILLY ORCHESTRA) **(79)**

12-inch records 5s. 6d.

C. 713
- Overture (ADELPHI THEATRE ORCH.) **(78)**
- Oyra's Dance (ADELPHI THEATRE ORCHESTRA) **(78)**

C. 719
- Tingle-ingleing Fox Trot (ADELPHI THEATRE ORCHESTRA) **(78)**
- Finale, Act II. (ADELPHI THEATRE ORCHESTRA) **(78)**

C. 720
- The Bubble (MARIE BLANCHE **(78)**
- Something seems tingle-ingleing (PETER GAWTHORNE and CHORUS) **(78)**

C. 721
- She says it with her eyes (MAISIE GAY and W. H. RAWLINS) **(78)**
- Love's own kiss—Waltz Song (PETER GAWTHORNE and MURIEL GRAY) **(78)**

C. 729
- "High Jinks"—One-Step or Fox Trot (METROPOLITAN DANCE BAND) **(78)**
- "The Bing Boys are Here"—Waltz (*Ayer*) (METROPOLITAN DANCE BAND) **(78)**

**The figures in brackets at end of selections
indicate the speed at which the records
. . . . should be played . . . .**

94

" HIGH JINKS ''—*continued*

12-inch records 5s. 6d.

C. 737 { Love's own kiss — Waltz Song (NELLIE TAYLOR and PETER GAWTHORNE) **(79)**
Honolulu Isle (*Melville Gideon*) (NELLIE TAYLOR) **(79)**

C. 750 { " High Jinks ''—Waltz (MAYFAIR ORCHESTRA) **(78)**
My heart is sad—Waltz (*Belabre*) (MAYFAIR DANCE ORCHESTRA) **(78)**

THE LIGHT OPERA COMPANY

12-inch records 5s. 6d.

C. 515 { " Dorothy," Gems from, Part I. (*Cellier*) **(81)**
" Dorothy," Gems from, Part II. (*Cellier*) **(81)**

C. 516 { " Florodora," Gems from (*Stuart*) **(81)**
" Duchess of Dantzig," Gems from (*Caryll*) **(81)**

C. 517 { " H.M.S. Pinafore," Gems from, Part I. (*Sullivan*) **(81)**
" H.M.S. Pinafore," Gems from, Part II. (*Sullivan*) **(81)**

C 518 { " Adèle," Gems from (*Briquet and Phillipp*) **(78)**
" Gipsy Love," Gems from (*Lehar*) **(80)**

C. 519 { " The Chocolate Soldier," Gems from (*Straus*) **(80)**
" The Girl in the Taxi," Gems from (*Jean Gilbert*) **(81)**

C .520 { " Véronique," Gems from (*Messager*) **(78)**
" The Dancing Mistress," Gems from (*Monckton*) **(80)**

C. 521 { " The Quaker Girl," Gems from, Part I. (*Monckton*) **(80)**
" The Quaker Girl," Gems from, Part II. (*Monckton*) **(80)**

C. 594 { " To-night's the night," Gems from (*Rubens*) **(78)**
NELSON KEYS and ARTHUR PLAYFAIR The Optimist and the Pessimist (" Bric-à-Brac ") (*Finck*) **(78)**

C. 596 { " Betty," Gems from, Part I. (*Rubens*) **(78)**
" Betty," Gems from, Part II. (*Rubens*) **(78)**

C 646 { " Tina," Gems from, Part I. (*Rubens*) **(78)**
" Tina," Gems from, Part II. (*Rubens*) **(78)**

C. 703 { " The Bing Boys are Here," Gems from, Part I. (*Nat D. Ayer*) **(78)**
" The Bing Boys are Here," Gems from, Part II. (*Nat D, Ayer*) **(78)**

C. 710 { " My Lady Frayle," Gems from, Part I. (*Finck and Talbot*) **(79)**
" My Lady Frayle," Gems from, Part II. (*Finck and Talbot*) **(79)**

C. 718 { " The Happy Day," Gems from, Part I· (*Jones and Rubens*) **(79)**
" The Happy Day," Gems from, Part II (*Jones and Rubens*) **(79)**

C. 735 { " Mr. Manhattan," Gems from, Part I (arr. by *Clifford Courtenay*) **(79)**
" Mr. Manhattan," Gems from, Part II. (arr. by *Clifford Courtenay*) **(79)**

C. 746 { " Some," Gems from, Part I. (*Tate and Powell*) **(78)**
" Some," Gems from. Part II. (*Tate and Powell*) **(78)**

C. 765 { " Theodore & Co.," Gems from, Part I. (*Novello and Kern*, arr. by *Jaxon*) **(78)**
" Theodore & Co.," Gems from, Part II. (*Novello and Kern*, arr. by *Jaxon*) **(78)**

C. 791 { " Vanity Fair," Gems from, Part I. **(79)**
" Vanity Fair," Gems from, Part II. **(79)**

C. 814 { " The Maid of the Mountains," Gems from, Part I. (*Fraser-Simson and Tate*) **(79)**
" The Maid of the Mountains," Gems from Part II. (*Fraser-Simson and Tate*) **(79)**

C. 824 { Musical Quartet (*Lassailly*) (" Carminetta ") **(79)**
Hypnotism Quintet (*Lassailly*) (" Carminetta ") **(79)**

C. 828 { " Arlette," Gems from, Part I. (*Le Feuvre and Novello*) **(78)**
" Arlette," Gems from, Part II. (*Le Feuvre and Novello*) **(78)**

" MR. MANHATTAN ''

10-inch record 3s. 6d.

B. 679 { 'Twas in September (DE GROOT and the PICCADILLY ORCHESTRA) **(79)**
When you're all dressed up and no place to go (DE GROOT and the PICCADILLY ORCHESTRA) **(79)**

12-inch record 6s.

02660 When you're all dressed up and no place to go (RAYMOND HITCHCOCK) **(78)**

12-inch records 5s. 6d.

C. 681 { Piccadilly (AUSTIN MELFORD) **(78)**
'Twas in September (PEGGY PHILLIPS and ERIC COURTLAND) **(78)**

C. 688 { " Mr. Manhattan," Selection I. (MAYFAIR ORCHESTRA) **(79)**
" Mr. Manhattan," Selection II. (MAYFAIR ORCHESTRA) **(79)**

C. 735 { Gems from " Mr. Manhattan," Part I. (LIGHT OPERA COMPANY) **(79)**
Gems from " Mr. Manhattan," Part II. (LIGHT OPERA COMPANY) **(79)**

"THE MAID OF THE MOUNTAINS"

10-inch records 3s. 6d.

B 805 { A Bachelor Gay (PETER DAWSON) (78)
A Paradise for two (The Key to your heart) LOUISE LEIGH and PETER DAWSON) (78)

B. 808 { Farewell (LOUISE LEIGH) (78)
New Moon (OLIVE BURTON) (78)

B. 828 { A Paradise for two (The Key to your heart) (DE GROOT and the PICCADILLY ORCHESTRA) (79)
My heart's just broke for you (*Dorothy Forster*) (DE GROOT and the PICCADILLY ORCHESTRA) (78)

12-inch records 5s. 6d.

C. 783 { "The Maid of the Mountains," Selection I. (MAYFAIR ORCHESTRA) (78)
"The Maid of the Mountains," Selection II. (MAYFAIR ORCHESTRA) (78)

C. 814 { "The Maid of the Mountains," Gems from, Part I. (THE LIGHT OPERA CO.) (79)
"The Maid of the Mountains," Gems from Part II. (THE LIGHT OPERA CO.) (79)

C. 817 { "The Maid of the Mountains," Waltz (METROPOLITAN DANCE BAND) (79)
Sphinx Waltz (*Popy*) (79)

C. 829 { "The Maid of the Mountains" Valse Song (Love will find a way) (DE GROOT and the PICCADILLY ORCHESTRA) (78)
Parted (*Tosti*) (DE GROOT and the PICCADILLY ORCHESTRA) (78)

"MY LADY FRAYLE"

10-inch record 3s. 6d.

B. 644 { Flappers (ARNOLD RICHARDSON) (78)
Since Chumley came back from London Town (*Nat D. Ayer*) ("Bric-à-Brac") (MURRAY JOHNSON) (78)

12-inch record 6s.

02659 Song of the Bowl (COURTICE POUNDS) (78)

12-inch records 5s. 6d.

C. 679 { What a naughty old gentleman father must have been (GRETCHEN YATES) (78)
Day by Day (ANNIE CROFTS) (78)

C 686 { "My Lady Frayle," Selection I. (PALACE THEATRE ORCHESTRA) (78)
"My Lady Frayle," Selection II. (PALACE THEATRE ORCHESTRA) (78)

C. 710 { "My Lady Frayle," Gems from, Part I (LIGHT OPERA COMPANY) (79)
"My Lady Frayle," Gems from, Part II. (LIGHT OPERA COMPANY) (79)

"PAMELA"

10-inch record 4s.

4-2957 Piccadilly, London, West (with Chorus) (OWEN NARES) (79)

12-inch records 6s.

03601 Cupid, Cupid (LILY ELSIE) (79)

03602 I loved you so (LILY ELSIE) (79)

04223 Waltz Theme and Cupid (Finale, Act II.) (LILY ELSIE and OWEN NARES) (79)

04224 I'm so very glad I met you (LILY ELSIE and OWEN NARES) (79)

04225 It's not the things you've got (LILY ELSIE and OWEN NARES) (79)

10-inch record 3s. 6d.

B. 903 { "Pamela"—Valse (DE GROOT and the PICCADILLY ORCHESTRA) (79)
"The Lilac Domino"—Waltz (*Cuvillier*) (DE GROOT and the PICCADILLY ORCHESTRA) (79)

12-inch record 5s. 6d.

C. 841 { "Pamela," Selection I. (MAYFAIR ORCHESTRA) (79)
"Pamela," Selection II. (MAYFAIR ORCHESTRA) (79)

"THE QUAKER GIRL"

10-inch record 3s. 6d.

B. 446 { Just like father used to do (HARRY CARLTON) (80)
My Motter ("The Arcadians") (HARRY CARLTON) (80)

12-inch records 5s. 6d.

C. 191 { "The Quaker Girl," Selection I. (COLDSTREAM GUARDS BAND) (81)
"The Quaker Girl," Selection II. (COLDSTREAM GUARDS BAND) (;81)

C. 521 { Gems from the "Quaker Girl," Part I. (THE LIGHT OPREA COMPANY) (80)
Gems from "The Quaker Girl,'" Part II. (THE LIGHT OPERA COMPANY) (80)

C. 529 { A Quaker Girl (GERTIE MILLAR) (80)
In Yorkshire (*Monckton*) ("Our Miss Gibbs") (GERTIE MILLAR) (80)

C. 530 { Tony from America (GERTIE MILLAR) (80)
Moonstruck (*Monckton*) ("Our Miss Gibbs") (GERTIE MILLAR) (80)

The figures in brackets at end of selections indicate the speed at which the records · · · · should be played · · · ·

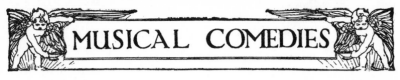

MUSICAL COMEDIES

" SOLDIER BOY "

10-inch record 3s. 6d.

B. 968
- The military stamp (with chorus) (LOUISE LEIGH and WALTER JEFFERIES) (79)
- I've got the sweetest girl in Maryland (*Donaldson*) ("Tabs") (COURTLAND and JEFFERIES) (79)

12-inch records 5s. 6d.

C. 866
- Mother (ERIC COURTLAND and JOSEPH REED) (79)
- En relisant vos lettres (valse lente) (*Masson-Kiek*) (DE GROOT and the PICCADILLY ORCHESTRA) (79)

C. 867
- "Soldier Boy" Selection I. (MAYFAIR ORCHESTRA) (79)
- "Soldier Boy," Selection II. (MAYFAIR ORCHESTRA) (79)

C. 868
- The lonely princess (LOUISE LEIGH) (79)
- The kiss waltz (LOUISE LEIGH and ERIC COURTLAND) (79)

" THEODORE & CO."

12-inch records 6s.

02692 Every little girl can teach me something new (GEORGE CROSSMITH and CHORUS) (78)

02693 Minor objections (GEORGE GROSSMITH (78)

04182 All I want is somebody to love me (GEORGE GROSSMITH and MADGE SAUNDERS) (78)

02691 My friend John (LESLIE HENSON) (78)

04181 Three hundred and sixty-five days (LESLIE HENSON and DAVY BURNABY) (78)

10-inch records 3s. 6d.

B. 753
- What a duke should be (DAVY BURNABY and CHORUS) (78)
- Oh how I want to marry all the little candy girls (HENRI LEONI) (78)

B. 754
- I'll make myself at home, dear (JULIA JAMES and FRED LESLIE) (78)
- Valse—Saracenne (GAIETY THEATRE ORCHESTRA) (78)

12-inch records 5s. 6d.

C. 748
- That "come hither" look (JULIA JAMES) (78)
- I'm getting such a big girl now (MADGE SAUNDERS and CHORUS) (78)

C. 749
- Any old where (HENRI LEONI and CHORUS) (78)
- Overture (GAIETY THEATRE ORCHESTRA) (78)

C. 753
- "Theodore & Co." Selection I. (MAYFAIR ORCHESTRA) (78)
- "Theodore & Co." Selection II. (MAYFAIR ORCHESTRA) (78)

C. 765
- Gems, "Theodore & Co.," Part I. (LIGHT OPERA COMPANY) (78)
- Gems, "Theodore & Co.," Part II. (LIGHT OPERA COMPANY) (78)

" TINA "

12-inch records 5s. 6d.

C. 632
- I've been to the pictures (MABEL SEALBY) (78)
- Let me introduce you to my father (W. H. BERRY and PHYLLIS DARE) (78)

C. 633
- The Violin Song (PHYLLIS DARE) (78)
- Something in the atmosphere (PHYLLIS DARE and PAUL RUBENS) (78)

C. 635
- "Tina," Selection I. (ADELPHI THEATRE ORCHESTRA) (78)
- "Tina," Selection II. (ADELPHI THEATRE ORCHESTRA) (78)

C. 636
- The Billsticker's Dance (ADELPHI THEATRE ORCHESTRA) (78)
- The Dance from "Tina" (ADELPHI THEATRE ORHCESTRA) (78)

C. 644
- Timbuctoo (W. H. BERRY) (78)
- I'm a self-made man (The Cocoa King) (W. H. BERRY) (78)

C. 646
- "Tina," Gems from, Part I. (LIGHT OPERA COMPANY) (78)
- "Tina," Gems from, Part II. (LIGHT OPERA COMPANY) (78)

C. 683
- Violin Song (DE GROOT and PICCADILLY ORCHESTRA) (78)
- Serenata (*Toselli*) (DE GROOT and PICCADILLY ORCHESTRA) (78)

C. 731
- "Tina," Waltz (METROPOLITAN DANCE BAND) (79)
- Maid in America Medley—Fox Trot (METROPOLITAN DANCE BAND) (79)

" TOM JONES "

10-inch record 5s.

2-3069 Waltz Song (RUTH VINCENT) (80)

10-inch record 3s. 6d.

B. 444
- Waltz Song (FLORENCE SMITHSON) (80)
- I know nothing of life (*Monkton and Talbot* ("Mousmé") (FLORENCE SMITHSON) (80)

MUSICAL COMEDIES

" TO-NIGHT'S THE NIGHT "

10-inch records 3s. 6d.

B. 484 ⎰ I'd like to bring my mother (MOYA MAN-
NERING and LESLIE HENSON) (78)
⎱ Meet me round the corner (MOYA MAN-
NERING and LESLIE HENSON) (78)

B. 501 ⎰ " To-night's the Night "—One step (MAY-
FAIR OCHESTRA) (80)
⎱ Love's garden of roses (*Haydn Wood*)
(DE GROOT and the PICCADILLY
ORCHESTRA) (78)

B. 576 ⎰ They didn't believe me (MURRAY'S SAVOY
QUARTET) (80)
⎱ I like to dance with the girls (*Nat D. Ayer*)
(MURRAY'S SAVOY QUARTET) (80)

12-inch records 5s. 6d.

C. 411 ⎰ " To-night's the Night " Selection I
(MAYFAIR ORCHESTRA) (78)
⎱ " To-night's the Night " Selection II.
(MAYFAIR ORCHESTRA) (78)

C. 574 ⎰ Murders (GEORGE GROSSMITH) (79)
⎱ Any old night is a wonderful night (GEORGE
GROSSMITH) (78)

C. 577 ⎰ The only way (GEORGE GROSSMITH) (78)
⎱ Little girl, little girl (from " Sunshine
Girl" (GEORGE GROSSMITH) (78)

C. 578 ⎰ They didn't believe me (GEORGE GROS-
SMITH and HAIDEE DE RANCE) (79)
⎱ GEORGE GROSSMITH
Tommy, won't you teach me how to
tango ? (*Penso*) (78)

·C. 623 ⎰ They didn't believe me (DE GROOT and the
PICCADILLY ORCHESTRA) (78)
⎱ A little bit of Heaven (*Ball*) (DE GROOT
and the PICCADILLY ORCHESTRA) (78)

C. 698 ⎰ " To-night's the Night " Fox Trot (MAY-
FAIR ORCHESTRA) (78)
⎱ A Dream of Delight Waltz (*Nicholls*)
(MAYFAIR ORCHESTRA) (78)

" YES, UNCLE ! "

10-inch record 4s.

4-2965 Carry on the good work (with Chorus)
(NORMAN GRIFFIN) (79)

12-inch records 6s.

02790 Ninny, Nonny, No (NORMAN GRIFFIN)
(79)

03609 Widows are wonderful (JULIA JAMES)
(79)

04231 Would you believe it ? (NORMAN
GRIFFIN and DAVY BURNABY) (79)

10-inch records 3s. 6d.

B. 908 ⎰ Think of me (with Chorus) HENRI LEONI
and MIMI CRAWFORD) (79)
⎱ You may take me round Paree (HENRI
LEONI and MIMI CRAWFORD) (79)

B. 909 ⎰ Play me that marching· melody (with
Chorus) (HENRI LEONI) (79)
⎱ Widows are wonderful (DE GROOT and the
PICCADILLY ORCHESTRA) (79)

B. 914 ⎰ Widows are wonderful (SAVOY QUARTET)
(79)
⎱ Hello ! New York (*Ayer*) (" The Bing
Boys on Broadway ") (SAVOY QUAR-
TET) (79)

12-inch records 5s. 6d.

C. 851 ⎰ The dear old days (with Chorus) (DAVY
BURNABY) (79)
⎱ Some day I'll make you love me (*Grey and
Ayer*, arr. *Stoddon*) (" Round the
Map ") (DE GROOT and the PICCADILLY
ORCHESTRA) (79)

C. 852 ⎰ " Yes, Uncle ! "—Selection I (MAYFAIR
ORCHESTRA) (79)
⎱ " Yes, Uncle ! "—Selection II (MAYFAIR
ORCHESTRA) (79)

🔲 🔲 🔲 🔲 🔲

**The figures in brackets at end of selections
indicate the speed at which the records
. . . . should be played . . . .**

REVUE RECORDS

REVUES

" AIRS AND GRACES "

12-inch records 6s.

03578   Pussy Cat in love (with Chorus) (GERTIE MILLAR) (78)

04208   Whisper to me (GERTIE MILLAR and ERNEST PIKE) (78)

12-inch record 5s. 6d.

C. 810 { Two dances from the Assyrian Scene— I. " Cup Bearer's Dance " ; " II. Bacchanale" (PALACE THEATRE ORCHESTRA, conducted by Mr. HERMAN FINCK) (78) Selection of Music from " Passionat Puppets "—1. " Doll Waltz " 2. " Harlequin Motif " 3. " Jack-in-the-Box Dance " 4. " Duet Dance "—Doll and Jack (PALACE THEATRE ORCHESTRA, conducted by Mr. HERMAN FINCK) (78)

" AS YOU WERE "

10-inch records 3s. 6d.

B. 986 { Back to Blighty (COURTLAND and JEFFERIES) (79) I'm the great big pot of Potsdam (COURTLAND and JEFFERIES) (79)

B. 987 { What ho ! Mr. Watteau (with Chorus) BLANCHE DARE (79) If you could care (ERIC COURTLAND) (79)

12-inch record 5s. 6d.

C. 874 { " As You Were "—Selection I. (MAYFAIR ORCHESTRA) (79) " As You Were "—Selection II. (MAYFAIR ORCHESTRA) (79)

" THE BING BOYS ARE HERE "

10-inch records 3s. 6d.

B. 640 { In other words (NAT D. AYER) (78) Dear Old Shepherd's Bush (NAT D. AYER) (78)

B. 641 { The Clock Song (NAT D. AYER) (78) Come round London with me (NAT D. AYER) (78)

B. 642 { Another little drink wouldn't do us any harm (NAT D. AYER) (78) The Whistler (ALHAMBRA ORCHESTRA) (78)

B. 678 { If you were the only girl—Fox-Trot (MAYFAIR ORCHESTRA) (78) Underneath the Stars—Fox-Trot (" We're all in it ") (MAYFAIR ORCHESTRA) (78)

B. 691 { The Languid Melody (DE GROOT and the PICCADILLY ORCHESTRA) (79) Down home in Tennessee (Donaldson) (DE GROOT and the PICCADILLY ORCH.) (79)

B. 702 { The Kipling Walk—One-Step (MURRAY'S SAVOY QUARTET) (80) Down home in Tennessee (Donaldson) (MURRAY'S SAVOY QUARTET) (80)

B. 703 { If you were the only girl (LUVAUN) (79) Yaaka Hula Hickey Dula (Goetz, Young and Wendling) (LUVAUN, sung with guitar) (79)

B. 725 { If you were the only girl—Fox-Trot (MURRAY'S SAVOY QUARTET) (83) Where did Robinson Crusoe go with Friday on Saturday night ?—One Step or Fox-Trot (Meyers) (MURRAY'S SAVOY QUARTET) (80)

12-inch records 5s. 6d.

C. 674 { " The Bing Boys are Here," Selection I. (ALHAMBRA ORCHESTRA) (78) " The Bing Boys are Here," Selection II. (ALHAMBRA ORCHESTRA) (78)

C. 676 { If you were the only girl in the world and I were the only boy (NAT D. AYER and PEGGY PHILLIPS) (78) The Languid Melody (ALHAMBRA ORCHESTRA) (78)

C. 677 { I stopped, I looked and I listened (NAT D. AYER) (78) The Kipling Walk (NAT D. AYER) (78)

C. 678 { Ragging the Dog and the Shoeblack (ALHAMBRA ORCHESTRA) (78) Heart of mine, come back to me (" The Passing Show of 1915 ") (GWENDOLINE BROGDEN) (78)

C. 703 { " The Bing Boys are Here," Gems from Part I. (THE LIGHT OPERA Co.) (78) " The Bing Boys are Here," Gems from, Part II. (The LIGHT OPERA Co.) (78)

C. 716 { If you were the only girl (DE GROOT and the PICCADILLY ORCHESTRA) (79) Every little while (" Some ") (DE GROOT and the PICCADILLY ORCHESTRA).

C. 729 { " The Bing Boys are Here "—Waltz (METROPOLITAN DANCE BAND) (79) " High Jinks "—One Step or Fox-Trot (arr. by Savino) (METROPOLITAN DANCE BAND) (79)

These records should be played with " His Master's Voice " needles, sold only in boxes bearing our copyright picture, " His Master's Voice," on the lid

REVUE RECORDS

" THE BING BOYS ON BROADWAY "

12-inch records 6s.

03605 College Days (with chorus) (VIOLET LORAINE) **(79)**

04227 Day after day (VIOLET LORAINE and WALTER JEFFERIES) **(79)**

04226 First love, last love, best love (VIOLET LORAINE and WALTER JEFFERIES) **(79)**

03606 Hello! New York (with chorus) (VIOLET LORAINE) **(79)**

03604 Something Oriental (with chorus) (VIOLET LORAINE) **(79)**

10-inch records 3s. 6d.

B. 907 { First love, last love, best love (DE GROOT and the PICCADILLY ORCHESTRA) **(79)** / For your love I am waiting (*Cuvillier*) (" The Lilac Domino") (DE GROOT and the PICCADILLY ORCHESTRA) **(79)**

B. 914 { Hello! New York (SAVOY QUARTET) **)79)** / Widows are wonderful (*Ayer*) (" Yes, Uncle!") (SAVOY QUARTET) **(79)**

12-inch records 5s. 6d.

C. 845 { " The Bing Boys on Broadway "—Selection I. (ALHAMBRA ORCHESTRA) **(79)** / " The Bing Boys on Broadway "—Selection II. (ALHAMBRA ORCHESTRA) **(79)**

C. 846 { The Fact is (DAN AGAR) **(79)** / Shurr-up! (DAN AGAR) **(79)**

" THE BING GIRLS ARE THERE "

12-inch records 6s.

04197 Do you like me? (VIOLET LORAINE and JOSEPH COYNE) **(79)**

03552 Let the great big world keep turning (VIOLET LORAINE and CHORUS) **(79)**

03553 So he followed me (VIOLET LORAINE) **(79)**

04196 That dear old home of mine (VIOLET LORAINE, JOSEPH COYNE and CHORUS) **(79)**

10-inch records 3s. 6d.

B. 807 { I bring my own girls along (NAT D. AYER) **(78)** / When your dancing with me—Fox-Trot (NAT D. AYER) **(78)**

B. 885 { That dear old home of mine (ERIC COURTLAND and WALTER JEFFERIES) **(79)** / Over there (the Great American War Song) (*G. M. Cohan*) (WALTER JEFFERIES) **(79)**

12-inch records 5s. 6d.

C. 779 { Yula Hicki Wicki Yacki Dula (NAT D. AYER and CHORUS) **(79)** / Oh yes! I remember (NAT D. AYER) **(79)**

C. 780 { " The Bing Girls are There," Selection I. (ALHAMBRA THEATRE ORCHESTRA) **(79)** / " The Bing Girls are There," Selection II. (ALHAMBRA THEATRE ORCHESTRA) **(79)**

C. 784 { That dear old home of mine (DE GROOT and the PICCADILLY ORCHESTRA) **(78)** / Let the great big world keep turning (DE GROOT and the PICCADILLY ORCH.) **(78)**

" BRIC-A-BRAC "

10-inch records 3s. 6d.

B. 520 { Glad to see you're back (TEDDIE GERARD) **(78)** / Naughty, naughty, one Gerrard (TEDDIE GERARD) **(78)**

B. 644 { Since Chumley came back from London Town (MURRAY JOHNSON) **(78)** / Flappers (*Talbot*) (" My Lady Frayle ") (ARNOLD RICHARDSON) **(78)**

B. 692 { Since Chumley came back from London Town (MURRAY'S SAVOY QUARTET) **(78)** / You've got to do it (" Pell Mell ") (MURRAY'S SAVOY QUARTET) **(79)**

12-inch records 5s. 6d.

C. 592 { Chalk Farm to Camberwell Green (GERTIE MILLAR) **(78)** / I'm simply crazy over you (GERTIE MILLAR and M. A. SIMON-GIRARD) **(78)**

C. 593 { Toy Town (GERTIE MILLAR) **(78)** / Neville was a devil (GERTIE MILLAR) **(78)**

C. 594 { The Optimist and the Pessimist (NELSON KEYS and ARTHUR PLAYFAIR) **(78)** / Gems from " To-night's the Night," including : " Please don't flirt with me," " The Only Way," " I'd like to bring my Mother," " Boots and Shoes " (*Rubens*) (THE LIGHT OPERA COMPANY) **(78)**

C. 607 { " Bric-à-Brac " Selections (THE PALACE THEATRE ORCHESTRA, conducted by HERMAN FINCK) **(78)**

C. 730 { " Bric-à-Brac " Waltz (METROPOLITAN DANCE BAND) **(78)** / You're here and I'm here—Medley—One step (*Kern*) (METROPOLITAN DANCE BAND) **(79)**

The figures in brackets at end of selections indicate the speed at which the records · · · · should be played · · · ·

REVUE RECORDS

" BUBBLY "

10-inch records 3s. 6d.

B. 848
{
Reckless Reggie (Davy Burnaby) (78)
Raggin' thro' the Rye (Eric Courtland and Walter Jefferies) (78)
}

B. 853
{
Hawaiian Butterfly (Eric Courtland and Walter Jefferies) (79)
Dream Boat (*Ivor Novello*) (Louise Leigh, Eric Courtland and Walter Jefferies) (78)
}

B. 861
{
Hawaiian Butterfly (De Groot and the Piccadilly Orchestra) (78)
Some girl has got to darn his socks (*H. Finck*) (" Round the Map ") (De Groot and the Piccadilly Orchestra) (78)
}

12-inch record 5s. 6d.

C. 800
{
" Bubbly," Sel. I. (Mayfair Orch.) (79)
" Bubbly," Sel. II. (Mayfair Orch.) (79)
}

" CHEEP ! "

12-inch records 6s.

04199   At the Calico Ball (Lee White and Clay Smith) (78)

04200   Don't blame me (Lee White and Clay Smith) (78)

03559   Good-bye Madame Fashion (Lee White) (78)

03558   I shall see you to-night (Lee White) (78)

02732   My Lily of Killarney (Clay Smith) (78)

03560   Somebody's coming to tea (Lee White) (78)

03561   Where did that one go to ? (Lee White) (78)

10-inch records 3s. 6d.

B. 859
{
Where the black-eyed Susans grow (Savoy Quartet) (79)
Hullo ! my dearie (*Stamper*) (" Zig-Zag ") (Savoy Quartet) (79)
}

B. 880
{
Where the black - eyed Susans grow (Courtland and Jefferies) (79)
Hezekiah Johnson's Jubilee (*Weston, Lee and The Two Bobs*) (Courtland and Jefferies) (79)
}

12-inch record 5s. 6d.

C. 794
{
" Cheep !"—Sel. I. (Mayfair Orch.) (78)
" Cheep !"—Sel. II. (Mayfair Orch.) (78)
}

" FOLLOW THE CROWD "

12-inch records 6s.

01133   The Wireless Scene (Talking) (Robert Hale and Tom Walls) (78)

03476   I love a piano (Ethel Levey) (78)
03477   That Hula Hula (Ethel Levey) (78)
03478   Where did Robinson Crusoe go wi h Friday on Saturday night ? (Ethel Levey) (78)

10-inch record 3s. 6d.

B. 725
{
Where did Robinson Crusoe go with Friday on Saturday night ?—One-step, or Fox-Trot (Murray's Savoy Quartet) (80)
If you were the only girl—Fox-Trot (" The Bing Boys ") (Murray's Savoy Quartet) (80)
}

" HANKY-PANKY "

10-inch records 3s. 6d.

B. 812
{
One hour of love with you (De Groot and the Piccadilly Orchestra) (79)
Come back to Ireland and me (De Groot and the Piccadilly Orchestra) (79)
}

B. 820
{
Come back to Ireland and me (Talbot O'Farrell) (78)
One hour of love with you (Harry Talbot and Louise Leigh) (78)
}

12-inch record 5s. 6d.

C. 792
{
" Hanky-Panky," Selection I. (Mayfair Orchestra) (78)
" Hanky-Panky," Selection II. (Mayfair Orchestra) (78)
}

" HOUP-LA ! "

10-inch records 4s.

2–3223   The Fool of the Family (Gertie Millar) (79)
7–33015   L'amour est bon (Madeleine Choiseuille and Chorus) (79)

12-inch records 6s.

03540   Houp-La ! (Gertie Millar) (79)
04191   I've saved all my loving for you (Gertie Millar and Nat D. Ayer) (79)
03542   Oh, how she could Yacki, Hacki, Wicki Wacki Woo (Ida Adams and Chorus) (79)
03541   Pretty Baby (Gertie Millar) (79)
04192   You can't love as I do (Gertie Millar and Nat D. Ayer) (79)
04193   Wonderful girl, wonderful boy, wonderful time (Ida Adams, Gertie Millar and Nat D. Ayer) (79)

These records should be played with " His Master's Voice " needles, sold only in boxes bearing our copyright picture, " His Master's Voice," on the lid

REVUE RECORDS

' HOUP-LA ! ''—*continued*

10-inch records 3s. 6d.

B. 786
Oh, how she could Yacki, Hacki, Wicki Wacki Woo (OLIVE BURTON and ERIC COURTLAND) (78)
Come on to Nashville Tennessee (*Donaldson*) (OLIVE BURTON and ERIC COURTLAND) (78)

B. 830
Oh, how she could Yacki, Hacki, Wicki Wacki Woo (MURRAY'S SAVOY QUARTET) (79)
They're wearin' them higher in Hawaii (79)

12-inch records 5s. 6d.

C. 768
I like the place where the peaches grow (NAT D. AYER and CHORUS) (79)
Any girl means everything to me (NAT D. AYER) (79)

C. 769
"Houp-La ! "—Selection I. (ST. MARTIN'S THEATRE ORCHESTRA) (79)
"Houp-La ! "—Selection II. (ST. MARTIN'S THEATRE ORCHESTRA) (79)

" THE PASSING SHOW ''

10-inch records 3s. 6d.

B 481
Gilbert the Filbert (BASIL HALLAM, the late) (78)
I'll make a man of you (GWENDOLINE BROGDEN) (78)

B. 488
You're here and I'm here (ELSIE JANIS and BASIL HALLAM, the late) (78)
Florrie was a Flapper (ELSIE JANIS) (78)

12-inch records 5s. 6d.

C. 382
"The Passing Show," Selection I. (conducted by HERMAN FINCK) (MAYFAIR ORCHESTRA) (78)
"The Passing Show," Selection II. (conducted by HERMAN FINCK) (MAYFAIR ORCHESTRA) (78)

C. 597
I've got everything I want but you (ELSIE JANIS and BASIL HALLAM) (78)
Piccadilly Grill Waltz (*De Groot*) (DE GROOT and the PICCADILLY ORCHESTRA) (78)

C. 730
You're here and I'm here Medley—One-Step (METROPOLITAN DANCE BAND) (79)
"Bric-à-Brac "—Waltz (*Monckton*, arr. by *Higgs*) (METROPOLITAN DANCE BAND) (79)

" THE PASSING SHOW OF 1915 ''

10-inch record 3s. 6d.

B. 485
Keep Smiling (*Berlin*, arr. by *Finck*) (BASIL HALLAM, the late) (79)
Ballin' the Jack Fox trot (ELSIE JANIS and BASIL HALLAM, the late) (79)

12-inch records 5s. 6d.

C. 405
"The Passing Show of 1915," Selection I. (PALACE THEATRE ORCHESTRA, conducted by H. FINCK) (78)
"The Passing Show of 1915," Selection II. (PALACE THEATRE ORCHESTRA) (78)

C. 565
The Constant Lover (BASIL HALLAM, the late) (79)
Good-bye, girls, I'm through (*Caryll*) (BASIL HALLAM, the late) (78)

C. 566
Prudence (ELSIE JANIS) (79)
Same old Song (ELSIE JANIS and BASIL HALLAM, the late) (79)

C. 678
Heart of mine, come back to me (GWENDOLINE BROGDEN) (78)
Ragging the dog and The Shoeblack (" The Bing Boys are Here ") (ALHAMBRA ORCHESTRA) (78)

" PELL MELL ''

10-inch records 3s. 6d.

B. 692
You've got to do it (MURRAY'S SAVOY QUARTET) (79)
Since Chumley came back from London Town (" Bric-à-Brac ") (MURRAY'S SAVOY QUARTET) (79)

B. 726
You've got to do it (LUVAUN) (79)
Moana Waltz (*Luvaun*) (LUVAUN) (79)

12-inch record 5s. 6d.

C. 696
" Pell Mell," Selection I. (MAYFAIR ORCHESTRA) (78)
" Pell Mell," Selection II. (MAYFAIR ORCHESTRA) (78)

" RAZZLE-DAZZLE ''

10-inch record 3s. 6d.

B. 674
You'll always be the same sweet baby (MAYFAIR ORCHESTRA) (78)
When we gather round the old home fires again (*Stærndale Bennett*) (WALTER JEFFERIES) (78)

12-inch record 5s. 6d.

C. 745
" Razzle-Dazzle," Selection I. (MAYFAIR ORCHESTRA) (78)
" Razzle-Dazzle," Selection II. (MAYFAIR ORCHESTRA) (78)

The figures in brackets at end of selections indicate the speed at which the records · · · · should be played · · · ·

REVUE RECORDS

" ROUND THE MAP "

12-inch records 6s.

03575 Here comes Tootsie (with Chorus) (VIOLET LORAINE) (78)

03576 Some girl has got to darn his socks (VIOLET LORAINE) (78)

03577 Some day I'll make you love me (VIOLET LORAINE) (78)

04207 "D.S.O. and V.A.D." (VIOLET LORAINE, ALFRED LESTER and NELSON KEYS) (78)

10-inch record 3s. 6d.

B. 861 { Some girl has got to darn his socks (DE GROOT and the PICCADILLY ORCH.) (78) / Hawaiian Butterfly (*Baskette and Santley*) (" Bubbly ") (DE GROOT and the PICCADILLY ORCHESTRA) (78)

12-inch records 5s. 6d.

C. 808 { When the right girl comes along (with chorus) (STANLEY LOGAN) (78) / "Round the Map" Fox Trot (MAYFAIR ORCHESTRA) (78)

C. 809 { "Round the Map," Selection I. (HERMAN FINCK and ORCHESTRA) (79) / "Round the Map," Selection II. (HERMAN FINCK and ORCHESTRA) (79)

C. 811 { A Conscientious Objector (ALFRED LESTER) (78) / Hurrah for the rolling sea (ALFRED LESTER) (78)

C. 851 { Some day I'll make you love me (DE GROOT and the PICCADILLY ORCHESTRA) (79) / The dear old days (with chorus) (*Ayer*) (" Yes, Uncle !") (DAVY BURNABY) (79)

" SAMPLES "

10-inch records 3s. 6d.

B. 631 { A Broken Doll (DE GROOT and the PICCADILLY ORCHESTRA) (78) / Tulip Song (" Joyland ") (*Darewski*) (DE GROOT and the PICCADILLY ORCHESTRA) (78)

B. 647 { My Honolulu Girl (DE GROOT and the PICCADILLY ORCHESTRA) (78) / A Perfect Day (*Jacobs-Bond*) (DE GROOT and the PICCADILLY ORCHESTRA) (78)

B. 701 { A Broken Doll (LUVAUN) (78) / Yaaka Hula Hickey Dula (*Goetz, Young and Wendling*) (79) (LENSEN and the TROCADERO ORCHESTRA) (78)

B. 762 { The Roses have made me remember (ERIC COURTLAND) (79) / A little Dutch Heaven for two (*Mills, Scott and Godfrey*) (COURTLAND) (79)

12-inch records 5s. 6d.

C. 672 { A Broken Doll (Miss AIMEE MAXWELL) (78) / When you come home (*Squire*) (AIMEE MAXWELL) (78)

C. 726 { A Broken Doll Fox Trot (METROPOLITAN DANCE BAND) (79) / "Half-Past Eight " Waltz (*Rubens*, arr. by H. M. Higgs) (METROPOLITAN DANCE BAND) (79)

" SOME "

10-inch records 3s. 6d.

B. 689 { Every little while (ERIC COURTLAND and CHORUS) (78) / We're all crazy (WALTER JEFFERIES) (78)

B 731 { They called it Dixieland (WALTON and CARTER) (80) / Put me to sleep with an old-fashioned melody (*Jentes*) (WALTON and CARTER) (80)

12-inch records 5s. 6d.

C. 704 { Jingle Johnnie (WALTER JEFFERIES and CHORUS) (78) / Have you seen the ducks go by ? (ERIC COURTLAND, WALTER JEFFERIES and CHORUS) (78)

C. 705 { "Some," Selection I. (MAYFAIR ORCHESTRA) (78) / "Some," Selection II. (MAYFAIR ORCHESTRA) (78)

C. 716 { Every little while (DE GROOT and the PICCADILLY ORCHESTRA) (79) / If you were the only girl (" The Bing Boys are Here ") (DE GROOT and the PICCADILLY ORCHESTRA) (79)

C. 746 { Gems from " Some," Part I. (THE LIGHT OPERA COMPANY) (78) / Gems from " Some," Part II. (THE LIGHT OPERA COMPANY) (78)

" TAILS UP ! "

10-inch records 3s. 6d.

B. 965 { Gnee-ah ! (DAVY BURNABY) (79) / Any little thing (DAVY BURNABY and LOUISE LEIGH) (79)

B. 966 { The twinkle in her eye (with Chorus) (LOUISE LEIGH) (79) / The Apache Rag (with Chorus) (LOUISE LEIGH) (79)

"TAILS UP!"—continued

10-inch records 3s. 6d.

B. 967 { Let's all go raving mad (LOUISE LEIGH, COURTLAND and JEFFERIES) (79)
Peter Pan (with Chorus) (LOUISE LEIGH) (79)

B. 982 { The Apache Rag (DE GROOT and the PICCADILLY ORCHESTRA) (79)
The tickle toe (*Hirsch*) ("Going Up") (DE GROOT and the PICCADILLY ORCHESTRA) (79)

12-inch record 5s. 6d.

C. 865 { "Tails Up!" Selection I (MAYFAIR ORCHESTRA) (79)
"Tails Up!" Selection II. (MAYFAIR ORCHESTRA) (79)

"THREE CHEERS"

12-inch records 6s.

04194 Hold me in your loving arms (ETHEL LEVEY and WALTER WILLIAMS) (79)
02685 I love to be a sailor (HARRY LAUDER) (79)
02572 Jean (HARRY LAUDER) (79)
03545 Just my love (BLANCHE TOMLIN) (79)
03546 Morning in the Highlands (BLANCHE TOMLIN and CHORUS) (79)
02688 The lads who fought and won (HARRY LAUDER) (79)
03544 The Ragtime Bagpipe Band (ETHEL LEVEY and CHORUS) (79)

10-inch records 3s. 6d.

B. 802 { There's a little bit of bad in every good little girl (OLIVE BURTON and ERIC COURTLAND) (78)
Arizona (*Melville Gideon*) (OLIVE BURTON and ERIC COURTLAND) (78)

B. 837 { There's a little bit of bad in every good little girl (DE GROOT and the PICCADILLY ORCHESTRA) (79)
Those bewitching eyes (*Mustal*) (BIJOU CINEMA ORCHESTRA) (79)

12-inch records 5s. 6d.

C. 770 { Don't all speak at once, little girls (WALTER WILLIAMS and CHORUS) (79)
Overture—"Three Cheers" (SHAFTESBURY THEATRE ORCHESTRA) (79)

C. 771 { "Three Cheers," Selection I. (MAYFAIR ORCHESTRA) (79)
"Three Cheers," Selection II. (MAYFAIR ORCHESTRA) (79)

C. 774 { Just my love (DE GROOT and the PICCADILLY ORCHESTRA) (78)
Désir Valse (*Stone*) (JEAN LENSEN, conductor, and the TROCADERO ORCHESTRA) (78)

"VANITY FAIR"

10-inch record 4s.

2·3218 The Kirchner Girl (TEDDIE GERARD) (79)

12-inch records 6s.

03539 A little love, a little kiss (REGINE FLORY) (79)
04190 Some sort of somebody (REGINE FLORY and NELSON KEYS) (79)

10-inch record 3s. 6d.

B. 788 { Marche blanche (PALACE THEATRE ORCHESTRA) (79)
Some sort of somebody (PALACE THEATRE ORCHESTRA, cornet solo played by PETER WILSON) (79)

12-inch records 5s. 6d.

C. 760 { Sunlight and Shadow—Waltz Song (GWENDOLINE BROGDEN) (79)
The Rainbow Song (GWENDOLINE BROGDEN and Chorus) (79)

C. 766 { The Romance of the Dragon Fly, No. 1 (PALACE THEATRE ORCHESTRA) (79)
The Romance of the Dragon Fly, No. 2 (PALACE THEATRE ORCHESTRA) (79)

C. 767 { "Vanity Fair"—Selection I. (PALACE THEATRE ORCHESTRA) (79)
"Vanity Fair"—Selection II. (PALACE THEATRE ORCHESTRA) (79)

C. 778 { Some sort of somebody (DE GROOT and the PICCADILLY ORCHESTRA) (79)
Any time's kissing time (*Norton*) ("Chu Chin Chow") (DE GROOT and the PICCADILLY ORCHESTRA) (79)

C. 791 { "Vanity Fair," Gems from, Part I. (LIGHT OPERA COMPANY) (79)
"Vanity Fair," Gems from, Part II. (LIGHT OPERA COMPANY) (79)

"WATCH YOUR STEP"

10-inch records 3s. 6d.

B. 290 { The Syncopated Walk (MAYFAIR ORCHESTRA) (78)
The Minstrel Parade (MAYFAIR ORCHESTRA) (78)

B. 552 { That Simple Melody (DE GROOT and the PICCADILLY ORCHESTRA) (78)
Settle down in a one-horse town (DE GROOT and the PICCADILLY ORCHESTRA) (78)

**The figures in brackets at end of selections
indicate the speed at which the records
. . . . should be played . . . .**

REVUE RECORDS

"WATCH YOUR STEP "—*continued*

12-inch records 5s. 6d.

C. 611
- The Simple Melody (ETHEL LEVEY and BLANCHE TOMLIN) (78)
- The Minstrel Parade (ETHEL LEVEY) (drums played by JOSEPH COYNE) (78)

C. 671
- My Bird of Paradise, Medley Fox-Trot (METROPOLITAN DANCE BAND) (78)
- I'm on my way to Dublin Bay, Medley One-Step (METROPOLITAN DANCE BAND) (78)

" ZIG-ZAG "

10-inch records 3s. 6d.

B. 803
- Louana Lou (LOUISE LEIGH and CHORUS) (78)
- In Grandma's days they never did the Fox-Trot (LOUISE LEIGH and CHORUS) (78)

B. 859
- Hullo! my dearie (SAVOY QUARTET) (79)
- Where the black-eyed Susans grow (Whiting) ("Cheep!") (SAVOY QUARTET) (79)

B. 870
- Hullo! my dearie (BLANCHE DARE and ERIC COURTLAND) (78)
- Down Texas Way (Godfrey, Mills and Scott) (ERIC COURTLAND and WALTER JEFFERIES) (78)

B. 899
- Hullo! my deárie (DE GROOT and the PICCADILLY ORCHESTRA) (79)
- Smoke Clouds (Darewski) ("Topsy Turvy") (DE GROOT and the PICCADILLY ORCHESTRA) (79)

12-inch records 5s. 6d.

C. 782
- "Zig-Zag," Selection I. (MAYFAIR ORCHESTRA) (79)
- "Zig-Zag," Selection II. (MAYFAIR ORCHESTRA) (79)

C. 793
- When the autumn leaves are falling (LOUISE LEIGH and FLORENCE BERENS, whistler) (78)
- ERNEST PIKE
- Roses of Picardy (Haydn Wood) (78)

UNIQUE BIRD RECORDS

10-inch records 3s. 6d.

B. 390
- Actual Bird Record made by a Captive Nightingale (No. I.) (78)
- Actual Bird Record made by a Captive Nightingale (No. II.) (78)

B. 392
- Actual Bird Record made by a Captive Thrush (78)
- Actual Bird Record made by a Captive Blackbird (80)

B. 467
- Actual Bird Record made by a Captive Nightingale (80). FLORENTINE QUARTET
- Narcissus from " Water Scenes " (Ethelbert Nevin) (78)

回 回 回

YODLE

BARTON, WARD, and FRANK CARROLL

10-inch record 3s. 6d.

B. 796
- Hawaiian Love Song (Barton) (78)
- Sleep, baby, sleep (New version by Barton) (78)

GERBER, PAUL

10-inch record 3s. 6d.

B. 474
- Kukulied mit Jodler (75)
- Min Vater isch e Appenzeller (77)

WATSON, G. P.

10-inch record 3s. 6d.

B. 475
- Life in the Alps (German Yodling) (79)
- Herr and Frau GERBER Jodlerpartien (76)

回 回 回 回 回

105

BAND RECORDS

BAND SELECTIONS

THE COLDSTREAM GUARDS

CONDUCTED BY

Major J. MACKENZIE-ROGAN, M.V.O.
Mus. Doc., Hon. R.A.M.

10-inch records 3s. 6d.

B. 102 { " La Czarine "—Mazurka (*Ganne*) (**80**)
La Mattchiche (*Borel Clerc*) (**78**)

B. 103 { Minuet, No. 1 (*Paderewski*) (**80**)
Spring Song (*Mendelssohn*) (**77**)

B. 104 { Through the Valley March (*Walker*) (**81**)
New Colonial March (*Hall*) (**82**)

B. 105 { God save the King (*Bull*) (**80**)
God bless the Prince of Wales (*Richards*) (**81**)

B. 106 { Rule Britannia (*Arne*) (**81**)
La Marseillaise (*Rouget de L'Isle*) (**78**)

B. 107 { O Sole Mio (*Di Capua*) (**80**)
The Rosary (*Nevin*) (Cornet Solo by Sergt. Hawkins) (**79**)

B. 108 { Bells of St. Malo (*Rimmer*) (**80**)
Christchurch Bells (**78**)

B. 109 { Coon Band Contest (*Pryor*) (**82**)
Ginger Two-Step (*Würm*) (**81**)

B. 110 { Hiawatha (*Neil Moret*) (**75**)
Liberty Bell March (*Sousa*) (**76**)

B. 111 { Stars and Stripes March (*Sousa*) (**81**)
Turkish Patrol (*Michaelis*) (**78**)

B. 112 { March Past of the Lancashire Brigade (**78**)
Regimental Marches of the Brigade of Guards (**77**)

B. 113 { " Poet and Peasant " Overture (*Suppé*) (**80**)
" William Tell," Storm (*Rossini*) (**78**)

B. 114 { Softly awakes my heart (" Samson and Delilah "—*Saint Saëns*) (Cornet Solo by Sergt. Hawkins) (**78**)
War March of the Priests (*Mendelssohn*) (**76**)

B. 115 { " Peer Gynt," Morning (*Grieg*) (**80**)
" Peer Gynt," Death of Ase (*Grieg*) (**78**)

B. 116 { Take a Pair of Sparkling Eyes (*Sullivan*) (Cornet Solo by Sergt. Hawkins) (**76**)
" Mikado," Selection III. (*Sullivan*) (**76**)

B. 117 { The Lost Chord (*Sullivan*) (Cornet Solo by Sergt. Hawkins) (**78**)
The Distant Shore (*Sullivan*) (Cornet Solo by Sergt. Hawkins) (**76**)

B. 119 { " Mikado," Selection I. (*Sullivan*) (**76**)
" Mikado," Selection II. (*Sullivan*) (**76**)

B. 120 { " Henry VIII.," Shepherds' Dance (*German*) (**78**)
" Henry VIII.," Morris and Torch Dance (*German*) (**77**)

B. 160 { " Merrie England," The English Rose (*German*) (**81**)
I know a lovely garden (*d'Hardelot*) (**81**)

B. 165 { Semper Fidelis March (*Sousa*) (**80**)
" Faust," " La Kermesse " (*Gounod*) (**80**)

B. 173 { Hungarian Dance (*Brahms*) (**80**)
Chanson de mon cœur (*Joyce*) (**80**)

B. 199 { Love in Arcady—Serenade (*Haydn Wood*) (**79**)
Hearts-ease Intermezzo (*Macbeth*) (**79**)

B. 200 { Swing Away March (*Cheeseman*) (**79**)
Our Director March (*Bigelow*) (**79**)

B. 206 { Distant Greeting March (arr. by *C. Godfrey*) (**78**)
Rose-Mousse Entr'acte (*Bosc*) (**78**)

B. 209 { Sleep on, beloved (*Adela Wodehouse*) (**78**)
(a) Abide with me (*Monk*) ; (b) All people that on earth (*Old Hundredth*) (**78**)

B. 218 { The Linnet (Piccolo Polka) (*Brockett*) (Piccolo Solo by Sergt. W. Valentine) (**78**)
Dance Intermezzo—" Sunbeams " (*Lane*) (**78**)

B. 220 { Little grey home in the west (*Löhr*) (Cornet Solo by Corpl. G. Moran) (**78**)
Süsse Küsse, Op. 10 (*Vollstedt*) (**78**)

B. 222 { The King's Command March (*Barnes*) (**79**)
Trot of the Cavalry (*Rubinstein*, arr. by *H. Saro*) (**79**)

B. 223 { Somewhere a voice is calling (*Tate*) (Cornet Solo by Corpl. G. Moran) (**78**)
My Little Jap Two-step (*B. Phelps*) (**80**)

B. 226 { " A Lover in Damascus " Suite—Beloved in your Absence—How many a lonely caravan (*Woodforde-Finden*, arr. by *Percy Fletcher*) (**78**)
" A Lover in Damascus " Suite—Allah be with us (*Woodforde-Finden*, arr. by *Percy Fletcher*) (**78**)

B. 227 { " A Lover in Damascus " Suite—Where the Albana flows (*Woodforde-Finden*, arr. by *Percy Fletcher*) (**78**)
" A Lover in Damascus " Suite—Far across the Desert (*Woodforde-Finden*, arr. by *Percy Fletcher*) (**78**)

The figures in brackets at end of selections
indicate the speed at which the records
. . . . should be played . . . .

106

BAND RECORDS

THE COLDSTREAM GUARDS—*continued*

10-inch records 3s. 6d.

B. 229 { " On Jhelum River "—Introduction and Boat Song (*Woodforde-Finden*, arr. by *Percy Fletcher*) **(78)** / " On Jhelum River "—Kingfisher Blue (*Woodforde-Finden*, arr. \ by *Percy Fletcher*) **(78)**

B. 234 { " On Jhelum River "—Will the red sun never set (*Woodforde-Finden*, arr. by *Percy Fletcher*) **(78)** / " On Jhelum River "—The Song of the Bride (*Woodforde-Finden*, arr. by *Percy Fletcher*) **(78)**

B. 236 { Nelson's Victory March (*Darewski*) **(78)** / Austria March (*Nowotny*) **(78)**

B. 247 { The Bullfighters—Quick March (*Kottaun*, arr. by *Ord Hume*) **(78)** / The Vedette—Quick March (*Alford*) **(78)**

B. 254 { " On Jhelum River "—Only a Rose (*Woodforde-Finden*, arr. by *Percy Fletcher*) **(78)** / " On Jhelum River "—Ashoo at her Lattice (*A. Woodforde-Finden*, arr. by *Percy Fletcher*) **(79)**

B. 255 { Colonel Bogey—March (*Clark*) **(80)** / Youth and Vigour—March (*Lautenschläger*) **(80)**

B. 256 { Marche Namur (*Richards*) **(78)** / La Ritirata Italiana (*Drescher*) **(78)**

B. 264 { National Emblem—March (*Bagley*) **(79)** / Imperial Echoes—Quick March (*Saffroni*, arr. by *Hume*) **(80)**

B. 268 { Pro Patria—March (*Clark*) **(80)** / Euterpe—March (*Clark*) **(80)**

B. 271 { A Humoreske on the Soldier's Song, " It's a long, long way to Tipperary," Part I. (*Shipley Douglas*) **(79)** / Ditto, Part II. (arr. by *Shipley Douglas*) **(79)**

B. 275 { Sambre et Meuse—Patriotic March (*Rauski*) **(79)** / Les Volontaires (*Metra*) **(79)**

B. 277 { A Lover in Damascus Suite, No. 5— " If in the Great Bazaars " (*Woodforde-Finden*, arr. by *Fletcher*) **(79)** / Holyrood—Quick March (*Alford*) **(79)**

B. 282 { Fall In ! March (*Cowen*, arr. by *C. Godfrey, Jr.*) **(80)** / King's Champion March (*Belcher*) **(80)**

B. 356 { The Maple Leaf for ever (*Muir*) **(78)** / Bugler GODARD / Trumpet and Bugle Calls **(78)**

B. 518 { Regimental Marches—The King's, Norfolk Regiment, Lincolnshire Regiment **(80)** / Regimental Marches—The Buffs, King's Own, Royal Warwickshire Regiment **(80)**

B. 580 { The Lamb's March (*Sousa*) **(78)** / The Pathfinder of Panama (*Sousa*) **(78)**

B. 782 { On the Plantation (Characteristic Piece) (*Puerner*) **(78)** / The Irish Patrol (*Puerner*) **(78)**

B. 809 { American National Airs (*a*) Yankee Doodle (*b*) Dixie (*c*) Hail Columbia **(78)** / American National Airs (*a*) Red, White and Blue (*b*) The Star-Spangled Banner **(78)**

B. 826 { When the great day comes—March (*I. Novello*) **(79)** / The Great Little Army—March (*K. Alford*) **(79)**

B. 835 { Sambre et Meuse—March (*Rauski*) **(79)** / Old Comrades—March (The favourite march of the changing of the Guards) (*Teike*) **(79)**

B. 849 { A Trieste March (*Carosio*) **(79)** / THE OPAL MILITARY BAND / Arabia March (*Buck*, arr. by *Alford*) **(79)**

B. 871 { A Perfect Day (*Carrie Jacobs-Bond*) (Cornet Solo by Corpl. G. Morgan) **(78)** / Until (*Sanderson*) (Cornet Solo by Corpl. G. MORGAN) **(78)**

B. 891 { Boston Tea Party—March (*Pryor*) **(79)** / Hands Across the Sea—March (*Sousa*) **(79)**

B. 915 { Manhattan Beach—March (*Sousa*) **(79)** / Uncle Sammy—March and Two-Step (*Holzmann*) **(79)**

B. 981 { Marche russe (*Ganne*) **(79)** / OPAL MILITARY BAND / Lorraine (March Majestic) (*Augarde*) **(79)**

THE REGIMENTAL MARCHES OF THE BRITISH ARMY

10-inch records 3s. 6d.

CAVALRY

B. 583 { Royal Horse and Field Artillery **(78)** / 1st and 2nd Life Guards / Royal Horse Guards (The Blues) **(78)**

B. 584 { 1st and 2nd Dragoon Guards **(78)** / 3rd Dragoon Guards / 4th Dragoon Guards **(78)**

B. 585 { 5th and 6th Dragoon Guards **(78)** / 7th Dragoon Guards and 1st Dragoons **(78)**

B. 586 { 2nd Dragoons and 7th Hussars, 3rd Hussars **(78)** / 4th Hussars, 5th Royal Irish Lancers **(78)**

THE COLDSTREAM GUARDS—*continued*

10-inch records 3s. 6d.

B. 587 { 6th Dragoons, 8th Hussars **(78)** / 9th Lancers, 10th Hussars **(78)**

B. 588 { 11th Hussars, 12th and 21st Lancers and 13th Hussars **(78)** / 14th and 15th Hussars **(78)**

B. 589 { 16th and 17th Lancers **(78)** / 18th, 19th and 20th Hussars **(78)**

B. 590 { Royal Artillery, Engineers, Grenadiers and all Fusilier Regiments / Scots Guards, Irish Guards, Welsh Guards **(78)** / Coldstream Guards **(78)**

INFANTRY

B. 591 { The Queen's (Royal West Surrey Regiment), "Braganza" / The East Surrey Regiment, "A Southerly Wind and a Cloudy Sky" **(78)** / The Hampshire Regiment, "The Hampshire" / The Dorsetshire Regiment, "The Dorsetshire" / The Duke of Edinburgh's (Wiltshire Regiment), "The Wiltshire" **(78)**

B. 592 { The Buffs (East Kent Regiment), "The Buffs" / The Queen's Own (Royal West Kent Regiment), "A Hundred Pipers" / The Essex Regiment, "The Essex" **(78)** / The Devonshire Regiment, "We've lived and we've loved together" / Prince Albert's (Somersetshire Light Infantry), "Prince Albert" / The Duke of Cornwall's Light Infantry, "One and All" **(78)**

B. 593 { The Border Regiment, "John Peel" / The Royal Sussex Regiment, "The Royal Sussex" / The King's Royal Rifle Corps, "Lutzow's Wild Hunt" **(78)** / The Suffolk Regiment, "Speed the Plough" / Princess Charlotte of Wales (Berkshire Regiment), "Dashing White Sergeant" **(78)**

B. 594 { The Sherwood Foresters (Derbyshire Regiment), "Young May Moon" / The Northamptonshire Regiment, "The Northamptonshire" **(78)** / The Cheshire Regiment, "Wha wadna' fecht for Charlie" / The South Wales Borderers, "Men of Harlech" / The Welsh Regiment "Ap shenkin" **(78)**

B. 595 { The Gloucestershire Regiment, "Kynegad Slashers" / The Worcestershire Regiment, "The Windsor"' **(78)** / The Royal Warwickshire Regiment "Warwickshire Lads" / The Norfolk Regiment, "Rule Britannia" / The Lincolnshire Regiment, "The Lincolnshire Poacher" **(78)**

B. 596 { The Rifle Brigade (The Prince Consort's Own), "I'm ninety-five" / Royal Marine Light Infantry and Royal Marine Artillery, "A Life on the Ocean Wave" / R.A.M.C., "Her bright smile haunts me still" **(79)** / (The Prince of Wales) North Staffordshire Regiment / The South Staffordshire Regiment, "Come lasses and lads" / The Durham Light Infantry, "The Light Barque" **(78)**

B. 597 { The King's (Liverpool Regiment), "Here's to the maiden of bashful fifteen" / 1st East Lancashire Regiment, "The Attack" / 2nd East Lancashire Regiment, "Lancashire Lad" **(78)** / The South Lancashire Regiment / The Loyal North Lancashire Regiment, "The Red Rose" / The Manchester Regiment, "The Manchester" **(78)**

B. 598 { The King's Own (Royal Lancaster Regiment), "Corn rigs are bonnie" / The York & Lancaster Regiment, "The York & Lancaster" / 2nd Yorkshire & Lancaster Regiment (84th), "The Jockey of York" **(78)** / The Prince of Wales's Own (West Yorkshire Regiment), "Ça ira" / East Yorkshire Regiment, "Yorkshire Lass" / The Princess of Wales's Own (Yorkshire Regiment), "Bonnie English Rose" / The Duke of Wellington's (West Riding Regiment), "The Wellesley" / The King's Own (Yorkshire Light Infantry), "Jock of York" **(78)**

B. 599 { Leicestershire Regiment, "Romaika" / The Oxfordshire Light Infantry, "Nachtlager in Grenada" / The 2nd Oxfordshire Light Infantry, "The Lower Castle Yard" **(78)** / 1st and 3rd Batt. Duke of Cambridge's Own (Middlesex Regiment) / 2nd and 4th Batt. Duke of Cambridge's Own (Middlesex Regiment) **(78)**

The figures in brackets at end of selections
indicate the speed at which the records
. . . . should be played . . . .

BAND RECORDS

THE COLDSTREAM GUARDS—*continued*

INFANTRY—*continued*

10-inch records 3s. 6d.

B. 600
- The Royal Irish Regiment, "Garry Owen"
- The Royal Irish Rifles, "Off, off, said the stranger"
- The Connaught Rangers, "St. Patrick's Day"
- The Prince of Wales Leinster Regiment (Royal Canadians), "The Royal Canadians" **(78)**
- The Bedfordshire Regiment, "Mandolinata"
- The King's (Shropshire Light Infantry), "Old Towler"
- Army Service Corps, "Wait for the wagon" **(78)**

B. 601
- The King's Own Scottish Borderers, "Blue Bonnets over the Border"
- The Cameronians (Scottish Rifles), "Within a mile of Edinboro' Town"
- The Highland Light Infantry, "Whistle o'er the lave o't"
- Highland Regiments, "Highland Laddie" **(78)**
- God save the King **(78)**

BUGLE CALLS OF THE BRITISH ARMY

10-inch records 3s. 6d.

B. 602
- The Charge, The Alarm, Officers' Call, Troops, Battery or Company Sergeant-Majors'. Colour-Sergeants', Quartermaster-Sergeant of the A.S.C. or R.A.M.C., Band Call, Drummers or Buglers, Orderly Sergeant, Orderly Corporal, Signallers, Pioneers, Cyclists, Orders, Orderly Room, Post Call, Warning for Parade **(78)**
- Quarter Calls before Parade, Fall In, Dismiss or No Parade, Recruits Parade or Ride; Watering Order—Mounted Infantry; Stables—Mounted Infantry; Feed—Mounted Infantry; Hay up or litter down, Parade for Guard, Parade for Picket, Fatigue, Defaulters, Sick, School, Rations, Forage, Alarm for troops to turn out under arms, Fire, Alarms **(78)**

B. 603
- Officers' Dress for Dinner, Officers' Dinner, Sergeants' Dinner. Men's Meal, 1st Call; Men's Meal, 2nd Call; Salute for Guard, Rouse, Reveillé **(78)**
- Retreat. Tattoo, First Post. Tattoo, Last Post. Lights Out. Continue, Stand Fast, Double **(78)**

12-inch records 5s. 6d.

C. 101
- "Lucrezia Borgia," Selection (*Donizetti*) **(80)**
- "Der Freischütz" Overture (*Weber*) **(81)**

C. 102
- "The Gondoliers," Selection I. (*Sullivan*) **(81)**
- "The Gondoliers," Selection II. (*Sullivan*) **(81)**

C. 104
- Victory and Thanksgiving (*Partridge*) **(81)**
- Valse Royale (*Partridge*) **(80)**

C. 105
- "Haddon Hall," Selection (*Sullivan*) **(81)**
- "The Coon's Patrol" (*Lotter*) **(81)**

C. 106
- "Messiah," All we like sheep (*Handel*) **(82)**
- "Messiah," O Thou that tellest (*Handel*) **(82)**

C. 107
- Triumphal March of Boyards (*Halvorsen*) **(81)**
- El Abanico (*Javaloyes*) **(81)**

C. 108
- "Merry Wives of Windsor" Overture (*Nicolai*) **(81)**
- "Fingal's Cave" Overture (*Mendelssohn*) **(80)**

C. 109
- "Trial by Jury," Selection (*Sullivan*) **(81)**
- "The Sorcerer," Selection (*Sullivan*) **(81)**

C. 110
- Coronation Bells (*Partridge*) **(80)**
- Folie Bergère (*Fletcher*) **(81)**

C. 111
- Reminiscences of Scotland, Part I. (arr. by *Fred Godfrey*) **(80)**
- Reminiscences of Scotland, Part II. **(80)**

C. 112
- Land of Hope and Glory (*Elgar*), Cornet Solo by Sergt. HAWKINS **(81)**
- Musica Proibita (*Gastaldon*) **(81)**

C. 113
- "L'Italiana in Algeri" Overture (*Rossini*) **(81)**
- Capricho Español ("Moriama"—*Espinosa*) **(81)**

C. 114
- "Pique Dame" Overture (*Suppé*) **(80)**
- Morning, Noon and Night Overture (*Suppé*) **(80)**

C. 115
- "Oberon" Overture (*Weber*) **(80)**
- Valse Triste (*Sibelius*) **(81)**

C. 116
- Norwegian Dance (*Greig*) **(80)**
- Marche Hongroise (*Berlioz*) **(81)**

C. 117
- Fanfare and March of the Silver Trumpets (*Viviani*) **(81)**
- Marche Russe ("Ballet Russe"—*Luigini*) **(81)**

C. 118
- The Dead March in "Saul" (*Handel*) **(80)**
- Chopin's Funeral March **(80)**

C. 119
- Fifinette Intermezzo (*Fletcher*) **(80)**
- Nell Gwyn Dances, Nos. II. and III. (*German*) **(81)**

C. 120
- Egmont Overture (*Beethoven*) **(81)**
- "Barber of Seville" Overture (*Rossini*) **(81)**

These records should be played with "His Master's Voice" needles, sold only in boxes bearing our copyright picture, "His Master's Voice," on the lid

BAND RECORDS

THE COLDSTREAM GUARDS—*continued*

12-inch records 5s. 6d.—*continued*

C. 121 { Students' Songs, No. I. (arr. by *Shipley Douglas*) **(81)**
Students' Songs, No. II. (arr. by *Shipley Douglas*) **(81)**

C. 122 { Students' Songs, No. III. (arr. by *Shipley Douglas*) **(81)**
Druid's Prayer Waltz (*Dawson*) **(81)**

C. 123 { "Yeomen of the Guard," Selection I. (*Sullivan*) **(81)**
"Yeomen of the Guard," Selection II. (*Sullivan*) **(81)**

C. 124 { "The Arcadians," Selection I. (*Monckton and Talbot*) **(80)**
"The Arcadians," Selection II. (*Monckton and Talbot*) **(80)**

C. 125 { Ballet Égyptien, Nos. I and II. (*Luigini*) **(81)**
Ballet Égyptien, No. III. (*Luigini*) **(81)**

C. 126 { Ballet Égyptien, No. IV. (*Luigini*) **(80)**
"Geneviève de Brabant," Selection (*Offenbach*) **(81)**

C. 127 { "Our Miss Gibbs," Selection I. (*Monckton and Caryll*) **(80)**
"Our Miss Gibbs," Selection II. (*Monckton and Caryll*) **(80)**

C. 128 { Evening Hymn and Last Post (*Mackenzie Rogan*) **(82)**
The Moon hath raised (*Benedict*) (Cornet Duet by Musicians HAWKINS and WEBB) **(81)**

C. 129 { "Faust," Selection (*Gounod*) **(81)**
"Les Cloches de Corneville," Selection (*Planquette*) **(80)**

C. 130 { Selection from Overture "1812" (*Tchaikovsky*) **(80)**
"Zampa" Overture (*Hérold*) **(81)**

C. 131 { "Patience," Selection (*Sullivan*) **(31)**
Graceful Dance from "Henry VIII." (*Sullivan*) **(82)**

C. 132 { "Tancredi" Overture (*Rossini*) **(79)**
"Fra Diavolo" Overture (*Auber*) **(81)**

C. 133 { Hungarian Rhapsody (*Liszt*) **(78)**
Symphonie Pathétique (*Tchaikovsky*) **(78)**

C. 134 { "Pirates of Penzance," Selection (*Sullivan*) **(81)**
"Iolanthe," Selection (*Sullivan*) **(77)**

C. 135 { "Peer Gynt," Anitra's Dance and In the Hall of the Mountain King (*Grieg*) **(80)**
Wedding March (*Mendelssohn*) **(76)**

C. 136 { "The Girls of Gottenburg," Selection (*Monckton and Caryll*) **(79)**
"Miss Hook of Holland," Selection **(77)**

C. 137 { "Tannhäuser," Grand March (*Wagner*)**(78)**
Overture "1812" (*Tchaikovsky*)(**78**)

C. 191 { "Quaker Girl," Sel. I (*Monckton*) **(81)**
"Quaker Girl," Sel. II. (*Monckton*) **(81)**

C. 192 { Policeman's Holiday One-step (*Ewing*) **(81)**
Wee Macgregor Highland Patrol (*Amers*) **(80)**

C. 193 { "Le Domino Noir" Overture (*Auber*) **(80)**
Bronze Horse Overture (*Auber*) **(81)**

C. 194 { Amina—Egyptian Serenade (*Lincke*) **(81)**
"Si j'étais Roi," Overture (*Adam*) **(81)**

C. 198 { "Sunshine Girl," Selection I. (*Rubens*) **(81)**
"Sunshine Girl," Sel. II. (*Rubens*) **(81)**

C. 199 { "The Geisha," Sel I. (*Sidney Jones*) **(81)**
"The Geisha" Sel. II. (*Sidney Jones*) **(81)**

C. 200 { Come sing to me (*Thompson*, arr. by *Frank Winterbottom*) (Cornet Solo by Corporal W. BRIGHT) **(81)**
Gipsy Love Waltz (*Lehar*) **(81)**

C. 203 { Mirella Overture (*Gounod*) **(81)**
Marco Spada Overture (*Auber*) **(81)**

C. 206 { "La Poupée," Selection I. (*Audran*) **(81)**
"La Poupée," Selection II. (*Audran*) **(80)**

C. 207 { Marche Militaire (*Schubert*) **(81)**
"La Reine de Saba," Grand March (*Gounod*) **(81)**

C. 211 { "Messiah," Lift up your Heads (*Handel*) **(80)**
"Messiah," And the Glory of the Lord (*Handel*) **(81)**

C. 216 { "Lurline" Overture (*Wallace*) **(81)**
Crown Diamonds Overture (*Auber*) **(81)**

C. 217 { "Gipsy Love," Selection I. (*Lehar*) **(81)**
"Gipsy Love," Selection II. (*Lehar*) **(81)**

C. 234 { "Polonia" Overture (*Wagner*) **(80)**
Preciosa Overture (*Weber*) **(81)**

C. 235 { "Utopia, Limited," Selection (*Sullivan*) **(81)**
"La Mascotte" Selection (*Audran*) **(81)**

C. 237 { La Sirène Overture (*Auber*) **(80)**
"Semiramide" Overture (*Rossini*) **(81)**

C. 238 { "Casse-Noisette (Nutcracker) Suite"—Miniature Overture (*Tchaikovsky*) **(80)**
"Casse-Noisette (Nutcracker) Suite"—Dance of the Sugar-plum Fairy (*Tchaikovsky*) **(80)**

C. 239 { "Casse-Noisette (Nutcracker) Suite"—March and Russian Dance (Trépak) (*Tchaikovsky*) **(80)**
"Casse-Noisette (Nutcracker) Suite"—Arabian Dance (*Tchaikovsky*) **(80)**

C. 240 { "Casse-Noisette (Nutcracker) Suite—" Reed Pipe Dance and Chinese Dance (*Tchaikovsky*) **(80)**
"Casse-Noisette (Nutcracker) Suite"—Flower Waltz (*Tchaikovsky*) **(80)**

C. 241 { "Falka," Selection I. (*Chaissaigne*) **(81)**
"Falka," Selection II. (*Chaissaigne*) **(81)**

**The figures in brackets at end of selections
indicate the speed at which the records
. . . . should be played . . . .**

BAND RECORDS

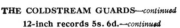

THE COLDSTREAM GUARDS—_continued_

12-inch records 5s. 6d.—_continued_

C. 242
- " Grand Duchess of Gerolstein " Selection I. (*Offenbach*) (81)
- " Grand Duchess of Gerolstein," Selection II.)*Offembach*) (81)

C. 243
- (*a*) Serenata (*Moszkowski*) ; (*b*) Pastorale ("Philémon et Baucis "—*Gounod*) (81)
- (*a*) Chanson Triste ; (*b*) Chanson Humoreske (*Tchaikovsky*) (81)

C. 244
- Light Cavalry Overture (*Suppé*) (79)
- " Le Prophête "—Grand March (*Meyerbeer*) (80)

C. 245
- Mazurka and Valse Ballet Music (" Coppelia "—*Délibes*) (80)
- " Bohemian Girl," Selection (*Balfe*) (81)

C. 246
- Il Conte d'Essex (*Mercadante*) (80)
- Raymond Overture (*Thomas*) (77)

C. 247
- " Boccaccio," Selection I. (*Suppé*) (81)
- " Boccaccio," Selection II. (*Suppé*) (81)

C. 248
- Three Symphonic Dances, No. 1. (*Grieg*) (81)
- The long day closes (*Sullivan*) (81)

C. 258
- Suite from " The Miracle "—Procession and Children's Dance (*Humperdinck* arr. by *Winterbottom*) (80)
- Suite from " The Miracle "—The March of the Army and Dead Motif, (80)

C. 264
- " Tannhäuser "—Pilgrims' Chorus (*Wagner*) (80)
- " Lohengrin "—Bridal Chorus (*Wagner*) (81)

C. 279
- " The Girl in the Taxi," Selection (*Jean Gilbert*) (81)
- " Rose of Castille," Selection (*Balfe*) (81)

C. 282
- " Il Trovatore," Miséréré (*Verdi*, arr. by *Franklin*) (81)
- Die Lorelei Paraphrase (*Nesvadba*) (81)

C. 283
- " Princess Ida," Selection I. (*Sullivan*, arr. by *Winterbottom*) (81)
- " Princess Ida," Selection II. (81)

C. 287
- " Mignon " Overture (*Thomas*, arr. by *Rogan*) (80)
- " Swan Lake Ballet "—Dance of the Swans ; Hungarian Dance—Czardas (*Tchaikovsky*) (80)

C 288
- Reminiscences of Verdi—Part I. (arr. by *F. Godfrey*) (80)
- Reminiscences of Verdi—Part II. (arr. by *F. Godfrey*) (80)

C. 293
- Reminiscences of Weber—Part I. (arr. by *F. Godfrey*) (81)
- Reminiscences of Weber—Part II. (arr. by *F. Godfrey*) (81)

C. 297
- Review of the Brigade of Guards (held in Hyde Park, April 28th, 1913), Part I. (78)
- Review of the Brigade of Guards (held in Hyde Park, April 28th, 1913), Part II. (78)

C. 310
- Fugue in G minor (*Bach*) (78)
- Fantasia in G Minor (*Bach*) (78)

C. 311
- " Fidelio " Overture (*Beethoven*) (79)
- Le Dieu et la Bayadère—Overture (*Auber*) (79)

C. 335
- " A Dream of Egypt " Suite—(2) Within the Sphinx's Solemn Shade—Pomegranate in your Mouth (*Woodforde-Fibden*, arr. by *Fletcher*) (78)
- " A Dream of Egypt " Suite—(4) I awakened when the moon (*Woodforde-Finden*, arr. by *Fletcher*) (78)

C. 337
- " Meistersinger " Selection, Part I. (*Wagner*) (78)
- " Meistersinger " Selection, Part II. (*Wagner*) (78)

C. 344
- " A Dream of Egypt "—Introduction and Beside the lonely Nile (*Woodforde-Finden*) (79)
- " A Dream of Egypt "—I envy every circlet (*Woodforde-Finden*) (79)

C. 359
- Sizilietta—Serenade (*von Blon*) (79)
- Turkish Idyll (*S. V. Hays*) (78)

C. 365
- Estudiantina—Valse (*Waldteufel*) (78)
- Morgenblätter—Valse (*J. Strauss*) (78)

C. 370
- Les Sirènes—Valse (*Waldteufel*) (79)
- Indigo Valse (*Strauss*) (79)

C. 388
- Bal Masqué—Valse Caprice (*Fletcher*) (78)
- Santiago—Spanish Valse (*Corbin*) (78)

C. 389
- Sicilian Vespers—Ballet Selection (*Verdi*, arr. by *Rogan*) (79)
- Sicilian Vespers—Selection (*Verdi*, arr. by *Rogan*) (79)

C. 393
- Orphée aux Enfers—Selection I (80)
- Orphée aux Enfers—Selection II. (*Offenbach*) (80)

C. 397
- Merrie England—Fantasia *German* (78)
- Demoiselle Chic—Intermezzo " Parisian Sketches " (*Fletcher*) (78)

C. 402
- Il Bacio (*Arditi*, arr. by *Rogan*) (Cornet Solo by Corporal G. MORGAN) (80)
- D'ye ken John Peel—Descriptive (arr. by *Shipley Douglas*) (80)

C. 403
- The Friendly Rivals (*C. Godfrey*) (Cornet Duet by Corp. G. MORGAN and Musician G. BARR) (80)
- By the Swanee River—Descriptive (arr. by *Myddleton*) (79)

C. 407
- Florodora—Selection I. (*Stuart*) (79)
- Florodora—Selection II. (*Stuart*) (79)

These records should be played with " His Master's Voice " needles, sold only in boxes bearing our copyright picture, " His Master's Voice," on the lid

111

BAND RECORDS

THE COLDSTREAM GUARDS—*continued*

12-inch records 5s. 6d.—*continued*

C 408
{ The Empire March (*Santley*, arr. *Fletcher*) (78)
A Dervish Chorus (*Sebek*) (80)

C. 415
{ The Emerald Isle, Selection I. (*Sullivan and German*) (80)
The Emerald Isle, Selection II. (*Sullivan and German*) (80)

C. 416
{ The Country Girl, Selection I. (*Monckton*) (80)
The Country Girl, Selection II. (*Monckton*) (80)

C. 463
{ Rêverie—Valse (*Waldteufel*) (78)
Valse—A Toi (*Waldteufel*) (78)

C. 465
{ "The Seasons"—Part I., Barcarolle and Valse (*Glazounov*) (78)
"The Seasons"—Part II., Petit Adagio Bacchanal (*Glazounow*) (78)

C. 466
{ The Sorcerer—Selection I. (*Sullivan*) (78)
The Sorcerer—Selection II. (*Sullivan*) (78)

C. 468
{ La Reine de Saba—Allegro, Andante Moderato, Allegro (*Gounod*) (78)
Le Domino Noir—Selection (*Auber*) (78)

C. 579
{ Olivette—Selection I. (*Audran*) (79)
Olivette—Selection II. (*Audran*) (79)

C. 593
{ (a) Song of the Boatman on the Volga (arr. by *Rogan*) (79)
(b) Russian Dance (arr. by *Rogan*) (79)
L'Etoile du Nord—Selection (*Meyerbeer*) (79)

C. 599
{ Romeo and Juliet—Ballet Music, Part I. (*Gounod*) (79)
Romeo and Juliet—Ballet Music, Part II. (*Gounod*) (79)

C. 614
{ Among the Flowers (*Mascheroni*) (80)
Rendezvous—Intermezzo (*Aletter*) (8)

C. 615
{ Carmen—Ballet Music, Part I. (*Bizet*) (79)
Carmen—Ballet Music, Part II. (*Bizet*) (79)

C. 627
{ Incidental Music to "Monsieur Beaucaire," Part I. (*Rosse*, arr. *Winterbottom*) (78)
Incidental Music to "Monsieur Beaucaire," Part II. (*Rosse*, arr. *Winterbottom*) (78)

C.628
{ Rose Mousse (*Bosc*) (79)
Minuet—"Samson" (*Handel*) (79)

C. 639
{ La Belle Héléne—Selection (*Offenbach*) (79)
Ruddigore—Selection (*Sullivan*) (79)

C. 650
{ Flower of the Forest (79)
A Sleigh Ride Polka—Descriptive (*Jullien*) (79)

C. 651
{ Reminiscences of Rossini (arr. by *F. Godfrey*) (78)
Three African Dances (*Montague Ring*) (79)

C. 700
{ Sextet "Lucia di Lammermoor" (*Donizetti*) (79)
Masaniello—Overture (*Auber*, arr. by *J Gready*) (79)

C. 706
{ Grand Patriotic Fantasia—Festival of Empire, Part I. (arr. by *Rogan*) (78)
Grand Patriotic Fantasia—Festival of Empire, Part II. (arr. by *Rogan*) (78)

C. 707
{ Grand Patriotic Fantasia—Festival of Empire, Part III. (arr. by *Rogan*) (78)
Grand Patriotic Fantasia—Festival of Empire, Part IV. (arr. by *Rogan*) (78)

C. 714
{ "H.M.S. Pinafore," Selection I. (*Sullivan*, arr. by *F. Godfrey*) (79)
"H.M.S. Pinafore," Selection II. (*Sullivan*, arr. by *F. Godfrey*) (79)

C. 744
{ Polonaise "Life for the Czar" (*Glinka*) (80)
"Norma" —Overture (*Bellini*) (78)

C. 757
{ "Maritana"—Selection I. (*Wallace*) (78)
"Maritana"—Selection II. (*Wallace*) (78)

C. 772
{ Military Tattoo—Part I. (Soloist, EDWARD HALLAND) (arr. by *Rogan*) (78)
Military Tattoo—Part II. (Soloists, ERNEST PIKE and EDWARD HALLAND) (arr. by *Rogan*) (78)

C. 786
{ Church Parade—Part I. (Soloist, PETER DAWSON) (arr. by *Rogan*) (78)
Church Parade—Part II (Soloists, ERNEST PIKE and PETER DAWSON) (arr. by *Rogan*) (78)

C. 799
{ Fantasia on American National Airs—Part I. (79)
Fantasia on American National Airs—Part II. (79)

C. 806
{ "Stabat Mater," Overture (*Rossini*) (78)
Soldiers' Chorus, "Faust" (*Gounod*) (79)

C. 812
{ "Madame Favart," Selection I. (*Offenbach*) (79)
"Madame Favart," Selection II. (*Offenbach*) (79)

C. 815
{ "La Fille du Tambour Major," Selection I. (The Daughter of the Drum Major) (*Offenbach*) (78)
"La Fille du Tambour Major," Selection II. (The Daughter of the Drum Major) (*Offenbach*) (78)

C. 825
{ A Comical Contest—Burlesque (C. *Godfrey*) (78)
American Fantasia—Happy Days in Dixie, or Life in the old Plantation (*Bidgood*) (78)

C. 837
{ "The Vikings"—Dramatic Overture, Part I. (*Hartmann*) (78)
"The Vikings"—Dramatic Overture, Part II. (*Hartmann*) (78)

The figures in brackets at end of selections indicate the speed at which the records . . . . should be played . . . .

112

BAND RECORDS

THE COLDSTREAM GUARDS—*continued.*

12-inch records 5s. 6d.—*continued*

C. 842 { Love's Garden of Roses (*Hayden Wood*) (Cornet solo by CPL. G. MORGAN) (79)
Solveig's Song (" Peer Gynt "—*Grieg*) (Cornet solo by CPL. G. MORGAN) (79)

C. 862 { Doges March (" Merchant of Venice "—*Rossi*) (79)
" L'Italiana in Algeri "—Overture (*Rossini*) (79)

C. 869 { " Scotland's Pride " (National Fantasia) Part I. (arr. and selected by *Charles Godfrey*) (79)
" Scotland's Pride " (National Fantasia) Part II. (79)

C. 870 { " Aïda," Selection I. (*Verdi*) (79)
" Aïda," Selection II. (*Verdi*) (79)

BLACK DIAMONDS BAND

10-inch record 3s. 6d.

B. 476 { New Year's Eve (with chorus) (80) DESCRIPTIVE
British Troops passing through Boulogne (78)

12-inch records 5s. 6d.

C 139 { Hunting Scene (*Bucalossi*) (81)
Turkish Patrol (*Michaelis*) (82)

C. 140 { Gold and Silver Waltz (*Lehar*) (81)
Venus on Earth Waltz (*Lincke*) (78)

THE GARDE REPUBLICAINE BAND

12-inch record 5s. 6d.

C. 725 { Marche italienne (*Rousseau*) (75)
Brune ou blonde—Valse (*Waldteufel*) (75)

METROPOLITAN BAND

10-inch record 3s. 6d.

B. 259 { Sympathy Waltz (*Friml*) (78)
Who paid the rent for Mrs. Rip Van Winkle ? Medley (79)

METROPOLITAN DANCE BAND

10-inch record 3s. 6d.

B. 269 { Valse June—Hesitation (*Baxter*) (79)
Hesitation Waltz (*Klickmann*) (79)

12-inch records 5s. 6d.

C. 384 { Isle d'Amour—Waltz Hesitation (*Edwards*) (79)
Barcarolle—" Tales of Hoffman " Waltz Hesitation (79)

C. 385 { All aboard for Dixieland—One-step (*Cobb*) (80)
Rose in the Bud—Valse (*Dorothy Forster*) (78)

C. 602 { Ticking Love Taps—Fox-trot (78)
By Heck—Fox Trot (*Henri*) (78)

C. 603 { Maurice—Waltz Hesitation (78)
Music Box Rag—Fox Trot (*Roberts*) (78)

C. 604 { Chin Chin—Fox Trot (*Caryll*) (78)
To-night's the Night Medley—Waltz Hesitation (*Rubens*) (78)

C. 671 { MyBird of Paradise—MedleyFoxTrot (78)
I'm on my way to Dublin Bay Medley—One-step (78)

C. 726 { " Half-Past Eight "—Waltz (*Rubens*, arr. by *Higgs*) (79)
A Broken Doll—Fox Trot (*J. W. Tate*, arr. by *Pether*) (79)

C. 727 { " The Happy Day "—Fox Trot (*Jones and Rubens*) (79)
" The Happy Day "—Waltz (*Jones and Rubens*, arr. by *Higgs*) (79)

C. 728 { The Long, Long Trail—Waltz (*Elliott*, arr. by *Yearsley*) (79)
The Peasant Girl—Waltz Medley (79)

C. 729 { " The Bing Boys are here "—Waltz (*Nat D. Ayer*) (79)
" High Jinks "—One-step or Fox Trot (arr. by *Savino*) (79)

C. 730 { " Bric-à-Brac "—Waltz (*Monckton*, arr by *H. M. Higgs*) (79)
You're here and I'm here—Medley One-step (*Kern*) (79)

C. 731 { " Tina "—Waltz (*Rubens and Wood*, arr. by *Higgs*) (79)
Maid in America Medley—Fox Trot (79)

C. 817 { Sphinx Waltz (*Francis Popy*) (79)
" The Maid of the Mountains "—Waltz (*H. Fraser-Simson*, arr. by *Melvin Morgan*) (79)

C. 818 { Welcome, Honey, to the old plantation home—Medley One-step (*Gamble*) (79)
Arizona—Fox Trot (*Melville Gideon*, arr. by *Herman Darewski*) (79)

C. 819 { Bugle Call Rag—Fox Trot (*Morgan*) (79)
Ole Virginny—One-step (*Zamecnik*) (79)

C. 820 { Loading up the Mandy Lee—Medley One-step (*Marshall*) (79)
That Dancing Melody—Fox Trot (arr. by *Darewski*) (" Topsy Turvy ") (79)

C. 821 { " Carminetta "—Valse (*Darewski*) (79)
Waltz we love—Waltz (La Valse que nous aimons) (*A. Vecsey*) (79)

 These records should be played with " His Master's Voice " needles, sold only in boxes bearing our copyright picture, " His Master's Voice," on the lid

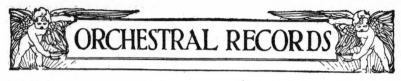

ORCHESTRAL RECORDS

METROPOLITAN MILITARY BAND

12-inch record 5s. 6d.

C. 378 {
Allies in Arms, Selection I. (Containing " Hearts of Oak," " La Brabançonne " (Belgium), " St. Patrick," " Russian Hymn," " Rule, Britannia," " See the Conquering Hero," Finale) **(78)**
Allies in Arms, Selection II. (Containing " La Marseillaise," " The Garb of Old Gaul," " The Maple Leaf," " Marcia Reale " (Italy), " Men of Harlech," " God Save the King ") **(78)**
}

PIPERS AND DRUMMERS OF HIS MAJESTY'S SCOTS GUARDS

10-inch records 3s. 6d.

B. 121 {
Land o' the leal (Traditional) **(80)**
Medley March (Traditional) **(80)**
}

B. 122 {
March Past of the Cameron Highlanders and Gordon Highlanders **(78)**
March Past of Royal Scots and Royal Highlanders **(78)**
}

OPAL MILITARY BAND

10-inch records 3s. 6d.

B. 635 {
The National Fencibles March (*Sousa*) **(79)**
The Thunderer March (*Sousa*) **(79)**
}

B. 690 {
The Gladiator March (*Sousa*) **(79)**
The Kansas City Star March (*Liberati*) **(79)**
}

B. 723 {
Big Guns—March (*Avolo*) **(79)**
Washington Grays—March (*Grafulla*) **(79)**
The London Scottish—March (*H. E. Haines*) **(79)**
}

B. 797 {
Up, Guards, and at 'em (*Gordon Mackenzie*) **(79)**
}

B. 849 {
Arabia March (*Buck*, arr. by *Alford*) **(79)**
THE BAND OF H.M. COLDSTREAM GUARDS.
A Trieste March (*Carosio*) **(79)**
}

B. 981 {
Lorraine (March Majestic) (*Augarde*) **(79)**
COLDSTREAM GUARDS BAND
Marcha russe (*Ganne*) **(79)**
}

PRYOR'S BAND

(conducted by ARTHUR PRYOR)

10-inch record 3s. 6d.

B. 244 {
Whistler and his dog (*Pryor*) **(78)**
The Warbler's Serenade (*Perry*) **(78)**
}

12-inch record 5s. 6d.

C. 356 {
" Madama Butterfly," Selection (*Puccini*) **(79)**
Dream Pictures (*Lumbye*) **(78)**
}

SOUSA'S BAND

(conducted by JOHN PHILIP SOUSA)

10-inch record 3s. 6d.

B. 246 {
At a Georgia Camp Meeting (*Mills*) **(78)**
Melinda's Wedding Day—Medley (*Piantadosi*) **(79)**
}

ORCHESTRAL SELECTIONS

ADELPHI THEATRE ORCHESTRA

12-inch records 5s. 6d.

C. 635 {
" Tina " Selection I. (*Paul Rubens*) **(78)**
" Tina " Selection II. (*Paul Rubens*) **(78)**
}

C. 636 {
The Billsticker's Dance (",Tina ") (*Paul Rubens*) **(78)**
The Dance from " Tina " (*Haydn Wood*) **(78)**
}

C. 713 {
Oyra's Dance (*Howard Talbot*) (" High Jinks ") **(78)**
Overture (" High Jinks ") **(78)**
}

C. 719 {
Tingle-ingleing—Fox Trot (" High Jinks ") **(78)**
Finale, Act 2 (" High Jinks ") **(78)**
}

ALHAMBRA ORCHESTRA

(conducted by John Ansell)

10-inch record 3s. 6d.

B. 642 {
The Whistler (" The Bing Boys are here ") (*Ayer*) **(78)**
NAT D. AYER.
Another little drink wouldn't do us any harm (" The Bing Boys are here ") (*Ayer*) **(78)**
}

12-inch records 5s. 6d.

C. 674 {
" The Bing Boys are here " Selection I. (*Ayer*) **(78)**
" The Bing Boys are here " Selection II. (*Ayer*) **(78)**
}

The figures in brackets at end of selections indicate the speed at which the records · · · · should be played · · · ·

ORCHESTRAL RECORDS

ALAMBRA ORCHESTRA—*continued*

12-inch records 5s. 6d.

C. 676 {
The Languid Melody (" The Bing Boys are here ") (*Ayer*) (78)
NAT D. AYER and PEGGY PHILLIPS
If you were the only girl in the world and I were the only boy (" The Bing Boys are here ") (*Ayer*) (78)
}

C. 678 {
Ragging the Dog and the Shoeblack (*Ayer*)
GWENDOLINE BROGDEN
Heart of mine, come back to me (" The Passing Show of 1915 ") (*Finck*) (78)
}

C. 780 {
" The Bing Girls are There," Sel. I. (79)
" The Bing Girls are There," Sel. II. (79)
}

C. 845 {
" The Bing Boys on Broadway "—Selection I. (79)
" The Bing Boys on Broadway "—Selection II. (79)
}

THE BEECHAM SYMPHONY ORCHESTRA

(conducted by Sir Thomas Beecham)

12-inch record 5s. 6d.

C. 431 {
" Die Fledermaus " Overture (" The Bat ") (*Johann Strauss*) (80)
Salut d'Amour (*Elgar*) (LA SCALA SYMPHONY ORCHESTRA) (78)
}

BIJOU CINEMA ORCHESTRA

10-inch record 3s. 6d.

B. 837 {
Those bewitching eyes (*Mustal*) (79)
DE GROOT and THE PICCADILLY ORCHESTRA
There's a little bit of bad in every good little girl (*Clarke and Darewski*) (" Three Cheers ") (79)
}

12-inch records 5s. 6d.

C. 647 {
The Call of the Angelus—Intermezzo (*Walton*) (78)
Seduction—Valse (*Crémieux*) (78)
}

C. 653 {
L'Automne Mélodie (*Lémune*) (79)
Nuit d'Egypte—Valse (*Arensky*) (79)
}

C. 717 {
Badinage (*Victor Herbert*) (78)
Les Cloches du Monastère (Monastery Bells) (*Wely*) (78)
}

C. 807 {
Alethea (*F. Manns*) (78)
The Dying Poet (*Gottschalk*) (78)
}

BOHEMIAN ORCHESTRA

10-inch records 3s. 6d.

B. 127 {
" Tales of Hoffmann," Barcarolle (*Offenbach*) (79)
" The Merry Widow " Waltz (*Lehar*) (81)
}

B. 128 {
Dresdine (76)
The Choristers' Waltz (*Phelps*) (78)
}

B. 129 {
La Petite Tonkinoise (*Scotto and Christine*) (77)
Intermezzo Rococo (*Aletter*) (78)
}

B. 155 {
Liselotte (*Leon Adam*) (80)
Lancelot (*Leon Adam*) (80)
}

12-inch records 5s. 6d.

C. 142 {
In the shadows (*Finck*)
" Chocolate Soldier " Waltz (*Oscar Straus*) (80)
}

C. 143 {
Gems from " Our Miss Gibbs " (with chorus) (*Monckton and Caryll*) (81)
Gems from " The Arcadians " (with chorus) (*Monckton and Talbot*) (80)
}

BORODIN SYMPHONIC ORCHESTRA

12-inch record 5s

C. 350 {
" Prince Igor "—Overture, Part I. (*Borodin*) (78)
" Prince Igor "—Overture, Part II. (*Borodin*) (79)
}

BOURNEMOUTH MUNICIPAL ORCHESTRA

(by permission of the Bournemouth Corporation)

(conducted by DAN GODFREY)

12-inch record 5s. 6d.

C. 340 {
Ballet Music of " Henry VIII." (*Saint-Saëns*) (78)
Norwegian Dances of Grieg (79)
}

THE CASTLE HOUSE ORCHESTRA

(conducted by Mr. F. W. McKEE, Director)

12-inch record 5s. 6d.

C. 375 {
Cecile—Waltz Hesitation (*McKee*) (78)
Esmeralda—Waltz Hesitation (*Carlos de Mesquita*) (78)
}

ORCHESTRAL RECORDS

DE GROOT AND THE PICCADILLY ORCHESTRA

10-inch records 3s. 6d.

B. 286
- What happened in the summer time (*Ayer*) (78)
- I want some loving (*Ben Styler*) (78)

B. 295
- Temple Bells, " Four Indian Love Lyrics " (*Woodforde-Finden*, arr. by *Fletcher*) (79)
- Till I wake, " Four Indian Love Lyrics " (79)

B. 501
- Love's Garden of Roses (*Haydn Wood*) (78)
- MAYFAIR ORCHESTRA "To-night's the Night "—One-step (*Rubens*, arr. by *Klein*) (80)

B. 502
- I wonder if love is a dream (*Dorothy Forster*) (80)
- A la hongroise (*Henri*) (80)

B. 552
- That simple Melody (" Watch your Step ") (*Irving Berlin*) (78)
- Settle down in a one-horse town (" Watch your Step ") (*Irving Berlin*) (78)

B. 631
- A Broken Doll (*J. W. Tate*) (" Samples " Revue) (78)
- Tulip Song (*H. Darewski*) (" Joyland") (78)

B. 647
- A Perfect Day (*Jacobs-Bond*) (78)
- My Honolulu Girl (*Melville Gideon* (" Samples " Revue) (78)

B. 675
- Underneath the Stars—A Romance (*Spencer*) (78)
- There's a long, long trail (*Elliott*) (78)

B. 679
- 'Twas in September (*Silvio Hein*) (" Mr. Manhattan ") (79)
- When you're all dressed up and no place to go (*Silvio Hein*) (" Mr. Manhattan ") (79)

B. 691
- Down home in Tennessee (*Donaldson*) (79)
- The languid Melody (*Ayer*) (" The Bing Boys ") (79)

B. 724
- Down in the Forest (*Landon Ronald*) (79)
- " La Tosca "—Fantasia (*Puccini*, arr. by *Tavan*) (79)

B. 747
- Bohemia (*Rubens*) (" The HappyDay ") (79)
- LENSEN and THE TROCADERO ORCHESTRA O Flower Divine (*Haydn Wood*) (79)

B. 769
- It's a long, long way to my home in Kentucky (*Nat D. Ayer*) (79)
- Something seems tingle-ingleing (" High Jinks ") (79)

B. 770
- Love, here is my heart (*Silesu*) (78)
- Arizona (*Melville Gideon*) (78)

B. 812
- One hour of love with you (*M. Darewski*) (" Hanky-Panky ") (79)
- Come back to Ireland and me (*R. Wakley*) (" Hanky-Panky ") (79)

B. 828
- My heart just broke for you (*Dorothy Forster*) (79)
- A Paradise for two (The key to your heart) (*Tate*) (" The Maid of the Mountains) (79)

B. 829
- 'Tis the Day (*Leoncavallo*) (79)
- JEAN LENSEN (conductor) and THE TROCADERO ORCHESTRA Until (*Sanderson*) (79)

B. 837
- There's a little bit of bad in every good little girl (*Clarke and Darewski*) (" Three Cheers ") (79)
- BIJOU CINEMA ORCHESTRA Those bewitching eyes (*Muskal*) (79)

B. 861
- Hawaiian Butterfly (*Baskette and Santley*) (" Bubbly ") (78)
- Some girl has got to darn his socks (*H. Finck*) (" Round the Map ") (78)

B. 892
- A Merry Farewell (Valse Song) (*Lassailly*) ("Carminetta") (78)
- Clicquot (*H. Darewski*) ("Carminetta") (78)

B. 893
- Didn't know the way to (*Novello*, arr. by *Stoddon*) (" Arlette ") (78)
- Poor Butterfly! (*Hubbell*) (78)

B. 899
- Hullo! my dearie (*Stamper*) (" Zig-Zag ") (79)
- Smoke Clouds (*Darewski*) (" Topsy Turvy ") (79)

B. 903
- " Pamela "—Valse (*Norton*) (79)
- " The Lilac Domino "—Waltz (*Cuvillier*) (79)

B. 907
- For your love I am waiting (*Cuvillier*) (" The Lilac Domino ") (79)
- First love, last love, best love (*Nat. D Ayer*) (" The Bing Boys on Broadway ") (79)

B. 909
- Widows are wonderful (*Nat D. Ayer*) (" Yes, Uncle!") (79)
- HENRI LEONI Play me that marching melody (with chorus) (*Le Feuvre*) ("Yes, Uncle ! ") (79)

B. 963
- Little Miss Melody (*Monckton*) (" The Boy") (79)
- If you look in her eyes (*Hirsch*) (" Going Up ") (79)

B. 982
- The tickle toe (*Hirsch*) (" Going Up ") (79)
- The Apache Rag (*Braham*) (" Tails Up !") (79)

12-inch records 5s. 6d.

C. 176
- Dreaming Waltz (*Joyce*) (78)
- Love and Life in Holland Waltz (*Joyce*) (78)

C. 177
- Ceylon Whispers Waltz (*Hopton*) (78)
- A Thousand Kisses Waltz (*Joyce*) (78)

C. 400
- When the Angelus is ringing (*Grant*) (79) MAYFAIR ORCHESTRA
- Penitence (*Jones*) (79)

The figures in brackets at end of selections indicate the speed at which the records . . . . should be played . . . .

ORCHESTRAL RECORDS

DE GROOT AND THE PICCADILLY ORCHESTRA—*continued*

12-inch records 5s. 6d.

C. 410
{ Less than the Dust, " Four Indian Love Lyrics " (*Woodforde-Finden*, arr. by *P. E. Fletcher*) (78)
Kashmiri Song, " Four Indian Love Lyrics " (*Woodforde-Finden*, arr. by *P. E. Fletcher*) (78) }

C. 585
{ Caresse d'Avril (*de Groot*) (78)
Le plus joli Rêve (*Azzezo*) (78) }

C. 597
{ Piccadilly Grill Waltz (*de Groot*) (78)
ELSIE JANIS and BASIL HALLAM
I've got everything I want but you (*Marshall*, arr. by *Finck*) (78) }

C. 623
{ A little bit of Heaven (*Ball*) (78)
They didn't believe me (*Kern*) ("To-night's the Night ") (78) }

C. 683
{ Violin Song (*Rubens*) (" Tina ") (78)
Serenata (*Toselli*) (78) }

C. 716
{ Every little while (*Tate*) (" Some ") (79)
If you were the only girl (*Ayer*) (" The Bing Boys are here ") (79) }

C. 774
{ Just my Love (*H. Darewski*) (" Three Cheers ") (78)
JEAN LENSEN (conductor) and THE TROCADERO ORCHESTRA
Désir Valse (*Stone*) (78) }

C. 778
{ Some Sort of Somebody (*Kern*) (" Vanity Fair ") (78)
Any time's kissing time (*Norton*) (" Chu Chin Chow ") (78) }

C. 784
{ That dear old home of mine (*Ayer*, arr. by *Parry*) (" The Bing Girls are There ") (78)
Let the great big world keep turning (*Ayer*, arr. by *Stoddon*) (" The Bing Girls are There ") (78) }

C. 816
{ Roses of Picardy (*Haydn Wood*) (78)
Any place is Heaven if you are near me (*Löhr*) (78) }

C. 829
{ Parted (*Tosti*) (78)
" The Maid of the Mountains "—Valse Song (Love will find a way) (*H. Fraser-Simson*) (78) }

C. 833
{ Valse Poudrée (*F. Popy*) (78)
NELLIE TAYLOR
Little Miss Melody (*L. Monckton*) (" The Boy ") (78) }

C. 850
{ The land of happy memories (*De Groot*) (78)
LOUISE LEIGH and RANDELL JACKSON
What is done, you never can undo (with chorus) Finale, Act II (*Cuvillier & Carr*) (" The Lilac Domino ") (79) }

C. 851
{ Some day I'll make you love me (*Grey and Ayer*, arr. by *Stoddon*) (" Round the Map ") (79)
DAVY BURNABY
The dear old days (with chorus) *Nat D. Ayer*) (" Yes, Uncle ! ") (79) }

C. 866
{ En relisant vos lettres Valse lente) *Masson-Kiek*) (79)
ERIC COURTLAND and JOSEPH REED
Mother (*Romberg*) (" Soldier Boy ") (79) }

HERMAN FINCK AND ORCHESTRA

(personally conducted by HERMAN FINCK)

12-inch record 5s. 6d.

C. 809
{ " Round the Map," Selection I. (78)
" Round the Map." Selection II. (*Herman Finck*) (78) }

THE GAIETY THEATRE ORCHESTRA

10-inch records 3s. 6d.

B. 754
{ Valse Saracenne (*Ivor Novello*) (" Theodore & Co.") (78)
JULIA JAMES and FRED LESLIE
I'll make myself at home dear (*Ivor Novello*))" Theodore & Co,") (78) }

B. 9 8
{ (*a*) I'll bet you (*b*) The touch of a woman's hand (*Hirsch*) (" Going Up ") (79)
Medley Two-step (*Hirsch*) (" Going Up ") (79) }

12-inch records 5s. 6d.

C. 749
{ Overture " Theodore & Co." (*Ivor Novello*) (78)
HENRI LEONI and CHORUS
Any old where (*Ivor Novello*) (" Theodore & Co.") (78) }

C. 861
{ " Going Up "—Selection I. (*Hirsch*) (79)
" Going Up "—Selection II (*Hirsch*) (79) }

GOTTLIEB'S ORCHESTRA

(personally conducted by Mr. GOTTLIEB)

12-inch records 5s. 6d.

C. 179
{ Autumn Voices Waltz (*Lincke*) (78)
Gipsy Love Waltz (*Lehar*) (78) }

C. 181
{ " Count o Luxemburg " Waltz (*Lehar*) (78)
" Chocolate Soldier " Waltz (*Straus*) (78) }

C. 186
{ Claudine Waltz (*Zulueta*) (78)
Druids' Prayer Waltz (*Davson*) (78) }

C. 189
{ Reviens Waltz (*Fragson-Christine*) (78)
Eternal Waltz (*Leo Fall*) (78) }

ORCHESTRAL RECORDS

GRAND OPERA ORCHESTRA
10-inch record 3s. 6d.

B. 174 { Præludium (*Järnefeldt*) **(80)** MAYFAIR ORCHESTRA
Cornwall March (*Bert Winson*) **(80)**

12-inch records 5s. 6d.

C. 144 { "Count of Luxemburg," Selection I (*Lehar*) **(81)**
"Count of Luxemburg," Selection II. (*Lehar*) **(81)**

C. 312 { "Surprise Symphony"—Allegro Molto (*Haydn*) **(78)**
"Surprise Symphony"—Andante(*Haydn*) **(78)**

C. 334 { "Pastoral Symphony"—Andante Molto Moto, 2nd movement, Part I. (*Beethoven*) **(78)**
"Pastoral Symphony"—Andante Molto Moto, 2nd movement, Part II. (*Beethoven*) **(78)**

HUNGARIAN GIPSY ORCHESTRA
10-inch record 3s. 6d.

B. 202 { "The Doll "(" Puppchen ")—Waltz (*Jean Gilbert*) **(79)**
"The Doll" (" Puppchen ")—Two-step (" You're the apple of my eye ") (*Jean Gilbert*) **(80)**

IFF'S ORCHESTRA
(personally conducted by Mr. IFF)
12-inch records 5s. 6d.

C. 164 { "Dollar Princess "Lancers, Figs. I and II (*Fall*) **(78)**
"Dollar Princess " Lancers, Figs. III. and IV. (*Fall*) **(78)**

C. 165 { "Dollar Princess " Lancers, Fig. V. (*Fall*) **(78)**
Waltz Dream " "Waltz (*Straus*) **(78)**

C. 166 { "The Merry Widow " Lancers, Figs. I. and II. (*Lehar*) **(78)**
"The Merry Widow " Lancers, Figs III. and IV. **(78)**

C. 167 { "The Merry Widow " Lancers, Fig. V. (*Lehar*) **(78)**
"The Merry Widow " Waltz (*Lehar*) **(78)**

C. 168 { Caledonian Quadrilles, Figs, I. and II. **(78)**
Caledonian Quadrilles. Figs. III. and IV. **(78)**

C. 169 { Caledonian Quadrilles, Fig. V. **(78)**
Valse Septembre (*Godin*) **(78)**

C. 229 { Foursome Reel 1 **(78)**
Foursome Reel 2 **(78)**

C. 230 { Eightsome Reel **(78)**
Highland Schottische **(78)**

C. 254 { Blue Danube Waltz (*Strauss*) **(78)**
Danse du Paraguay Two-step (*Valverde*) **(78)**

JACOBS AND HIS TROCADERO ORCHESTRA
10-inch records 3s. 6d.

B. 162 { "La Bohême " Fantaisie, Part I. (*Puccini*) **(80)**
"La Bohême" Fantaisie Part II. (*Puccini*) **(80)**

B. 231 { "Puppchen " — Two-step Intermezzo (*Jean Gilbert*) **(79)**
When love creeps in your heart (*Mills and Scott*) **(79)**

B. 274 { Pleading (*Wood*) **(80)**
Demoiselle Chic (*Fletcher*) **(80)**

12-inch records 5s. 6d.

C. 233 { "The Girl in the Taxi " Waltz (*Jean Gilbert*) **(81)**
Un peu d'amour—Mélodie (*Lao Silesu*) **(81)**

C. 354 { You're my baby (*Nat D. Ayer*) **(78)**
Je sais que vous êtes jolie (*Christine*) **(79)**

C. 373 { A Tango Dream (*Maxwell*) **(80)**
Smiles then Kisses—Waltz (*Ancliffe*) **(80)**

JEAN LENSEN (CONDUCTOR) AND THE TROCADERO ORCHESTRA
10-inch records 3s. 6d.

B. 701 { Yaaka Hula Hickey Dula (*Goetz, Young and Wendling*) **(78)**
LUVAUN (Guitar Solo)
A Broken Doll (*Tate*) (" Samples ") **(78)**

B. 747 { O Flower divine (*Haydn Wood*) **(79)**
DE GROOT and the PICCADILLY ORCHESTRA
Bohemia (*Rubens*) (" The Happy Day ") **(79)**

B. 829 { Until (*Sanderson*) **(79)**
DE GROOT and the PICCADILLY ORCHESTRA
'Tis the day (*Leoncavallo*) **(79)**

12-inch records 5s. 6d.

C. 715 { Bird of Love Divine (*Haydn Wood*) **(79)**
Destiny Waltz (*S. Baynes*) **(79)**

C. 774 { Désir Valse (*D. Stone*) **(78)**
DE GROOT and the PICCADILLY ORCHESTRA-
Just my love (*H. Darewski*) (" Three Cheers ") **(78)**

The figures in brackets at end of selections indicate the speed at which the records . . . . should be played . . . .

ORCHESTRAL RECORDS

JOYCE'S ORCHESTRA

(personally conducted by ARCHIBALD JOYCE)

12-inch records 5s. 6d.

C. 196 { Mickey's Birthday Two-step (*Joyce*) (**78**)
Dreaming Waltz (*Joyce*) (**78**)

C. 232 { A Thousand Kisses Waltz (*Joyce*) (**78**)
Vision d'amour Valse (*Joyce*) (**78**)

C. 255 { Remembrance Waltz (*Joyce*) (**78**)
The Passing of Salome Waltz (*Joyce*) (**78**)

THE IMPERIAL ORCHESTRA

(conducted by Bro. ARTHUR CRUDGE)

12-inch record 5s. 6d.

C. 418 { Grand Masonic Selection, "Companions and Brethren," Part I. (arr by *Crudge*) (**78**)
Grand Masonic Selection, "Companions and Brethren," Part II. (arr. by *Crudge*) (**78**) (containing traditional Melodies, Hymns, Processionals, &c.)

LA SCALA SYMPHONY ORCHESTRA

10-inch record 3s. 6d.

B. 311 { "The Valkyrie," Ride of the Valkyries (*Wagner*) (**79**)
"Lohengrin," Prelude Act III. (*Wagner*) (**79**)

12-inch records 5s. 6d.

C. 428 { "Carmen," Overture (*Bizet*) (**77**)
"Carmen," Selection (*Bizet*) (**77**)

C. 429 { "Cavalleria Rusticana," Intermezzo (*Mascagni*) (**77**)
"Cavalleria Rusticana," Preludio (*Mascagni*) (**78**)

C. 430 { "Faust," Preludio (*Gounod*) (**77**)
"Lohengrin," Overture (*Wagner*) (**79**)

C. 431 { Salut d'amour (*Elgar*) (**78**)
THE BEECHAM SYMPHONY ORCHESTRA (conducted by Sir Thomas Beecham)
"Die Fledermaus" Overture ("The Bat") (*Johann Strauss*) (**80**)

LINCKE'S ORCHESTRA

12-inch record 5s. 6d.

C. 141 { Amina Serenade (*Lincke*) (**80**)
Luna Waltz (*Lincke*) (**80**)

MAYFAIR ORCHESTRA

10-inch records 3s. 6d.

B. 164 { Baby's Sweetheart—Pizzicato Serenade (*Corri*) (**81**)
Pizzicato "Sylvia" (*Délibes*) (**80**)

B. 174 { Cornwall March (*Bert Winson*) (**80**)
GRAND OPERA ORCHESTRA
Praeludium (*Järnefeldt*) (**80**)

B. 287 { At the Fox Trot Ball, that's all (*Nat D. Ayer*) (**79**)
I want to go back to Michigan (*Irving Berlin*) (**79**)

B. 290 { The Syncopated Walk (*Irving Berlin*) (**78**)
The Minstrel Parade (*Irving Berlin*) (**78**)

B. 674 { You'll always be the same sweet baby (*A. Seymour Brown*)(" Razzle Dazzle ") (**78**)
WALTER JEFFERIES
When we gather round the old home fires again (*T.C. Sterndale-Bennett*) (**78**)

B. 677 { Valse d'Amour (*Crémieux*) (**79**)
Vision of Salome—Valse Orientale (*Joyce*) (**79**)

B. 678 { Underneath the Stars—Fox Trot (*Spencer*) (**79**)
If you were the only girl—Fox Trot (*Ayer*) (**79**)

B. 746 { Love in my garden—Valse (*Benson*) (**78**)
The Early Bird—Two-step and Fox Trot (*N. Kennedy*) (**78**)

B. 768 { Danses miniatures de Ballet, No. I, (*Ansell*) (**78**)
Danses miniatures de Ballet, No. II. (*Ansell*) (**79**)

B. 783 { Love me at Twilight (*Bert Grant*) (**78**)
Mélodie d'Amour (*Engelmann*) (**78**)

B. 810 { Three Irish Pictures—No. I.—(*Ansell*) (conducted by John Ansell) (**78**)
Three Irish Pictures—No. II. — (*Ansell*) (conducted by John Ansell) (**79**)

B. 811 { Poppies — A Japanese Intermezzo (*Moret*) (**79**)
When it's night-time in Dixieland (*Irving Berlin*) (**79**)

B. 827 { Three Irish Pictures—No. III.—(*Ansell*) (conducted by John Ansell) (**79**)
Les Sylphides — Dance Intermezzo (*Cussans*) (**79**)

B. 836 { Danses Miniature de Ballet, No. 4 (*Ansell*) (conducted by John Ansell) (**79**)
Intermezzo — "Tales of Hoffmann" (*Offenbach*) (**79**)

B. 872 { Amerinda Intermezzo (*Smith*) (**78**)
In a Monastery Garden (*Ketelbey*) (**78**)

These records should be played with " His Master's Voice " needles, sold only in boxes bearing our copyright picture, " His Master's Voice," on the lid

ORCHESTRAL RECORDS

MAYFAIR ORCHESTRA—*continued*

12-inch records 5s. 6d.

C. 147 { "Pink Lady," Selection I. (*Caryll*) **(81)**
"Pink Lady," Selection II. (*Caryll*) **(81)**

C. 148 { "Pink Lady," Valse (*Caryll*) **(81)**
Vision d'Amour (*Byford*) **(80)**

C 149 { "Pagliacci," Selection I. (*Leoncavallo*) **(81)**
"Pagliacci," Selection II.(*Leoncavallo*) **(81)**

C. 150 { Valse Triste (*Sibelius*) **(81)**
La Mariposa (*G. Diaz*) **(80)**

C 197 { "La Bohême " Fantasia, Part I. (*Leoncavallo*) **(80)**
"La Bohême " Fantasia, Part II .(*Leoncavallo*) **(81)**

C. 205 { Echo des Bastions (*H. King*) **(81)**
Un peu d'amour (*Leo Silesu*) **(80)**

C. 208 { Rêverie Interrompue, Op. 40, No. 4 (*Tschaikovsky*, arr. by *Schmid*) **(70)**
Polonaise, Op. 40, No. 1 (*Chopin*, arr. by *C. Fenn-Leyland*) **(80)**

C. 215 { Toy Symphony (*Haydn*) **(80)**
Christmas Melodies (arr. by *W. Partridge*) **(80)**

C. 250 { "La Source " Ballet, Selections I. and II. (*Delibes*) **(80)**
"La Source " Ballet, Selections III. and IV. (*Delibes*) **(80)**

C. 261 { Nights of Gladness Valse (*Ancliffe*) **(80)**
De Groot's Orchestra
Dance of the Little Feet—Gavotte (*de Bréville*) **(80)**

C. 305 { "Monsieur Beaucaire," Incidental Music Part I.— (*Rosse*, arr. by *Bucalossi*) **(78)**
"Monsieur Beaucaire," Incidental Music, Part II.—(*Rosse*, arr. by *Bucalossi*) **(78)**

C. 333 { Destiny—Valse Lente (*Baynes*) **(78)**
Dance of the Disappointed Fairies (*La Touch*) **(78)**

C. 338 { Laughing Eyes (*Finck*) **(78)**
March of the Giants (*Finck*) **(78)**

C. 343 { The Land of Roses— Valse (*Finck*)**(78)**
Ecstasy—Valse (*Sidney Baynes*) **(78)**

C. 355 { "La Bohême "—Selection I. (*Puccini*) **(78)**
"La Bohême "—Selection II. (*Puccini*) **(78)**

C. 382 { "The Passing Show," Selection I. (*Finck*) **(78)**
"The Passing Show," Selection II. (conducted by Herman Finck) (*Finck*) **(78)**

C. 400 { Penitence (*Jones*) **(79)**
De Groot and the Piccadilly Orchestra
When the Angelus is ringing (*Grant*) **(79)**

C. 411 { "To-night's the Night "—Selection I. (*Rubens*) **(78)**
"To-night's the Night "—Selection II. (*Rubens*) **(78)**

C 413 { " Betty "—Selection I. (*Rubens*) **(78)**
" Betty "—Selection II. (*Rubens*) **(78)**

C. 414 { " Betty " Waltz (*Rubens*) **(78)**
" For Valour "—Military Valse (*Ancliffe*, arr. by *Lotter*) **(78)**

C. 643 { " Joyland "—Sel. I. (*H. Darewski*) **(78)**
" Joyland "—Sel. II. (*H. Darewski*) **(78)**

C. 648 { "The Magic Flute," Overture, Part I. (*Mozart*) **(80)**
"The Magic Flute," Overture, Part II. (*Mozart*) **(80)**

C. 684 { Valse Bluette (for strings only) (*Drigo*) **(79)**
Valse from Ballet, "La Belle au Bois Dormant " (*Tchaikowsky*) **(79)**

C. 687 { "The Happy Day," Selection I. (*Rubens and Jones*, arr. by *Higgs*) **(78)**
"The Happy Day," Selection II. (*Rubens and Jones*, arr. by *Higgs*) **(78)**

C. 688 { "Mr. Manhattan," Sel. I. (*Talbot*) **(79)**
"Mr. Manhattan," Sel. II. (*Talbot*) **(79)**

C. 689 { "Toto," Sel. I. (*Joyce and Morgan*) **(79)**
"Toto," Sel. II. (*Joyce and Morgan*) **(79)**

C. 696 { "Pell Mell," Selection I. (*Ayer*) **(78)**
"Pell Mell," Selection II. (*Ayer*) **(78)**

C. 697 { "Half-Past Eight," Selection I. (*Rubens*, arr. by *Higgs*) **(78)**
"Half-Past Eight," Selection II. (*Rubens*, arr. by *Higgs*) **(78)**

C. 698 { A Dream of Delight, Waltz (*Nicholls*) **(78)**
"To-night's the Night," Fox Trot (*Rubens*) **(78)**

C. 701 { Welsh Rhapsody, Part I. (*German*) **(79)**
Welsh Rhapsody, Part II. (*German*) **(79)**

C. 705 { " Some," Sel. I. (*Tate and Powell*) **(78)**
" Some," Sel. II. (*Tate*) **(78)**

C. 745 { " Razzle-Dazzle," Sel. I. (*Darewski*) **(78)**
" Razzle-Dazzle " Sel. II. (*Darewski*) **(78)**

C. 750 { " High Jinks " Waltz (*78*)
Mayfair Dance Orchestra
My heart is sad Waltz (*Belabre*) **(78)**

C. 752 { "Jingleland," Medley of Popular Songs Part I. **(78)**
"Jingleland," Medley of Popular Songs, Part II. **(78)**

C. 753 { "Theodore & Co.," Selection I. (*Novello and Kern*) **(78)**
"Theodore & Co.," Selection II. (*Novello and Kern*) **(78)**

C. 754 { "All the Winners," Part I. **(78)**
"All the Winners," Part II. **(78)**

C. 755 { "Chu Chin Chow," Sel. I. (*Norton*) **(79)**
"Chu Chin Chow," Sel. II. (*Norton*) **(79)**

C. 771 { "Three Cheers "—Selection I. **(79)**
"Three Cheers "—Selection II. **(79)**

C. 773 { "See Saw "—Selection I. (*Novello and Braham*) **(79)**
"See-Saw "—Selection II (*Novello and Braham*) **(79)**

The figures in brackets at end of selections indicate the speed at which the records . . . . should be played . . . .

ORCHESTRAL RECORDS

MAYFAIR ORCHESTRA—*continued*

12-inch records 5s. 6d.

C. 781
{ " Young England "—Selection I. (*Clutsam and Bath*) **(79)**
" Young England "—Selection II. (*Clutsam and Bath*) **(79)**

C. 782
{ " Zig-Zag "—Selection I. (*Stamper*) **(79)**
" Zig-Zag "—Selection II. (*Stamper*) **(79)**

C. 783
{ " The Maid of the Mountains "—Selection I. (*Fraser-Simson and Tate*) **(78)**
" The Maid of the Mountains "—Selection II. (*Fraser-Simson and Tate*) **(78)**

C. 792
{ " Hanky-Panky " — Selection I. (*M. Darewski*) **(78)**
" Hanky-Panky " — Selection II. (*M. Darewski*) **(78)**

C. 794
{ " Cheep !"—Selection I. **(78)**
" Cheep !"—Selection II. **(78)**

C. 800
{ " Bubbly "—Selection I. (*Braham, Adams and Gideon*) **(79)**
" Bubbly "—Selection II.(*Braham, Adams and Gideon*) **(79)**

C. 801
{ " Suzette "—Sel. I. (*M. Darewski*) **(79)**
" Suzette "—Sel. II. (*M. Darewski*) **(79)**

C. 808
{ " Round the Map "—Fox Trot (*Finck*) **(79)**
STANLEY LOGAN
When the right girl comes along (with chorus) (*Finck*) (" Round the Map") **(78)**

C. 813
{ " The Better 'Ole "—Selection I. **(79)**
" The Better 'Ole "—Selection II. **(79)**

C. 823
{ " Carminetta "—Selection I. (*E. Lassailly, H. Finck and H. Darewski*) **(79)**
" Carminetta "—Selection II.(*E. Lassailly, H. Finck and H. Darewski*) **(79)**

C. 826
{ " John and Jonathan," Selection of British and American Airs— Part I. (arr. by *Arthur Crudge*) **(79)**
" John and Jonathan," Selection of British and American Airs—Part II. (arr. by *Arthur Crudge*) **(78)**

C. 831
{ " Arlette "—Selection I. (*Novello and Le Feuvre*) **(78)**
" Arlette "—Selection II. (*Novello and Le Feuvre*) **(78)**

C. 835
{ " The Boy "—Selection I. (*Monckton and Talbot*) **(78)**
" The Boy "—Selection II. (*Monckton and Talbot*) **(78)**

C. 840
{ " Here and There," Selection I. (*Chappelle*) **(78)**
" Here and There " Selection II. (*Chappelle*) **(78)**

C. 841
{ " Pamela," Selection I. (*Norton*) **(78)**
" Pamela," Selection II. (*Norton*) **(78)**

C. 843
{ " Any Old Thing "—Selection I. **(79)**
" Any Old Thing "—Selection II. **(79)**

C. 847
{ " The Lilac Domino "—Selection I. (*Cuvillier and Carr*) **(79)**
" The Lilac Domino "—Selection II. (*Cuvillier and Carr*) **(79)**

C. 852
{ " Yes, Uncle !"—Selection I. (*Ayer*) **(79)**
" Yes, Uncle !"—Selection II. (*Ayer*) **(79)**

C. 853
{ " The Beauty Spot "—Sel. I. (*Tate*) **(79)**
" The Beauty Spot "—Sel. II. (*Tate*) **(79)**

C. 863
{ Three Dale Dances " " Nos. I. and II. (On Yorkshire Folk Tunes) (*Arthur Wood*) (conducted by the Composer) **(79)**
" Three Dale Dances "—Nos. II. (contd.) and III. (On Yorkshire Folk Tunes) (*Arthur Wood*) **(79)**

C. 865
{ " Tails Up !"—Selection I **(79)**
" Tails Up !"—Selection II. **(79)**

C. 867
{ " Soldier Boy "—Selection I. (*Romberg, Crawford and Barrett*) **(79)**
" Soldier Boy "—Selection II. (*Romberg, Crawford and Barrett*) **(79)**

C. 874
{ "As You Were !" Selection I. (*Darewski*) **(79)**
"As You Were ! " Selection II. (*Darewski*) **(79)**

MAYFAIR DANCE ORCHESTRA

12-inch records 5s. 6d.

C. 306
{ Smiles, then Kisses (*Ancliffe*) **(78)**
Mighty like a rose—Waltz (*Nevin*) **(78)**

C. 323
{ Little grey home in the West — Valse (*Löhr*) **(78)**
Myrra—Valse Orientale (*Clutsam*, arr. by *Morette*) **(78)**

C. 336
{ Je sais que vous êtes jolie—Two-step (*Christine*) **(78)**
Maxixe Bresilienne (*Salabert*) **(78)**

C. 601
{ Black Rose—Waltz Hesitation (*Aubry*) **(79)**
Illusion—Valse Hesitation (*Nove*) **(80)**

C. 708
{ The Magic Melody—Fox Trot (*Kern*) (" We're all in it ") **(78)**
Underneath the Stars—Fox Trot (*H. Spencer*) (" We're all in it ") **(78)**

C. 750
{ My heart is sad—Waltz **(78)**
MAYFAIR ORCHESTRA
" High Jinks "—Waltz **(78)**

MENY'S ORCHESTRA

12-inch records 5s. 6d.

C. 156
{ Eton Boating Song Waltz (*Kaps*) **(78)**
Over the Waves Waltz **(78)**

C. 159
{ Post Horn Galop (*Koenig*) **(78)**
Sir Roger de Coverley Galop (*Daykin*) **(78)**

ORCHESTRAL RECORDS

METROPOLITAN ORCHESTRA

10-inch records 3s. 6d.

B. 158 {
"Tales of Hoffmann," Barcarolle (*Offenbach*) (81)
The way to the heart (*Lincke*) (81)
}

B. 233 {
Rendezvous Intermezzo (*Alletter-Komrak*) (78)
Danse Styrienne—Czardas (*Michiels*) (78)
}

12-inch records 5s. 6d.

C. 146 {
Phantom Brigade (*Myddleton*) (82)
Glow-Worm Idyll (*Lincke*) (86)
}

C. 376 {
A Hunt in the Black Forest—A Descriptive Musical Episode (*Voelker*) (78)
In a Clock Store—Descriptive Fantasia (*Orth*) (78)
}

METROPOLITAN ORCHESTRA
(conducted by DAN GODFREY)

12-inch record 5s. 6d.

C. 314 {
Prelude (*Rachmaninoff*) (79)
Kutschke Polka, Op. 155 (*Stasny*) (79)
}

NEUES TONKÜNSTLER ORCHESTER

12-inch record 5s. 6d.

C. 432 {
"Der Rosenkavalier," Walzer, I. Teil (*Richard Strauss*) (80)
"Der Rosenkavalier," Walzer, II. Teil (*Richard Strauss*) (80)
}

PALACE THEATRE ORCHESTRA
(conducted by HERMANN FINCK)

10-inch record 3s. 6d.

B. 788 {
Marche Blanche (*Finck*) (" Vanity Fair ") (79)
Some sort of somebody (Cornet solo played by Peter Wilson) (*Kern*) (" Vanity Fair ") (79)
}

12-inch records 5s. 6d.

C. 405 {
"The Passing Show of 1915 "—Selection I. (*Finck*) (78)
"The Passing Show of 1915 "—Selection II. (*Finck*) (78)
}

C. 607 {
"Bric-à-Brac "—Selection I. (*Monckton and Finck*, arr. by *Higgs*) (78)
"Bric-à-Brac "—Selection II. (*Monckton and Finck*, arr. by *Higgs*) (78)
}

C. 686 {
"My Lady Frayle "—Sel. I. (*Finck*) (78)
"My Lady Frayle "—Sel. II. (*Finck*) (78)
}

C. 766 {
The Romance of the Dragon Fly, No. I. (*Finck*) (" Vanity Fair ") (79)
The Romance of the Dragon Fly, No. II. (*Finck*) (" Vanity Fair ") (79)
}

C. 767 {
"Vanity Fair "—Selection I. (79)
"Vanity Fair "—Selection II. (79)
}

C. 810 {
Two dances from the Assyrian Scene— 1. "Cup Bearers' Dance "; 2. "Bacchanale " (*Finck*) (" Airs and Graces") (78)
Selection of Music from "Passionate Puppets "—1. "Doll Waltz "; 2. "Harlequin Motif "; 3. "Jack-in-the-Box Dance "; 4. Duet Dance "Doll and Jack " (*Finck*) (" Airs and Graces") (78)
}

PALAIS DE DANSE ORCHESTRA (BERLIN)
(personally conducted by GIORGI VINTILESCU)

10-inch record 3s. 6d.

B. 203 {
Waltz from "The Cinema Star " (*Jean Gilbert*) (78)
Two-step from "The Cinema Star " (*Jean Gilbert*) (78)
}

12-inch record 5s. 6d.

C. 277 {
Laughing Love (L'amour qui rit)—Two-step (*Christine*) (80)
Love's Dance—Two-step (*Hoschna*) (81)
}

SHAFTESBURY THEATRE ORCHESTRA

12-inch record 5s. 6d.

C. 770 {
Overture—"Three Cheers " (79) WALTER WILLIAMS and CHORUS
Don't all speak at once, little girls (*H. Darewski*) (" Three Cheers ") (79)
}

ST. MARTIN'S THEATRE ORCHESTRA

12-inch record 5s. 6d.

C. 769 {
"Houp-la !"—Selection I. (arr. by *R. S. Stoddon*)(79)
"Houp-La !"—Selection II. (arr. by *R. S. Stoddon*) (79)
}

TZIGANE ORCHESTRA (PARIS)

10-inch record 3s. 6d.

B. 126 {
Tesoro Mio (*Becucci*) (79)
Mon Etoile (*Denisly*) (79)
}

The figures in brackets at end of selections indicate the speed at which the records . . . . should be played . . . .

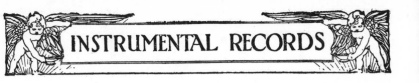

INSTRUMENTAL RECORDS

INSTRUMENTAL

ACCORDION

DEIRO, PIETRO

10-inch records 3s. 6d.

B. 510 { This is the Life—Medley (*Irving Berlin*) (79) / Italian Favourites (79)

B. 704 { Down in Chattanooga—Medley (*Irving Berlin*) (79) / International Rag (*Irving Berlin*) (79)

12-inch record 5s. 6d.

C. 762 { Romeo and Juliet—Selection (*Gounod*) (78) / Barber of Seville—Overture (*Rossini*) (78)

BAGPIPES

10-inch record 3s. 6d.

B. 135 { Highland Fling (80) / Sword Dance (80)

SMITH, PIPE-MAJOR D.

(assisted by Corpl. WHITE)

10-inch record 3s. 6d.

B. 980 { Cock o' the North / Hielan' laddie / Miss Drummond o' Perth (Highland Fling) / Reel of Tulloch (Reel) (79)

BANJO

OAKLEY, OLLY

10-inch records 3s. 6d.

B. 136 { Danse Arlequin (*Oakley*) (80) / Uncle Johnson (*Papworth*) (81)

B. 137 { Sweep's Intermezzo (*Rubens*) (81) / Matador Two-step (*Penn*) (78)

B. 138 { Oakleigh Quick-step (*Oakley*) (76) / Whistling Rufus (76)

B. 139 { Queen of Burlesque (76) / Fusilier Patrol (77)

B. 140 { Under the Double Eagle (*J. F. Wagner*) (77) / Menuet (*Paderewski*) (76)

B. 141 { Harvest Barn Dance (77) / The Dandy Fifth (*Farland*) (76)

B. 142 { Cocoanut Dance (77) / Jolly Boys March (*Sullivan*) (76)

12-inch record 5s. 6d.

C. 286 { Lancashire Clogs (*Grimshaw*) (80) / A Black Coquette (*Grimshaw*) (80)

VAN EPPS, FRED

10-inch record 3s. 6d.

B. 834 { Ragging the Scale—Fox Trot (*Claypoole*) (79) / W. H. REITZ (Xylophone) / Eldorado March (*Victor Herbert*) (79)

BELLS

10-inch record 3s. 6d.

B. 166 { Chimes of the Old Garrison Church, Potsdam (80) / The Coming of the Year (with organ) (78)

THE BELLS O' BOURNVILLE

The finest carillon in Britain. By kind permission of the Bournville Village Trust, the Cadbury Model Village.

10-inch records 3s. 6d.

B. 507 { (a) Killarney (*Balfe*) (78) / (b) Eileen Alannah (*Thomas*) (78) / (a) Blue Bells of Scotland (78) / (b) Annie Laurie (78)

B. 508 { Lead, kindly Light (tune—Sandon) (*Purday*) (78) / Harvest Home (78)

B. 509 { Huntsman's Chorus (78) / Change on 10 bells (78)

12-inch record 5s. 6d.

C. 586 { Evening bells, ¼ to 6 o'clock, introducing " The day Thou gavest, Lord, is ended " (*Scholefield*) (78) / THE TRINITY ORATORIO CHOIR / It came upon the midnight clear (*Willis*) (78)

These records should be played with " His Master's Voice " needles, sold only in boxes bearing our copyright picture, " His Master's Voice," on the lid

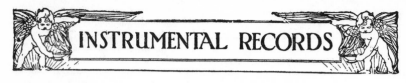

INSTRUMENTAL RECORDS

BELLS—*continued*

BORLAND and CHRIS CHAPMAN
10-inch record 3s. 6d.

B. 143 { Peal of Church Bells (**80**)
Southern Girl Gavotte (*Kremer*) (**79**)

CHAPMAN, CHRIS
10-inch record 3s. 6d.

B. 176 { Twilight Shadows (*Tobani*) (**78**)
Westminster Chimes and Big Ben (**78**)

REITZ, W. H.
10-inch record 3s. 6d.

B. 242 { Heather Bells (*Losey*) (**78**)
Dance California (*Gregory*) (**78**)

CELESTE

HOPKINS, CHARLES
10-inch records 3s. 6d.

B. 527 { O come, all ye faithful (**79**)
Hark the Herald Angels sing (**79**)

B. 700 { Lead, kindly Light (*Rev. J. B. Dykes*) (**78**)
MINSTER CHOIR
Ring out with jocund chime (*Sir F. Bridge*) (**78**)

B. 863 { Rock of Ages (**78**)
Oft in the stilly night (**78**)

CLARINET

DRAPER, CHARLES
12-inch record 5s. 6d.

C. 487 { Concertino (*Weber*) (**81**)
ELI HUDSON (Flute)
Du, du liegst mir im Herzen (You live in my heart) (*Boehm*) (**80**)

CORNET SOLOS

BRIGHT, Corporal W.
12-inch record 5s. 6d.

C. 200 { Come sing to me (*Thompson*) (**81**)
COLDSTREAM GUARDS BAND
Gipsy love Waltz (*Lehar*) (**81**)

HAWKINS, Sergeant
10-inch records 3s. 6d.

C. 107 { The rosary (*Nevin*) (**79**)
COLDSTREAM GUARDS BAND
O Sole Mio (*Di Capua*) (**80**)

B. 114 { Softly awakes my heart (" Samson and Delilah "—(*Saint-Saëns*) (**80**)
COLDSTREAM GUARDS BAND
War march of the priests (*Mendelssohn*) (**76**)

B. 116 { Take a pair of sparkling eyes(*Sullivan*) (**76**)
COLDSTREAM GUARDS BAND
" The Mikado "—Sel. III. (*Sullivan*) (**76**)

B. 117 { The lost chord (*Sullivan*) (**78**)
The distant shore (*Sullivan*) (**76**)

B. 220 { Little grey home in the west (*Löhr*) (**78**)
COLDSTREAM GUARDS BAND
Süsse Küsse, Op. 10 (*Voll tedt*) (**78**)

B. 223 { Somewhere a voice is calling (*Tate*) (**78**)
COLDSTREAM GUARDS BAND.
My little Jap two-step (*Phelps*) (**80**)

12-inch record 5s. 6d.

C. 112 { Land of hope and glory (*Elgar*) (**81**)
COLDSTREAM GUARDS BAND
Musica proibita (*Gastaldon*) (**81**)

MORGAN, Corporal G.
12-inch records 5s. 6d.

C. 402 { Il bacio (Ardili arr. by *Mackenzie Rogan*) (**80**)
COLDSTREAM GUARDS BAND
D'ye ken John Peel (Descriptive) (arr. by *Shipley Douglas*) (**80**)

C. 842 { Love's garden of Roses (*Haydn Wood*) (**79**)
Solveig's Song (" Peer Gynt " (*Greig*) (**79**)

CORNET DUETS

HAWKINS, Corporal, and WEBB
12-inch record 5s. 6d.

C. 128 { The moon hath raised (*Benedict*) (**81**)
COLDSTREAM GUARDS BAND
Evening Hymn and Last Post (*Mackenzie-Rogan*) (**82**)

MORGAN, Corporal, and BARR
12-inch record 5s. 6d.

C. 403 { The friendly rivals (*Godfrey*) (**79**)
COLDSTREAM GUARDS BAND
By the Swanee river (Descriptive) (arr. by *Myddelton*) (**79**)

The figures in brackets at end of selections indicate the speed at which the records . . . . should be played . . . .

INSTRUMENTAL RECORDS

FLUTE

HUDSON, ELI

12-inch record 5s. 6d.

C. 487 { Du, du liegst mir im Herzen (You live in my heart) (*Boehm*) (80)
  CHARLES DRAPER (Clarinet)
  Concertino (*Weber*) (81)

FLUTE DUETS

BARTON, GILBERT, and
W. GORDON WALKER

10-inch record 3s. 6d.

B. 611 { Comin' thro' the Rye (80)
  Annie Laurie (80)

HAWAIIAN GUITAR SOLO

LUVAUN

10-inch records 3s. 6d.

B. 701 { A broken Doll (*Tate*) (" Samples ") (78)
  LENSEN and THE TROCADERO ORCHESTRA
  Yaaka Hula Hickey Dula (*Goetz, Young and Wendling*) (78)

B. 703 { Yaaka Hula Hickey Dula (sung, with Guitar) (*Goetz, Young and Wendling*) (79)
  If you were the only girl (*Ayer*) (" The Bing Boys are Here ") (79)

B. 726 { Moana Waltz (*Luvaun*) (79)
  You've got to do it (sung with Guitar) (*Ayer*) (" Pell Mell ") (79)

HAWAIIAN GUITAR DUETS

LOUISE, HELEN, and
FRANK FERERA

10-inch records 3s. 6d.

B. 815 { Hawaiian Hula Medley (78)
  Pua Carnation (78)

B. 897 { Waiu Luliluli—March, (Old Hawaiian Melody) (78)
  Kai Maia O Ka Maoli—Medley March (*Kekupuohi*) (78)

LUA, PALE K., and
DAVID K. KAILI

10-inch records 3s. 6d.

B. 297 { Kilima Waltz (79)
  HawaiianWaltz Medley (Native Hawaiian Melodies) (79)

B. 529 { Kohala March (78)
  Honolulu March (78)

B. 773 { My Hula Love—Medley March (79)
  Kawaihau—Waltz (79)

OBOE

FOREMAN, ARTHUR

10-inch record 3s. 6d.

B. 389 { Drei Romanzen, No. 1 (*Schumann*) (81)
  MELVILLE GIDEON
  (American Ragtime Pianist)
  Ragtime Improvisation on Rubinstein's Melody in F (80)

ESTEY PIPE ORGAN

BIGGS, RICHARD K.

12-inch record 5s. 6d.

C. 788 { Funeral March, Op. 35, No. 2 (*Chopin*) (79)
  Estey Automatic Pipe Organ
  REGINALD L. McALL
  Hallelujah Chorus, " Messiah " (*Handel*) (79)

GRAND ORGAN

MARTIN, EASTHOPE

12-inch records 5s. 6d.

C. 270 { " Lohengrin," Prelude, Act III. (*Wagner*) (81)
  Wedding March (" Midsummer Night's Dream "—*Mendelssohn*) (81)

C. 271 { Grand Chorus in E flat, Op. 40 (*Guilmant*) (81)
  Cuckoo and Nightingale (*Handel*) (81)

C. 273 { Offertoire in E flat (*Lefébure-Wely*) (81)
  Hallelujah Chorus (" Messiah "—*Handel* (81)

C. 298 { The Lost Chord (*Sullivan*) (78)
  Communion in E, Op. 29, No. 8 (*Batiste*) (78)

C. 461 { Marche Triomphale (*Lemmens*) (78)
  Symphony in F minor (*Widor*) (78)

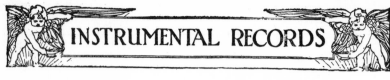

INSTRUMENTAL RECORDS

PICCOLO

HUDSON, ELI

10-inch records 3s. 6d.

B. 146 { The Electric Polka (81)
Hornpipe Medley (78)

B. 147 { Birds of the Field (*Le Thiere*) (80)
Danse des Satyrs (76)

B. 148 { Silver Birds (76)
The Wren Polka (76)

PIANOFORTE

BOURNE, UNA

10-inch records 3s. 6d.

B. 266 { Caprice (*Bourne*) (79)
Petite Valse Caprice (*Bourne*) (79)

B. 291 { Danse Créole (*Chaminade*) (79)
Pierrette (*Chaminade*) (79)

B. 353 { Callirhöe 4th Air de Ballet, Op. 37 (*Chaminade*) (78)
Valse Caprice (*Chaminade*) (78)

B. 706 { Hark ! Hark ! the Lark (*Schubert*, transcribed by *Liszt*) (79)
Interlude, Op. 152 (*Chaminade*) (79)

B. 771 { Les Sylvains (*Chaminade*) (78)
Tarantelle (*Heller*) (78)

B. 845 { Humoreske (*Bourne*) (79)
Gavotte (*Bourne*) (79)

12-inch records 5s. 6d.

C. 391 { La Fileuse, Op. 35 (*Chaminade*) (80)
Etude Romantique, Op. 35 (*Chaminade*) (78)

C. 427 { 4me Valse (*Chaminade*) (78)
Automne (*Chaminade*) (78)

C. 733 { Spinning Song (" The Flying Dutchman ") (*Wagner*) (79)
Quartet ("Rigoletto") (*Verdi*, transcribed by *Liszt*) (79)

C. 787 { Pas des écharpes (*Chaminade*) (78)
Air de Ballet (*Chaminade*) (78)

C. 839 { March (" Tannhäuser "—*Wagner*, arr. *Liszt*) (79)
Liebestod (" Tristan und Isolde "—*Wagner*, arr. *Liszt*) (79)

FORSTER, DOROTHY

10-inch records 3s. 6d.

B. 499 { Jeannette (*Dorothy Forster*) (79)
Happy Memories (*Dorothy Forster*) (79)

B. 560 { Coquette (*Dorothy Forster*) (79)
M. ZACHAREVITSCH (Violin)
Un peu d'amour (Silesu) (78)

GIDEON, MELVILLE

(American Ragtime Pianist)

10-inch record 3s. 6d.

B. 389 { Ragtime Improvisation on Rubinstein's Melody in F (80)
ARTHUR FOREMAN (Oboe)
Drei Romanzen No. I. (*Schumann*) (81)

PIANOFORTE ACCOMPANIMENTS

FOR SOPRANO

10-inch record 3s. 6d.

B. 822 { Still as the night—in D flat (*Bohm*) (79)
All through the night (Old Welsh Song)—in B. flat (79)

FOR SOPRANO OR TENOR

10-inch records 3s. 6d.

B. 713 { The Rosary—in D flat (*Nevin*) (79)
A Perfect Day—in C (*Jacobs-Bond*) (79)

B. 715 { Down in the Forest—in E (*Landon Ronald*) (79)
O dry those tears—in A (*Teresa del Riego*) (79)

B. 717 { Until—in G (*Sanderson*) (79)
Little grey home in the West—in E flat (*Löhr*) (79)

B. 719 { Somewhere a voice is calling—in G (*Tate*) (79)
Parted —in B flat (*Tosti*) (79)

B. 721 { I hear you calling me—in C (*Marshall*) (79)
Because—in C (*Guy d'Hardelot*) (79)

B. 821 { Wait—in G (*Guy d'Hardelot*) (79)
The Green Hills o' Somerset—in E flat (*Eric Coates*) (79)

12-inch records 5s. 6d.

C. 723 { Beloved it is morn—in F (*Aylward*) (79)
Good-bye—in A flat (*Tosti*) (79)

C. 795 { I'll sing thee songs of Araby—in A flat (*Clay*) (79)
Where my caravan has rested—in A flat (*Löhr*) (79)

C. 796 { O Lovely Night—in D flat (*Landon Ronald*) (79)
Any place is heaven if you are near me—in E flat (*Löhr*) (79)

C. 797 { She wandered down the mountain side—in E flat (*Clay*) (79)
Solveig's Song (" Peer Gynt ")—in A minor (for Soprano) (*Grieg*) (79)

The figures in brackets at end of selections indicate the speed at which the records • • • • should be played • • • •

INSTRUMENTAL RECORDS

PIANOFORTE
ACCOMPANIMENTS—*continued*
FOR SOPRANO OR TENOR—*continued*
12-inch record 5s. 6d.

C. 836 { Roses of Picardy—in D (*Haydn Wood*) (79)
Love's Garden of Roses—in B flat (*Haydn Wood*) (79)

FOR CONTRALTO
10-inch record 3s. 6d.

B. 824 { Still as the night—in B flat (*Bohm*) (79)
All through the night (Old Welsh Song)— in G major (79)

FOR CONTRALTO OR BARITONE
10-inch records 3s. 6d.

B. 714 { The Rosary—in B flat (*Nevin*) (79)
A Perfect Day—in F (*Jacobs-Bond*) (79)

B. 716 { Down in the Forest—in B flat (*Landon Ronald*) (79)
O dry those tears—in E (*Teresa del Riego*) (79)

B. 718 { Until—in D flat (*Sanderson*) (79)
Little grey home in the west—in B flat (*Löhr*) (79)

B. 720 { Somewhere a voice is calling—in D (*Tate*) (79)
Parted—in F (*Tosti*) (79)

B. 722 { I hear you calling me—in G (*Marshall*) (79)
Because—in A flat (*Guy d' Hardelot*) (79)

B. 823 { The green hills o' Somerset—in C (*Eric Coates*) (79)
Wait—in E flat (*Guy d' Hardelot*) (79)

12-inch records 5s. 6d.

C. 724 { Beloved, it is morn—in C (*Aylward*) (79)
Good-bye—in E flat (*Tosti*) (79)

C. 798 { O 'lovely night—in B flat (*Landon Ronald*) (79)
Daddy—in F (*Behrend*) (79)

FOR BARITONE OR BASS
10-inch record 3s. 6d.

B. 825 { Father O'Flynn—in A flat (arr. by *Chas. V. Stanford*) (79)
Ho! Jolly Jenkin (" Ivanhoe ")—in D (*Sullivan*) (79)

TUBAPHONE
MILLER, A.
10-inch record 3s. 6d.

B. 149 { Boulanger March (76) (Tubaphone)
Carnival of Venice (78) (Xylophone)

TYMPANON
VOTITCHENKO, SACHA
(with pianoforte accompaniment)
10-inch record 3s. 6d.

B. 285 { Douleur, Part I. (*Votitchenko*) (79)
Douleur, Part II. (*Votitchenko*) (79)

VIOLIN
DE GROOT
10-inch records 3s. 6d.

B. 772 { La Paloma (*Yradier*) (78)
Sérénade, " Millions d'Arlequin," Suite de Ballet (*Drigo*) (79)

B. 814 { Auld Robin Gray (Old Scotch Song) with pianoforte and organ accompaniment (78)
Bonnie Mary of Argyle (Old Scotch Song) (with pianoforte and organ accompaniment) (78)

B. 846 { Intermezzo (" Cavalleria Rusticana ") (*Mascagni*) (with pianoforte and organ accompaniment) (78)
Ave Maria (*Gounod*) (with pianoforte and organ accompaniment) (78)

B. 878 { Träumerei (*Schumann*) (78)
Miss HELEN SEALY
The Bonnie Banks of Loch Lomond (Traditional) (78)

FELLOWES, HORACE
10-inch records 3s. 6d.

B. 310 { (*a*) Charlie is my darling ; (*b*) Stirling Castle ; (*c*) Timour the Tartar (78)
(*a*) Ye banks and braes ; (*b*) Marquis of Huntley—Highland Fling ; (*c*) De'il amang the tailors—Reel (78)

B. 388 { (*a*) Flowers o' the forest ; (*b*) Stumpie Strathspey ; (*c*) The Mason's Apron Reel (arr. by *Alfred Moffat*) (78)
FRANZ VON VECSEY (Violin)
Träumerei (*Schumann*) (76)

INSTRUMENTAL RECORDS

VIOLIN—*continued*

FELLOWES, HORACE—*continued*

12-inch record 5s. 6d.

C. 488 { Scotch Fantasia (*a*) Auld Robin Gray ; (*b*) Duncan Gray (arr. by *Sainton*) (80)
TIVADAR NACHEZ (Violin)
Träumerei (*Schumann*) (78)

HAYWARD, MARJORIE

10-inch records 3s. 6d.

B. 705 { Canzonetta, Op. 6 (*d'Ambrosio*) (79)
La Serenata (Angel's Serenade) (*Braga*) (79)

B. 748 { L'Extase (*Thomé*) (79)
Madrigale (*Simonetti*) (79)

B. 853 { Spring Song (*Mendelssohn*) (79)
HELEN SEALY
Romance (*Rubinstein*) (79)

12-inch record 5s. 6d.

C. 722 { Henry VIII. Dances—(*a*) (Morris Dance (*German*) (79)
Henry VIII. Dances—Shepherd's Dance (*German*) (79)

LAW, MARY

12-inch records 5s. 6d.

C. 802 { (*a*) Moment Musical(*Schubert*) ; (*b*) Mazurka (*Wieniavski*) (79)
7th Concerto, Op 76—Ist Movement (*De Beriot*) (79)

C. 873 { Adagio religioso from 4th Concerto (*Vieux-temps* (79))
Fantasie ou scène de ballet, Op. 100 (*De Bériot*) (79)

NACHEZ, TIVADAR

12-inch record 5s. 6d.

C. 488 { Träumerei (*Schumann*) (78)
HORACE FELLOWES (Violin)
Scotch Fantasia (*a*) Auld Robin Gray ; (b) Duncan Gray (arr. by *Sainton*) (80)

SEALY, HELEN

10-inch records 3s. 6d

B. 858 { Romance (*Rubinstein*) (79)
Miss MARJORIE HAYWARD
Spring Song (*Mendelssohn*) (79)

B. 878 { The Bonnie Banks of Loch Lomond (Traditional) (78)
DE GROOT
Träumerei (*Schumann*) (78)

VIOLIN—*continued*

VON VECSEY, FRANZ

10-inch record 3s. 6d.

B. 388 { Träumerei (*Schumann*) (76)
HORACE FELLOWES (Violin)
(*a*) Flowers of the Forest ; (*b*) Stumpie Strathspey ; (*c*) The Mason's Apron Reel (arr. by *Alfred Moffat*) (78)

ZACHAREVITSCH, M.

10-inch records 3s. 6d.

B. 517 { The Sunshine of your Smile (*Ray*) (78)
(*a*) Dance of Ivan Ivanovitch (*Zacharewitch*) (78)
(*b*) A Don Cossacks' Dance (*Zacharewitch*) (78)

B. 560 { Un peu d'amour (*Silesu*) (78)
Miss DOROTHY FORSTER (Piano)
Coquette (*Dorothy Forster*) (79)

B. 578 { Sextet, " Lucia di Lammermoor " (unacc.) (*Donizetti*, arr by *St. Lubin*) (79)
Berceuse, Op. 16 (*Faure*) (79)

VIOLIN AND PIANOFORTE DUETS

HAYWARD, MARJORIE, and UNA BOURNE

12-inch records 5s. 6d.

C. 844 { Kreutzer Sonata I., First movement (*Beethoven*) (79)
Kreutzer Sonata II., Andante, with variations, Part I (*Beethoven*) (79)

C. 854 { Kreutzer Sonata III., Andante, with variations, Part II. (*Beethoven*) (79)
Kreutzer Sonata IV., Finale (*Beethoven*) (79)

VIOLONCELLO

BOURDON, ROSARIO

10-inch record 3s. 6d.

B. 664 { The Broken Melody (*Van Biene*) (78)
Silver threads among the gold (*Danks*) (79)

The figures in brackets at end of selections
indicate the speed at which the records
. . . . should be played . . . .

INSTRUMENTAL RECORDS

XYLOPHONE

MILLER, A.

10-inch record 3s. 6d.

B. 149 { Carnival of Venice (78) (Xylophone)
Boulanger March (78) (Tubaphone)

REITZ, W. H.

10-inch records 3s. 6d.

B. 177 { Zallah (An Egyptian Intermezzo)(*Loraine*)
(81)
The Waterfall Polka (*Stobbs*) (81)

B. 834 { Eldorado March (*Victor Herbert*) (79)
FRED VAN EPS (Banjo)
Ragging the Scale — Fox Trot (*Claypoole*) (79)

TRIOS

MURRAY'S RAGTIME TRIO
(acc. by the MAYFAIR ORCHESTRA)

12-inch record 5s. 6d.

C. 399 { Beets and Turnips—Fox Trot (78)
Hors d'œuvres—Fox Trot (78)

NEAPOLITAN TRIO

10-inch records 3s. 6d.

B. 633 { O sole mio (Neapolitan Serenade) (*di Capua*) (7)
Across the still lagoon (*Loge*) (79)

B. 680 { Idyll, Op. 134 (*Theo. Lack*) (78)
Fedora Gavotte (*Lapetino*) (78)

B. 774 { I hear you calling me (*Marshall*) (78)
VENETIAN TRIO
Little grey home in the West (*Löhr*) (78)

B. 857 { Addio a Napoli (Farewell to Naples) (78)
VENETION TRIO
Forget-me-not—Intermezzo (Op. 22)
Allen Macbeth) (78)

HUDSON, OLGA, ELGAR
and ELI

(Flute, Celeste, Piano and Orchestra)

12-inch records 5s. 6d.

C. 446 { The sunshine of your smile (*Ray*) (78)
MARION BEELEY
The Call of the Homeland (*Teschemacher*)
(78)

C. 489 { Angels guard thee (*Godard*) (80)
Youth and Love (*Saker*) (81)

TRIOS—*continued*

ORGAN, CELESTE AND BELLS

10-inch record 3s. 6d.

B. 272 { O come, all ye faithful (78)
Hark! the Herald Angels sing (78)

VENETIAN TRIO

10-inch records 3s. 6d.

B. 355 { Berceuse de Jocelyn (*Godard*) (78)
Humoreske (*Dvorak*) (78)

B. 561 { Love's dream after the ball (*Czibulka*) (78)
FLORENTINE QUARTET
Melody of Love, Op 600 (*Engelmann*) (78)

B. 774 { Little grey home in the West (*Lohr*) (78)
NEAPOLITAN TRIO
I hear you calling me (*Marshall*) (78)

B. 857 { Forget - me - not—Intermezzo (Op. 22)
(*Allen Macbeth*) (78)
NEAPOLITAN TRIO
Addio a Napoli (Farewell to Naples) (78)

QUARTETS

FLORENTINE QUARTET

10-inch records 3s. 6d.

B. 467 { Narcissus from " Water Scenes " (*Ethelbert Nevin*) (78)
BIRD RECORD
Actual Bird Record made by a Captive
Nightingale (80)

B. 561 { Melody of Love, Op. 600 (*Engelmann*) (78)
VENETIAN TRIO
Love's dream after the ball (*Czibulka*) (78)

MURRAY'S SAVOY QUARTET

10-inch records 3s. 6d.

B. 575 { Every morn you'll hear them say " Goodnight " (*Tierney*) (80)
Hide and seek (*Comer*) (80)

B. 576 { I like to dance with the girls (*Ayer*) (80)
They didnt believe me (*Kern*) (" To-night's
the Night ") (80)

B. 577 { We'll have a jubilee in my old Kentuck
home (*Donaldson*) (80)
Oh, man, you'd hang around (*Ayer*)
(80)

B. 692 { You've got to do it (*Ayer*) (" Pell Mell ")
(79)
Since Chumley came back from London
Town (*Ayer*) (" Bric-à-Brac ") (79)

INSTRUMENTAL RECORDS

QUARTETS—*continued*

MURRAY'S SAVOY QUARTET—*continued*
10-inch records 3s. 6d.

B. 702
- Down home in Tennessee—Fox Trot (*Donaldson*) **(80)**
- The Kipling Walk—One-step (*Ayer*) ("The Bing Boys are here") **(80)**

B. 725
- Where did Robinson Crusoe go with Friday on Saturday Night—One-step or Fox Trot (*Meyers*) **(80)**
- If you were the only girl—Fox Trot (*Ayer*) ("The Bing Boys") **(80)**

B. 813
- Fancy you fancying me (*Lee and Weston*) **(79)**
- Hello! Hawaii, how are you? (*Schwartz*) **(79)**

B. 830
- Oh! how she could Yacki, Hacki, Wicki Wacki Woo (*Von Tilzer*) **(79)**
- They're wearin' them higher in Hawaii **(79)**

SAVOY QUARTET

(Vocalist : JOE WILBUR.)
10-inch records 3s. 6d.

B. 847
- Welcome, Honey, to the old plantation home (*Gumble*) **(79)**
- How's ev'ry little thing in Dixie? (*Gumble*) **(79)**

B. 859
- Hullo! my dearie (*Stamper*) ("Zig-Zag") **(79)**
- Where the black-eyed Susans grow (*Whiting*) ("Cheep!") **(79)**

B. 867
- What do you want to make those eyes at me for? (*McCarthy, Johnson and Monaco*) **(79)**
- Beware of Chu Chin Chow **(79)**

B. 879
- Mammy's little coal-black Rose (*R. A. Whiting*) **(79)**
- He may be old, but he's got young ideas (*Johnson, Gerber and Jentes*) **(79)**

B. 890
- Over There (The Great American War Song) (*Cohan*) **(79)**
- Oh, boy! when you're home on leave (*Ayer*) **(79)**

QUARTETS—*continued*

SAVOY QUARTET—*continued*
10-inch records 3s. 6d.

B. 896
- Down Texas Way (*Godfrey, Mills and Scott*) **(79)**
- For me and my gal (*Meyer*) ("Here and There") **(79)**

B. 905
- You oughtn't to do it, when you don't belong to me (*Carlton and Whidden*) **(78)**
- Honey, will you miss me? (*Wilbur and Rice*) **(79)**

B. 914
- Hello! New York (*Ayer*) ("The Bing Boys on Broadway") **(79)**
- Widows are wonderful (*Ayer*) ("Yes, Uncle!") **(79)**

B. 962
- The wild women are making a wild man of me (*Piantadosi*) **(79)**

B. 985
- I don't want to get well (*H. Jentes*) **(79)**
- Some Sunday morning (*Whiting*) **(79)**
- Indian rag (*Ayer*) **(79)**

THE VERSATILE FOUR

12-inch records 5s. 6d.

C. 645
- Circus day in Dixie (*Gumble*) **(80)**
- Araby (*Irving Berlin*) **(80)**

C. 654
- Winter Nights (*Schwartz*) **(79)**
- Down Home Rag (*Sweatman*) **(79)**

SEXTET

THE SIX BROWN BROTHERS
(Saxophone)

10-inch record 3s. 6d,

B. 526
- The Moaning Saxophone Rag **(79)**
- VAN EPS TRIO (Banjo, Piano & Drum)
- The Original Fox Trot (*Klickmann*) **(79)**

☐ ☐ ☐ ☐ ☐

The figures in brackets at end of selections
indicate the speed at which the records
. . . . should be played . . . .

NEW RECORDS

"His Master's Voice" RECORDS

AUGUST 1914

12-inch Records 5s. 6d.; 10-inch 3s. 6d.

Orchestral

BERLIN PHILHARMONIC ORCHESTRA
(conducted by NIKISCH)

12-inch Records, 5s. 6d. each.

040790	Fifth Symphony—Finale, Part III.	*Beethoven*
040791	Fifth Symphony—Finale, Part IV.	*Beethoven*

THIS month's issue of records brings to a conclusion the set which together covers the whole of the wonderful Fifth Symphony. We have already had the three complete movements— the 1st Movement Part I., the 1st Movement Part II., and the Scherzo, as well as a portion of the Finale. The remaining portion of the Finale is dealt with in the present two records.

Again in these records do we remark the delicate and poetical precision of the maestro Nikisch in the soft passages that lead to the Presto. The definition of those celebrated pianissimos is superb, alike in the

Nikisch

actual performance and in the reproduction. The entire movement carries but few fortissimo pages; the Finale, following without break on the Scherzo, pursues an even tenor of attractively - flowing themes. A modulatory passage for the entire orchestra takes us to a striking second subject which chains the attention; this is given out by violins, bassoons and clarinets. With the foregoing thematic material we hear the working-out of the last movement. There is an increase in animation as we approach the end, and the final Presto seems to us an expression of peaceful happinesss after troublous journeying.

The importance of being able to have in the home the complete colossal Fifth Symphony, played by a world-famous organisation, and (more important still) conducted by the genius-leader Nikisch himself, cannot be over-estimated.

How many millions have flocked to the world's concert halls since Beethoven's time in order to enjoy this inspired musical poem, it would be impossible to say. Yet now, how many millions can have this enjoyment at any time, and without the trouble of a visit to a perhaps distant capital! "His Master's Voice" Gramophone has accomplished nothing more wonderful than this crystallization of the masterpiece of a genius. (*Speed 78*)

Ballads

Mr. JOHN McCORMACK (tenor)
(with orchestral accompaniment)
10-inch Record, 4s. 6d.

4-2378   **Genevieve**   *Tucker*

John McCormack

WHEREVER a tuneful tenor song is appreciated, "Genevieve" is still a great favourite. Its cloying strains are known the world over, and its sentiment never fails to go home, no matter how often heard. Such a song as this, John McCormack can sing perhaps better than any other modern vocalist. The great Irishman throws a wealth of feeling into its rendition, and brings out the rare beauty of the ballad. The lines

"I bless the hour when first we met,
The hour that gave me love and thee"

are voiced with the ardour and fire we know McCormack to be master of, yet the note of tenderness is maintained to the end. One of the great tenor's most admirable efforts of late. (*Speed 77*)

O Genevieve I'd give the world
To live again the lovely past!
The rose of youth was dew impearl'd,
But now it withers in the blast.
I see thy face in ev'ry dream,
My waking thoughts are full of thee;
Thy glance is in the starry beam
That falls along the summer sea.
O Genevieve, sweet Genevieve,
The days may come, the days may go,
But still the hands of mem'ry weave
The blissful dreams of long ago.
Fair Genevieve, my early love,
The years but make thee dearer far!
My heart shall never, never rove;
Thou art my only guiding star.
For me the past has no regret,
Whate'er the years may bring to me;
I bless the hour when first we met,
The hour that gave me love and thee!
O Genevieve, etc.   (*George Cooper*)

Words printed by permission of the publishers, Messrs. Boosey & Co.

Sir GEORGE HENSCHEL (bass)

(with pianoforte accompaniment by himself)

10-inch Record, 4s. 6d.

7-42006   **Das Wandern**   *Schubert*

Henschel

NOW that it has been possible to collect the opinions of the Press generally upon the Birthday Honours bestowal of a Knighthood upon Henschel, one sees clearly the wonderful prestige this truly great artist has built up. No finer tribute to Henschel could be conceived than the fact that the Knighthood is regarded as much as an honour to *music* as a fitting recognition of the life-work of a great musician.

Once again we have the pleasure to be able to offer a record of German lieder by Sir George Henschel —one of Schubert's most lovely songs. The fascinating air is sung with the artistry we all know belongs so peculiarly to the great Anglo-German; the voice is as remarkable as ever, and the self-accompaniment is as accomplished as in the previous records by the master-bass.   (*Speed 78*)

Mr. HUBERT EISDELL (tenor)
(with pianoforte and violin accompaniment)
12-inch Record, 5s. 6d.

02526   **Speak**   *Tosti*

Hubert Eisdell

A DOUBLY welcome return of that favourite of favourites, Mr. Hubert Eisdell. Again we present the light tenor in a love-song, and again does he delight every ear with the intensity of his feeling and the striking warmth of vocal colouring.

Throughout the song there is no diminishing of the fervour with which the opening verse — "Speak with those eyes of thine"—is delivered. One is carried on, entranced, to the lovely final bars, which are breathed in Eisdell's purest notes. Effect is added to the record by the apt, errant appearance of a violin obbligato to the pianoforte accompaniment.

(Speed 78)

Published by Messrs. G. Ricordi & Co.

Miss ALICE LAKIN (contralto)
(with pianoforte, organ and celeste accompaniment)
10-inch Record, 3s. 6d.

2-3025   **Just**   *Bradford*

A DELICIOUS little morceau, which is rendered particularly telling through its quaint terseness. The exquisite tenderness of Miss Alice Lakin's noble contralto is used in the rendition with great taste and feeling, and the song receives remarkably fine treatment.

A fine effect is gained by the change of melody at the last verse, the full beauty of which is brought out in this splendid record.   *(Speed 78)*

Published by Messrs. Metzler & Co.

Miss EVELYN HARDING (soprano)

(with pianoforte accompaniment)
12-inch Record, 5s. 6d.

03381   **Spring's Awakening**   *Sanderson*

Evelyn Harding

A TALE of the sweetness of life, sweetly sung by Miss Evelyn Harding whose first record, published last month, was warmly received.

The new young soprano brings us a fresh, pure voice with a pleasing timbre. She has a happy manner of singing, and is very well suited by a swinging, bright ballad like Sanderson's "Spring's Awakening." There's a world of understanding in this rendering, which is instinct with the beauty of the quaint little verses. Miss Harding's voice "records" cleanly and sweetly, and the reproduction is everything that could be desired artistically.   (*Speed 79*)

Come along, come along, life is so sweet,
Gather the flowers that bloom at your feet,
Blossoms will fade away ere the year's gone ;
Winter's before us, so dreary and long.
       Ah !

Smile when your troubles come, they will away,
Troubles won't last if you smile ev'ry day ;
For the sun shines behind ev'ry cloud in the sky ;
And the lilt of a laugh smothers many a sigh.
       Ah !
       Come along, etc.
       Ah !

Lift up your eyes to the dawn coming through,
Bringing a new world for me and for you ;
Birth of the sunshine, the shadows have gone,
A new world is breaking away into song.
       Ah !
       Come along, etc.
       Ah !   (*Maud Cunningham*)

Words printed by permission of the publishers, Messrs. Boosey & Co.

Miss GERTIE DICKESON (soprano)

(with pianoforte accompaniment)

10-inch Record, 3s. 6d.

2-3026   **Our Land of Dreams**   *Thompson*

Miss Gertie Dickeson

WE all nod off into the land of dreams at times! So listen to the song of one who is just from that fairy land. The singer is our *débutante* of July, Miss Gertie Dickeson, who is, although a *débutante* to the record world, an established favourite on the concert platform.

She sings to us with a considerable amount of sincerity, and maintains a velvetiness of tone that secures the most earnest hearing. The final passage with its message of hope is quite strikingly done.   *(Speed 79)*

Oft in my dreams I linger
In a fairy land,
Where once we wandered, dearest,
Hand in hand.
Birds sang their joyous song,
Flow'rs decked our way,
No thought of care had we
That happy day.
Come back and meet me in that land of dreams,
Where skies are always blue and sunshine gleams;
There I will tell you of my love so true;
Come back to that dear land, that once we knew.

And in that land of dreams no other face I see,
Once more I hear sweet words
You said to me.
My heart cries out in vain,
My tears must fall,
Dearest, come back to me.
You are my all!
Come back and meet me in that land of dreams,
Where skies are always blue and sunshine gleams;
There I will tell you of my love so true;
Come back to that dear land,
I wait for you!
(Jack Thompson)

Words printed by permission of the publishers, Messrs. Enoch & Sons.

Mr. ROBERT RADFORD (bass)

(with pianoforte accompaniment)

12-inch Record, 5s. 6d.

02525 **Sombre Woods**   *Lully (arr. by A. L.)*

Robert Radford

A FINE record of a very fine song, which is also well known under the French title, "Bois Epais." Not for many a long day have we been able to enjoy the profound beauty of Radford's majestic lower register so much as here; the song is one which would lose one half of its effect in the hands of a moderately good singer. The master-art and magnificent organ of Radford are matched by the intensity of feeling which the author has tried to convey to us. England's greatest basso achieves a really remarkable performance here, and he is heard in gloriously fine voice.

The recording of this great bass voice is notably good, and as a reproduction this will vie with the best.   (*Speed 79*)

Sombre woods, ye glades dark and lonely,
Where midnight gloom enters only,
Oh! hide my slighted love
In your unbounded night.

If now this broken heart
Never more may enfold her,
If no more these eyes may behold her,
Then evermore I hate the light.
                   (*Theo. Marzials*)

***Words** printed by permission of the publishers, Messrs. Boosey & Co.*

Mr. HARRY DEARTH (bass)

(with pianoforte accompaniment)

12-inch Record, 5s. 6d.

02533   ### Joe the Gipsy   *Batten*

Harry Dearth

ROLLICKING Harry Dearth makes us catch the spirit of devil-may-care in his new record of Batten's " Joe the Gipsy." He rolls out the merry autobiography in his most breezy style : you can hear every word too.

That rattling chorus goes with tremendous *entrain*, you can just imagine yourself " under the wide blue sky." The popular baritone gets many a smile into his lines. You are with him all the time !

Unexpectedly comes a new phase. The reticent reference to the loved one who has gone before, is portrayed very sympathetically by the accomplished baritone. An admirable example of the all-round art of Mr. Harry Dearth.   *(Speed 78)*

Of course, you know I'm Gipsy Joe,
  For ev'ryone knows me.
I've jest and joke for all good folk
  Wherever I chance to be.
My pockets are bare, I haven't a care,
  I live as the Romanys do,
If I find a good fowl on my nightly prowl,
  Well, what does it matter to you ?

Ha, ha ! ho, ho ! A rollicking cove am I,
  None so gay and free,
  Happy as can be,
  Under the wide blue sky.
  I fear no foe
  Wherever I may go,
For Gipsy Joe am I.

I make a call at Court or Hall,
  P'r'aps I'm asked to tea,
I help myself from pantry shelf
  To the choicest bits there be.
If luck is mine, on the best I dine,
  A partridge, poult or hare,
Then my wares I sell and fortunes tell
  For the good cheer I get there.

'Twas long ago at Walthamstow,
  The fair was on that day,
That Gipsy Nan danced near my van
  And stole my heart away,
Oh ! never you'd meet a lass so sweet,
  Such tender laughing eyes,
Now oft at night when stars are br'ght
  I see them in the skies,
And I lay a rose when no-one knows,
  There where my dear one lies.
    (G. Hubi-Newcombe)

Words printed by permission of the publishers, Messrs. Enoch & Sons

"His Master's Voice"

ERNEST CRAMPTON and
MARJORIE VERNON

of the

CRAMPTON CONCERT PARTIES

(with pianoforte accompaniment)

10-inch Record, 3s. 6d.

2-4190   Great-Grandmamma

Crampton

"Seven Gavotte Songs," No. 4

Ernest Crampton

A NOTHER one of the series of aptly-named " Gavotte Songs" which have made these seaside concert-parties famous.

The present number deals deftly with old-world loves and fancies, and musings and yearnings. It is offered as a duet by the clever chief soprano of the party, Miss Marjorie Vernon and the author-composer himself, Mr. Crampton.

(Speed 79)

Years ago, when this old, old world was young,
Love you know, so the amorists have always sung,
Ruled the land, with a bow and arrow in his hand,
But to-day, Cupid's put his shafts away.

If you'd been your great-gran'-pa-pa,
And liv'd quite long ago,
Would you have been just as you are ?
Oh I I often long to know,
And if I'd been my great-gran'mamma,
I think I'd have caught your eye,
Great-gran'mamma loved great-gran'-pa-pa,
And I often wonder why.

You and I, now this world is cold and grey, soon will fly,
On wings, but not of love they say ;
Aeroplanes, though they're taxing the inventors' brains,
Are a bore, if Cupid's going to fly no more.

(E. Crampton)

Words printed by permission of the publishers, Messrs. Cary & Co.

CRAMPTON GAVOTTE SONG RECORDS PREVIOUSLY ISSUED			
No. I. "A Hundred Years Ago" *(Crampton)*	10-inch	3s. 6d.
No. II. "Lack-a-day" *(Crampton)*	12-inch	5s. 6d.
No. III. "An Old Spinet" *(Crampton)*	10-inch	3s. 6d.
No. VII. "An Old-World Garden" *(Crampton)*	12-inch	5s. 6d.

10

LIGHT OPERA COMPANY

(with orchestral accompaniment)

12-inch Record, 5s. 6d.

04552   **Gems from " The Night Birds " ("Die Fledermaus ")**   *Strauss*

SPARKLING vocal gems from Strauss' melodious and original musical play which is better known to many as "Die Fledermaus." One of the most astonishing vocal performances in our catalogue is that of Selma Kurz in the Czardas from "Die Fledermaus" (Record No. 043180, 12-inch, 9s.).

The merry members of the Light Opera Company score a rousing success in their combined singing of these gems.   (*Speed 79*)

THE MINSTER SINGERS

(with orchestral accompaniment)

12-inch Record, 5s. 6d.

04589   **Sea Songs**

(introducing "Sailing," "Larboard Watch," "Rocked in the Cradle of the Deep," "Life on the Ocean Wave," "Asleep in the Deep," "Nancy Lee," "Anchored")

HERE is a real novelty which will appeal to sea-lovers and all mankind. The best-loved old sea-songs such as "Asleep in the Deep," "Rocked in the Cradle of the Deep," "Larboard Watch" and so on have been worked into a coherent medley of infectious melody, and the rendition of the pot-pourri is breezily done by the Minster Singers. As an original record it can be recommended to everyone.   (*Speed 78*)

Mr. TOM CLARE

(with pianoforte accompaniment by himself)

12-inch Record, 5s. 6d.

02535   **Souvenirs**   *Clare*

Tom Clare

BY his piano and Tom Clare. That piano, that eye-glass, and that Tom —well, what a trio ! To lovers of vaudeville they bring up a whole crop of—we were going to write " remembrances," but " Souvenirs " will be more apropos seeing that Tom has favoured you by making a record of his song of that name for August. This quaint little number gives us the popular entertainer in his very best vein, and the recording leaves nothing to be desired—every word audible. Altogether a very bright contribution.

If you are one of the millions that are going to the " briny " during the holiday month, don't fail to take Tom Clare's record of " Souvenirs " with you ! It will ensure a mirthful holiday !   (*Speed 77*)

Published by Messrs. Reynolds & Co.

Instrumental

VIOLIN

Miss MARIE HALL

(with pianoforte accompaniment)

10-inch Record, 3s. 6d.

3-7974 **Canzonetta, Op. 6** *d'Ambrosio*

A BEAUTIFULLY broad violin piece by d'Ambrosio, played with that serene beauty of bowing that has lifted Marie Hall into her position of pre-eminence among English violinists. The splendour of her art is reflected in the delightfully easy thing she makes of this work—the art which conceals art. Her tone is deliciously broad and fulsome, distinctive as is all of this artist's playing. Of the composition itself it can be said that the Canzonetta is a lilting piece which one will play over and over again out of enthusiasm for the sheer sweetness of it.

(Speed 78)

Marie Hall

Capt. Mackenzie Rogan
(Senior Bandmaster of the British Army)

NEW
DOUBLE-SIDED
RECORDS

Bands

BAND OF H.M. COLDSTREAM GUARDS
(conducted by Capt. J. Mackenzie Rogan, M.V.O., Mus. Doc., Hon. R.A.M.)

12-inch double-sided Record, 5s. 6d.

C 359
{ **Sizilietta—Serenade**   *von Blon*
Published by Hawkes & Son
Turkish Idyll   *S. V. Hays*
Published by Boosey & Co.

IN the promotion of Dr. Mackenzie Rogan to a captaincy, the army honours itself and its greatest musician, as well as its greatest band. The Senior Bandmaster of the British Army can well be proud of the splendid honour.

Two very fine programme pieces are published this month in record form in "Sizilietta" and the "Turkish Idyll." The woodwind have excellent opportunities here, and well do they take advantage of them. *(Speeds 79)*

10-inch double-sided Record, 3s. 6d.

B 255
{ **Colonel Bogey—March**   *Alford*
Youth and Vigour—March   *Lantenchläger*
Published by Hawkes & Son

A COUPLE of scintillating marches that make the blood course through the veins. We all know by now what a march can be when performed by the Coldstreamers under Rogan, and these two are among the finest on the catalogue. *(Speeds 80)*

METROPOLITAN BAND

12-inch double-sided Record, 5s. 6d.

C 357 {
Peg o' my heart—One-step or Turkey Trot   *Fischer*
Horse Trot—One-step or Turkey Trot   *Davies*

"PEG O' MY HEART" is one of the biggest successes of the year, and it makes a fine band record. "Horse Trot" is quaint and original.
(*Speeds 78*)

MAYFAIR ORCHESTRA

(conducted by HERMAN FINCK)

12-inch double-sided Record, 5s. 6d.

C 358 {
Two little Dances—A la Minuette, A la Gavotte
(From the "Tapestry Scene" in "THE PASSING SHOW" Revue)   *Finck*
Valse Joyeuse   *Finck*
Published by Hawkes & Son

THE smartest Revue of the summer is perhaps "The Passing Show," which is packing the Palace Theatre nightly. Among the jewels of orchestral music played (and composed) by Herman Finck is this number, comprising two charming little dances. It is a record you will long remember. The "Valse Joyeuse" is altogether sweet.   (*Speeds 78*)

Herman Finck

JACOBS AND HIS TROCADERO ORCHESTRA

12-inch double-sided Record, 5s. 6d.

C 373 {
A Tango Dream   *Maxwell*
Published by Enoch & Sons
Smiles then Kisses—Waltz   *Ancliffe*
Published by Hawkes & Son

A DOUBLE-SIDED record that ought to sell in tens of thousands. Look at the titles! Elsa Maxwell's fascinating "A Tango Dream" and Ancliffe's "Smiles then Kisses." The playing of Jacobs and his men is wonderful.   (*Speeds 80*)

"His Master's Voice"

The Splendid JULY RECORDS

ORCHESTRAL—12-inch Records, 5s. 6d.

BERLIN PHILHARMONIC ORCHESTRA
(Conducted by Herr ARTHUR NIKISCH)

040788	Fifth Symphony—Scherzo and Part I. Finale	(*Beethoven*)
040789	Fifth Symphony—Finale Part II.	*do*

VOCAL—12-inch Record, 6s. 6d.

02527	By the Waters of Babylor	Sir George Henschel

12-inch Records, 5s. 6d.

053264	Mi chiamano Mimi "La Bohême," Act I.	Mme. Claudia Muzio
02518	All hail, thou dwelling lowly, "Faust"	Charles W. Harrison
02524	Pals	Harry Dearth
04584	Gems from "The Prince of Pilsen"	Light Opera Company

10-inch Record, 4s. 6d.

2–3015	Carmena (Vocal Waltz)	Mme. Alma Gluck

10-inch Records, 3s. 6d.

2–3011	Twickenham Ferry	Miss Lucy Marsh
4–2460	A Wild, Wild Rose	Hubert Eisdell
2–3024	Come, for it's June	Miss Evelyn Harding
4–2461	Rosa Machree	Stewart Gardner
4–2447	Tom Bowling	John Harrison
4–2444	Donnegan's Daughter	Charles Tree
2–3020	Bird of Blue	Miss Paola St. Clair
2–3022	Bonny Blue Kerchief	Miss Gertie Dickeson
2–4195	An Old Spinet "Seven Gavotte Songs," No. 3	
	Ernest Crampton and Marjorie Vernon of the	
		Crampton Concert Parties

INSTRUMENTAL

VIOLIN—12-inch Record, 6s. 6d.

07985	Praeludium	Kreisler

'CELLO—12-inch Record, 5s. 6d.

07879	Silver threads among the gold (with orchestral accomp.)	W. H. Squire

DOUBLE-SIDED RECORDS

12-inch Record, 5s. 6d.

C 361	Aubade Printanière Under the Stars March	} Mayfair Orchestra

10-inch Records, 3s. 6d.

B 254	On Jhelum River—Only a Rose On Jhelum River— Ashoo at her Lattice	The Band of H.M. Coldstream Guards (Cond. by Capt. Dr. J. Mackenzie Rogan)
B 231	Puppchen—Two-step Intermezzo When love creeps in your heart	} Jacobs and His Trocadero Orchestra
B 232	Crickets' Serenade Dance of the Songbirds	} Metropolitan Orchestra
B 233	Rendezvous Intermezzo Czardas	} Metropolitan Orchestra

'His Master's Voice' RECORDS

SEPTEMBER 1914

12-inch Records 5s. 6d.; 10-inch 3s. 6d.

Orchestral

NEW SYMPHONY ORCHESTRA
(Conducted by Mr. LANDON RONALD)

12-inch Record, 5s. 6d.

0852   Pizzicato from "Sylvia"   *Délibes*

Photo: Dover Street Stud.os.

D ÉLIBES, prince of ballet-writers, lived and
   worked in the troublous times of the Franco-
   Prussian wars that scarred the Continent over
forty years back. It was in 1870 that he produced in

Landon Ronald

Photo by   Claude Harris

Paris his ballet "Coppélia" which made his reputation.

The tragic events of the war were an interruption, as is the present conflict, to the success of these lighter-hearted entertainments, and there was an interval of six years before the composer brought out his second ballet.

"Sylvia" is not less delightful than "Coppélia." "My 'Swan Lake' is poor stuff compared with 'Sylvia'," wrote Tchaikovsky. "Nothing during the last few years has charmed me so greatly as this ballet and 'Carmen.'"

Délibes shows himself in "Sylvia" delightfully creative and artistic, a trait usually not found in works appertaining to the dance. He introduced art into a style of composition which in its highest form calls for art above all else: before Délibes one had seen nothing of art in dance-music.

The New Symphony Orchestra probably perform the favourite "Pizzicato" movement with greater virtuosity than any other musical body in the world. The delicacy of the swinging passages for strings is brought out in masterly fashion and the performance, as produced on this record, is unapproachable. Lovers of orchestral playing will find in this number a lovely specimen of Landon Ronald's genius in interpreting, and a fascinating jewel of composition.

(Speed 79)

Celebrity

McCORMACK and KREISLER

(with pianoforte accompaniment)
12-inch Record, 9s.

02540   **Angel's Serenade**   *Braga*

ALTHOUGH we have previously issued a record of the "Angel's Serenade" (by Alma Gluck and Zimbalist), we have no hesitation in offering a fresh version of it by

McCormack and Kreisler listening to this actual record on "His Master's Voice" Cabinet Grand Instrument.

Photo:
Underwood & Underwood.

such international celebrities as McCormack and Kreisler. We believe that the many who acquired the soprano record of the piece will one and all buy the new record, for this latter is, if possible, even more wonderful. The cloying melody is perfectly suited to the luscious tone-colour of McCormack, who is here heard in his very finest voice.

And when it is added that the obbligato is poured forth by no less a hand than that of Kreisler, one can understand that here is a record that stands alone in its sphere of music.   (*Speed 78*)

Ballads

Mr. STEWART GARDNER (baritone)

(with pianoforte accompaniment)

12-inch Record, 5s. 6d.

02532   **My Lady's Bower**   *Temple*

Stewart Gardner

THE poetic feeling instilled into this lovely song is such as we could expect from few living artists : and to say that it is characteristic of Mr. Stewart Gardner's work is to give it the highest praise.

The interesting verses are sung with sympathetic power ; pleasing restraint is noticed in the more narrational parts. The final disclosure is given with real grandeur and impressiveness. That noble baritone quality which makes Mr. Gardner's voice among the best loved of to-day, is in abundance throughout this admirable record.   (*Speed 78*)

Thro' the moated grange at twilight,
  My love and I we went,
By empty rooms and lonely stairs,
  In lovers' sweet content,
And round the old and broken casement
  We watch'd the roses flow'r,
But the place we lov'd the best of all
  Was call'd "My Lady's Bower."

And with beating hearts we enter'd,
  And stood and whisper'd low
Of the sweet and lovely lady
  Who liv'd there years ago !
And the moon shone in upon us
  Across the dusty floor,
Where her little feet had wander'd
  In the courtly days of yore.

And it touch'd the faded arras,
  And again we seem'd to see
The lovely lady sitting there,
  Her lover at her knee.
And we saw him kiss her fair white hand,
  And, oh ! we heard him say :
" I shall love thee, love, for ever,
  Tho' the years may pass away !
I shall love thee for ever,
  Tho' the years may pass away ! "

But then they vanish'd in a moment,
  And we knew 'twas but a dream,
It was not they who sat there
  In the silver moon-light gleam !
Ah ! no, 'twas we, we two together,
  Who had found our golden hour,
And told the old, old story
  Within "My Lady's Bow'r.

              (*Frederic E. Weatherly*)

Words printed by kind permission of the publishers, Messrs. Boosey & Co.

Mr. HARRY DEARTH (bass)

(with pianoforte accompaniment)

12-inch Record, 5s. 6d.

02534
(a) **The Sandwich Man**
(b) **The Fortune Hunter**—Song Cycle
"**Bow Bells**"
Willeby

THIS fine new song-cycle, "Bow Bells," contains vivid *clichés* of London life. Who better fitted than London-born Harry Dearth to put them into song?

The verses are terse, quaint, clever, full of true observation. Dearth's finely-produced bass is used with the acme of expressiveness in bringing out the beauty of the music. His diction, as usual, is beautifully clear, and the record is a little masterpiece. (*Speed 79*)

Harry Dearth

THE SANDWICH MAN

Up an' down the street I goes
Advertisin' pleasure shows,
In the drizzlin' dampin' rain,
Down the street an' back again.

Grumblin' to meself all day,
Toilin' on while others play,
Watchin' folks go smiling by,
Feelin' blue an' wond'rin' why.

Then she brings my can o' tea,
Lizzie does an' talks to me,
An' I know though folks look fine,
None has got a lass like mine !
(*Dorothy Dickinson*)

THE FORTUNE HUNTER

Lunnon is a big place,
Lots o' people in it,
Heaps o' folks a-toilin'
Every single minute ;
Everybody's movin',
Comin' or a-goin',
Sort o' makes me giddy—
Takes a lot o' knowin'.

Lunnon is a fine place,
Often 'mid its noises
Think about the country
And the quiet voices ;
Dream about a cottage,
Lips that wait to kiss me.
Hear the children's laughter—
Wonder if they miss me.

Down the street the flower girls
Lilac sprays are sellin',
Makes me think in passin'
How the country's smellin' ;
Have to stop and buy some—
(Wish my heart would harden !)
Just because the lilac
Grows in mother's garden.
(*Dorothy Dickinson*)

Words printed by kind permission of the publishers, Messrs. Boosey & Co.

Miss EVELYN HARDING (soprano)

(with pianoforte accompaniment)

10-inch Record, 3s. 6d.

2-3023   **The Fairy Pipers**   *Brewer*

Evelyn Harding

THRICE unhappy the one whose ears will not hear the pipes of the fays these sunny days. Who can resist Evelyn Harding's joyous appeal to "come out and listen"? This deservedly popular song is sung by our new light soprano with all the joyousness and lilt that are the essentials of the song itself. The charming artist imparts her delightful personality to the sprightly ballad, and the resulting record is a joy indeed. *(Speed 79)*

When all the birds are gone to sleep,
  And all the frogs are still,
If you would hear the fairy pipes
  Come out upon the hill.

  Come out! come out! listen on the
    air!
  Up there! down there! playing
    ev'rywhere!
  Oh hark! oh hear! don't you hear
    the tune?
  Airy fairy pipers underneath the
    merry moon?

They'll play to you of Cupid's tricks,
  Of lovely queens and kings,
Of fights and fun and politics,
  And lots of other things.

  Oh hark! oh hear! can't you hear
    them play?
  Up there! down there! till the
    break of day!
  Oh hark! oh hear! don't you love
    the tune?
  Airy fairy pipers underneath the
    silver moon!

But if you doubt that this can be
  And question what I say,
You'll never hear the melody
  The fairy pipers play.

Then come! come out! listen while you can,
Up there! down there! since the world began.
Oh hark! oh hear! oh, the happy tune!
Airy fairy pipers underneath the silver moon!
    Come! Come!   *(Weatherly)*

Words printed by kind permission of the publishers, Messrs. Boosey & Co.

Miss ALICE LAKIN (contralto)

(with organ and orchestral accompaniment)

12-inch Record, 5s. 6d.

03384   **The Promise of Life**   *Cowen*

THIS classic song, of which we already possess a record by Mme. Clara Butt, is here very finely sung by Miss Alice Lakin in the black-label series. The haunting beauty of Cowen's immortal music, to which are so aptly wedded the eloquent words of Clifton Bingham, is brought out memorably by the great, round, striking vocal organ of this renowned contralto, who excels herself. The recording leaves nothing to be desired.   (*Speed 79*)

> There is no song, of all our hearts are singing,
>> But has some note whose haunting sadness grieves ;
> There is no rose, of all the year is bringing,
>> But has some thorn, unseen amid the leaves.
> There is no garden but some weed encloses,
>> There is no day but hath its hour of pain ;
> Yet still we sing and gather earth's bright roses,
>> Walk in its garden and forget the rain !
>>> Sing on, O heart, although the tears may glisten,
>>>> Gather life's flowers, although the rain be rife ;
>>> Earth is not all—His angels ever listen,
>>>> Heaven shall make perfect our imperfect life.
>
> There are no eyes whose light has ne'er been blinded
>> By silent tears of pity or of pain ;
> There is no heart that has not been reminded
>> By some chance word of what comes not again.
> There is no life that hath not held some sorrow,
>> There is no soul but hath its secret strife ;
> Still our eyes smile, our hearts pray for to-morrow,
>> Fair in its promise of more perfect life !
>>> Smile on, sweet eyes, although the pathway darken,
>>>> Pray on, O heart, amid the busy s rife ;
>>> Earth is not all—His angels ever hearken,
>>>> Heaven shall make perfect our imperfect life.
>>>>> (*Clifton Bingham*)

Words printed by kind permission of the publishers, Messrs. Boosey & Co.

Elsie Baker

Miss ELSIE BAKER and
Mr. FREDERICK WHEELER

(with orchestral accompaniment)

12-inch Record, 5s. 6d.

(by permission of Messrs. Chappell & Co., Ltd.)

04115 The day is done *Löhr*

Frederick Wheeler

HERMANN LÖHR has finely set to music these restful verses from Longfellow's "Hiawatha," and we have succeeded in obtaining a beautiful duet record of the morceau by Miss Baker and Mr. Wheeler, whose duet work is renowned the world over.

The singing of both these artists is marked with excellent feeling and strength. It would not be possible to better the interpretation. The fragrant closing lines of this excerpt were used by us a summer or two ago with a striking Simpson poster. *(Speed 80)*

The day is done, and the darkness
Falls from the wings of Night,
As a feather is wafted downward
From an eagle in his flight.
Come, read to me some poem,
Some simple, heartfelt lay,
That shall soothe this restless feeling,
And banish the thoughts of day.

Such songs have power to quiet
The restless pulse of care,
And come like the benediction
That follows after prayer.
Then read from the treasured volume—
The poem of thy choice,
And lend to the rhyme of the poet
The beauty of thy voice.

And the night shall be filled with music,
And the cares that infest the day
Shall fold their tents, like the Arabs,
And as silently steal away.

(Longfellow)

Words printed by kind permission of the publishers, Messrs. Chappell & Co., Ltd.

NEW RECORDS

Mr. HUBERT EISDELL (tenor)

(with celeste and violin accompaniment)

10-inch Record, 3s. 6d.

4-2446 **My Memories** *Tosti*

A SWEET lyric which will leave the most fragrant memories with all happy enough to hear the record. It represents one of Mr. Eisdell's best efforts for some months, and is a really delightful specimen of tenor singing. The artist's middle register is heard to unusual advantage. His tone is beautifully mellow, while the well-known Eisdell *timbre* is recorded perfectly.

By-the-by, this popular singer is an officer in the Royal Naval Reserve, and is now serving with our gallant fleet. *(Speed 79)*

Published by Messrs. G. Ricordi & Co.

MISS ETHEL LEVEY

(with orchestral accompaniment)

12-inch Record, 5s. 6d.

03385 {Goodbye Summer, " So Long " Fall, Hello, Wintertime !} *Wenrich*

A N international favourite sings us a song of international fame. The air is haunting, and the Queen of Revue invests the verses with all that piquant personality which still draws packed houses to the London Hippodrome these days of war and high temperatures. As a record it is one of Ethel Levey's brightest efforts. This means much.

(Speed 79)

Humorous

GEORGE ROBEY
(with orchestral accompaniment)
12-inch Record, 5s. 6d.

02538   The Witness   *Wick*

George Robey

Published by Messrs. Francis, Day & Hunter

THE Prime Minister of Mirth will lose his Cabinet rank if he doesn't keep out of these specious professions. This month he is actually a professional marriage-witness! Of course we — we — of course we know that—er —criminals are not allowed to carry canes that go "swish"—but nevertheless we hope and trust the Witness will not extend his Sessions experience further.

Seriously (if one *can* be serious in speaking of the Arch-Humorist) Robey is "killing" in this new outburst. Hear it, and relieve the tension of these days of war by a long, long laugh.

(Speed 78)

TOM CLARE
(with pianoforte accompaniment)
12-inch Record, 5s. 6d.

02536   I've seen it on the pictures   *Clare*

THE title conjures up many a humorous picture episode we have all seen at the "Palaces" of Light and Darkness. Tom Clare discursively treats his piquant subject with the easy, sure, but clean, humour with which his performances of Songs at the Piano are associated. His singing is smart and his self-accompaniment most clever. *(Speed 79)*

SHACKLETON
off to the Pole

ø

Explorer takes "His Master's Voice" Gramophone with him

Sir Ernest Shackleton is now on the high seas in his good ship the *Endurance* on his way to the Antarctic. He intends to cross Antarctica from sea to sea.

Before sailing he had an audience of the King and formally offered himself for service in the Fleet. His Majesty. however, prefers that the expedition be proceeded with, so important is its work.

As with his previous Polar voyage, Sir Ernest takes a gramophone and a bright lot of records with him to cheer the weary months in the snow-bound regions.

Capt. Mackenzie Rogan
(Senior Bandmaster of British Army)

NEW

DOUBLE-SIDED

RECORDS

Bands

BAND OF H.M. COLDSTREAM GUARDS

(conducted by Capt. J. Mackenzie Rogan, M.V.O., Mus. Doc., Hon. R.A.M.)

12-inch double-sided Record, 5s. 6d.

C 368

Yankiana, American Suite
—The Song of the Bells
—Mighty America

Yankiana, American Suite
—Arrival of the Coon-
town Cadets   *Thurban*

A PICTURESQUE work which calls up memories of the characteristics of the New World. Much of it is in the patriotic strain and is impressive music. The finest military band on earth, under Capt. Mackenzie Rogan, achieve an astonishingly fine performance in this record. (*Speeds 78*)

Published by Messrs. Boosey & Co.

METROPOLITAN BAND

10-inch double-sided Record, 3s. 6d.

B 259 { Who paid the rent for Mrs. Rip van Winkle?—Medley
Sympathy Waltz *Friml*

THE quaint interrogative title, "Who paid the rent for Mrs. Rip van Winkle?" covers a song which has stormed the American continent and has already captured several army corps of admirers on this side. The tune is alluring and quickly remembered, and will be whistled everywhere to-morrow. The waltz is unusually pretty. *(Speeds 79 & 78)*

JACOBS AND HIS TROCADERO ORCHESTRA

10-inch double-sided Record, 3s. 6d.

B 257 { When Mr. Moon is shining (from "Mam'selle Tra-la-la") *Gilbert*
My little Persian Rose *Friedland*

TWO of the "hits" of the day, rendered in Jacobs' own characteristic way. The cloying harmonies of the violins are most effective. The well-known Moon-song from the Lyric Theatre success "Mam'selle Tra-la-la" is an especially fine bit of playing. *(Speeds 80)*

Published by Messrs. Feldman & Co.

METROPOLITAN ORCHESTRA

12-inch double-sided Record, 5s. 6d.

C 374 { Military Symphony—Allegretto *Haydn*
Military Symphony—Allegro *Haydn*

TWO of the most stirring movements of Haydn's well-known Military Symphony, given with great understanding and the utmost impressiveness. At a time when war is the one topic of conversation among European peoples this double-sided record should be very acceptable. *(Speeds 79)*

METROPOLITAN ORCHESTRA

10-inch double-sided Record, 3s. 6d.

B 256 {**Marche Namur** *Richards*
{**La Riterata—Italian March** *Drescher*

HERE is a record of the greatest topicality. The great fortress Namur is greatly in the public eye at present. Italian sympathies in the war seem to be all on the side of their fellow-Latins, and the Riterata March is welcome just now. Both titles are stirring, and are finely played. (*Speeds 78*)

Published by Messrs. Hawkes & Son

10-inch double-sided Record, 3s. 6d.

B 260 {**All aboard for Dixieland—Turkey Trot** *Cobb*
{**Ninette—One or Two-step** *Christine*

THE finest and newest Turkey Trot tune is the inviting "All aboard for Dixieland." It is one of the very greatest successes of the day. Ninette is an alluring two-step. Grand playing.
(*Speeds 80 & 79*)

PATRIOTIC RECORDS

A small selection from our Special Brochure bearing the flags of the Allies in colour

VOCAL

Madame CLARA BUTT
(with the Guards' Band)

These two records are accompanied by the Band of H.M. Coldstream Guards, conducted by Captain J. Mackenzie Rogan, M.V.O., Mus. Doc., Hon. R.A.M.
12-inch Record, 6s. 6d.
03240 God save the King
12-inch Record, 12s. 6d.
03239 Land of Hope and Glory   *Elgar*

MARCEL JOURNET
12-inch Record, 9s.
032038 La Marseillaise   *de L'Isle*

Mr. THORPE BATES
10-inch Record, 3s 6d.
4-2147 The Admiral's Broom   *Bevan*
12-inch Records, 5s. 6d.
02228 The Midshipmite   *Adams*
02312 The Deathless Army   *Trotere*

Mr. PETER DAWSON
10-inch Record, 3s. 6d.
4-2229 The Blue Dragoons
Kennedy Russell

Mr. HARRY DEARTH
12-inch Records, 5s. 6d.
02230 A Sergeant of the Line   *Squire*
02291 My Old Shako   *Trotere*
02465 They all love Jack   *Adams*

Mr. STEWART GARDNER
02284 Danny Deever   *Damrosch*

Mr. ROBERT RADFORD
10-inch Record, 3s. 6d.
4-2319 Drake goes West   *Sanderson*
12-inch Record, 5s. 6d.
02399 When the King went forth to War
Koenemann

Mr. ROBERT HOWE
12-inch Record, 5s. 6d.
02464 A Soldier's Song   *Mascheroni*

Mr. R. KENNERLEY RUMFORD
12-inch Record, 5s. 6d.
02198 Three for Jack   *Squire*

Mr. CHARLES TREE
12-inch Record, 5s. 6d.
02507 Up from Somerset   *Sanderson*

CHURCH CHOIR (Mixed)
Solo by Mr. THORPE BATES
10-inch Record, 3s. 6d.
4910 The National Anthem

CHORUS OF LA SCALA OPERA, MILAN
10-inch Record, 3s. 6d.
54564 Soldiers' Chorus ("Faust")   *Gounod*

HARRY LAUDER
12-inch Record, 5s. 6d.
02478 Ta-ta, my bonnie Maggie darling

LEWIS WALLER
10-inch Record, 3s. 6d.
1443 The Charge of the Light Brigade
Tennyson

BANDS

BAND OF H.M. COLDSTREAM GDS.
Conducted by Captain J. Mackenzie Rogan, M.V.O., Mus. Doc., Hon. R.A.M.
10-inch double-sided Records, 3s. 6d.
B 105 { God save the King
       { God bless the Prince of Wales
                       Brinley Richards
B 106 { La Marseillaise   *de L'Isle*
       { Rule Britannia   *Arne*
B 118 { Trooping the Colour
       { In a Clockmaker's Shop
       { La Czarine (composed for the last
B 102 { ceremonial visit of the Czar of
       { Russia to Paris)   *Ganne*
       { La Mattchiche   *Borel Clerc*
       { Regimental Marches of the Brigade
B 112 { of Guards
       { March Past of the Lancashire
       { Brigades
12-inch double-sided Records, 5s. 6d.
C 130 { 1812 Overture   *Tschaikowsky*
       { Zampa Overture   *Herold*
       { Review of the Brigade of Guards,
C 297 { Part 1.
       { Review of the Brigade of Guards,
       { Part 2.
       { (Held in Hyde Park, April 28, 1913)
C 112 { Land of Hope and Glory   *Elgar*
       { Musica Proibita   *Gastaldon*

DESCRIPTIVE

GRAMOPHONE BAND
10-inch Record, 3s. 6d.
2-108 Departure of a Troopship

Get your copy of the Patriotic List

'His Master's Voice' RECORDS

OCTOBER 1914

12-inch Records 5s. 6d. ; 10-inch 3s. 6d.

Orchestral
NEW SYMPHONY ORCHESTRA
(conducted by LANDON RONALD)

12-inch Record, 5s. 6d.

0833   **Danse Persane (Persian Dance)**   *Guiraud*

Landon Ronald

Photo by   Claude Harris

THE accomplished New Symphony Orchestra, under their world - renowned leader, Landon Ronald, have now given the world of music a veritable library of the classics, from which hardly any important page is missing. All the great classical overtures, symphonies, suites, marches, tone-poems are enshrined for to-morrow and the great thereafter : difficult indeed is it to realise the stupendous truth of this, but every musician should bring himself to grasp this fact and avail himself of the huge stores of orchestral gems that are at his hand.

"His Master's Voice"

A little out of the beaten track is this month's offering, Guiraud's Danse Persane. It is a most vivid piece of writing, alive with Eastern colour, palpitating with Oriental feeling. The performance is unforgettably delicate and the tonal beauty of the record altogether rare. *(Speed 78)*

LONDON SYMPHONY ORCHESTRA
(conducted by NIKISCH)

12-inch Record, 5s. 6d.

2-0502 **Nozze di Figaro—Overture** *Mozart*

Nikisch

MOZART'S Marriage of Figaro, with its merry plot and music, is one of the most delightful of comedy operas. The complications of the story, the quick changes of mood and the sparkling humour are all well reflected in music of an exceedingly interesting kind. In no other single opera, perhaps, is there such a succession of musical gems as in Figaro. Each is perfect in its way and each seems to enhance the beauty of the others.

The overture, written in true Mozartian style, is a delightful one. It is one of the best-known items on modern concert programmes, and indeed it must be admitted that it fully deserves its popularity.

We present a particularly brilliant version of it played by no less a body than the London Symphony Orchestra under the leadership of the *maestro* Nikisch. The reproduction is well worthy of the enthralling performance given. *(Speed 79)*

2

THE SYMPHONY ORCHESTRA
(conducted by Sir EDWARD ELGAR)

12-inch Record, 5s. 6d.

2-0511   Pomp and Circumstance March, Cp. 29   *Elgar*

(introducing " Land of Hope and Glory ")

Sir Edward Elgar

AT a time when patriotism is welling up in the breast of every British-born citizen, Elgar's super-patriotic suite is doubly welcome, especially a performance conducted by the great composer himself.

In "Pomp and Circumstance" Elgar reaches great heights of national feeling. The patriotism of the artist shows itself as vividly in this work as in his acceptance, despite his age, of an active part in protective work during the war : Sir Edward Elgar has become a Special Constable in Hampstead.

That thrillingly broad march-melody now known to every British ear, "Land of Hope and Glory," is played with unspeakable breadth of tone and majesty by these fine players directed by Elgar. No one can listen without experiencing feelings of noble patriotism, such is the nature of its immediate appeal. Every Britisher should possess this unique record. (*Speed 79*)

Published by Messrs. Boosey & Co.

Previously issued
ELGAR ORCHESTRAL RECORD
12-inch, 5s. 6d.
0967   **Carissima**   *Elgar*
Conducted by the Composer

Ballads

DESTINN (soprano)

(with orchestral accompaniment)
12-inch Record, 12s. 6d.

2-053104   **Gioconda**—*Suicidio!* (*Suicide Only Remains!*)
Act IV. (*Sung in Italian*)   Ponchielli

Destinn

L A GIOCONDA is a work of great beauty, full of wonderful arias, duets and ensembles, with fine choral effects and a magnificent ballet. The book is founded on Hugo's " Tyrant of Padua," and tells a most dramatic story, which, however, cannot be called inviting, as the librettist has crowded into it nearly all the crimes he could think of !

This great air for *Gioconda* is from the final act, which represents a ruined palace on an island in the Adriatic, with Venice visible in the distance. To this desolate island *Gioconda* has managed to bring the unconscious *Laura*, in an endeavour to save her from the vengeance of her husband. As the curtain rises two men are carrying the insensible form into the ruin. As they depart for Venice, *Gioconda* asks the men to seek out her mother, whom she fears never to see again. Left alone, she approaches the table, looks fixedly at a glass of poison, and begins her terrible song, one of the most dramatic of the numbers in Ponchielli's work.

Mme. Destinn's *Gioconda* is one of the greatest impersonations of the rôle ever witnessed. She delivers this great final air of the opera with dramatic power, singing it, as she always does the music of Ponchielli's work, with superb effect.   (*Speed 78*)

Published by Messrs. Ricordi & Co.

Mr. JOHN McCORMACK (tenor)

(with male chorus and orchestral accompaniment)

10-inch Record, 4s. 6d.

4-2472   Come where my Love lies dreaming   *Foster*

IRELAND'S song-genius has this month the collaboration of a male chorus for his song "Come where my Love lies dreaming," and wonderfully effective is the combination. The loveliest tones of McCormack are lavished in profusion on this idyllic number, and one could hear the record a thousand times without tiring of it. With what fire he vocalises the passionate lines! How velvety is that tone! A really charming record.

(Speed 80)

John McCormack

SOME SPECIALLY FINE RECORDS BY OUR WORLD-FAMOUS NATIVE TENOR

12-inch Records, 9s.

2-052022	Furtiva lagrima, Una ("Elisir d'Amore") *In Italian*	*Donizetti*
2-052021	Racconto di Rodolfo ("Boheme") *In Italian*	*Puccini*

12-inch Records, 6s. 6d.

02244	Come back to Erin	*Claribel*
02323	Evening Song, An	*Blumenthal*
02327	In a Persian Garden—Ah! moon of my delight	*Lehmann*
02400	Maire, my girl	*Aitken*
02324	She is far from the land	*Lambert*

10-inch Records, 6s.

7-52033	Dai campi, dai prati ("Mefistofele")	*Boito*
7-52032	Mi par d'udire ancora	*Bizet*

10-inch Records, 4s. 6d.

4-2326	At Dawning	*Cadman*
4-2076	I hear you calling me	*Marshall*
4-2215	Silver threads among the gold	*Danks*
4-2070	When shadows gather	*Marshall*

Mme. ALMA GLUCK (soprano)

(with pianoforte accompaniment)

10-inch Record, 4s. 6d.

3980   Will o' the Wisp   *Spross*

Alma Gluck

MANY concert-goers will remember the sensationally successful interpolation of this little morceau at the Gluck-Zimbalist concert in the late Spring at the Albert Hall. All hearts had been captured by the brilliant performance of the Angel's Serenade (in which Mr. Zimbalist, the new Benedict, played the obbligato) and the enthusiastic audience clamoured for an encore piece.

The pretty gossamer-gowned soprano took recall after recall before consenting to reappear with the accompanist. Then—Will o' the Wisp !—and with such success was it sung that we at once determined to record it. It is Alma Gluck at her daintiest.

(Speed 79)

Published by Messrs. The John Church Co.

Miss JULIA CULP (mezzo-soprano)

(with orchestral accompaniment)

10-inch Record, 4s. 6d.

2-3027 **All through the night** *Old Welsh Air*

LOVERS of vocal music of two Continents are agreed that the greatest exponent of *lieder* to-day (now that Henschel has retired) is **Miss** Julia Culp.

This gifted mezzo-soprano is of Dutch birth, having been born at The Hague, Holland. She made her first appearance at a concert in Magdeburg in 1903, and is now everywhere acclaimed Queen of Lieder-singers.

Not only does she sing these old ballads in their original language, but she sings in English also, and without accent. Her lusciously round, resonant voice is of remarkable warmth and colouring, and the expression conveyed into the rendering of this fine old Welsh air is enchanting. A notable first record of an artist of world-fame.

Miss Culp now lives at Zehlendorff, a suburb of Berlin, where she has a charming Dutch home. She loves her native land, however, and every summer spends ten days as a special guest of the Queen at Het Loo. The Queen Mother of Holland has been a patroness of the artist for many years.

The editor has heard Miss Culp many times, but feels that her singing can best be described by famous critics.

"The exquisite art of Miss Culp, her power of colouring her voice, of spinning out a pianissimo to the barest thread of silver, of sending out a fortissimo with splendid dramatic power, of giving expression to the most delicate of sentiments, was beautifully exhibited in her songs by Schubert, Strauss and Brahms." "Miss Culp is a Dutch woman, but most English-speaking singers might well go to school to her."

(Speed 78)

Mr. HUBERT EISDELL (tenor)

(with pianoforte accompaniment)

10-inch Record, 3s. 6d.

4-2442   I don't suppose   *Trotère*

Hubert Eisdell

OUR popular light tenor, who is serving his King and Country, fortunately made a set of records before mobilising, and we are able to give the delight of his singing month by month to his host of admirers, though the artist is no longer near us.

It takes but little effort of the imagination to believe that he *is* with you when you hear this charming record "I don't suppose," one of Trotère's most finished lyrics. The glorious middle voice is used freely and with exquisite effect. A beautiful little record.   (*Speed 79*)

I don't suppose the gift meant much to you—
Your parting gift to me—an opening flow'r ;
To you 'twas but a rose-bud sweet with dew,
     It's life—an hour !

I don't suppose the gift cost much to give—
A touch of hands, a glance, a fleeting smile ;
A whispered hope in sweetness it might live
     A little while !

That you would care, if ever you should know,
Not even in my dreams do I suppose !
Still one sweet mem'ry sets the past aglow—
     It is a rose,
     A faded rose !
        (Leslie Cooke)

Words printed by kind permission of the publishers, Messrs. J. B. Cramer & Co., Ltd.

Mr. STEWART GARDNER (baritone)
(with pianoforte accompaniment)
10-inch Record, 3s. 6d.

4-2475   **Beloved, at your feet**   *Chumleigh*

AN intense love-song of the type that brilliant Stewart Gardner knows how to bring close to your heart. His noble voice comes from the horn with the maximum of effect, and his ringing top notes are a joy.

The verses are prettily set and form a charming little cameo, as it were. The master-artist who delivers them enjoys the singing, surely ; else he could not impart such fervency to every line. (*Speed 79*)

> Beloved, at your feet I lay a gift
>   Of roses red and lilies passing fair,
> Oh ! lift them to your lips when I am gone,
>   And let them linger for a moment there.
> Beloved, in your hands I lay my life,
>   For good or ill, oh ! hold it for a space,
> And I will strive to go a nobler way,
>   And make it worthy of its dwelling-place.
> Beloved, to your heart I give my love,
>   Oh ! smile on it, be pitiful to me,
> And it shall blossom there like some young rose,
>   In perfect beauty through eternity.
>   (*Ed. Teschemacher*)

Words printed by kind permission of the publishers, The Newman Publishing Co.

Miss MARION BEELEY (contralto)
(with organ and pianoforte accompaniment)
12-inch Record, 5s. 6d.

03383   **The Call of the Homeland**   *Teschemacher*

A FINELY-proportioned ballad of Teschemacher, the sentiment of which is especially welcome now, when everyone's heart is warmed more than ever to the Homeland. Miss Marion Beeley's striking contralto is heard to great advantage in these tuneful verses, and the effect of the organ and piano accompaniment is excellent. This is a record which should attain considerable popularity, for do we not all " feel it night and day—the call of the Homeland " ?

                  (*Speed 80*)

Published by Messrs. Boosey & Co.

Mr. ROBERT RADFORD (bass)

(with pianoforte accompaniment)

10-inch Record, 3s. 6d.

4-2494   ### Shipmates o' Mine   *Sanderson*

Robert Radford

OUR great bass has happily chosen a song of the waves for October. Sanderson's "Shipmates o' mine" will find an echo in every breast now that Jack is doing such magnificent work in sweeping and cleansing the seas.

Mr. Robert Radford's God-given organ has never been heard more richly and with more pleasing resonance than here. The tone is especially true to life, and the recording generally above praise. A really exceptional record.   (*Speed 80*)

Tell me, tell me, where are you sailing,
　Shipmates o' mine ?
The morn is cold and the great winds are wailing,
　Shipmates o' mine !
"Forth we must go," their brave words are falling,
"Forth to the new land that ever is calling ! "
Fortune attends you there ! good luck go with you !
　Shipmates o' mine !

Tell me, tell me, where are you roaming,
　Shipmates o' mine ?
O'er blue seas or where the grey waves are foaming,
　Shipmates o' mine ?
Never a message, oh ! tell us your story,
All Fate has given you, sorrow or glory ;
Send us one word, for our lone hearts are waiting,
　Shipmates o' mine !

Tell me, tell me, where are you sleeping,
　Shipmates o' mine ?
Down, deep down, where no rough tide is leaping,
　Shipmates o' mine !
There in your slumber the great guns you're hearing,
Over your heads the proud ships are steering,
Till the trumpet shall sound, and your Captain shall wake you,
　Shipmates o' mine !

(*Ed. Teschemacher*)

Words printed by permission of the publishers, Messrs. Boosey & Co.

Instrumental

Miss MARIE HALL (violin)
(with pianoforte accompaniment)
10-inch Record, 3s. 6d.

3-7973   **La Précieuse**   *Kreisler*

L A PRÉCIEUSE is one of Kreisler's favourite
works (he arranged Couperin's score for the
violin) and it is high praise to be able to say
that Marie Hall's characteristic interpretation of it is
as fine as any we have heard.   The noble beauty of
tone, masterly bowing, complete sense of rhythm—
withal the poetical feeling instilled into the morceau—all
these belong to Miss Marie Hall's superb gifts.

Published by Messrs. Schott & Co.   (*Speed 78*)

Mr. PERCY GRAINGER (piano)
12-inch Record, 5s. 6d.

05554   **Toccata**   *Debussy*

W E are proud to be able to
offer first records of Australia's greatest instru-
mental son, Mr. Percy Grainger,
who, during the thirty or so years
of his life, has achieved renown
in many continents. He now tours
the European continent regularly,
fulfilling over 100 engagements
annually in Holland, Scandinavia,
Switzerland, and Germany. He
played by command before Queen
Alexandra at Buckingham Palace,

Photo   Holman & Paget

and before the Danish Court in 1905.   In this superb
" Toccata " of Debussy's composition, one finds an incomparable beauty of touch and tone, striking definition and intense poetical feeling. The recording
expert has surpassed himself in the clarity and the
fidelity of the reproduction.   (*Speed 79*)

Published by Messrs. Fromont

Popular Lyric

GEORGE CARVEY

(with orchestral accompaniment)

12-inch Record, 5s. 6d.

02539　　　**Why don't you love me?**

Mayer—Haines—Waid

M R. GEORGE CARVEY, who was such a popular member of the famous Gaiety Theatre Company which has recently been broken up, has made a great hit with this song in a special Gramophone Sketch he has been showing at the London Pavilion and other Variety Theatres. He makes as successful a record of it as he did of his enormously popular "Come to the ball." *(Speed 78)*

Humorous

GEORGE ROBEY

(with orchestral accompaniment)

12-inch Record, 5s. 6d.

02546　　　**We parted the best of friends**　　*P. Edgar*

Robey—P.R.A.M.

W HAT can we say new of the Prime Minister of Mirth ? He is more unctuous every week, and his " stunts " get more ingenious every day. You'll roar when you hear about the bad sovereign episode where he diddled a " Strand Auction " merchant.

"We parted the best of friends."—Can you not imagine the little storyettes that end up with this sanctimonious utterance ? George, you are really incorrigible ! *(Speed 78)*

NEW
DOUBLE-SIDED
RECORDS
Bands

BAND OF H.M. COLDSTREAM GUARDS

(conducted by Capt. J. Mackenzie Rogan, M.V.O., Mus. Doc., Hon .R.A.M.)

12-inch Double-sided Records, 5s. 6d.

C 370 { Valse—Les Sirènes   *Waldteufel*
        Indigo Valse   *Strauss*

(Popularly known as "A Thousand and One Nights")

BEAUTIFUL playing by the greatest band in the world. The cloying melody of these waltzes is grandly brought out by the masterly playing under Mackenzie Rogan. Remarkably good definition.

(Speeds 79)

C 366 { Wine, Women and Song—Waltz   *Strauss*
        Entry of the Bulgars   *arr. by Winterbottom*

Published by Messrs. Hawkes & Son.

THE wood-wind is very life-like in these reproductions of lilting sound-pictures. How wonderfully together are the men! The volume is massive and the tone pleasing throughout.

(Speeds 79 & 80)

MAYFAIR ORCHESTRA

(conducted by Herman Finck)

10-inch double-sided Record, 3s. 6d.

B 263 { Bal Masque—Valse Caprice   *P. E. Fletcher*
        Handle Wakes   *Morresay*

Published by Messrs. Hawkes & Son.

WE do not remember any record made by the Mayfair Orchestra more intrinsically lovely than the present. The strings are thrilling.

(Speeds 79)

METROPOLITAN ORCHESTRA

12-inch double-sided Record, 5s. 6d.

C 376

A Hunt in the Black Forest—A Descriptive Musical Episode *Voelker*

"Day breaks—birds sing — cocks crow — huntsman's horn—village chimes—the hunters assemble—they start —full gallop—horns sound halt—at the blacksmiths—the smith at work—start again—hounds scent game—in full cry—game run to earth—cheers—finale."

In a Clock Store—Descriptive Fantasia *Orth*

"Apprentice opens store—ticking clocks—they strike— cuckoo, grandfather's clock, etc.—boy whistles—clocks run down and are wound—musical clock plays a popular air—four o'clock strikes on various clocks."

DESCRIPTIVE records played in stirring fashion. The "Hunt in the Black Forest" is full of extraordinarily fine effects. The picture of a hunt is really vivid. The Clock Store Fantasia is wonderfully well played.

CASTLE HOUSE ORCH.

12-inch double-sided Record, 5s. 6d.

C 375

Cecile—Waltz Hesitation *F. W. McKee*
Esmeralda—Waltz Hesitation *Carlos de Mesquita*

AMERICA is just about "Hesitation"-mad. She is certainly dance-mad, and the "Hesitation"—a variant of the waltz with a curious limp at certain intervals—is one of the very biggest favourites. We offer a grand double-sided record by the celebrated Castle House Orchestra. Castle House is the Mecca of society dancers across the Pond, where the two Castles have made a fortune in a twinkling. (*Speeds 78*)

Mr. and Mrs. Castle dancing the Hesitation for our records

NEW
Patriotic Records

Mr. STEWART GARDNER

10-inch Records, 3s. 6d.

4-2493	One United Front	*Bradwell*
4-2498	Sons of Old Britannia	*Forster*
4-2492	Little Mother	*Buchanan*
4-2497	Sons of the Motherland	*Monckton*
4-2496	The Soldiers of the King	*Stuart*
4-2495	Private Tommy Atkins	*Potter*

12-inch Record, 5s. 6d.

02548	England! Thy Name!	*Lewis Barnes**

(*Composer of The King's Command March coupled with Trot of the Cavalry, by Coldstream Guards Band, No. B222, 10-inch, 3/6).

DESCRIPTIVE RECORD

10-inch Record, 3s. 6d.

9473   British Troops passing through Boulogne

12-inch Record, 5s. 6d.

C 377 { **A Drill Sergeant** Words of Command **A Signalling Sergeant-Instructor** Morse Code—Alphabet and Message

METROPOLITAN MILITARY BAND

12-inch Records, 5s. 6d.

C 378 { "Allies in Arms." Selection I.* "Allies in Arms." Selection II.†

*Selection I. contains Opening, "Hearts of Oak (England)," "La Brabanconne" (Belgium). "St. Patrick" (Ireland), "Russian Hymn" (Russia). "Rule Britannia" (England), "See the Conquering Hero" (England). Finale.

†Selection II. contains "La Marseillaise" (France), "The Garb of Old Gaul" (Scotland), "The Maple Leaf" (Canada), "Marcia Reale" (Italy), "Men of Harlech" (Wales), "God Save the King" (England).

C 379 { Salut à Liège (dedicated to the Brave Belgians) *Entwistle* United Forces March

C 380 { "Our Sailor King," Patriotic March *Gay* "Fighting for Liberty," Patriotic March *Kaye*

BUGLERS OF H.M.
COLDSTREAM GUARDS

10-inch Record, 3s. 6d.

B 261 { Regimental Calls, No. 1 " 2

B 262 { Camp Calls, No. 1 " 2 " " " "

OUR SEPTEMBER SUPPLEMENT

REPRINTED FOR GENERAL CONVENIENCE

ORCHESTRAL—12-inch Records, 5s. 6d.

NEW SYMPHONY ORCHESTRA
(conducted by LANDON RONALD)

0852	Pizzicato from "Sylvia"	*Délibes*

CELEBRITY—12-inch Record, 9s.

02540	Angel's Serenade	McCormack and Kreisler

VOCAL—12-inch Records, 5s. 6d.

02532	My Lady's Bower	Stewart Gardner
02534	{ (a) The Sandwich Man { (b) The Fortune Hunter—Song Cycle "Bow Bells"	} Harry Dearth
03384	The Promise of Life	Miss Alice Lakin
04115	The day is done	Miss Elsie Baker and Mr. Frederick Wheeler
03385	Goodbye Summer; "So Long" Fall, Hello, Wintertime!	Miss Ethel Levey

10-inch Records, 3s. 6d.

2–3023	The Fairy Pipers	Miss Evelyn Harding
4–2446	My Memories	Hubert Eisdell

HUMOROUS—12-inch Records, 5s. 6d.

02538	The Witness	George Robey
02536	I've seen it on the pictures	Tom Clare

DOUBLE-SIDED RECORDS

12-inch Records, 5s. 6d.

C 368	Yankiana, American Suite —The Song of the Bells —Mighty America Yankiana, American Suite —Arrival of the Coontown Cadets	The Band of H.M. Coldstream Guards (Cond. by Capt. Dr. J. Mackenzie Rogan)
C 374	Military Symphony—Allegretto Military Symphony—Allegro	} Metropolitan Orchestra

10-inch Records, 3s. 6d.

B 259	Who paid the rent for Mrs. Rip van Winkle?—Medley Sympathy Waltz	} Metropolitan Band
B 257	When Mr. Moon is shining (from "Mam selle Tra-la-la) My little Persian Rose	} Jacobs and his Trocadero Orchestra
B 256	Marche Namur La Riterata—Italian March	} Metropolitan Orchestra
B 260	All aboard for Dixieland—Turkey Trot Ninette—One or Two-step	} Metropolitan Orchestra

NEW RECORDS

'His Master's Voice' RECORDS

MARCH 1915

12-inch Records 5s. 6d. ; 10-inch 3s. 6d.

Orchestral

NEW SYMPHONY ORCHESTRA (conducted by LANDON RONALD)

12-inch Record, 5s. 6d.

0850 "William Tell" Overture—Opening
Andante   *Rossini*

PREFACING our analytical notes, we must observe at once that the record under review is one of the most lovely, soul-satisfying achievements on our catalogue.

The story of Tell, the patriot who was chief instrument of the revolution which delivered the Swiss cantons from the German yoke in 1207, was taken by Rossini for the theme of one of his best-known operas, the dramatic interest being heightened by the introduction of love scenes and other episodes.

Landon Ronald
Photo by   Claude Harris

The overture, played probably as often as any other single work at concerts the world over, was called by Berlioz a symphony in four parts. It is a fitting prelude to a noble work and abounds in beautiful contrasts.

The opening Andante depicts the serene solitude of Nature at dawn. From the slowly-climbing figure on the 'cello

the music is enchantingly reposeful. The wayward, elusive air resolves after a time into a more definite rhythmic tune, which soon lapses into dreamy meditation. This is short-lived, however, for the measured flow is resumed until the blissful termination of this andante comes along to throw the witchery of its spell over the fortunate hearer.

The full beauty of the orchestra can be admired, albeit the movement almost amounts to a ravishing 'cello solo with orchestral background. Unforgettable is the close, with sustained shake of the richest 'cello string, while the orchestra slips gently away, downwards, climbing up to serenity again just at the last.

To hear is to be bewitched.

Landon Ronald and his renowned players in inspired mood.   (*Speed 78*)

Ballads

Mme. KIRKBY LUNN (contralto)

(with pianoforte accompaniment by Mr. Percy Pitt and organ by Mr. E. Stanley Roper, of St. Stephens, Walbrook, and the Danish Royal Chapel)

12-inch Record, 6s. 6d.

03395 Entreat me not to leave thee

Gounod, arr. by Percy Pitt

THE serene beauty of Mme. Kirkby Lunn's peerless vocal organ shines out in this fervent number. The aria is given with such perfection of phrasing and finish that the lines stand out each one like a finely-cut jewel. Here indeed is an artist—an English artist—worthy to rank with the greatest song-genius any Latin country ever produced. The voice is enchanting—the artistry is sublime.

The pleasing pianoforte accompaniment is by Mr. Percy Pitt, musical director of Covent Garden Opera, and Mr. Stanley Roper plays the organ obbligato with great effect. Altogether an exceptional record.   (*Speed 78*)

And Ruth said—

Entreat me not to leave thee,
Or to return from following after thee,
For whither thou goest I will go,
And where thou lodgest I will lodge,
Thy people shall be my people,
And thy God, my God.
Where thou diest I will die,
And there will I be buried ;
The Lord do so to me, and more also,
If aught but death part thee and me.
Thy people shall be my people,
And thy God, my God.

Words printed by permission of the publishers, Weekes & Co.

Photo   Dover Street Studios

Miss RUTH VINCENT (soprano)

(with pianoforte accompaniment by the composer)

10-inch Record, 4s. 6d.

2-3049   The stars that light my garden
Kennedy Russell

Ruth Vincent

AN appealing little love-song of that modern shape and terseness that carries intensity and conviction. It is much sung just now.

It could not be better sung than by accomplished Miss Ruth Vincent, whose crystalline tones carry with them the fragrance of the verses. Her voice soars easily upward into the loftiest tonal altitudes.

Here is ballad-singing of high artistic value.

(Speed 79)

The stars that light my garden,
 That make it paradise,
Are dear to me because they are,
 O love of mine, your eyes !

The song that fills my garden,
 That bids my heart rejoice,
Is sweeter than all other songs,
 Because it is your voice !

The rose that decks my garden,
 Through sunshine, cloud and dew,
Is dearer than all earth's fair flowers,
 Because, my love, 'tis you !

(Edward Teschemacher)

Words printed by permission of the publishers, Chappell & Co., Ltd.

OTHER RUTH VINCENT RECORDS

2-3044	I wonder if love is a dream	10-inch	4s. 6d.
2-3004	A Birthday (*F. H. Cowen*)	10-inch	4s. 6d.
03350	Lilac Time (*Willeby*)	12-inch	6s. 6d.

Mr. HUBERT EISDELL (tenor)

(with pianoforte accompaniment)

10-inch Record, 3s. 6d.

4-2529   **O Flower Divine**   *Haydn Wood*

Hubert Eisdell

ENCHANTING love-song, the Fairest One being apostrophised in flower metaphor.

This new morceau is having a tremendous vogue at present. Tenors—good, bad and indifferent—are all singing it : they could all well go to school to Hubert Eisdell in this particular instance, for our lyric tenor sings here as though inspired. The brilliant series of what one might call songs - of - appeal that we have had from him are crowned by this month's jewel. Idle to attempt to word-paint the colouring of the vocal performance—no lover of music must miss the treat of hearing. A record fragrant as a rose-garden.   *(Speed 79)*

Whence came you to this lonely place,
　　O flower divine ?
Giving such wondrous peace and grace
　　This heart of mine.
From some fair garden of the light,
To bless my weary aching sight,
Or from some valley to the night,
　　O flower divine !

I may but dream it whence you came,
　　O flower divine !
I can but call you by one name,
　　Find love of mine !
Sweetheart and friend and dearest one,
Be with me till my days are done,
Lead me to God at set of sun,
　　O flower divine !

　　　　　　　(*Edward Teschemacher*)

Words printed by permission of the publishers, Chappell & Co., Ltd.

Mr. JOHN HARRISON (tenor)
(with orchestral accompaniment)
10-inch Record, 3s. 6d.

4-2528 The Indian Soldier (Shabash Bhaiyan)
Kennedy Russell

Harrison in "Tales of Hoffmann," in which he is now delighting all London at the Shaftesbury.

A LOYAL record of an exceedingly novel order. There is no Britisher but has been thrilled with the manner in which India has rallied to the flag. The shiploads of Indian fighting-men who have raced to the French firing-line have been the admiration of the world—and the astonishment of the Teutons!

This swinging song extols Gurkha, Sikh, and the various tribesmen who are renowned as fighters.

A feature of the record is the grandly vivid orchestral prelude and accompaniment, which bring to one the scent of the Orient. The minor melodies are vastly picturesque, and the whole work is strikingly original. (*Speed 80*)

From all the slopes of Hindu Kush,
  To where the long seas play,
Around Comorin's jutting point,
  From thence to fair Bombay ;
To where the sacred river flows,
  To where the Indus runs,
They gather, gather, horse and foot,
  They hasten to the guns.
Swart brothers of the northern crags,—
  Mahrattas of the plain,—
Pathan and Rajput,—Gurkha,—Sikh,—
  We fight with you again !

Far back in days of long ago,
  When Akbar ruled by sword,
Then Ind first rose as one domain
  When Aurungzeb was lord ;
Full many factions fought since then,
  Before the British came
And met your sires in knightly strife,
  And won the gallant game.
Another game 'tis now to play,
  And one of different strain,
Pathan and Rajput,—Gurkha,—Sikh,—
  We fight with you again !

Bravo ! Bravo !
So we greet you, brother !
Coming from your Eastern home
  To help your war-worn mother !
Shabash Bhaiyan !
Couch your knightly lance,
And sally forth to fight with us
  And all the sons of France !

Words printed by permission of the publishers, Messrs. Boosey & Co.

(Charles Biron Minter)

NEW RECORDS

Miss RUBY HELDER (Lady tenor)
(with pianoforte accompaniment)
10-inch Record, 3s. 6d.

2-3051 **Courage** *Vanden Heuvel*
(The "Daily Telegraph" Recruiting Song)

THE palpitating feeling which Ruby Helder imparts to the delivery of these loyal verses is a thing to be heard. The song is the official Recruiting Song of the London "Daily Telegraph," and has enjoyed big sales as sheet music ; it has been, and is, a feature of many an important concert these war months.

Miss Ruby Helder vitalises the song in the most delightful fashion. Her intensity of tone is quite remarkable. (*Speed 79*)

Published by Enoch & Sons

Ruby Helder

ELGAR HEARS CARILLON ON "HIS MASTERS VOICE" GRAND

A characteristic pose of Sir Edward

Madame EDNA THORNTON (contralto

(with pianoforte accompaniment)

10-inch Record, 3s. 6d.

2-3052 Danny Boy (Old Irish Air)

SONG of the glens peculiarly suited to treatment by a contralto voice. It will be admitted that Mme. Edna Thornton scores a great success with her rendition. Her diction is clear-cut and invariably pleasing, and the way she leaps from middle to high register is an example of effortless vocalisation.

The earnest note is struck at once and well maintained. We do not remember to have heard Mme. Thornton in better voice. *(Speed 78)*

Oh, Danny Boy, the pipes, the pipes are calling
From glen to glen, and down the mountain side,
The summer's gone and all the roses falling,
It's you, it's you must go and I must bide.
But come ye back when summer's in the meadow,
Or when the valley's hushed and white with snow,
It's I'll be here in sunshine or in shadow.
Oh, Danny Boy, oh, Danny Boy, I love you so

But when ye come, and all the flowers are dying,
If I am dead, as dead I well may be,
Ye'll come and find the place where I am lying,
And kneel and say an Ave there for me ;
And I shall hear, though soft you tread above me,
And all my grave will warmer, sweeter be,
For you will bend and tell me that you love me,
And I shall sleep in peace until you come to me!

Edna Thornton

(Fred E. Weatherly)

Words printed by permission of the publishers, Boosey & Co.

Miss EVELYN HARDING (soprano)

(with pianoforte accompaniment)

10-inch Record, 3s. 6d.

2-3050   **A Song of Gladness**   *Sanderson*

Evelyn Harding

SONG of the softer, brighter days soon to be with us. It demands delicate treatment : Evelyn Harding weaves the gossamer threads with the sure manipulation of the artist of skill.

Her light soprano voice trips airily through the gay verses, seeming to take the most awkward leaps in the most facile way! Such is flexibility of voice, when a true artist possesses the voice. For the rest, who among us wishes to be deaf to the sweet call of spring ?   (*Speed 80*)

The golden broom has spread its wings,
And the warm brown bee he softly sings.
The cherry tree in purest white
Dances with delight !
    And the sky is blue, as sky can be,
    And the world is glad, as the world can be.

The cuckoo now is blithe with song,
And the mavis pipes the whole day long,
Apple blossoms float in the air,
Joy-bells ringing everywhere.
    And the sky is blue as sky can be,
    And the world is glad, as the world can be.

Rejoice and sing the live-long day,
For time is sweet when the year's at May !
There's fresh delight in all things near.
In the Springtime of the year.
    And the sky is blue, as sky can be,
    And the world is glad, as the world can be.

(*Ruth Rutherford*)

Words printed by permission of the publishers, Boosey & Co.

TETRAZZINI

(with orchestral accompaniment)

12-inch Record, 12s. 6d.

03336   **Bonnie Sweet Bessie**   *Gilbert*

(Sung in English)

Tetrazzini

IT seems a coincidence that the Florentine Nightingale has conceived the idea of singing in English for you at the same time as her fellow - countryman, Caruso.

Anyway, it is a treat, for Tetrazzini brings to the performance of the old Scotch ballad a vocal clarity quite crystalline in its beauty. She endows the rare old Gilbert air with a beauty which time will never dim. Her diction is remarkably pleasing, and constitutes even an improvement on her previous efforts in our language, efforts which have proved acceptable to Britons, to judge by the big favour shown to these records. We reprint below the previous three records-in-English by the *diva*. *(Speed 79)*

OTHER TETRAZZINI RECORDS IN ENGLISH

12-inch Records, 12s. 6d.

03286   Home, sweet Home   03241   The last Rose of Summer

03280   The Swallows (*Cowen*)

CARUSO

sings in English

(with orchestral accompaniment)

10-inch Record, 8s. 0d.

4-2480 **Trusting Eyes** *Gartner*

THE Prince of Song once more pays court to our language by deigning to leave his softer Italian for our terser, squarer, English. Charmingly he sings, too : his English is very 'taking' and the amount of fire he infuses into his rendering is just remarkable.

The little ballad is quite in the manner of those choice little Neapolitan songs that Caruso knows so well how to perform. It is a song and a record that everyone will enjoy, for Caruso is in grand voice. (*Speed 79*)

Photo   Bert, Paris

Caruso

O trusting eyes, when in your depths I'm gazing,
    No sorrow in my heart can be,
The clouds are parted, wakes again the sunshine,
    Making a golden way for me ;
Light as from Heaven gleams above me
    O trusting eyes ! because you love me !

O trusting heart, I fain would dwell for ever
    With you beside me till life's close.
As in some garden that kind fate has given,
    Guarding you there my perfect rose :
God keep you mine and may heaven shine above you,
    O trusting heart, because I love you !

(*Edward Teschemacher*)

Words printed by permission of the publishers, Gould & Co.

Mr. STEWART GARDNER (baritone)

(with pianoforte accompaniment)

10-inch Record, 3s. 6d.

4-2530 **Clieveden Woods** *F. S. Breville-Smith*
(The Call of the River)

Stewart Gardner

NOBLE-VOICED Stewart Gardner excels in bringing out the depth of meaning in this type of nature-song. He nurses, as it were, the rocking phrases of invocation. The music is of cradle-song type and teems with emotion when voiced so gorgeously as by this artistic baritone. The upward swing of the opening lines is poetry itself. Recording and interpretation alike admirable.

(Speed 80)

Where the Clieveden Woods mount heav'nward
In the sunset cool and deep,
I can hear you softly calling,
Mighty river n your sleep.
What is it your voice is saying,
Through the silence ot the night?
Speak to me O mighty river,
Bring me back my lost delight.

Where the Clieveden Woods mount heav'nward,
Through the dusk your voice is borne,
See the stars above you gleaming,
They shall lead you to the morn,
Life is jus' a flowing river.
Joy must come and tears must be,
But beyond there lies the morning,
Far beyond there waits the sea!!

(Teschemacher)

Words printed by permission of the publishers, Keith, Prowse & Co., Ltd.

Talking

Mr. ARTHUR BOURCHIER

12-inch Record, 5s. 6d.

01110 Speech of the Rt. Hon. H. H. Asquith, M.P. on "Causes of the War"

Arthur Bourchier

IT is fitting that we should follow up Mr. Lloyd George's speech on the War by the companion oration of the Prime Minister, this second one, like the first, being delivered for the purpose of the record (and for the enjoyment of the multitude and of posterity) by Mr. Arthur Bourchier.

Many were the encomiums passed on the masterly speech Bourchier so stirringly 'recorded' for us last month; no less enjoyable and 'gripping' will his second speech be found.

Mr. Asquith's statement is marked by that simplicity of form and directness of phrasing that have gained for him the reputation of possessing, perhaps, the most lucid intellect of any public man living. No Britisher can consider his patriotic equipment quite complete unless his home contains this record of the Premier's Speech, delivered by one of the most telling orators on the stage to-day. Every word is distinct—every phrase sinks into the mind. (*Speed* 78)

Mr. CHARLES TREE (baritone)
(with pianoforte accompaniment)
12-inch Record, 5s. 6d.

02555   The Crocodile—"English County Songs"
Fuller Maitland

Charles Tree

A VASTLY entertaining ditty from Fuller Maitland's "English County Songs." Charles Tree serves up the "tall" stories with rare gusto and lots of sly humour. What a crocodile that must have been, to be sure! Skin eight miles thick, for it took ten years to cut a way out!— Phew!

Nothing could be more enjoyable than the breezy singing of this popular artist, who lives up to his big reputation. (*Speed 79*)

Published by Cramer & Co.

GRAND OPERA COMPANY
(with orchestral accompaniment.)   *(Sung in English)*
10-inch Record, 3s. 6d.

4626   Anvil Chorus—"Il Trovatore"   *Verdi*

THE ceaseless swinging harmonies of the celebrated Anvil Chorus are brought out wonderfully in the spirited performance by the Grand Opera Company, with a rousing orchestral accompaniment. Everyone will admire the superb *élan* and beautiful *ensembles*. Grand value.   Speed 79)

PREVIOUSLY ISSUED RECORDS BY THE GRAND OPERA COMPANY 12-inch Records, 5s. 6d.	
Gems—"Cavalleria Rusticana"	04539
Gems—"Faust"	04562
Sextette ("Lucia di Lammermoor")	2-054024
The Bridal Chorus from "Lohengrin"	04527
Gems—"Mignon"	04537
Gems—"Pagliacci"	04553
Gems—"Rigoletto"	04573
Gems—"Tales of Hoffmann"	04572

Mr. LAMBERT MURPHY and
Mr. REINALD WERRENRATH

(with orchestral accompaniment)

10-inch Record, 3s. 6d.

7-54004   **Ah Mimi tu più non torni "La Bohême"**

Puccini

Lambert Murphy

AS we anticipated the duet "Solene in quest'ora" by this combination of artists was received with acclamation : everyone agreed that it was one of the best records issued for some time.

It would seem rash to prophesy even greater success for this favourite Bohème number, but it is certain that everyone who hears this rendering will wish to possess the record. Both voices are superb and the effect is quite electrical. Lambert Murphy is advancing with giant strides in his American Grand Opera career, and Werrenrath is accepted as a truly great baritone. Their combined singing is a revelation.

Act IV. shows the garret in the Quartier Latin in which Rodolfo, poet, and Marcel, painter, live. Bereft of their sweethearts, each is trying to conceal from the other that he is secretly pining for the absent loved one. Marcel pretends to work at his easel : Rodolfo appears to be writing—but is gazing furtively at Mimi's little pink bonnet.—He sings—"Ah Mimi, thou false one!" Marcel joins in, and the two voices are heard magnificently. (*Speed 80*)

Reinald Werrenrath

CARIL

(conducted by SIR EDWARD E

Two 12-inch records, 5s. 6d. eac

Verses delivered by Mr. HENRY AINLEY, accompanied b

2-0522 CARILLON—Part I.   " Sing, Belgians, Sing "   (t
2-0523   ,,   ,, II.   ,,   ,,   ,,   p

THE " heart-broken cry of the patriot poet weeping for his ru
—yet disclaiming vengeance—has inspired Sir Edward E
of his loftiest utterances." Thus writes a well-known c
Daily News. And the description is admirable. Cammaerts, thou
among the greatest of living poets, surely wrote his tense lines
Belges, Chantons " in a moment of finest inspiration.   If the
were inspired, then inspired too were the composer of the musical
read that he has " produced here one of the most effective and
things in existence." None will deny this after hearing these
lovely records, made under the guiding hand of the *maestro* hims

orchestra, no less an artist than Henry Ainle
the poem.

The whole performance is uplifting in its
sincerity, its majestic sweep. We have inde
an artistic triumph that will serve to carry the
of outraged Belgium to every corner of the g

The music, rich yet simple, rings as true a
It calls for no analysis : the series of me
conveyed are sharp and real.

HENRY AINLEY

the celebrated Actor who
recited the verses. His
many admirers will declare
the reproduction of his
voice extraordinarily fine.

But a very slight accompaniment is heard
actual recitation : the work opens with a perf
prelude that is almost an overture. Betweer
is an interlude reflecting the poet's moods.
figure becomes at once familiar. The danc
strikingly original. The mournful lines that open the
lead on to a pulse-quickening culmination, the orche
Ainley's impassioned " In Berlin ! " and bursting into
triumphal joy. Nothing could be more moving, more
Henry Ainley's superbly dramatic utterance.

" HIS MASTER'S VOICE

LON

R, O.M.)

E SYMPHONY ORCHESTRA

tion of Emile Cammaerts'   *Elgar*
Chantons, Belges, Chantons")   ,,

THE TRANSLATION

SIR EDWARD ELGAR, O.M.

PART ONE

Sing, Belgians, sing,
Although our wounds may bleed, although
*   our voices break,*
Louder than the storm, louder than the
*   guns,*
Sing of the pride of our defeats,
'Neath this bright autumn sun,
And sing of the joy of honour
When cowardice might be so sweet.

To the sound of the drum, to the sound
*   of the bugle.*
On the ruins of Aerschot, Dinant and
*   Termonde,*
Dance, Belgians, dance,
And our glory sing,
Although our eyes may burn,
Although our brain may turn,
Join in the ring!

PART TWO

With branches of beech, of flaming beech,
To the sound of the drum,
We'll cover the graves of our children,
We'll choose a day like this,
When the poplars tremble softly
In the breeze.
And all the woods are scented
With the smell of dying leaves,
That they may bear with them, beyond,
The perfume of our land.

We'll ask the earth they loved so well,
To rock them in her great arms,
To warm them on her mighty breast,
And send them dreams of other fights,
Re-taking Liege, Malines,
Brussels, Louvain and Namur,
And of their triumphant entry, at last
IN BERLIN!

Part Two (continued)

Sing, Belgians, sing!
Although our wounds may bleed, although
*   our voices break,*
Louder than the storm, louder than the
*   guns,*
Although our wounds may bleed, although
*   our hearts may break,*
Sing of hope and fiercest hate,
'Neath this bright autumn sun;
Sing of the pride of charity
When vengeance would be so sweet.

(Translated from the French
of Emile Cammaerts, by
Tita   Brand   Cammaerts).

Words printed by permission of the
publishers, Elkin & Co.

Original French given on page 19

RECORD—A MILESTONE IN MUSIC

Humorous

Miss ELSIE JANIS

(with orchestral accompaniment)

10-inch Record, 3s. 6d.

2-3053   When we tango to the Wearing of the Green   *Elsie Janis*

THAT beautiful and phenomenally successful Revue, "The Passing Show," which is just coming off after a big run, owed much of its success to the great American Star, Elsie Janis. Her original style, and dainty, alluring manner, "fetched" the audience immensely.

She sings this bright little song with heaps of smartness and humour. You might imagine yourself in the stalls at the Palace, so lifelike is the reproduction.

By the by, Miss Janis is just back in London for rehearsals of "The Passing Show of 1915" at the Palace. She came over on the 'Lusitania' and saw 'Old Glory' go up and the Union Jack go down — the famous *ruse de guerre !*   (*Speed* 79)

TOM CLARE at the PIANO

12-inch Record, 5s. 6d.

02556   Waltzing Willie   *Tom Clare*

Tom Clare

THE great Fun-at-the-Piano Merchant sparkles more scintillatingly than ever this month. His newest verses anent light-toed Willie end up smartly with various first lines of melodies of the day, worked in most cutely. His last Kaiser-verse culminates in Tipp——no we mustn't give it away !

(*Speed* 78)

THE FOLLOWING TWO RECORDS OF CELEBRATED SCHOOL SONGS ARE NOW PLACED ON 'HIS MASTER'S VOICE' CATALOGUE

(They are only sent out to dealers' against special order and are not being sent with other Supplementary Records unless specially asked for).

SHERBORNE SCHOOL SONGS
THE CECILIAN QUINTETTE
(with pianoforte accompaniment)
12-inch Record, 5s. 6d.

04123   **Fair and grey and ancient " Sherborne School So :gs "** *Louis N. Parker*
Published by Weekes & Co.

10-inch Record, 3s. 6d.   (Sung in Latin)

2-4243   **Carmen Sæculare " Sherborne School Songs "**   *Louis N. Parker*
Published by Weekes & Co.

ISSUED LAST CHRISTMAS
12-inch Record, 5s. 6d.

04120   **A Solemn Carol for Christmastide**

Old Sherburnians—and countless others—will welcome these records of the School classics. "Fair and grey and ancient" is a grand melody. "Carmen Sæculare" is the school's most popular song, corresponding with the world-famous "Dulce Domum" of Winchester. The Christmas Carol is a noble work. All are rendered with excellent feeling by the Cecilian Quintette.

ORIGINAL WORDS OF CAMMAERTS' GREAT POEM

"Chantons, Belges, Chantons"   (See pages 12 & 13)

Chantons, Belges, chantons,
  Même si les blessures saignent, même si la voix se brise,
Plus haut que la tourmente, plus fort que les canons,
  Chantons l'orgueil de nos défaites,
Par ce beau soleil d'automne.
  Et la joie de rester honnêtes
Quand la lâcheté nous serait si bonne.

Au son du tambour. au son du clairon,
  Sur les ruines d'Aerschot, de Dinant de Termonde,
Dansons, Belges, danson ,
  En chantant notre gloire.
Même si les yeux brûlent, si la tête s'égare,
  Formons la ronde !

Avec des branches de hê:re, de hêtre flamboyant,
  Au son du tambour,
Nous couvrirons les tombes de nos en'ants.

  Nous choisirons un jour.
Comme celui-ci,
  Où les peupliers tremblent doucement
Dans le vent,

Et où l'odeur des feuilles mortes
Embaume les bois,
  Comme aujourd'hui,
Afin qu'ils emportent
  Là-bas
Le parfum du pays.

Nous prierons la terre qu'ils ont tant aimée
  De les bercer dans ses grands bras,
De les réchauffer sur sa vaste poitrine
  Et de les faire rêver de nouveaux combats ;
De la prise de Bruxelles, de Malines,
  De Namur, de Liège, de Louvain,
Et de leur entrée triomphale, là-bas A Berlin!
Chantons, Belges, chantons,
  Même si les blessures saignent, et si la voix se brise,
Plus haut que la tourmente, plus fort que les canons,
  Même si les blessures saignent, même si le cœur se brise.
Chantons l'espoir et la haine implacable,
  Par ce beau soleil d'automne,
Et la fierté de rester charitables
  Quand la Vengeance nous serait si bonne!
         (Emile Cammaerts)

Reprinted by permission

Capt. Mackenzie-Rogan
(Senior Bandmaster of British Army)

NEW
DOUBLE-SIDED
RECORDS
Bands
BAND OF H.M.
COLDSTREAM GUARDS

(conducted by Capt. J. Mackenzie Rogan, M.V.O., Mus. Doc., Hon. R.A.M.)

12-inch double-sided Record, 5s. 6d.

C 389 {
Sicilian Vespers — Ballet Selection
Sicilian Vespers — Selection *Verdi, arr. by Mackenzie-Rogan*
}

THE first London production of this lesser-known opera of Verdi was at Drury Lane in 1859 with Tietiens in the cast. Although a brilliant work it has never been very popular as a stage production. The Ballet Music, however, is exceedingly fine and offers splendid material for a band record. The Coldstreamers play with stimulating aplomb and achieve some fine ensembles. The clarinets are specially grand. (*Speeds* 79)

BAND OF H.M. COLDSTREAM GUARDS

(conducted by Capt. J. Mackenzie Rogan, M.V.O., Mus. Doc.)

10-inch double-sided Record, 3s. 6d.

B 279 {
The Four Flags   *Winson*
Wake Up England!   *Winson*
}

STILL more sparkling march tunes aflame with the spirit of Britain in Arms. The brass makes one's eyes brighten and sets one's blood running fast and hot. The playing is superb. (*Speeds 79 & 81*)

MAYFAIR ORCHESTRA

(conducted by HERMAN FINCK)

12-inch double-sided Record, 5s. 6d.

C 390 {
Day Dreams   *Haydn Wood*
Published by Hawkes & Sons
Ye Olden Chimes   *Batten*
Published by Chappell & Co
}

"DAY DREAMS" is a languorous, cloying composition in Haydn Wood's most restful vein. The record will at once become everybody's favourite. The "Chimes" number on the reverse will appeal to everyone.; it is at once charming and lilting and will make every toe keep time with it.

(*Speeds 78 & 81*)

Miss UNA BOURNE (Piano)

12-inch double-sided Record, 5s. 6d.

C 391 {
La Fileuse, Op. 35   *Chaminade*
Etude Romantique, Op. 32 *Chaminade*
Published by Enoch & Sons
}

AMONG the most accomplished pieces of execution heard on the pianoforte is Miss Una Bourne's rendering of Chaminade's celebrated Spinning number, La Fileuse. The technique is as amazing as her dexterity is delightful. It is such records as this that literally "fill the home with melody." The Etude is a most poetical piece of meditative playing. Recording excellent.

(*Speeds 80 & 78*)

VENETIAN TRIO (Instrumental Trio)

10-inch double-sided Record, 3s. 6d.

B 280 { **Come where my love lies dreaming** *Foster*
{ **Mélodie** *Lalo*

THE haunting beauty of the playing of this accomplished instrumental combination will remain long in the mind. No greater favourites are found on our instrumental pages than this kind of record. Both melodies are treated with indescribable delicacy, and the harmonies are entrancing. (*Speeds* 79)

TABLE OF APPEARANCES
of
WELL-KNOWN CONCERT ARTISTS
who make "His Master's Voice" Records

Artist	Town	Date
ROBERT RADFORD ...	Kettering......................	March 1
	Edinburgh	„ 3
	Port Glasgow	„ 4
	Manchester	„ 11
	Huddersfield	„ 16
	Ayr	„ 18
	Perth	„ 19
GERVASE ELWES	Bournemouth	„ 9
	Sherborne	„ 13
	Wakefield	„ 17
	Doncaster	„ 18
	London.........................	„ 24
	Amsterdam ... ... }	„ 27, 28,
	Rotterdam .... }	30, 31
JOHN HARRISON	Shaftesbury Theatre	
	("Tales of Hoffmann")	
PALGRAVE TURNER ..	Brighton	„ 3
	London	„ 6
	Stroud	„ 10
	London	„ 15
	Reigate.......................	„ 16
	Westminster	„ 19
	Esher.........................	„ 25
	Oxford	„ 28
HERBERT HEYNER ...	London.........................	„ 2
	Worcester	„ 4
	Bristol	„ 6
	London............	„ 8
	Eastbourne.............. {	„ 9, 10, 11, 12, 13
	London.........................	„ 14
	Glasgow	„ 17
	Halifax........................	„ 18
	Bradford	„ 19
	Manchester..................	„ 20
	Nottingham	„ 22
	Derby	„ 23
	London............	„ 28

NEW RECORDS

Records issued in DECEMBER, JANUARY and FEBRUARY

REPRINTED FOR GENERAL CONVENIENCE

ORCHESTRAL—12-inch Records, 5s. 6d.
NEW SYMPHONY ORCHESTRA
(conducted by LANDON RONALD)

2–0513	Danse Macabre	*Saint-Saens*
0843	Les Phœniciennes—Herodiade	*Massenet*
ʃ853	Midsummer Night's Dream Overture	*Mendelssohn*
0844	Les Gauloises—Finale from "Hérodiade"	*Massenet*

THE SYMPHONY ORCHESTRA
(conducted by Sir EDWARD ELGAR)

2–0512	Salut d'Amour	*Elgar*
2–0517	Pomp and Circumstance March (No, 4 in G), Op 39	*Elgar*
2–0519	Bavarian Dances, No. 2	*Elgar*

CELEBRITY—10-inch Record, 8s. 0d.

4–2375	Your eyes have to'd me what I did not know	Caruso

12-inch Record, 25s. 0d.

2–054050	E scherzo, od è folia—"Un Ballo in Maschera," Act I.	
	Caruso, Hempel, Duchene, Rothier and De Segurola	

12-inch Record, 12s. 6d.

032261	La Marseillaise	Chaliapin
2–053085	D'amor sull alli rosee—"Il Trovatore"	Tetrazzini
03369	Comin' thro' the Rye	Melba

10-inch Record, 12s. 6d.

7–54003	O soave fanciulla—"La Bohême"	Lucrezia Bori and McCormack

10-inch Record, 8s. 0d.

7–52035	Buona Zaza, del mio buon tempo—"Zaza," Act II.	Titta Ruffo

10-inch Record, 6s. 0d.

7–52056	Donna non vidi mai—"Manon Lescaut," Act I.	Martinelli

VOCAL—12-inch Record, 6s. 6d.

2–033045	Berceuse de Jocelyn (Angels guard thee)	Mme. Alma Gluck

12-inch Records, 5s. 6d.

02551	The Garden of Sleep	Stewart Gardner
03391	Our Country's Call	Mme. Edna Thornton
2–054051	Solenne in quest'ora (Swear in this hour)—"Forza del Destino"	
		Lambert Murphy and Reinald Werrenrath
02552	Thy Sentinel am I	Robert Radford
03393	Call of the Motherland	Miss Ruby Helder
02553	Thou'rt passing hence	Peter Dawson
03394	Carry on	Miss Ethel Levey

10-inch Records, 4s. 6d.

4–2513	It's a long, long way to Tipperary	John McCormack
2–3042	Harvest	Mme. Kirkby Lunn
4–2396	Dear Love, remember me	John McCormack
2–3044	I wonder if Love is a Dream	Miss Ruth Vincent

10-inch Records, 3s. 6d.

4–2504	The King's Highway	Robert Radford
4–2505	A Lullaby	Hubert Eisdell
2–4210	Russian National Anthem	
2–4212	Nautical Airs, Part I., containing : "A Life on the Ocean Wave," "Bay o' Biscay," "Tom Bowling"	
2–4211	Nautical Airs, Part 2, containing : "Death of Nelson," "Red, White and Blue," "Rule Britannia"	The Cecilian Quartette
2–4214	The Girl I left behind me	
2–4216	Who Killed Cock Robin ?	
2–4215	Little Brown Jug	

"His Master's Voice"

2-3039	Somebody's Rose	Miss Marion Beeley
4-2506	A Yeoman's Yarn	Harry Dearth
2-4213	March of the Men of Harlech	Stewart Gardner and Ernest Pike
2-3040	I want a dancing man	Miss Elsie Janis
4-2462	The Song of Aiche	Hubert Eisdell
2-4202	When the Angelus is ringing	Mixed Quartette
2-3041	The Voice of Home	Miss Paola St. Clair
4-2474	Linden Lea—A Dorset Song	Charles Tree
4-2523	I dream of a garden of sunshine	John Harrison
2-3045	Dearest, I bring you daffodils	Miss Evelyn Harding
4-2520	England's Battle Hymn (Send him Victorious)	
		Stewart Gardner and Chorus
4-2524	Friends again	Charles Tree
4-2521	The Sedan Chair "Seven Gavotte Songs," No. 6	Ernest Crampton
2-3046	Irish Love Song	Miss Alice Lakin
2-4220	When Johnny comes marching home	The Cecilian Quartette
4-2522	March on to Berlin	George Carvey

TALKING—12-inch Records, 5s 6d.

01108	Mr. Lloyd George's Speech at the Queen's Hall, Part I.	Arthur Bourchier
01109	Ditto	Part II.	Arthur Bourchier

INSTRUMENTAL

PIANO—12-inch Records, 5s. 6d.

05558	Mock Morris Dances	Percy Grainger
C 383	A Scottish Rhapsody, Part I. / A Scottish Rhapsody, Part II.	A. J. Lancashire
05561	The Harmonious Blacksmith	Mark Hambourg
05562	Nocturne No. 18 in E major	Mark Hambourg

VIOLIN—12-inch Record, 6s. 6d.

07995	Ave Maria (Schubert–Wilhelmj)	Mischa Elman

12-inch Record 5s. 6d.

2-07916	Moto Perpetuo	Miss Marie Hall

'CELLO—12-inch Record, 5s. 6d.

07880	Eglantine—Melody	W. H. Squire

HUMOROUS—12-inch Records, 5s. 6d.

02550	Here we are again	Mark Sheridan
02537	Every Time	Tom Clare
02545	I don't think it matters	George Robey
02554	It's refined	Tom Clare

10-inch Records, 3s. 6d.

1454	Laughteritis	Charles Penrose
4-2511	Belgium put the Khibosh on the Kaiser	Mark Sheridan
4-2512	All Aboard for Dixieland	Murray Johnson

DOUBLE-SIDED RECORDS

12-inch Records, 5s. 6d.

C 388	Bal Masque—Valse Caprice / Santiago—Spanish Valse	The Band of H.M. Coldstream Guards (cond. by Capt. Dr. J Mackenzie Rogan)
C 382	"The Passing Show," Selection I. / "The Passing Show," Selection II.	Mayfair Orchestra (conducted by Herman Finck)

10-inch Records, 3s. 6d.

The Band of H.M. Coldstream Guards (cond. by Capt. Dr. J. Mackenzie Rogan)

B 268	Pro Patria—March / Euterpe—March	B 276	Conquering Heroes / The Gallant Knight
B 275	Sambre et Meuse—Patriotic March / Les Volontaires	B 277	A Lover in Damascus Suite, No. 5 —"If in the great Bazaars" / Holyrood—Quick March
B 274	Pleading / Demoiselle Chic		Jacobs and his Trocadero Orchestra
B 273	Indian Blood / The Ride of the Janissaries		Mayfair Orchestra (conducted by Herman Finck)
B 278	Lazy Dance / Gloriana—Ragtime		ditto

'His Master's Voice' RECORDS

MAY 1915

12-inch records 5s. 6d.; 10-inch 3s. 6d.

Orchestral

THE SYMPHONY ORCHESTRA
(conducted by Sir EDWARD ELGAR)

12-inch record, 5s. 6d.

2-0530   **Bavarian Dances, No. 3**   *Elgar*

THIS is the third of the Three Bavarian Dances of Elgar, which form such a delightful feature of concert programmes throughout the kingdom.

It may be remembered that these dances are the first, third and sixth numbers from a choral suite entitled "From the Bavarian Highlands," in which Sir Edward perpetuated in melodic form his impressions of a holiday spent one summer at Garmisch. The dance

Sir Edward Elgar

which is numbered Two has already been issued on record No. 2-0519. The delight it gave to lovers of orchestral picture-music will ensure a fervent welcome being accorded to another of the trio.

Number Three is marked *allegro vivace*, and corresponds with the number entitled "The Marksman"

in the choral suite. The scene is a village shooting-match. The ceaseless swinging subjects are intended to depict the scene of animation, with its parties of peasant-garbed dancers— the men in their heavy shoes, thick stockings to the bare knees, short knickers, decorative coatee and swagger hat—the women in full-waisted short skirts, with the peasant "bun" of hair.

The joyousness of the music is easily depictive of the rustic scene with its background of heavily-gabled booths and towering green and grey peaks searching the hearts of the cloud-lands.

The interpretation is not only authentic, but is also uplifting in the sweep and majesty of the master-guided grand orchestra.   (*Speed 78*)

Published by J. Williams

Ballads

Mr. JOHN McCORMACK (tenor)
(with orchestral accompaniment)
10-inch record, 4s. 6d.

4-2473   **Who knows?**   *Ball*

John McCormack

A PLEASING ballad in the fervent vein. Just as in the ditties of " Ould Ireland " and in popular tunes like " Tipperary " (McCormack's record made this sublime !)—the great tenor's art is of the rollicking, breezy kind—so in the serious type of song McCormack sinks his personality in the work and becomes for the nonce the profound and meditative artist. Such is the note struck in "Who knows?" whose cadences, as sung, carry the beauty of a striking piece of poetry declaimed by an artist of genius.

The serene strength of McCormack's singing is dazzling and his quality of tone and half-tone has never been surpassed. When, added to this, we have perfect recording, the record will surely take its place high among tenor successes.   (*Speed 77*)

> Thou art the soul of a summer's day,
> Thou art the breath of the rose ;
> But the summer is fled and the rose is dead ;
> Where are they gone ?—Who knows, who knows ?
>
> Thou art the blood of my heart of hearts,
> Thou art my soul's repose ;
> But my heart's grown numb, and my soul is dumb,
> Where art thou lo e ?—Who knows, who knows ?
>
> Thou art my hope of my after years,
> Sun of my winter snows ;
> But the years go by 'neath a clouded sky,
> When shall we meet ?—Who knows, who knows ?
>
> (*Paul Lawrence Dunbar*)

Words printed by permission of the publishers, Feldman & Co.

Mme. KIRKBY LUNN (contralto)

(with pianoforte accompaniment by Mr. Percy Pitt and organ by Mr. E. Stanley Roper of St. Stephen's, Walbrook, and the Danish Royal Chapel)

10-inch record, 4s. 6d.

2-3063 **Soul of Mine** *Ethel Barns*

Photo   Dover Street Studios

Kirkby Lunn

WHEN Kirkby Lunn sings, one is reminded of the sun-flooded interior of a great cathedral, richly shaded with the many hues of stained glass. Such is the rare and strange beauty of the voice. It is a voice, indeed, that one can love for itself alone.

Such a voice could delight one in any collection of musical sounds, even though they were haphazard.

The song for May is a devotional love-song of touching brevity. It is deeply impressive, sung as it is with ineffable feeling.

(Speed 80)

O soul of mine,
Out of the void, out of the vast,
Out of the deep I cry to thee.
Out of the mist, from the ages past.
From the arms of God come thou to me
O soul of mine.

O heart of mine,
Into the light, into the dawn,
Into the day thou callest me ;
Into thy heart, from the dark of sleep
To the sun of love I come to thee
O soul of mine.

(Teresa Hooley)

Words printed by permission of the publishers, Chappell & Co., Ltd.

Mr. HUBERT EISDELL (tenor)

(with pianoforte accompaniment)

10-inch record, 3s. 6d.

4-2535   **Mother Mine**   *Lewis Barnes*

WHEN this sweet record is on sale, its creator will be "somewhere on the high seas" in an armed merchantman. We secured a few records from this idol of the people three or four days before his departure for the coast. We also got the finely typical snapshot shown, in which the rather quizzical look and easy bear-

ing that are characteristics of Eisdell are most happily registered. Here's to the safe return of such a sterling artist!

Of his singing one can say nothing new. It is a delightful morceau, and the enchanting loveliness of tone that picks Eisdell out from the ruck is a feature that will endear the record to all. *(Speed* 79)

Lieut. Eisdell, R.N.D.   *H.M.V. Photo.*

In your eyes I see the stars of Heaven.
In your voice is matchless music given.
On your cheek, fair as the morning light,
Are lovely roses, delicate and white.

All your thoughts are beautiful and holy,
All your ways unselfish, kind and lowly.
Where you go, no matter what the place
You leave the memory of an angel's face.

Wealth I've none, yet I have riches rare,
Your dear self, priceless beyond compare,
None can replace, or match your oble worth.
Oh Mother mine, best mother on the earth.

Duty calls! and I must face the foe.
Kiss me once, and bless me ere I go.
Mother of mine, when I am far away
You care I leave to God, ever and alway.
(Lewis Barnes)

Words printed by per ission of the publishers, Leonard & Co.

Miss FLORA WOODMAN

(with pianoforte accompaniment)

10-inch record, 3s. 6d.

2-3062 Oh tell me Nightingale   *Liza Lehmann*

Photo   Vandyk

FLORA WOODMAN
the sensational 18-year-old soprano who promises to become a world celebrity.

" NOT only does she possess a voice which may ultimately place her amongst the most famous singers, but already she sings in a way that makes singing appear the most supremely natural thing in the world." Thus wrote recently a famous critic of Flora Woodman. He went on: "From D to the upper A her voice has a challenging power which need fear no comparison."

The occasion was nothing less than a Hallé concert. At the Albert Hall since then Flora Woodman has astounded and delighted the the critics. This charming 18-year-old girl, who made quite a sensational début in 1914, has all the skill and finish and style of an experienced

Published by J. Williams   *(continued opposite)*

—the New Nightingale

Miss Flora Woodman's Début on Records

(continued from page 6)

celebrity.   The serenity of nature is in her voice
Her shake is miraculous in its long sustained
purity.   Just listen for a minute to her record
—to listen is to be enraptured.   A new Nightingale indeed!

What is perhaps a unique distinction for a
vocalist—to be the *only* artist with the New
Symphony Orchestra and Landon Ronald at
the Albert Hall Sunday Concerts—is already
to the credit of Flora Woodman.   To see that
graceful figure, bosom still graced by a long
curl slipping over the shoulder, stand by the
conductor's dais—send forth crystalline note
with unheard-of ease, note upon note of matchless beauty: this is an experience of a lifetime.
Such a girl was *born* to sing, to sing her way
into the war-worn hearts of all music-lovers
to-day.

We have engaged this
artist exclusively for "His
Master's Voice" records.
This is the nation's gain.
(Speed 79)

" His Master's Voice " Record

Another New Artist

Miss VIOLET ESSEX (soprano)

(with orchestral accompaniment) (*sung in English*)

12-inch record, 5s. 6d.

03398   **The Kiss (Il Bacio)**   *Arditi*

Violet Essex at the recording horn
H.M.V. photo

PROMINENT among the bevy of famous new artists presented in this month's supplement is charming little Miss Violet Essex. This accomplished soprano is one of the biggest favourites on the London concert platform : she is well-known for her work at the best West-end theatres, and is an especial star at Sunday League concerts.

Her voice and art are as lovely as her personality. Endowed by nature with a charming presence, and the knowledge of *style* in singing (that rare attribute!) Violet Essex has quickly reached a high pinnacle.

For her first number she has essayed the delightful "Il Bacio" in English with accompaniment of orchestra. Her success is striking. The voice is beautifully "placed," and recorded fittingly. (*Speed 78*)

Mr. HARRY DEARTH (bass)

(with pianoforte accompaniment)

12-inch record, 5s. 6d.

02561   **Cloze-Props**   *Wolseley Charles*

Photo   Dover Street Studios
Harry Dearth

THE artless confessions of Jim, clothes-prop merchant, are rhymed in delightful form and set to original music. The song might have been *built* for Harry Dearth, whom it suits down to the very ground.

The rollicking baritone gives out the quaint tale with peerless touches of character and rare insight.

The reason why the " widdy" at Bow was not for Jim is touchingly brought out in the strangely effective final verse, which is dealt with most tenderly. Here is a song and a record in the finest vein of popular Harry Dearth.   (*Speed 79*)

O I'm Cloze-prop Jim, an' I ain't so slim
  As fifty years ago.
But one and all can hear my call,
  From Bethnal Green to Bow :
An' many's the time when a fog looks prime,
  I pop in a backyard door,
Folks' props I borrow, and on the morrow
  I sell 'em their props once more.

Cloze-props ! Cloze-props !
  Who ll buy ? who'll buy ?
I've short and long, and all of 'em strong,
  Come, ladies, come and buy.
I troll my song as I jog along,
  From mo n till night is nigh,
  Will yer, won't yer buy ?

Come rain, come snow, I tramping go,
  Gay as a bird I be,
I've a joke or a pun for ev'ry one,
  And all have a smile for me.
There's a widdy I know that lives at Bow,
  With a dainty waist and trim,
Folk say that she is sweet on me,
  But widdies is not for Jim.

Cloze-props ! Cloze-props !
  Who'll buy ? who'll buy ?
I've props for all, some short, some tall,
  Come, ladies, don't be shy.
And the pretty maids come when they hear me call,
  Nobody can deny,
  Will yer, won't yer buy ?

Some nights I slip with a guttering dip,
  Upstairs to an old locked drawer,
Her picture's there, and she looks so fair,
  In the neat little gown she wore ;
Now lone I be, " Good-bye," said she,
  " Don't, don't forget me, dear,"
And I thinks she waits by the Go den Gates
  For me, this many a year.
But here I be with my props, you see,
  And everyone knows my cry.   *(Hub'-Newcombe)*

Words printed by permission of the publishers, Boosey & Co.

Mr. STEWART GARDNER (baritone)
(with pianoforte accompaniment)
12-inch record, 5s. 6d.

02562 **The Island of Love** *Haydn Wood*

A NOTHER song by the composer of that beautiful air, "O Flower Divine" (did you hear Eisdell's superb record of it?) will demand attention apart from its singer. When the latter is Stewart Gardner, attention is doubly quickened.

The rich, vibrant tone-quality that belongs to the art of this favourite baritone is present in bountiful measure in this record.

Stewart Gardner   *Published by Boosey & Co.*   (*Speed 78*)

Mr. ROBERT RADFORD in English Opera
(with orchestral accompaniment)
12-inch record, 5s. 6d.

02560 **Hear me, gentle Maritana—**
"Maritana"   *Wallace*

O NE of the priceless boons conferred on the world by "His Master's Voice" Gramophone is the breathing of new life into old-time favourites, infusing long-familiar airs with fresh beauty through the medium of great artists of to-day. It is in this spirit that we conceived the making of the present record.

Wallace's flowing "Maritana" air has taken its place among Old English classics. Its haunting sweetness is brought out remarkably by the lovely singing of our great bass, Mr.

Robert Radford

Robert Radford, who has lavished all that is finest in his art and voice in the rendition offered here. (*Speed 79*)

NEW **Celebrity** RECORD

JOURNET & Chorus

(with orchestral accompaniment) *(sung in French)*

12-inch record, 9s. 0d.

**2-032009 Benediction des Poignards
"Les Huguenots"**   *Meyerbeer*

This tuneful opera is by an Italian, it should be noted; Meyerbeer's Christian name was Giacomo. It is a pity the work is not now heard in London.

THE famous Benediction music from the "Huguenots" sung by Journet, who is in really grand voice. To think that his voice is classed as "bass"—with *that* range! His high notes are almost tenor. But are they not rich, every jewel of them?

Journet first sang in London in 1897, when the power and flexibility of his voice made a remarkable impression. Again in London, in 1905, he replaced Plançon with great success. These were great shoes to fill, but the younger artist was equal to the test. In the United States, Journet is a particular favourite, having been for many years a leading member of the Metropolitan Opera. The sustained singing of the bass in this "Huguenots" excerpt is lovely, and a well-balanced chorus adds to the effect. (*Speed 79*)

NEW **Celebrity** RECORD

McCORMACK & Chorus

(with orchestral accompaniment) (*sung in Italian*)

10-inch record, 6s. 0d.

7-52061 **Funiculi, Funicula** *Denza*

In addition to the lovely ballad record on page three, we have the pleasure to present John McCormack in an Italian air often attempted by tenors. McCormack's success is striking.

D ENZA's familiar operatic composition is attacked by McCormack with real zest. No Italian could improve on the style and finish of the singing. McCormack is as much at home in this difficult work as in a simple ballad. His articulation of the Italian is delightfully crisp—this indeed is one of the joys of the record. There is absolute *abandon* in parts that tell of the temperamental blood of our great Irish tenor. The effects are enhanced by chorus and fine orchestra. (*Speed 79*)

NEW Celebrity RECORD

CHALIAPIN

(with orchestral accompaniment) *(sung in Italian)*
12-inch record, 12s. 6d.

052387 Recit.: " Le rovine son queste,"
Evocazione : " Donne, che riposate,"
" Roberto il Diavolo " *Meyerbeer*

UNIVERSALLY acknowledged to be the world's greatest dramatic bass, Chaliapin has been throwing his personality into efforts for charitable funds in Russia. A stalwart helper indeed.

His singing of the striking music "The Ruins are here" brings to the mind the moonlit scene with Robert the Devil. The shuddering music, extraordinarily poignant singing, vivid effects of voice, all combine to produce a record comparable with his famous " Death of Boris."

When this unique voice breaks into the orchestration dramatically, as often happens in this scene, one feels almost in the presence of this most dominating of actor-singers, so realistically does the record convey the magnetism of Chaliapin. The intensity of feeling and expression which a single sound can take is a revelation of the art of the great Russian. In every way a striking record. *(Speed 79)*

NEW **Celebrity** RECORD

MELBA

(with pianoforte accompaniment) *(sung in French)*

12-inch record, 12s. 6d.

2-033042 { (*a*) **Romance**   *Bourget*
{ (*b*) **Mandoline**   *Debussy*

TWO exquisite morceaux in the modern French style in the most translucent, crystalline tones of the Golden Voice. Bourget's Romance is delicately woven as a silken fabric. The inflections of the voice might be the shimmer of the silk. The morceau enchants. The second piece on the record is entitled " Mandoline," and shows Debussy's muse in characteristic form. But such a voice would transform even banal music into celestial guise. There is a fittingly accomplished pianoforte accompaniment.

Melba is said to be about to organise Red Cross Concerts on a large scale here, as she has been doing "down under." This would mean a fortune for charity.   (*Speed 79*)

NEW **Celebrity** RECORDS

CARUSO

(with orchestral accompaniment) *(sung in Italian)*

12-inch record, 12s. 6d.

2-052077   Fenesta che lucive
                (Neapolitan Song)   *Bellini*

BELLINI'S gay Neapolitan song is delivered by Caruso in a cascade of finest gem-notes. His heart and soul are in the rendition of the folk-tune. The beauty of tone is as wonderful as ever, and the fire is peerless.
(Speed 79)

10-inch record, 8s. 0d.

(with orchestral accompaniment) *(sung in French)*

7-32008   Serenade Espagnole *Landon Ronald*

A SERENADE composed by our own Landon Ronald, whose songs rival in popularity those of almost any living writer. The famous conductor of the New Symphony Orchestra has here written a serenade redolent of Southern skies. The lilting, passionate air is voiced with great charm by Caruso, and the beauty of utterance is remarkable.
(Speed 78)

Published by Enoch & Sons

NEW Celebrity RECORD

TITTA RUFFO

(with orchestral accompaniment) (*sung in Italian*)

10-inch record, 8s. 0d.

7-52062 **Oh che m'importa ?**

Ettore Titta Ruffo

WITH the world's greatest soprano, tenor and bass we are fortunate to be able to present the world's greatest operatic baritone this month. He sings with his rich, magnetically alluring voice a swinging expressive Italian air of pleasing shape and melody. The characteristic tone of this rare voice is caught finely, and the ease of delivery is extraordinary. One awaits with more and more impatience the coming of Ruffo to England. True, we have his records, which are simply wonderful reproductions of the great original voice. When Ruffo himself does come here, his tens of thousands of record-admirers will enjoy a rare treat.

(*Speed 80*)

NEW **Celebrity** RECORD

FARRAR & CARUSO

(with orchestral accompaniment) *(sung in French)*

12-inch record, 20s. 0d.

2-034018 On l'appelle Manon "Manon" *Massenet*

The spirited singing of these two great vocalists, who are often actually heard together in grand opera in New York, is a revelation of artistic ensembles.

THE lovely duet from "Manon" receives a memorable interpretation at the hands of Geraldine Farrar and Caruso. Farrar is still remembered with delight by opera-goers here who had the joy of hearing her in Europe. The two great voices are heard in perfect form. The record is attractive, right out of the ordinary.

Massenet's "Manon" must not be confused with the more frequently played "Manon lescaut" of Puccini. This air, "They call her Manon," is one of the most striking in the opera. The spirited dialogue ensures high interest in the music, and the expressionful vocalization of these two great artists is quite charming. Such finish is rarely heard in combined singing. (*Speed 79*)

"His Master's Voice"

NEW **Celebrity** RECORD

CLEMENT & FARRAR

(with pianoforte accompaniment) *(sung in French)*

10-inch record, 8s. 0d.

7-34002   **Au clair de la Lune**   *Lully*

This record strikes quite a new note in celebrity duets. Its simplicity is most appealing.

CLEMENT is a superb operatic tenor with a big reputation in France and an even bigger one in the States. Since the war he has been doing great deeds in the firing line and has distinguished himself greatly. Lully's fragrant, simple little verses bring a catch to the throat when sung so divinely as in this beautiful duet. "In the Moonlight"! One sees Pierette shyly knocking at Pierrot's door, begging a pen to "write a word." Begging, too, warmth and shelter, lest she starve. Her candle is finished, her fire is out.

The pair of artists sing in glorious harmony, here gently, there with increased spirit, finally with much feeling. The Spirit of Montmartre! (*Speed 79*)

Miss RUBY HELDER (Lady tenor)
(with pianoforte accompaniment)
12-inch record, 5s. 6d.

03397   **Beauty's Eyes**   *Tosti*

A TYPICALLY intense song in the real Tosti style, Weatherly being librettist. The depth of meaning in this grand tenor love-song is plumbed as could be done by few artists living to-day —a tribute to Miss Ruby Helder which every hearer must endorse. Her performance is not only well-nigh perfect—it is striking, for the fervour she imparts to her vocalization is a thing only realizable on hearing. To hear this lovely piece of singing is to realize that in the Lady Tenor we have an English artist who takes her place with the world's greatest vocalists.   (*Speed 80*)

I want no stars in heav'n to guide me,
  I need no moon, no sun to shine
While I have you, sweetheart, beside me,
  While I know that you are mine.
I need not fear whate'er betide me,
  For straight and sweet my pathway lies ;
I want no stars in heav'n to guide me,
  While I gaze in your dear eyes.

I hear no birds at twilight calling,
  I catch no music in the streams
While your golden words are falling,
  While you whisper in my dreams.
Ev'ry sound of joy enth alling
  Speaks in your dear voice alone,
While I hear your fond lips calling,
  While you speak to me, mine own.

I want no kingdom where thou art, love,
  I want no throne to make me glad,
While within thy tender heart, love,
  Thou wilt take my heart to rest
Kings must play a weary part, love,
  Thrones must ring with wild alarms,
But the kingdom of my heart, love,
  Lies within thy loving arms. (*Weatherly*)

Words printed by permission of the publishers, Chappell & Co., Ltd.

NEW TONGUE-TWISTER
MURRAY JOHNSON
(with orchestra) 10-inch, 3s. 6d.

4-2538 Which switch is the switch Miss for Ipswich?

as featured in "ROSY RAPTURE" Revue at the Duke of York's, London

Another New Artist

Miss IVY ST. HELIER
(with pianoforte accompaniment)
10-inch record, 3s. 6d.

2-3061   **Mary from Tipperary**   *Darewski*

ANOTHER artist new to " His Master's Voice " catalogue makes her bow in vivacious Miss Ivy St. Helier, whose name will surely go down to posterity as one of the band of artists who went across to the firing line in France to give concerts to Tommy in the trenches and Tommy in the hospitals. This topping artist, who was in the recent revival of " Fanny's First Play," has won her spurs in many spheres of entertainment. That breathless song-hit " Mary from Tipperary," featured in new revues, is warbled with splendid spirit and raciness by the sweet-voiced Ivy. *Pub. by Francis, Day & Hunter* (*Speed 79*)

TABLE OF APPEARANCES
of
WELL-KNOWN CONCERT ARTISTS
who make " His Master's Voice " Records

Artist	Town	Date	
CLARA BUTT	Albert Hall	May	13
	Eastbourne	„	22
	Rhyl	„	24
ALICE LAKIN	London	„	2, 5 & 6
	Ipswich	„	4
VIOLET ESSEX	Folkestone	„	3, 4, 5, 6, 7, 8
	Brighton	„	17, 18, 19, 20, 21, 22
	Hull	„	24, 25, 26, 27, 28, 29
	Liverpool	„	31

Another New Artist

F. CHATTERTON HENNEQUIN
(SOCIETY ENTERTAINER) (with piano)
12-inch record, 5s. 6d.

01112   The Scrapper and the Nut   *Hennequin-Parker*

THIS artist is new to our supplement, and strikes a new note in records of elocution and story-telling. He is a favourite London society entertainer, and has appeared at Queen's Hall and many big provincial concerts. His voice is beautifully manly and "records" with extreme clearness.

"The Scrapper and the Nut" is a vivid verse-story (composed, be it noted, by himself) of the war and—getting into khaki. At the call "Hoxton and Belgravia each did their duty as a man." The horny-handed pugilist and the manicured "nut" were side by side in the ranks. Later, Bill called Cecil "Lizzie—his mother's only joy"— Cecil struck—and—well, the telling of what happened is heart-stirring.   *Published by Reynolds & Co.*   (*Speed 79*)

LIGHT OPERA COMPANY (with orch.)
12-inch record, 5s. 6d.

04604   Gems from "Veronique"   *Messager*
Containing :—" Opening Chorus," " When not engaged in fighting," " The bloom of an apple-tree," " Trot here," " Now my little story's ended "

VERONIQUE is being revived at the Adelphi Theatre with great *éclat*. Messager's tuneful music is making it one of the draws of the day. What could be finer than this choral record of the gems of the comic opera ? The singing is full of snap.
Published by Chappell & Co., Ltd.   (*Speed 80*)

Miss MARGARET COOPER at the Piano

12-inch record, 5s. 6d.

03396   **I don't seem to want you when you're with me**   *Rubens*

Margaret Cooper

THIS much-liked artist in songs at the piano has a rather different type of ditty for the present moment. It is almost serious—a tear with a smile. The title tells of a panicky lover. Margaret Cooper sings it with strong point and rare piquancy of voice. A smart and pleasing record.   (*Speed 78*)

Published by Chappell & Co., Ltd.

DESCRIPTIVE RECORD

(prayer and exhortation by the Rev. J. R. Parkyn)

12-inch record, 5s. 6d.

09283 Divine Service on a Battlefield *arr. by Vivian Bennetts*

LAST month we issued a record embodying "Divine Service on a Battleship." We follow it up fittingly with the form of service adopted on a battlefield.

There are effects of the whistling of "Jack Johnsons" during the service, bringing home to the listener the ever-present dangers of every minute of life in the firing line and just behind. The prayers and exhortations are impressively given by the Rev. J. R. Parkyn and the singing of the hymns and playing of the band are splendid. As is usual, the band breaks into a lively air at the finish.   (*Speed 78*)

𝒯𝒽𝑒 FOX-TROT VOGUE—NEW RECORDS

MURRAY'S RAGTIME TRIO acc. by MAYFAIR ORCH.

Beets & Turnips—Fox-Trot & Hors d'Oeuvres—Fox-Trot, C399, 12-in. 5/6

And Elsie Janis' New Record (with Basil Hallam) of Ballin' the Jack (see p. 24) *tells* you how to dance the Fox-Trot. Another fine tune to 'fox-trot' is Elsie Janis' record of "I want a dancing man," No. 2-3040, 10-in. 3/6

Humorous

ALFRED LESTER

(assisted by the author, Frank Leo)
12-inch record, 5s. 6d.

09282 **Higgins on the River** *Frank Leo*

NOW that the sun sometimes shines, visions are conjured up of flannels, the river, the crush, the recriminations! A ripping burlesque on a river collision is turned by Alfred Lester into a sparkling and laughable record. And there's a gramophone in it!

Alfred Lester

The Lugubrious One shows himself an artful cuss this month. His argument with the howling swell whose boat has collided with his own (Higgins') craft is screamingly funny. "If you'd spent more time in practising rowing instead of plastering your 'air down, this wouldn't 'ave 'appened!"—It ends up with the Nut paying backsheesh for damage done to——his own skiff! (*Speed 79*)

MURRAY JOHNSON

(with orchestral accompaniment)
10-inch record, 3s. 6d.

4-2534 **This is the Life** *Irving Berlin*

A REVUE type of song with an astonishing amount of "go" in it. The words are really funny. While extolling the pleasures of country life—chickens—and all the rest of it—Murray Johnson sighs for the Joys of the Town. This song is a hit of the spring. Finely sung. (*Speed 79*)

Published by Feldman & Co.

NEW
DOUBLE-SIDED
RECORDS
Bands

BAND OF H.M. COLDSTREAM GUARDS

(conducted by Capt. J. Mackenzie Rogan, M.V.O., Mus. Doc., Hon. R.A.M.)

12-inch double-sided records, 5s. 6d.

C 397
Merrie England—Fantasia *German*
Published by Chappell & Co. Ltd.

Demoiselle Chic—Intermezzo "Parisian Sketches" *Fletcher*
Published by Hawkes & Son

C 395
Mother Machree *Olcott, arr. by Ball*
(cornet solo by Corporal Morgan)
Published by Feldman & Co.

Chilperic *Herve, arr. by Mackenzie-Rogan*

EDWARD GERMAN'S "Merrie England" is served as a Fantasia for band, wonderfully played. The intermezzo, "Demoiselle Chic," will delight everybody, so haunting are its strains. This record drives home the fact that on "His Master's Voice"

Capt. Mackenzie-Rogan
(Senior Bandmaster of British Army)

records *only* can one have the first band of the army (conducted by the Army's Senior Bandmaster), a band without a rival in the world. "Mother Machree," as a band piece with cornet solo, is superb. "Chilperic" is very taking and original. (*Speeds 78*)

10-inch double-sided record, 3s. 6d.

B 284 {
Seraphine—March   *Clarke*
Published by Hawkes & Son

Fairy Dreams—"Pas de Fascination"
Arthur Wood
Published by Chappell & Co., Ltd.
}

THE march brings out the matchless aplomb of the great Guards' Band. Wood's Fairy number is extremely dainty. (*Speeds 79*)

MAYFAIR ORCHESTRA

12-inch double-sided records, 5s. 6d.

C 398 {
Naval Revue—Part I.   *Eric Jones*

Naval Revue—Part II.   *Eric Jones*
}

LILTING presentation of sea tunes woven into striking harmony. This record is redolent of the salt sea ridden so majestically by our world-gripping Navy. (*Speeds 79*)

C 396 {
San-Su-Wa—Japanese Intermezzo   *Janin*
Published by Francis, Day & Hunter

La Fille de Madame Angot—Selection
Lecocq
}

EXCEEDINGLY fine orchestral selections, which tell their own tale in the language of harmony. The string effects are sweet. (*Speeds 78 & 80*)

10-inch double-sided record, 3s. 6d.

B 283 {
Charmeuse   *Clarke*

Hamadryad   *Benyon*
Published by Chappell & Co., Ltd.
}

A COUPLE of lighter pieces of much charm, quaintness and delicacy. Just the sort of music to give your instrument its first look at the garden this year. (*Speeds 79 & 78*)

OUR MARCH AND APRIL SUPPLEMENTS

REPRINTED FOR GENERAL CONVENIENCE

ORCHESTRAL—12-inch records, 5s. 6d.

NEW SYMPHONY ORCHESTRA
(conducted by LANDON RONALD)

0850	"William Tell" Overture—Opening Andante	*Rossini*
0840	"Le Prophète"—Galop	*Meyer beer*

VOCAL

12-inch record, 6s. 6d.

03395	Entreat me not to leave thee	Mme. Kirkby Lunn

12-inch records, 5s. 6d.

02557	We Sweep the Seas	Mr. Harry Dearth
02555	The Crocodile—"English County Songs"	Charles Tree
04123	Fair and grey and ancient—"Sherborne School Songs"	The Cecilian Quintette
03386	Husheen	Miss Alice Lakin

10-inch records, 4s. 6d.

2-3049	The stars that light my garden	Miss Ruth Vincent
2-4205	The Moon hath raised her lamp above—"The Lily of Killarney"	John McCormack and Reinald Werrenrath
2-3054	A Psalm of Love	Mme. Kirkby Lunn
2-3030	Little Grey Home in the West	Mme. Alma Gluck

10-inch records, 3s. 6d.

4-2529	O Flower Divine	Hubert Eisdell
4-2528	The Indian Soldier (Shabash Bhaiyan)	John Harrison
2-3055	Roses of Forgiveness	Miss Carmen Hill
2-3051	Courage ("Daily Telegraph" Recruiting Song)	Miss Ruby Helder
2-3052	Danny Boy (Old Irish Air)	Mme. Edna Thornton
2-3050	A Song of Gladness	Miss Evelyn Harding
4626	Anvil Chorus—"Il Trovatore"	Grand Opera Company
7-54004	Ah Mimi tu più non torni—"La Bohême"	Lambert Murphy and Reinald Werrenrath
4-2530	Clieveden Woods	Stewart Gardiner
2-4243	Carmen Sæculare –"Sherborne School Songs"	The Cecilian Quintette
4-2531	Megan	Mr. Hubert Eisdell
4-2532	Sussex by the Sea—Marching Song	Mr. Stewart Gardner
2-4244	The Children of Britain	The Cecilian Quartette

CELEBRITY

12-inch record, 20s. 0d.

2-054052	La rivedrà nell' estasi "Un Ballo in Maschera," Act I.	Caruso, Hempel, Rothier, De Segurola and Chorus

12-inch records, 12s. 6d.

2-052086	Cujus Animam "Stabat Mater"	Caruso
03336	Bonnie Sweet Bessie	Tetrazzini

10-inch record, 8s. 0d.

4-2480	Trusting Eyes	Caruso

(continued on inside cover)

NEW

RECORDS

for the month of

December
1915

This list is Supplementary to
the Main Record Catalogue

Orchestral

NEW SYMPHONY ORCHESTRA
(conducted by LANDON RONALD)

12-inch records 5s. 6d.

| 2-0571 | Zampa Overture, Part I | *Herold* |
| 2-0572 | Zampa Overture, Part II | *Herold* |

Landon Ronald

LIKE "Egmont" and "Leonora," which retain their concert-platform popularity through the ages despite the fact that the operas to which they are the preludes are no longer performed, "Zampa" is undying in its appeal to lovers of orchestral music. The extraordinary vitality of the music of Herold's overture captures the interest at every bar, and can even be said to stimuate.

Many are the interpretations of the work: none more strikingly original and vital than Landon Ronald's.

The Press has shown great interest in Landon

Ronald's return to the theatre for the first performance in English of "Carmen" at the Shaftesbury Theatre, since this the greatest of English conductors has not wielded the *báton* in a theatre for twenty years.

It was, of course, in the theatre that Landon Ronald began to climb the ladder of fame. From solo pianist he rose to conductor, thence to a similar position with an operatic touring company. Becoming Melba's accompanist for a term, he also showed outstanding ability as a composer. There followed a conductorship at Covent Garden Royal Opera, and ultimately the formation of what is now London's supreme orchestral body, the New Symphony Orchestra. . . . Yes, back to the theatre for a night's performance, after twenty years of concert work (which the maestro holds to be immeasurably loftier than theatre activities) —this must claim our sentimental interest.

To return to the current record-issue, "Zampa" forms a glowing addition to the New Symphony Orchestra's reproductions. The *verve* of the opening, the elusive pastoral episode that follows, the lilting, unceasing, rhythmic, march-like melodies that bring one to a convincing finale—all are delivered with the precision and feeling that invest every performance of this renowned combination.   (*Speed 79*)

Mr. JOHN McCORMACK (tenor)

(with orchestral accompaniment)

10-inch record 4s. 6d.

4-2368   **Mother o' mine**   *Tours*

Photo   Underwood

AMONG the shorter ballads of recent years none has attained more lasting success than Tours' "Mother o' mine." A song of this kind demands the acme of sustained vocalization, as well as real fervency, for a perfect performance —which is one way of saying that no man in the world can sing it so well as John McCormack.

The characteristic way in which the dulcet McCormack tones give out the haunting air seems to be the only possible one, you think, when under the spell of the rendition. Yet how different to the average unconvincing performance of "Mother o' mine" is this inspired singing of our great tenor.

The record is haunting, right up to the throbbing final note. (*Speed 77*)

Published by Chappell & Co , Ltd.

NEW ENGLISH SINGER
with a GOD-GIVEN VOICE

Mr. WILLIAM SAMUELL (baritone)
(with orchestral accompaniment conducted by Mr. Hubert Bath)
12-inch record 5s. 6d.

2-032019 Vision Fugitive "Herodiade" *Massenet*

THE Promenade Concerts, and subsequently the Shaftesbury Opera Season, will go down to history if only for serving to reveal amongst us a native singer of talents comparable with those of world-renowned artists of foreign birth. In Mr. William Samuell we have an operatic baritone who, at a bound, has entered the first rank. The critics have been so amazed that they have thrown off their prejudices and welcomed an *English* singer as a master.

Samuell's baritone voice is of immense range and flexibility, of the most silken quality and the loveliest "colour." But the voice is not his all; he has temperament, *style* (that rare attribute), emotional feeling. These features are strikingly reproduced in his first record, Massenet's "Vision Fugitive," delivered with sublime artistry.

Naturally, Samuell has become an exclusive "His Master's Voice" collaborator.   (*Speed 76*)

Mr. HUBERT EISDELL (tenor)

(with pianoforte accompaniment)
10-inch records 3s. 6d.

4-2622 Thank God for a garden *Teresa del Riego*

(with orchestral accompaniment)

4-2623 **Blue eyes I love** *Clarke*

Published by Chappell & Co., Ltd.

TWO impressive little songs whose appeal will be lasting. "Thank God for a garden" shows the song-writing muse of Teresa del Riego in its most enthralling vein. The serenely pure voice of Hubert Eisdell delivers the sweet verses with a distinctive loveliness of tone that belongs to the art of this polished young tenor. The passionate utterance is also remarkable for its clearness of enunciation.

Thank God for a garden,
Be it ever so small,
Thank God for the sunshine
That comes flooding it all !
Thank God for the flowers,
For the rain and the dew,
Thank God for summer,
That brings me you !

Thank God for the sunrise,
For the new morning bright,
Thank God for the sunset
That is "Shepherd's delight";
Thank God for the cornfields
In the moonlight of blue,
Thank God for summer,
Thank God for you.
(Teresa del Riego)

"Blue eyes I love" will capture every heart with its gentle, rocking cadence. It serves to show the roundness and power of Eisdell's rarely used lower register. "Blue eyes" is a really exquisite record.

(Speeds 78)

Words printed by permission of the publishers, Chappell & Co., Ltd.

6

"Opera in English"

Madame KIRKBY LUNN

(with orchestral accompaniment)

12-inch record 12s. 6d.

**03440   O Righteous God (Gerechter Gott)
"Rienzi"** *Wagner*

ANOTHER page is added to our series of "Opera in English" records by the aid of Madame Kirkby Lunn, our greatest English contralto, whose triumphs in the Grand Season at Covent Garden have been such a supreme feature these many years.

In the impressive aria, "O Righteous God," from "Rienzi," we hear Kirkby Lunn at the zenith of her matchless powers. The ease of delivery is remarkable. The velvety quality of voice betokens the contralto of peerless vocal production.

Against the wandering orchestral accompaniment the voice rises and falls with devotional stateliness. At the close there is a grand cadenza, showing off the control of the celebrated singer. (*Speed 79*)

Photo Dover Street Studios

"Opera in English"

Miss VIOLET ESSEX (soprano)

(with orchestral accompaniment)

12-inch record 5s. 6d.

03436   **Jewel Song—"Faust"**   *Gounod*

FROM accomplished Miss Violet Essex we garner the Jewel Song in English, to add to our operatic repertoire. Her performance is a sparkling one.

Gounod's masterpiece, it is said, is now sung throughout the world more than any other five operas combined. At the Paris Opera alone it has been given 1,500 times. Such lovely music can never die.

It is in the Garden Scene, Act III., that the present morceau is sung. In no humour to spin, Marguerite moves towards the house : she catches sight of the box of jewels. Opening it, she expresses her childish glee in the scintillating Jewel Song. This coloratura air is attacked brilliantly by Violet Essex, who overcomes the difficulties of the song with conspicuous ease.

A highly interesting record.   *(Speed 79)*

"Opera in English"

Mr. STEWART GARDNER (baritone)

(with orchestral accompaniment conducted by Mr. Hubert Bath)

12-inch record 5s. 6d.

02604   **Prologue—"Pagliacci"**   *Leoncavallo*

NO more popular operatic record could be offered than an English version of the famous Prologue. The singing is by Stewart Gardner, an earnest of sterling work.

The masterfully-constructed libretto of "Pagliacci," its compelling and moving story, the skilful orchestration, and, finally, the intensely dramatic plot, always hold an audience rapt.

During the orchestral prelude, Tonio, in clown costume, suddenly appears in front of the curtain and begs leave to revive the ancient Greek prologue. He then comes forward as Prologue and explains that the subject of the play is taken from real life—observing that actors are but men and that the author has tried to express the passions and sentiments of the characters he will introduce. He then orders up the curtain.

Stewart Gardner acquits himself with splendid ability, his virile voice being heard with great expressiveness.   (*Speed 78*)

"Opera in English"

THE GRAND OPERA COMPANY

(with orchestral accompaniment)

12-inch record 5s. 6d.

04575   Gems from "Il Trovatore"   *Verdi*

THE opera to be treated this month by the Grand Opera Company is Verdi's "Il Trovatore," or, as we ought to term it for an English version, The Troubadour. At the first production in English, however, the title used was The Gipsy's Vengeance, under which name the play met .with success at Drury Lane nearly sixty years ago.

This tragic work is permeated with an atmosphere of romance and mystery. The many melodious numbers contained in it have endeared it to all nations.

All the familiar airs, sung in English, are woven into this exhilarating record. The voices are rarely blended and the ensembles perfectly managed.

One relishes especially the Soldier's Chorus, Tempest of the Heart (Il Balen), and Home to our Mountains. To wind up, we have the undying Miséréré with its dramatic climax.

A record for every collection.   (*Speed 78*)

RECORDS *for* XMAS

You are recommended to the complete "His Master's Voice" Catalogue for a wide selection of records, vocal and instrumental, suitable for Christmas.   All the old hymns, devotional solos, choral numbers, bell reproductions, descriptive pieces, etc., are to be found on our Catalogue.   These records will add two-fold to the enjoyment of Christmas parties.

Miss FLORA WOODMAN (soprano)

(with orchestral accompaniment)

10-inch record 3s. 6d.

2-3124 Shepherd, thy demeanour vary

Brown, arr. by Lane Wilson

EACH day brings fresh triumphs to Flora Woodman, whom we termed recently " the new nightingale." Time confirms the appellation.

Included in her average concert programme is usually an Old English tune—such as "Shepherd, thy demeanour vary." This gives scope for the graceful and fluent delivery in which the charming young artist excels.

She takes an evident pleasure in the quality and gradation of her pure and resonant tone—thus affording additional delight to the listener.

Her exceptional gifts of voice and expression find a happy vehicle in this exquisite pastoral air, with its artless flow. (*Speed 79*)

Shepherd, thy demeanour vary
Dance and sing, be light and airy;
Would you win me, you must woo
As a lover brave and true.
Hum's and ha's, dull looks and sighing,
And such simple methods trying,
Never will this heart subdue,
I must catch the flame from you.
Fa la la!

Words printed by permission of the publishers, Boosey & Co.

11

New tenor of great gifts—first records

Mr. HERBERT TEALE (tenor)

(with pianoforte accompaniment)

10-inch double-sided record 2s. 6d.

B 525 { Love's Devotion *A. Tate*
{ Melisande *Ashleigh*

IN Mr. Herbert Teale we present a new tenor, whose appealing voice and refined style will give keen enjoyment to every ballad-lover. He bids fair to become one of the biggest favourites on records. As a singer of love-songs, he is a master. Hear these. (*Speeds 79*)

Published by J. H. Larway

Mr. JULIAN KIMBELL (baritone)

(with orchestral accompaniment conducted by Mr. HUBERT BATH)

10-inch double-sided record 2s. 6d.

B 524 { The Tempest of the Heart (Il Balen)
{ "Il Trovatore" *Verdi*
{ For a Carousal (Fin ch' han dal vano)
{ "Don Giovanni" *Mozart*

Published by Novello & Co.

FURTHER contributions of unusual merit from the popular baritone, Mr. Julian Kimbell. The full beauty of these two sustained operatic airs is brought out by the excellent artistry of this fine young singer. (*Speeds 78 & 79*)

NEW RECORDS

Miss NORA D'ARGEL (soprano)

**(with orchestral accompaniment,
conducted by Mr. Hubert Bath)**

12-inch record 5s. 6d.

03437   **La Villanelle**   *dell' Acqua*

WHAT soprano gifted with powers of coloratura fails to essay the "Villanelle" of dell' Acqua? In the natural course, Miss d'Argel offers the brilliant air to us, and a splendid record does she make of it.

The swing of the song is caught deliciously, and the bird-like flights are attained with an ease of production that sets the seal on the art and technique of the Australasian prima donna. At no point of this favourite old classic is there any diminution of enthusiastic attack. One can but marvel at an artistic equipment of so complete a nature.

We have had no more enjoyable record from Miss Nora d'Argel.   (*Speed 80*)

Published by Ashdown, Ltd.

Another star——romantic soprano's bow
Miss STELLA CAROL (soprano)
(with orch. accompaniment, conducted by Mr. Hubert Bath)

12-inch double-sided record 4s. 0d.

C 605
The Swallows *Cowen*
Published by Boosey & Co.
Lo, here the gentle lark *Sir H. Bishop*

IN Stella Carol, we introduce an artist new to records, but whose romantic story is as well-known to the musical public as her great gifts of song. She essays, on her début, two classics whose performance she accomplishes with sensational success. She will be, of course, exclusive to "His Master's Voice."

(By the by, Stella Carol was a survivor of the torpedoed "Arabic.") *(Speeds 79)*

THE LIGHT OPERA COMPANY
(with orchestral accompaniment)

12-inch double-sided record 4s. 0d.

C 596
Gems from "Betty"—Part I. *Rubens*
containing—
"I love the girls," "Can it be love," "We ought to combine," "The right side."
Gems from "Betty"—Part II. *Rubens*
containing—
"Duchess of dreams," "Jotte," "If it was true," "Opposite the ducks."
Published by Chappell & Co., Ltd.

A SPLENDID vocal medley from the prosperous Daly's Theatre hit, "Betty," which is among the brightest musical shows of the town. All the plums are given, and a fine double-sided record they make. *(Speeds 78)*

PADEREWSKI

12-inch record 12s. 6d.

05565   Le Carillon de Cythère (The Chimes of Cythera)   *Couperin*

THE magnetic Polish virtuoso makes an appropriate re-appearance on our supplementary list. For a long time past he has been working strenuously in England for the fund to relieve Poland in her agony. His intense love of his native land is the dominating passion of this celebrated artist.

In Couperin's Carillon composition Paderewski shows us the warmly temperamental side of his character. Technique he subordinates to feeling. The phrasing is massively sonorous, and the interpretation of the Chime passages is a revelation of poetic accomplishment.

The recording of the famous artist's playing is admirable.   (*Speed 80*)

TITTA RUFFO

(with orchestral accompaniment)

10-inch record 8s. od.

7-52031 Zaza piccola Zingara—" Zaza "

Leoncavallo

THE king of operatic baritones is known and loved in Italy for his impersonation of the rôle of Cascart in Leoncavallo's "Zaza." The air, "Zaza, little gipsy," is sung in Act IV. by Milio Dufresne, but the melody attracts Ruffo and makes him wish to sing it for record purposes, although it does not fall to him in the opera. It is a highly effective number, emotional yet melodious. There are many of those incomparably resonant declamatory notes that distinguish this master singer.

The orchestral accompaniment is rich, but is dominated by the great voice. *(Speed 79)*

TETRAZZINI

(with orchestral accompaniment)

12-inch record 12s. 6d.

2-053117 Tre giorni son che—" Nina "

Pergolese

THE Florentine nightingale gives a typical offering of crystalline singing replete with that bird-like ease of delivery that has made her name renowned in every corner of the earth.

While Covent Garden Opera remains closed, we suppose we cannot expect to have the *diva* back in England.

The many wonderful records of this supreme voice, however, reconcile one somewhat to the loss. Verily, the Tetrazzini records *are* Tetrazzini.

The " Nina " aria is given with superb grace and a quality of voice comparable only with the plash of a rippling brook. (*Speed 80*)

GLUCK and ZIMBALIST

(with pianoforte accompaniment)

10-inch record 6s. 0d.

2-3107 Old Folks at Home (Swanee River)
('with violin obbligato of Dvorák's "Humoreske")

THE editor of these notes recalls the thrill which stirred the great Albert Hall audience when first the opening notes of "Old Folks" were carolled by Gluck while Zimbalist simultaneously played — the "Humoreske"! The item was set down on the programme, innocently enough, simply as "Old Folks at Home."

The ovation that greeted the novelty caused pretty Alma Gluck to beam, the while her modest husband, Zimbalist, nodded approval.

No - one hearing this novel record can fail to be touched by the appeal of the sweet old tune with the haunting and appropriate obbligato.   (*Speed 78*)

CARUSO and ELMAN

(with pianoforte accompaniment)

12-inch record 16s. 6d.

2-032018   Si vous l'aviez compris—
Melodie   *Denza*

Caruso

WITH what a thrill of anticipation one sets in position for the first time a new record by Caruso of Italy and Elman of Russia! Nay, are they not, both of them, possessions of the world itself?

The memorable records of these two in combination are treasures of many music lovers. To them can well be added this enchanting ballad in French, by Denza. Caruso sings with the feeling and golden-throated ease that he alone can impart to a song. His tone is set off worthily by the temperamental bowing of Elman.

Elman

(*Speed 78*)

DESTINN & DUCHENE

(with orchestral accompaniment)

12-inch record 16s. 6d.

2-034020   Mio dolce pastorale—"Pique Dame," Act II.   *Tschaikowsky*

Destinn

TSCHAIKOWSKY'S colourful opera has been much in the limelight since the very notable performances of it some months ago at the London Opera House, where Vladimir Rosing was the guiding spirit. Rosing gave us a record of the gem of Act I.: "Forgive me, oh Divinity." The loveliest air of Act II. is now offered by Destinn and Duchene, whose combined singing is indescribably sweet.

The original writing of the Russian composer is noticed in the formation of this operatic morceau. Destinn performs gloriously, her fellow artist aiding admirably.

An unusual and beautiful record.   (*Speed 79*)

McCORMACK and Miss LUCY MARSH

(with orchestral accompaniment)

12-inch record 9s. 0d.

2-054059　O terra addio—" Aïda," Act IV.

Verdi

THE last scene of Verdi's "Aïda" shows the interior of the Temple of Venus, with a subterranean apartment below. Above, the priests and priestesses chant their strange songs. Below, a dark vault, in which Rhadames, condemned to burial alive, discovers Aïda, who had concealed herself there that she might die with her lover.

The lovers sing their plaintive "farewell to earth" in haunting strains, voiced impressively by McCormack and Lucy Marsh.

"The work finishes in serenity and peace, and such terminations are the most beautiful. Their song of love and death is among the most beautiful of all music," writes a French critic.

(Speed 80)

MARTINELLI

(with orchestral accompaniment)

10-inch record 6s. od.

7-52067   **Ideale—Melodia**   *Paoli Tosti*

SO marked was the favour with which the public received the recent ballad record of Martinelli, that we follow it up with another. This second one is Tosti's popular and haunting "Ideale."

Many will remember the beautiful Caruso record of this lilting melody.

Martinelli's interpretation is characteristic of his own personal style, and makes an interesting comparison. The big, open, full-throated tone of this young celebrity can be enjoyed in perfection in "Ideale." The technical finish of this piece of singing is amazing. And the style is enthrallingly refined. Superb singing by an accomplished Italian.   (*Speed 80*)

NEW RECORDS

Celebrated Dramatic Actress recites

Miss CONSTANCE COLLIER

12-inch double-sided record 4s. od.

C 606 { **The Hellgate of Soissons, Pt. I.** *Kaufman*
{ **The Hellgate of Soissons, Pt. II.** *Kaufman*

THE celebrated actress, Miss Constance Collier, has consented to make a record of the tale of Soissons during the famous attack there. Hellgate it assuredly was.

The poignant verses of a Frenchman were vividly translated into English, and Constance Collier declaims them with dramatic effect. This vocalised story makes the heart beat faster. *Published by Fisher Unwin* (*Speeds* 77)

NEW Celebrity Records ISSUED

This Supplement presents no fewer than nine records by Celebrity Artists, including Caruso, Tetrazzini, Titta Ruffo and Paderewski. See pages 7, 15, 16, 17, 18, 19, 20, 21 and 22 for these reproductions.

NEW ARTISTS

New artists on our Supplement this month include

WILLIAM SAMUELL	CONSTANCE COLLIER
STELLA CAROL	ADA REEVE
HERBERT TEALE	MANNY and ROBERTS

Mr. HARRY DEARTH (bass)

(with pianoforte accompaniment)

10-inch record 3s. 6d.

4-2624 **Devon mine** *Geehl*

THE popular and versatile basso pays cordial tribute to "the land of crag and tor." The already admirable art of this well-known artist has seemed recently to have become even more mature. There is a striking nobility of tone in his singing.

The sentiment of the song will reach every heart these days of expressed loyalty to one's native soil. Set to rousing music by Geehl, the ditty has a snap and a depth of sincerity that will carry it to success.

Harry Dearth is indeed in grand voice; his rich low notes are of vibrant resonance and pleasing quality. *(Speed 80)*

Where's the land of crag and tor, home of winds that wake and roar,
 Where's the land our hearts adore, land of hill and heather?
Where's the place of dale and stream, deep in snows, with rain agleam,
 Home of glory, home of dream, calling us for ever?

Homeland! homeland! homeland down in Devon,
 Western land of sun and cloud, kissed and blessed by heaven!
Men of other lands may boast, here's our land of crag and coast!
 Join with me and drink this toast, my homeland down in Devon!

Who are they that dwell down there, tann'd by good untainted air,
 Faithful, strong to do and dare, one in hope together?
Who, when evil days shall fall, who will rally, one and all,
 Who will answer England's call, men of hill and heather.

Homeland, homeland, etc. *(E. Teschemacher)*

Words printed by permission of the publishers, Gould & Co.

World=loved comedienne makes superb début

Miss ADA REEVE

(with orchestral accompaniment)

10-inch double-sided record 2s. 6d.

B 523 {
Father's little man   *Elton*
Published by Francis, Day & Hunter

Foolish Questions   *Hone*
Published by Feldman & Co.

YET another new artist for this rich supplement —Miss Ada Reeve. Few Vaudeville artists ever attain world-fame, like Harry Lauder and Chevalier. To be classed with world-celebrities is Ada Reeve, whose name is as familiar "down under" as in London town. In her own line she is undoubtedly without a rival to-day. Just hear her version of "Foolish Questions"; it is astonishingly clever. The other title is an effective contrast. (*Speeds 77*)

See page 3 of cover for New Records by the Original Cast of

"BRIC-A-BRAC," the Palace REVUE

Miss MARGARET COOPER
at the piano

10-inch record 3s. 6d.

2-3125   **Hello ! Martha**   *Smith*

THIS song explains the unique success of Margaret Cooper in two spheres at one and the same time. A ballad-singer who gives allegiance to Vaudeville is not always *persona grata* with concert audiences, on returning. But what concert audience can resist that refinement of style that accompanies Margaret Cooper's ditties anent foibles and fancies of the day ?

When we recently heard her sing "Hello! Martha" at the London Coliseum, she literally brought the house down. The cleverness of impersonation of Martha's various and hypothetical types of suitor tickled the vast audience immensely, and the singer was recalled again and again.

Give ear to this little song and be delighted.

(Speed 77)

Published by Chappell & Co., Ltd.

See page 36 for New Records by the Original Artists of
"WATCH YOUR STEP"
the huge Revue-hit of the Empire

Ragtimers who are the rage of London

CHAS. MANNY and BOB ROBERTS

10-inch double-sided record 2s. 6d.

B 521
All night long *Brooks*
Published by Francis, Day & Hunter

International Rag *Irving Berlin*
Published by Feldman & Co.

ALHAMBRA Revue artists make their bow. They are ragtime specialists of the real undiluted 100% order. One expert rips out the melody with rare vim, while  the black-faced accomplice chips in with an irresponsible sort of obbligato. The Alhambra audience just dote on this pair. (*Speeds 78*)

COLLINS and HARLAN

10-inch double-sided record 2s. 6d.

B 515
My Croony Melody *Goetz-Goodwin*

WILL HALLEY

I'm glad my wife's in Europe *Gottler*

THE famous American duo make a hugely effective harmonized record of the haunting "My Croony Melody," while, on the reverse, humorous-voiced Halley scores heavily with a quaint avowal of pleasure at his wife not being able to return to U.S.A. for fear of submarines. (*Speeds 79*)

Instrumental

Miss IRENE SCHARRER (piano)

12-inch record 5s. 6d.

05571   **Danse Nègre**   *Scott*

THE thousands of admirers of this fascinating artist will welcome her return to our Supplementary List. Miss Scharrer has been adding to her already great name by many appearances at symphony concerts in the metropolis, where her solo playing has been a great attraction.

The brilliant, crisp execution which is a feature of the Scharrer records, is present notably in this tripping Danse Nègre, which is performed with rare feeling. Among pianoforte solos, this number must take a high place.

Miss Scharrer, the Press states, is now affianced to a house master of Eton. (*Speed 79*)

Published by Elkin & Co., Ltd.

Miss UNA BOURNE (piano)

10-inch double-sided record 2s. 6d.

B 528 { **A Little Song**   *Una Bourne*
{ **Cradle Song**   *Una Bourne*

THE well-known and accomplished pianist, Miss Una Bourne, gives further delightful evidence of her ability. The execution is fluent and pleasing throughout, while the recording is excellent too. (*Speeds 79 & 78*)

Miss ELSIE JANIS & Mr. BASIL HALLAM

(with orchestral accompaniment)
12-inch double-sided record 4s. 0d.

C 597
{
I've got every-thing I want but you, *Marshall, arr. by Finck* — "The Passing Show"

DE GROOT & PICCADILLY ORCHESTRA

Piccadilly Grill—Waltz *de Groot*
(*Published by West & Co.*)
}

Photo: Foulsham & Banfield.

Elsie Janis & Basil Hallam in "The Passing Show."

SOME of the tunes introduced into "The Passing Show" at the Palace Theatre outlived even that highly successful revue. Among them "I've got everything I want but you" by the two stars of the cast was a gem. Coupled with this is de Groot's new waltz. (*Speeds 78*)

DORIS COWAN and GEORGE BAKER

10-inch double-sided record 2s. 6d.

B. 513
{
Prithee pretty maiden, "Patience" *Sullivan*

None shall part us, "Iolanthe" *Sullivan*
}

SULLIVAN'S most tuneful duet-songs delivered with lots of arch humour and the maximum of melodic charm. (*Speeds 78 & 80*)

Published by Chappell & Co., Ltd.

Miss OLIVE KLINE and
Miss ELSIE BAKER
(with orchestral accompaniment)
10-inch double-sided record 2s. 6d.

B 522 { **Abide with me** *Monk*
{ **Whispering Hope** *Hawthorne*

FOR the Christmas month we judge nothing
will be more acceptable than devotional
ballads like these two grand favourites. The
soprano blends gloriously with the contralto,
securing striking harmonies. *(Speeds 79)*

Mr. CHARLES HOPKINS (Celeste)
10-inch double-sided record 2s. 6d.

B 527 { **O come all ye faithful**
{ **Hark the Herald Angels sing**

THE first celeste records were entirely successful. The charm of this little-heard instrument
gave added beauty to the devotional airs
played by Mr. Charles Hopkins, and everyone liked
them. For December are offered two more high
favourites. *(Speeds 79)*

New "SHELL OUT" Records—Comedy Revue
THE MAYFAIR ORCHESTRA
12-inch double-sided records 4s. 0d.

C 608 { **SELECTIONS I & II,** containing
{ all the Hits

C 609 { One Step and March—"SHELL OUT"
{ The Girl in the Box Waltz *Yearsley*

DORIS COWAN and GEORGE BAKER
10-inch double-sided record 2s. 6d.

B 533 { Canoeing
{ **DORIS COWAN**
{ Little Miss Lancashire

DORIS COWAN
10-inch double-sided record 2s. 6d.

B 534 { I want loving all the time
{ **CLARA BECK**
{ At the Fox Trot Ball, that's all—"5064 GERRARD!" *Ayer*

TOM CLARE at the piano

12-inch double-sided record 4s. od.

C 595 {
**You're a great big bouncing wonderful
bundle of girl** *Sterndale Bennett*
The Awfully Chap *Murray*
}

TOM'S long title covers a vocal recipe for the modern type of syncopated love ballad. It is full of hits.

"The Awfully Chap" deals with a Johnnie with the Bond Street manner and a Hyde Park air! Screams both! *Published by Reynolds & Co.* (*Speed 78*)

Hawaiian Guitar Duets
PALIE K. LUA & DAVID K. KAILI

of the Irene West Royal Hawaiians

10-inch double-sided record 2s. 6d.

B 529 {
Kohala March
Honolulu March
}

THE first record of Hawaiian Guitar Duets turned out quite the big success we prophesied.

New numbers by Lua and Kaili feature original marches, which go with plenty of fire and precision. The peculiar tone quality of their strings is very fascinating. (*Speeds 78*)

THE SIX BROWN BROTHERS (Saxophone)

10-inch double-sided record, 2s. 6d.

B 526 {
That Moaning Saxophone Rag
VAN EPS TRIO (Banjo, Piano & Drum)
The Original Fox Trot *Klickmann*
}

STILL another novelty. The six saxophonists secure rare and pleasing effects in their gentle ragtime air. The record has a charm of its own. With it is a fox-trot performance of astonishing vigour and volume by an instrumental trio. Spicy fare! (*Speeds 79*)

Mr. CEDRIC SHARPE ('cello)

(pianoforte accompaniment by Mr. HAMILTON HARTY)

10-inch record 3s. 6d.

7898   **Serenade**   *Pierné*

PIERNÉ'S glowing sere-
nade makes a fragrant
'cello solo with piano
accompaniment. The latter,
by the way, is done by Mr.
Hamilton Harty, whose skill
as accompanist is only
excelled by his gifts as
orchestral conductor.

Mr. Cedric Sharpe draws
a strangely beautiful tone
from his instrument. The
reproduction, too, is completely faithful. (*Speed 78*)

PHILHARMONIC STRING QUARTETTE

10-inch record 3s. 6d.

8104   Slow movement from Quartette

in D major   *Tschaikowsky*

LOVERS of chamber music will find a feast of
restful melody in this famous Slow Movement
from Tschaikowsky's D Major Quartette.

The three celebrated instrumentalists who col-
laborate with Cedric Sharpe show themselves artists
of poetic feeling. The simply-woven strains are of
ineffable appeal : the lovely tremolo passages give
one a throb of emotion. (*Speed 79*)

*Many fascinating Instrumental Trios and Quar-
tettes are given on pages 113 and 244 of the complete " His Master's Voice " Record Catalogue.*

GRAND NEW DANCE RECORDS

Just the thing for your Winter Party

METROPOLITAN DANCE BAND

12-inch double-sided records 4s. od.

C 604
{ Chin Chin—Fox Trot *Caryll*
To-night's the Night Medley—
  Waltz Hesitation *Rubens*

C 603
{ Maurice—Waltz Hesitation
Music Box Rag—Fox Trot *Roberts*

C 602
{ Ticking Love Taps—Fox Trot
By Heck—Fox Trot *Henri*

C 600
{ Midnight Whirl Rag—One-step *Hein*
Whilst they were dancing around
  Medley—One-step

MAYFAIR DANCE ORCHESTRA

C 601
{ Black Rose—Waltz Hesitation *Aubry*
Illusion—Valse Hesitation *Nove*

FOR parties and dances these specially fine records, of large volume, will be found of immense value.

"Chin Chin" is due to follow "Watch Your Step" at the Empire Theatre in the New Year. We are out in advance with the spirited Fox Trot. The Maurice and Music Box numbers are both of unusual interest and beauty.

These fox trots are among the snappiest and raciest yet composed. Their entrain is irresistible. Then you have the choice of a lively one-step, and some very alluring waltz hesitations. Ideal for dancing to. *(Speeds 79 & 80)*

BAND OF H.M. COLDSTREAM GUARDS

**(conducted by Capt. J. MACKENZIE-ROGAN, M.V.O.,
Mus. Doc., Hon. R.A.M., Senior Bandmaster of the British Army)**

12-inch double-sided records 4s. od.

C 599 { **Romeo and Juliet—Ballet Music, Pt. I.**
Romeo and Juliet—Ballet Music, Pt. II.
Gounod

C 598 { **(a) Song of the Boatmen on the Volga**
(b) Russian Dance *arr. by Capt.*
Mackenzie-Rogan
L'Etoile du Nord—Selection *Meyerbeer*

THE Army's premier band have grand material again this month. Gounod's Ballet Music is richly done.

Mackenzie-Rogan's arrangement of the Ei Ukhnem song of the "Volga Boatmen" is full of original and pleasing harmonies, while the lively Russian Dance is played with masterly aplomb. Two records of the very highest class.

(Speeds 79)

METROPOLITAN MILITARY BAND

10-inch double-sided record 2s. 6d.

B 505 { **The Victors' March** *Elbel*
Aloha Oe—Hawaiian Medley Waltz

STIRRING band music, executed by the Metropolitan, with all that wealth of brass and percussion and richness of woodwind that make this band a big favourite. *(Speeds 79)*

MUSIC-HALL APPEARANCES of MANNY & ROBERTS (see p. 27)
Dec. 6 The Palace, Manchester   Dec. 20 Wood Green Empire, London
„ 13 Chiswick Empire, London   „ 27 The Coliseum, London

MAYFAIR ORCHESTRA

10-inch double-sided record 2s. 6d.

B 530 { The Dixie Bazaar *Alleyn*
{ Moontime Serenade—Waltz *Edridge*

THE Mayfair show what *can* be done with a lively rag tune. Their incomparable strings sing out the gay melody of "The Dixie Bazaar"; the waltz is dreamily played with a certain abandon. (*Speeds 80 & 78*)

Published by West & Co.

DE GROOT and the PICCADILLY ORCHESTRA

12-inch double-sided record 4s. 0d.

C 585 { Caresse d'Avril *de Groot*
{ *Published by Keith Prowse & Co.*
{ Le plus joli Rêve *Azzezo*

CLOYING orchestral works full of vivid passages of strong contrast. De Groot's wizard wand gets wonderful effects out of his Piccadilly artists. "Caresse d'Avril" is the very latest composition of fertile de Groot, and is destined to be one of the most frequently heard dances of the winter. (*Speeds 78*)

36

Orchestral

ROYAL ALBERT HALL ORCHESTRA
(late The New Symphony Orchestra)
(conducted by LANDON RONALD)

12-inch record 5s, 6d.

2-0599 Angelus—"Scènes Pittoresques"
Massenet

Photo   Claude Harris
Landon Ronald

THE Angelus number from Massenet's vivid "Scènes Pittoresques" needs little description. The carillon motif brings quickly to the mind the picture of belfried church and devout peasantry. There is a devotional note of great feeling and even poignancy running through the strangely beautiful performance of the newly-named Royal Albert Hall Orchestra, under the bâton (and the spell) of Landon Ronald. (*Speed 78*)

Madame ALMA GLUCK (soprano)
10-inch record 4s. 6d.
2-3119 The Braes o' Balquhidder (Scotch Air)

WHEN first we introduced charming Alma Gluck to the record world a couple of years ago, we presented her, among early offerings, in an old Scotch song, Burns' "Red, red rose," to a setting of R. L. Cottenet. Everyone was surprised at the facility with which this gifted Roumanian-American prima donna delivered the folktune-like melody. These old airs are great favourites with Gluck. "The Braes o' Balquhidder" is just such another lilting old tune. *(Speed 79)*

Miss MARIE HALL (violin)
10-inch record 3s. 6d.
3-7990   Vaggsang   *Tor Aulin*

THE great English violinist has just had one of the greatest triumphs of her triumphal life, in the ovations she has nightly received at her February engagement at the London Coliseum. This wonderful hall, a kind of super-entertainment hall head and shoulders above the usual Music Hall, has "starred" the eminent violinist with amazing success.

The Scandinavian melody forming her new record is exquisitely bowed. *(Speed 79)*

Mr. WILLIAM SAMUELL (baritone) (the late)

(with orchestral accompaniment)
10-inch record 3s. 6d.

4-2671   **The Wanderer's Song**   *Harrison*

WITH profound regret we have to record the passing-away of our new operatic star, Mr. William Samuell, who succumbed to an attack of typhoid a few weeks ago.

This brilliant young life, nipped so early in the bud, gave promise of great things. The gay-hearted Welshman had fought hard and finely for recognition; he had toured the Colonies with the Quinlan Opera Company and polished and perfected his vocal equipment the while, waiting for the chance to submit his art to the audience of Great London.

His chance came. An engagement at the Shaftesbury for the English Opera Season brought him lavish praise from the critics. Concert audiences, too, rose at him. He had his foot on the ladder—when illness took him away. His 'record' admirers wrote us condolences from everywhere. We issue a new ballad by the artist. (*Speed 78*)

Published by Enoch & Sons

Miss NORA D'ARGEL (soprano)
(with orchestral accompaniment)
12-inch record 5s. 6d.

2-033052   **Una voce poco fa**   *Rossini*
"Il Barbiere di Siviglia"

THE many admirers of this accomplished young Australasian have just had the opportunity of hearing her in a recital at the Æolian Hall, where she gave songs in many languages and of many types. The Press "notices" rightly acclaimed both her versatility and her vocal perfection.

The trying but alluring aria "Una voce" from The Barber forms her new record which is a revelation of effortless singing.   (*Speed 79*)

Miss NORA D'ARGEL and
Mr. WILLIAM SAMUELL (the late)
(with orchestral accompaniment)
12-inch record 5s. 6d.

04139   **Sincerity**   *Emilie Clarke*

THE late William Samuell had collaborated in a few duets with Nora d'Argel before the musical world lost him. The telling harmonies and deep feeling of Clarke's "Sincerity" render it a vocal record of outstanding merit. Both singers are inspired.   (*Speed 78*)

Published by Cramer & Co.

4

Mr. HUBERT EISDELL (tenor)

(with pianoforte accompaniment)

10-inch record 3s. 6d.

4-2670   Red Devon by the sea   *Clarke*

OUR favourite young tenor gives us an enthusiastic rendition of a song in praise of much-belauded Devon. We get many a one of those appealing, fulsome notes in the middle register that give character to Eisdell's lovely voice. And withal, we have that refinement of style and treatment that make his every note a delight. (*Speed 80*)

Published by Chappell & Co., Ltd.

Mr. STEWART GARDNER (baritone)

(with pianoforte accompaniment)

12-inch record 5s. 6d.

02618   O Star of Eve "Tannhäuser" *Wagner*

THE weighty timbre of Gardner's voice is fitted to attack the strains of Wagner's undying air. The recitative is delivered impressively and with great tone-trueness, and the air proper with swinging and virile power. A masterly effort. (*Speed 78*)

Miss CARMEN HILL (soprano)

(with pianoforte accompaniment)

10-inch record 3s. 6d.

2-3143   **The Bonny Curl**   *M. V. White*

CARMEN HILL, charming singer of dainty songs, has material worthy of her translucent voice in Maude Valerie White's sweet air "The Bonny Curl." That extraordinary finish and polished style, features which betoken faultless production, are lavished on the lines with the full beauty of Carmen Hill's voice. The effect is enchanting.   *(Speed 79)*

Published by Chappell & Co., Ltd.

Mr. CHARLES TREE (baritone)

(with pianoforte accompaniment)

12-inch record 5s. 6d.

02619   Wonnerful wise man o' Tawton
Kennedy Russell

THE ballad-monger of Zumerzet ditties is completely at home with this tale of the Tawton man. Charles Tree gives full many a turn of deeply-studied character to the utterance of the verses, showing himself once more a master of the art of rustic song singing.   *(Speed 78)*

Published by Chappell & Co., Ltd.

Mr. JOHN HARRISON (tenor)

(with pianoforte and organ accompaniment)

12-inch record 5s. 6d.

02617   **Beloved, it is morn**   *Ay'ward*

FLORENCE AYLWARD bids fair to go down to history at all events for her exquisite composition "Beloved, it is morn." The unconventional construction and spontaneous flow of this song carry conviction and delight with every honeyed note of the silver-voiced tenor, Mr. John Harrison. Organ and piano are used to support the voice, and the combined effect is indescribably beautiful.   (*Speed 79*)

Published by Chappell & Co., Ltd.

Mdme. EDNA THORNTON (contralto)

(with pianoforte, and 'cello by Cedric Sharpe)

12-inch record 5s. 6d.

03459   **Hindoo Song**   *Bemberg*

BEMBERG'S "Hindoo Song," usually performed by a soprano (Melba herself sings it) makes a surprisingly effective contralto record. Hardly could it be otherwise with Edna Thornton singing, anyway. This velvety contralto, singing at times against a 'cello, has never been heard to greater advantage than in the present record. We recommend it warmly to every devotee. (*Speed 79*)

CARUSO and DESTINN

(with orchestral accompaniment)

12-inch record 20s. od.

2-054053   Sento una forza indomita
" Il Guarany "

THE pleasurable anticipation that the Caruso - Destinn combination evokes is more than fulfilled by the hearing of this " Guarany " record.

This Opera was produced at La Scala in 1870 and at Covent Garden in

Camera Portrait by Hoppé

1872. It contains some brilliant music and many picturesque effects. The scene is laid in Brazil, in the seventeenth century.

This aria is quite the most famous number; it is the duet between Pery and Emilia. The balance between the two celestial voices is preserved exquisitely.   *(Speed 79)*

MARTINELLI

(with orchestral accompaniment)

10-inch record 6s. 0d.

7-52052 Cielo e mar "Gioconda" *Ponchielli*

Photo   Dover Street Studios

PONCHIELLI is perhaps the most famous of the contemporaries of Verdi. His "Gioconda," famous for its lovely airs, is based on a play of Victor Hugo, and deals with the sacrifices made by Gioconda, a singer, for Enzo a noble who in spite of the singer's devotion, deserts her.

Alone on the deck of Enzo's ship, awaiting Laura in the gloom, his thoughts turn to the scene about him and he sings "Heaven and Ocean." His performance is instinct with the poetry of the situation.

Martinelli displays that glorious ringing quality we all know so well.

(*Speed 79*)

NORA D'ARGEL, EDNA THORNTON, WALTER HYDE & ROBT. RADFORD

(with chorus and orchestra)

12-inch records 5s. 6d.

04145   **Elijah Memories—Part I.**

04146   **Elijah Memories—Part II.**
           (Mendelssohn) *arr. by Hubert Bath*

WITH the near approach of Easter this well-woven arrangement of the best-loved of Mendelssohn's airs from Elijah, arranged by the deft hand of Mr. Hubert Bath, will give delight to oratorio lovers. The artists responsible are among the very finest that could be found in this or any country. The best-known numbers are heard to glorious effect. The singing of the artists, solo and ensemble, is memorable.   (*Speed 79*)

Mr. CAMPBELL McINNES (baritone)

10-inch double-sided record 2s. 6d.

B 581 { **Jenny Nettle**   *arr. by Graham Peel*
        { **Duncan Gray**   *arr. by Graham Peel*

THIS favourite Scotch baritone makes his bow in two universally-loved ditties, sung with polish and endearing tenderness. His voice is rich and nicely modulated.   (*Speeds 78*)

Mr. HARRY DEARTH (bass)

(with pianoforte accompaniment)

10-inch record 3s. 6d.

4-2672   Little lass o' mine   *Morgan*

POPULAR Harry Dearth gives us the story of a little damsel who has entwined herself round his heart-strings. And right cheerily does he expound her charms and virtues. That great, rich, vibrant, manly bass is used to extraordinary effect in the recital. The recording is superb.   (*Speed 79*)

Published by Boosey & Co.

Mr. HERBERT TEALE (tenor)

(with pianoforte accompaniment)

10-inch double-sided record 2s. 6d.

B 573

Friend and Lover   *Landon Ronald*
Published by Keith Prowse & Co., Ltd.

Little Rose Clad Window   *Dorothy Forster*
Published by Chappell & Co., Ltd.

NO better pair of songs could be picked for the display of the peculiar art of this rising young singer. Landon Ronald's endearing song is given with feeling and Dorothy Forster's haunting tune is made the most of.   (*Speeds 80*)

Miss VIOLET OPPENSHAW (contralto)

10-inch double-sided record 2s. 6d.

B 572
{ When I am dead, my dearest ("Six
Sorrow Songs")   *Coleridge Taylor*
Published by Augener, Ltd.

Ici-bas (The Perfect Love) *Guy d'Hardelot*
Published by Chappell & Co., Ltd.

THIS distinguished young contralto, who has acquitted herself finely at the Royal Albert Hall Sunday Concerts on occasion, is heard in two excellent airs. Guy d'Hardelot's "Ici-bas" promises to have a vogue. (*Speeds 78 & 79*)

Mr. JULIAN KIMBELL (baritone)

(with orchestral accompaniment)

10-inch double-sided record 2s. 6d.

B 574
{ Brian of Glenaar   *Graham*
Published by Enoch & Sons

A Heap of Rose Leaves   *Willeby*
Published by Chappell & Co., Ltd.

THE picturesque baritone who once was a cartoonist, and who might have remained so had he not had a habit of humming to himself and (unconsciously) to a neighbour of the name of Gervase Elwes, has sung us that stirring ditty "Brian of Glenaar." It is magnificent. The other song is sung with distinction.

(*Speeds 80 & 78*)

Mr. MARK HAMBOURG (piano)

12-inch records 5s. 6d.

05574 Prelude in C Sharp minor, Op. 3, No. 2
Rachmaninoff

05575 { (*a*) **Waltz in D flat** *Chopin*
{ (*b*) **Etude in G flat**

THE great Russian pianist has been recorded superbly in Rachmaninoff's impressive prelude and two exquisitely crisp Chopin morceaux, which show his touch and interpretation to perfect advantage.

The massive chords and dictatorial "statements" of the prelude are the work of a virtuoso among virtuosi.

It is said that the prelude depicts the strivings and knockings of a man who has been closed down in a coffin as dead, but revives. This grisly suggestion is startlingly akin to the 'build' of the Prelude. (*Speeds 78*)

M. ZACHAREWITSCH (violin)

10-inch double-sided record 2s. 6d.

B 578 { **Sextette "Lucia di Lammermoor"**
Donizetti, arr. by St. Lubin
{ **Berceuse, Op. 16** *Faure*

A finely-contrasted double-sided record by the eminent violinist Zacharewitsch. The sextette is bowed with astonishing fire and the Berceuse with tender feeling. (*Speeds 79*)

MURRAY'S SAVOY QUARTETTE
10-inch double-sided records 2s. 6d.

B 577
We'll have a jubilee in
my old Kentucky home *Donaldson*
Published by Feldm n & Co.

Oh, man, you'd hang around *Ayer*
Published by Fe'dman & Co.

B 576
I like to dance with the girls *Ayer*
Published by Feldman & Co.

They didn't believe me
"To-night's the Night" *Kern*
Published by Francis Day & Hunter

B 575
Every morn you'll hear them
say "Good-night" *Tierney*
Published by Feldman & Co.

Hide and seek *Comer*
Published by Feldman & Co.

THE renowned combination at the Savoy Hotel, which makes the Supper Room the haunt of fashionable London, are heard in a set of rattling ragtime tunes, in which their unusual banjo, drum, vocal and other effects are potted in diverting fashion. (*Speeds 80*)

DESCRIPTIVE ORCHESTRA
10-inch double-sided record 2s. 6d.

B 579
Women of Britain *Crudge*
Our Whistling Tommies *Crudge*

TWO splendid new pieces offered in a very novel guise. (*Speeds 79*)

LESLIE FORBES
10-inch double-sided record 2s. 6d.

B 570
Flannigan Recruiting—Part I.
Do   do   Part II.

A NOVEL vocal record of a bright and breezy nature depicting one Flannigan with a blarneying tongue. (*Speeds 79*)

BAND of H.M. COLDSTREAM GUARDS
**(conducted by Capt. J. MACKENZIE-ROGAN, M.V.O.
Mus. Doc., Hon. R.A.M.)**

12-inch double-sided record 4s. od.

C 639 { **La belle Hélène—Selection**   *Offenbach*
          Ruddigore—Selection   *Sullivan*
Published by Chappell & Co., Ltd.

ENTRANCING selections from melodious works, played with that snap and finish which everyone associates with Mackenzie Rogan and the finest band in the army. (*Speeds 79*)

METROPOLITAN DANCE BAND
12-inch double-sided record 4s. od.

C 638 { **Vanity—Valse** *Published by Gould & Co.*   *Wade*
          Valse Jeune *Pub. by John Church Co., Ltd.* *Virgo*

Mr. WALTER JEFFERIES
10-inch double-sided records 2s. 6d.

B 567 { **Everybody's crazy on the Fox Trot**   *Scott*
           Published by The Star Music Publishing Co.
           There's a long, long trail   *Elliott*
           Published by West & Co.

B 571 { **Tip Top Tipperary Mary**   *Carroll*
            Published by Francis Day & Hunter

AIMEE MAXWELL
What is love, "Watch your Step"
Irving Berlin
Published by Gen. Musical Publishing Co.

MURRAY JOHNSON
10-inch double-sided record 2s. 6d.

B 566 { **When the Kilty lads come home (Pipes
            by Pipe-Major Burns)**   *Glen & Wright*
            Published by Lawrence Wright Co.
            Somebody knows, Somebody cares
            Herman Darewski
            Published by Francis, Day & Hunter

TOPICAL hits, including some irresponsible ragtime ditties and some haunting chorus songs, delivered with spirit and vivacity. (*Speeds 78*)

Miss MAIDIE SCOTT
(with orchestral accompaniment)
10-inch double-sided record 2s. 6d.

B 568

I'm glad I took my Mother's advice
Langley

Published by Francis Day & Hunter

Father got the sack from the Water-Works *Collins & Terry Sullivan*
Published by Francis Day & Hunter

THIS hugely popular comedienne with the dainty style makes her début with two typical songs of rare humour and piquancy, recorded with amazing clearness. *(Speeds 79)*

LIGHT OPERA COMPANY
(with orchestra)
12-inch double-sided record 4s. 0d.

C 637

Gems " The Only Girl " *Victor Herbert*
Containing : " Here's a health," " When you're wearing the ball and chain," "You have to have a part," " When you're away."
Published by Feldman & Co.

Gems "The Purple Road" *Reinhardt & Peters*
Containing : "To claim our pretty brides," " Mysterious kiss," " Diplomacy," " Feed me with love," " Pretty little Chi-Chis."
Published by Francis Day & Hunter

THESE brilliant vocal gems will need no praise of ours. They are as crisply sung as usual. *(Speeds 80)*

WALTON and CARTER
(with orchestral accompaniment)
10-inch double-sided record 2s. 6d.

B 569

Alabama Jubilee *Yellen*
Published by Francis Day & Hunter

Listen to that Dixie Band *Yellen*
Published by Francis Day & Hunter

A RAGTIME pair whose syncopated efforts are ripping in their irresponsible frivolity.
(Speeds 80)

Orchestral

ROYAL ALBERT HALL ORCHESTRA
(late The New Symphony Orchestra)
(conducted by LANDON RONALD)
12-inch record 5s. 6d.

**2-0609 Danse des Bacchantes—
"Philemon et Baucis"** *Gounod*

Photo   Claude Harris

Landon Ronald

A MONG the many charming numbers that have been written by great composers for the ballet, Gounod's Bacchantes' Dance takes an exalted place.

The fluttering, shimmery passages of the work bring to mind a Genée or a Karsavina pirouetting through flocks of dainty, posing coryphées.

The pompous opening carries us on to a stately and graceful passage suggesting the formal bowing of the prima ballerina. A more animated episode sets toes a-twirl. Soon we are in the midst of a tempestuous dance, and the delightfully crisp playing of the strings gives rare delight. The Finale is instinct with the abandon of the stage. Breathless whirls, bouquets.

The standard of the performance is the glorious one of the unequalled Royal Albert Hall combination, with Landon Ronald's genius gilding every bar.

(Speed 79)

Mr. WALTER HYDE (tenor)

(with pianoforte accompaniment)

12-inch record 6s. 6d.

02626   **Once again**   *Sullivan*

L OVERS of polished tenor singing will welcome the return to our supplement, after a long absence, of Mr. Walter Hyde. This finished artist, who has the rare ability to 'hold' the critical Sunday audience of the Albert Hall, with its vast auditorium seeking to swallow up the strongest voice, has more recently been surprising America with his vocal resources. Many a triumph is to his name.

In "Once again" we hear the intensity of vocal colouring that marks Hyde's voice as great. The fervour of the performance is remarkable. We have recorded him brilliantly.

(Speed 77)

Published by Boosey & Co.

Mme. JEANNE BROLA (soprano)

(with orchestra conducted by Mr. PERCY PITT)

12-inch record 5s. 6d.

03464 They call me Mimi, "La Bohême"
Puccini

BROLA won a million hearts with her first record, her singing of "Vissi d'Arte" being pronounced ravishing.

What can one say of her Bohême number? It is the undying "They call me Mimi" with which Melba associated herself so intimately, singing it in French and in Italian.

Brola's English version, which has many times enthralled the Opera audiences of the Shaftesbury Season, is of extraordinary refinement and pathos. From the opening "They call me Mimi, but my name is Lucy"—to the narrative portion, describing her pitifully simple life: her toilsome day of artificial flower-making, her lonely existence in her chambrette up among the housetops—all is sung with enchanting ease, purity of intonation and flawless artistry. This record can well be labelled "great." *(Speed 78)*

Leading new contralto makes her bow

Miss PHYLLIS LETT (contralto)
(with pianoforte accompaniment)
12-inch record 5s. 6d.

03462   **The Hills of Donegal**   *Sanderson*

IN Miss Phyllis Lett we present, for the first time on "His Master's Voice" records, an artist on whom honours are thick.

She first appeared at the Albert Hall in 1906 as principal contralto in "Elijah," and has since sung at all the great festivals up and down the kingdom. Her voice is characterised by a noble roundness and organ-like richness. She sings with the grace and polish and finish that betoken high training combined with the soul of an artist. Sanderson's little song as performed is a cameo of sound.   *Published by Boosey & Co.*   (*Speed 79*)

Mr. HERBERT TEALE (tenor)
(with orchestra conducted by Mr. HUBERT BATH)
10-inch double-sided record 2s. 6d.

B 610 { **O Flower of Memory**   *Fothergill*
The Sleep of Even "The Rose Maiden"
Published by Boosey & Co.   *Cowen*

THE appealing art of this fine young tenor finds splendid scope in two charming ballads.
(*Speeds 79*)

Miss FLORA WOODMAN (soprano)
(with orchestra conducted by Mr. HUBERT BATH)

12-inch record 5s. 6d.

03463 Come to the dance *Herbert Oliver*

OUR new nightingale distinguishes herself (and the supplement) with an irresistible vocal waltz this month. The spirit of merriment permeates Oliver's alluring number. The tripping stanzas are sung with that amazing lack of effort and crystalline purity of tone we have all learned to look for in a Flora Woodman record. To listen is to be enraptured. (*Speed 78*)

Photo.   Foulsham & Banfield

Published by Boosey & Co.

Mr. HUBERT EISDELL (tenor)
(with pianoforte accompaniment)

10-inch record 3s. 6d.

4-2696 A Little world of Love *Kennedy Russell*

A PLAINTIVE little love ditty that stands out from the ruck of love songs. It has a pleasing 'build' and quickly fixes itself in one's affections. Eisdell utters the intense phrases with his own perfection of style and wonderful feeling. The delicacy of the finish is ineffable. (*Speed 77*)

Published by Chappell & Co., Ltd.

The late WILLIAM SAMUELL (baritone)
(with orchestra conducted by Mr. HUBERT BATH)
10-inch record 3s. 6d.

4-2695   **The Yeomen of England**
       "Merrie England"   *Edward German*

THE rousing song from German's classic work is often heard on the concert platform, but it is safe to say that it has never before been sung with such majestic strength as we have it here by the late William Samuell. The articulation is astounding in its finish and clearness. Every final consonant is heard with jewel-like clarity. The singing is gorgeous.

Published by Chappell & Co., Ltd.   (*Speed* 79)

Mr. ROBERT RADFORD (bass)
(with orchestra under Mr. HUBERT BATH)
10-inch record 3s. 6d.

4-2694   **Father o'Flynn (old Irish Melody)**
          arr. by Sir C. V. Stanford

WHAT greater favourite is there than the dear old "Father o'Flynn"? Radford gives it with the right home touch and any amount of enthusiasm. It does one good to hear it. (*Speed* 78)

Published by Boosey & Co.

CARUSO

(with orchestral accompaniment)

12-inch record 12s. 6d.

2-032012 Les Rameaux (The Palms) *Fauré*

Photo
Bert

FAURÉ the composer was for many years the leading baritone at the Paris Opera. He wrote many songs, of which "Les Rameaux" is by the far greatest.

We have asked Caruso to sing for Easter this noble song of the Resurrection. He has complied and the world is the better for a thrilling rendition of the memorable phrases. The triumphant climax is taken with indescribable glory. The glowing voice—surely the greatest since song was first heard on this planet—shows not a trace of lessening beauty. And a Caruso record *is* a Caruso. *(Speed 78)*

OTHER GREAT EASTER RECORDS

CARUSO & JOURNET
12-inch record 20s. 0d.

| 2-034013 | The Crucifix | *Faure* |

CARUSO
12-inch record 12s. 6d.

| 02470 | Agnus Dei | *Bizet* |

CLARENCE WHITEHILL
12-inch record 6s. 6d.

| 02422 | Why do the nations "Messiah" | |

ROBERT RADFORD & WESTMINSTER CATH. CHOIR
12-inch record 5s. 6d.

| 02451 | The Palms | *Faure* |

Mme. CLARA BUTT (contralto)

(with orchestra conducted by Mr. ARTHUR GODFREY)

12-inch record 12s. 6d.

03399 **God shall wipe away all tears**
"The Light of the World" *Sullivan*

FOR Easter we make offering of Sullivan's great aria in the striking tones of the famous contralto. The recording is worthy of the voice itself. It is indeed Clara Butt who is singing to you from the record.

The declamatory passages are rendered strikingly, a high level of interest being maintained throughout. All lovers of Clara Butt's singing should secure this record and the many other unequalled numbers of hers on the catalogue. *(Speed 78)*

Published by Cramer, Ltd.

Mr. CHAS. HOPKINS (celeste solos)

(with organ accompaniment)

10-inch double-sided record 2s. 6d.

B 612 {**Jesus Christ is risen to-day**
{**O Sons and Daughters**

LOVELY celeste solos of devotional songs. The effect is exquisite. *(Speeds 79)*

Mme. EDNA THORNTON
(contralto)
(with organ by STANLEY ROPER, violin by JOHN SAUNDERS, and pianoforte)

12-inch record 5s. 6d.

03461   **Agnus Dei (Lamb of God)**   *Bizet*

BIZET'S "Agnus Dei," of which we have a record by Caruso, forms the subject of Edna Thornton's Easter record. The grand air brings forth some of the most luscious notes from the organ throat of the great contralto. There is majesty in her manner of singing, as in her actual tone. (*Speed 79*)

Published by Metzler & Co., Ltd.

WESTMINSTER CATHEDRAL CHOIR
(under the direction of Dr. R. R. TERRY) (unaccompanied)

12-inch records 5s. 6d.

04806   **Te Deum—Part I.**   *Francesco Anerio*
04807   **Te Deum—Part II.**   *Francesco Anerio*

ANERIO was born in Rome in 1567. In 1600 he was made Maestro at the Lateran. He wrote many masses and other works of sacred music, and his "Te Deum" is a fine example. The famous choir who sing it here under Dr. Terry secure a memorable performance. (*Speeds 79*)

NEW Easter Records

NORA D'ARGEL, EDNA THORNTON, WALTER HYDE, ROBT. RADFORD
(with orchestra and chorus under Mr. HUBERT BATH)

12-inch records 5s. 6d.

04148 "Elijah" Memories—Part III.
04149 "Elijah" Memories—Part IV.
Mendelssohn (specially arr. by Hubert Bath)

IN March we issued Parts I. and II. of this deftly-woven arrangement of Elijah airs by the famous quartette. The new parts are excellent. Ideal fare for Easter. *(Speeds 79)*

MAYFAIR ORCHESTRA, AIMEE MAXWELL & GEORGE BAKER
(with organ and bells)

12-inch double-sided record 4s. 0d.

C 619 { Intercessory Hymns, including "Lead Kindly Light" and "Abide with me" A Sabbath Evening Scene introducing Jude's 'A Sabbath Evening Hymn' *(Descriptive)* *arr. by Crudge*

STRIKING devotional work distinguished by variety and picturesqueness. *(Speeds 79)*

MAYFAIR ORCH. & GEORGE BAKER
(with organ, celeste and bells)

12-inch double-sided record 4s. 0d.

C 620 { Sacred Selection—Grant us Thy Peace Part I. *arr. by Crudge* MAYFAIR ORCHESTRA AND AIMEE MAXWELL Sacred Selection—Grant us Thy Peace Part II. *arr. by Crudge*

NOTABLE singing and playing of grand religious music. *(Speeds 80)*

Miss EVELINE MATTHEWS and
Mr. JOHN HARRISON

(with orchestra under Mr. PERCY PITT)

12-inch record 5s. 6d.

04147   **Let me gaze—" Faust "**   *Gounod*

A NOTHER page is added to our issues of Opera in English by this stirring duet, in which an accomplished new soprano, Miss Eveline Matthews, collaborates with favourite John Harrison.. The spirited dialogue from the third act of Gounod's tuneful opera is sung with great fervour and assurance by the splendid duettists, who are supported by a rich orchestra under Percy Pitt.

A treat for lovers of " Faust."   (*Speed 79*)

Miss MARGARET COOPER at the piano

10-inch record 3s. 6d.

2-3154   **Daddie and Babsie**   *Levey*

A SPARKLING delineation in song by the best-known of all singers-at-the-piano. The arch delivery is supplemented by singing of real worth, and the record is a complete delight.
(*Speed 79*)

Published by Chappell & Co., Ltd.

"His Master's Voice"

Another fine New Artist

Mr. C. WARWICK EVANS ('cello)
(with organ by Mr. STANLEY E. ROPER)

12-inch record 5s. 6d.

07886   **Solemn Melody**   *Walford Davies*

THIS grand young artist is principal 'cellist in the Queen's Hall Orchestra and ranks with the finest British performers. This estimate of his powers will be agreed to by all who hear his masterly bowing of Walford Davies' impressive "Solemn Melody." There is wonderful breadth, a nobility of tone, poetry of phrasing, as well as perfection of technique in this notable performance. The tone is extraordinarily big, without being forced. Lovers of the 'cello will rave over this record. *(Speed 78)*

Published by Novello & Co.

M. ZACHAREWITSCH (violin)

10-inch double-sided record 2s. 6d.

B 613 { **Scherzo** *Arensky*
{ **Ronde des Lutins, Op. 25** *Bazzini*

THE genius of Zacharewitsch is displayed in glorious guise in two well-contrasted pieces showing the artist to be a virtuoso. Exquisite playing. *(Speeds 79)*

Miss IRENE SCHARRER (piano)

12-inch record 5s. 6d.

05576 "Tipperary"—Five Variations   *Goodhart*
(founded on the immortal song)

TOMMY'S National Anthem dressed in its Sunday best. These musicianly variations (on a somewhat hackneyed theme) give new life to the tune. Miss Scharrer plays with wonderful strength and fire the massive and difficult runs of the grandiose versions: the delicate forms are fingered with dainty crispness. This is a record for everybody. *(Speed 79)*

Published by Feldman & Co.

Miss ISOLDE MENGES (violin)
(with pianoforte by Mr. HAMILTON HARTY)

12-inch record 5s. 6d.

2-07925 Staccato Valse, Op. 128, No. 6   *Godard*

A STACCATO valse is a novelty. It is, too, something of a contradiction in terms. It is a delightful conceit, perfectly played by Miss Menges. *(Speed 79)*

Mr. GILBERT BARTON and
Mr. W. GORDON WALKER (flute duets)

10-inch double-sided record 2s. 6d.

B 611 { Comin' thro' the Rye
{ Annie Laurie

A NOTHER novelty, two flutes with orchestra. The fussy flutes are splendid and wonderfully 'together' in the variations. *(Speeds 80)*

Miss VIOLET OPPENSHAW (contralto)

10-inch double-sided record 2s. 6d.

B 607
{
Shepherd's Cradle Song *Somervell*
(with piano)
Published by E. Ashdown, Ltd.

Massa's in de cold, cold ground *Foster*
(with orch.)
}

THE celebrated contralto reveals a power of imparting tender feeling to her singing, such as is confined only to the best contralto artists. *(Speeds 79)*

Mr. TOPLISS GREEN (baritone)

(with pianoforte accompaniment)

10-inch double-sided record 2s. 6d.

B 609
{
The love of my heart *Godfrey Nutting*
Published by Gould & Co.

Barnicombe Fair *Kennedy Russell*
Published by Boosey & Co.
}

THIS grand young baritone with the quality-laden voice and manly style is at his best in this nicely chosen double record. A first-class performance. *(Speeds 79)*

Miss RENÉE MAYER (soprano)

(with orchestral accompaniment)

10-inch double-sided record 2s. 6d.

B 608
{
Up there *Ivor Novello*
Slumber Tree *Ivor Novello*
}
Published by Boosey & Co.

THE composer of "Till the boys come home" has written these new songs, which dainty Renée Mayer sings very bewitchingly.
(Speeds 79)

THE VERSATILE FOUR
(from Murray's Club)
12-inch double-sided record 4s. 0d.

C 645 { **Circus day in Dixie** *Gumble*
  Published by Francis Day & Hunter
  Araby *Published by Feldman & Co.* *Irving Berlin*

THIS black-faced quartette comprises Haston, Johnson, Mills and Tuck. They are the rage of Murray's and the Alhambra Theatre, where their intimate performances of ragtime proclaim them " some coons " in this line. (*Speeds 80*)

PHIL KAUFFMAN
(with orchestral accompaniment)
10-inch double-sided record 2s. 6d.

B 606 { **Jenny**
  Ida, sweet as apple cider

ANOTHER new ragtime criminal, who puts a tremendous amount of intensity into his business. (*Speeds 80*)

LIGHT OPERA COMPANY
(with orchestral accompaniment)
12-inch double-sided record 4s. 0d.

C 646 { **Gems from "Tina," Parts I. and II.**
  containing :—Opening chorus, Cheri, Timbuctoo.
  Opening chorus, Act III., Let me introduce you to
  my father. The violin song. Something in the
  atmosphere. I come from Holland. *Paul Rubens*

A LOVELY vocal pot-pourri of the gems from the Adelphi hit. (*Speeds 78*)

MURRAY JOHNSON
(with orchestral accompaniment)
10-inch double-sided record 2s. 6d.

B 605 { **Pack up your troubles in your old kit-bag** *Powell*
  Published by Francis Day & Hunter
  Auntie Skinner's Chicken Dinner *Morse*
  Published by Feldman & Co.

TWO tuneful little ticklers for which ragtime is directly responsible. (*Speeds 79*)

MAYFAIR ORCHESTRA
12-inch double-sided records 4s. od.

C 648 { The Magic Flute Overture, Part I. *Mozart*
{ The Magic Flute Overture, Part II. *Mozart*

C 649 { **"Samples" Revue—Selections I. & II.**
containing :—How things have changed. When I
leave the world behind. Winter Nights. I work
eight hours. Moana Aloa Dance. My bird of
paradise. Peter. That dancing Jubilee. The
clarinet's love. *arr. by Crudge*

Published by Feldman & Co.

MOZART'S enthralling overture secures a
wonderful performance by the Mayfair.
"Samples" started at the Playhouse and is
now running merrily at the Vaudeville. The
wonderfully tuneful songs make a superb record for
orchestra. *(Speeds 80)*

OPAL MILITARY BAND
10-inch double-sided record 2s. 6d.

B 604 {
Till the boys come home *Ivor Novello*
Published by Boosey & Co. *arr. by J. Ord Hume*
MAYFAIR ORCHESTRA
Our boys *P. E. Smith*
Published by Hill & Co., Sunderland

THE new favourite tune of Tommy is played
beautifully in B 604. *(Speeds 79)*

BAND of H.M. COLDSTREAM GUARDS
(conducted by Capt. J. MACKENZIE-ROGAN, M.V.O., Mus. Doc., Hon. R.A.M.)
12-inch double-sided record 4s. od.

C 650 { **Flowers of the Forest**
{ **A Sleigh ride Polka-Descriptive** *Jullien*

RICH fare from the premier band of the British
Army. *(Speeds 79)*

NEW ISSUE.—Complete Regimental Marches of the British
Army, played by the Coldstream Guards Band under
Capt. ROGAN. *Ask for special list*

NEW

RECORDS

for

April - May

1917

This list is Supplementary to
the Main Record Catalogue

MARTINELLI

with harp accompaniment

10 inch record 6s. 0d.

7–52087 Mattinata ('Tis the Day)

Leoncavallo

Photo Dover Street Studios

MARTINELLI, who was so popular at Covent Garden and appeared here five seasons in succession, we hear has more than fulfilled the expectation of his English admirers at the Metropolitan Opera House, New York, where he has appeared with instantaneous success. Thus following in the footsteps of the other great Italian tenors, who have sung in New York, Martinelli has proved himself a truly great Artist. He is now 'appearing' in the ranks of the Italian Army.

In this record we hear him in "MATTINATA" which has become a standard in the repertoire of all great tenors.

Our friends will remember that this song was specially composed by Leoncavallo for the Gramophone Company, and was first sung by Caruso.

(*Speed* 78)

AMELITA GALLI-CURCI

(soprano)

with orchestral accompaniment

12 inch record 9s. 0d.

2-063006 La Partida (Canción Española)

Alvarez

MADAME GALLI-CURCI (pronounced Kour-chee), who in private life is the Marchioness Amelita Galli-Curci, is an Italian by birth. She has sung in opera in Madrid and in half-a-dozen European Capitals. Not long ago she made her début in America at the Chicago Opera House, when she was greeted with such scenes of frantic enthusiasm as have seldom been witnessed in that great theatre.

Photo   Victor Georg

Her voice is one that haunts the memory, and it is at its best in " La Partida," by Alvarez, the famous Spanish Composer. The melody is a beautiful one with its passionate, long-drawn phrases, and in the accompaniment can be heard the clang of the castanets which serve to enhance the Moorish character of the song. Altogether a magnificent record.

(Speed 78)

3

Mr. M. MURRAY-DAVEY (bass)

with orchestral accompaniment

12 inch record 6s. 6d.

2-032023   Piff ! Paff ! " Les Huguenots "
Meyerbeer

Photo   Arbuthnot

MR. M. MURRAY DAVEY, who gives us this splendid song from Meyerbeer's greatest opera, is by birth a Scotchman. He received his musical education in France and his wonderful rich bass, round, full and resonant, brings back to our minds memories of the good old Covent Garden days when Plançon, greatest of bassos reigned supreme. This is one of the finest records that has ever been produced and reveals the singer's voice in all its splendour.

(Speed 80)

4

Miss FLORA WOODMAN (soprano)

with orchestral accompaniment

12 in. record 5s. 6d.

2-053127 Ah, che assorta (Forest Fairy)

Venzano

THIS brilliant young Soprano's voice is always heard at its best in lilting waltz songs, which enable her to display the wonderful flexibility and elasticity of her pro-

Photo   Vandyck

duction. Very few singers have her gift of absolute ease and perfect intonation.   It is sure delight to listen to this birdlike carolling of limpid music.

(Speed 78)

Mr. EVAN WILLIAMS (tenor)

with orchestral accompaniment

12 inch record 6s. 6d.

02529 The Holy City *Stephen Adams*

THE brilliant vocal qualities, allied to a keen dramatic sense, which have given to Evan Williams a place apart among singers of Oratorio both in England and in America have never been better displayed than in this splendid record of THE HOLY CITY.

Every word rings out clear and true, and the chorus, " Jerusalem, Jerusalem," thrills the listener through and through till the final note swells to a mighty crescendo and dies away.

(Speed 78)

Mr. HERBERT CAVE (tenor)

with orchestral accompaniment

12-inch record 5s. 6d.

02716 **Mavis** *Craxton*

THIS delightful tenor, whose first record was published in February, has established himself a great favourite, not only with London Concert audiences, but also with the thousands who heard his delightful singing in " YOUNG ENGLAND," first at Daly's Theatre and afterwards at Drury Lane.

Herbert Cave sings this charming song in his usual manly style and conveys into his interpretation those qualities of light and shade which are perfectly rendered by this record, which should enjoy a wide popularity. (*Speed* **78**)

Published by Boosey & Co.

Madame EDNA THORNTON (contralto)
with pianoforte accompaniment
and 'cello obbligato by Mr. Cedric Sharpe

10 inch record 3s. 6d.

2-3226   **Time's Garden**   *Goring Thomas*

THE great contralto's voice gives us this song in thrilling tones which blend in perfect harmony with the sobbing strains of the 'cello obbligato played with perfect taste and restraint by Cedric Sharpe. All who purchase this brilliant record will feel sorry when Goring Thomas's beautiful melody comes to an end.   (*Speed* 79)

Photo   Elliott & Fry

Published by J. B. Cramer & Co., Ltd.

Mr. HARRY LAUDER
with orchestral accompaniment

10 inch record 3s. 6d.

4-2840   **Bonnie Mary of Argyle** (traditional)

DOUBTLESS there have been some people who imagined that Harry Lauder, by reason of his being a Music Hall singer, could not do justice to a good Concert Room Ballad. They will admit themselves mistaken when they have heard this record of a fine baritone song rendered with perfect taste and feeling by the versatile Scotch Artist.   (*Speed* 79)

NEW RECORDS

Miss EDITH EVANS (soprano)
with pianoforte accompaniment
12 inch record 5s. 6d.

03548   The Reason   *Teresa del Riego*

THIS is a remarkably fine ballad, emotionally sung by Edith Evans. Every word rings out pure and clear, giving one the illusion that the great singer is herself present. This is a record that will be in great demand among all lovers of fine singing.   (*Speed* **78**)

Published by Chappell & Co., Ltd.   Photo   Swaine

Mr. CHARLES TREE (baritone)
with pianoforte accompaniment
10 inch record 3s. 6d.

4–2839   Uncle Tom Cobbley at War
(Devonshire Folk Song)   *W. Masland*

THAT sympathetic baritone, Mr. Charles Tree, gives a boisterous rendering of that famous Devonshire Folk Song, brought up-to-date. Our old friends, Bill Brewer, Jack Sewer, Peter Gurney, Peter Davey and 'Arry Awke' are met again, but not in sweet Devonshire lanes. They are on the war-path after Kaiser Bill, and right glad we are to hear their merry notes.   (*Speed* **79**)

Published by Reid Bros.

"His Master's Voice"

THE SYMPHONY ORCHESTRA

conducted by Sir ALEXANDER C. MACKENZIE

12 inch record 5s. 6d.

**2-0721   Saltarello—Ballet Music from
"Colomba"**   *A. C. Mackenzie*

SIR ALEXANDER MACKENZIE has already been introduced to "His Master's Voice" patrons in his Suite, "London, Day by Day." We are glad to give lovers of good English music another opportunity of hearing the famous Composer at his best in the Ballet Music from "Saltarello." The delicacy and charm of the music are apparent throughout, and we would call attention to a certain, what we might call. Scottish effect in the music. You can almost hear the drone of the bagpipes in certain portions of the work. This is indeed a record to be secured.

(Speed 78)

Published by Novello & Co., Ltd.

NEW RECORDS

ROYAL ALBERT HALL ORCHESTRA
conducted by LANDON RONALD

12 inch record 6s. 6d.

2–0720 Casse Noisette Suite—Danse Arabe
Tschaikowsky

THIS is another delightful number of the famous Casse-Noisette, *Anglice* Nut-Cracker Suite, in the form of a weird and wonderful Arab Dance. The great Russian Composer shows his wonderful sympathy and understanding of the East in his scoring and instrumentation.

Photo   Claude Harris

The melody is Oriental in its strange and sensuous cadence, and as one listens one seems to feel the heavy laden atmosphere of Araby.

Of the playing itself nothing more need be said in its praise than that Landon Ronald's genius as a conductor is once again revealed.

(Speed 79)

VLADIMIR DE PACHMANN

12 inch record 5s. 6d.

05593 {
(a) **Prelude, Op. 28, No. 24**   *Chopin*
(b) **Etude, Op. 10, No. 5**   *Chopin*
}

Photo   Matzene Chicago

PACHMANN, as the whole world knows, is one of the greatest, if not the greatest exponent of Chopin. He gives us to-day these two gems by the great master in his inimitable style. The famous Etude, written for black notes only, flows from his fingers in limpid cadences like clear water flowing over the pebbles of some woodland stream. All piano lovers will secure this delightful record.   (*Speeds* 78)

Miss HELEN SEALY (violin)
with pianoforte accompaniment

10 inch double-sided record 2s. 6d.

B 798 {
Rosemary   *Sealy*
(a) Sybilla   (b) Pekinese   *Sealy*
}

THREE charming drawing-room pieces, beautifully rendered by a gifted violinist. A record that will be a great favourite with all who love to hear this sweet instrument well played. Special attention is called to the fine double-stopping in "Sybilla."   (*Speeds* 78)

BENNO MOISEIWITSCH

12 inch record 6s. 6d.

05598 Nocturne (for the left hand only)

Scriabine

Photo   Claude Harris

THE wonderful young Russian pianist attains the greatest heights of virtuosity in his perfect rendering of this unique NOCTURNE written for the left hand only. It begins with wonderful arpeggios and chords which are followed by passages of sustained melody. These lead up to a fine cadenza in which the master's technique is shown to its perfection It is well-nigh impossible to realize that one hand and that the left, is utilized in this complex, though beautiful nocturne.   (*Speed* 78)

Mr. C. WARWICK EVANS ('cello)

with pianoforte accompaniment

10 inch record 3s. 6d.

2-7853 When you're away " The Only Girl "

Victor Herbert

THIS famous and popular song from that well-known Musical Comedy: " The Only Girl," is here rendered on the 'cello by that gifted English artist, Mr. Warwick Evans. There is no instrument like the 'cello for rendering the *cantabile* quality of the human voice and Mr. Evans rises to the occasion in his interpretation of this sweet melody.

(*Speed* 79)

Published by Feldman & Co.

THE BAND OF H.M. COLDSTREAM GUARDS

conducted by Capt. J. MACKENZIE-ROGAN
M.V.O., Mus. Doc., Hon. R.A.M.

12 inch double-sided record 4s. 0d.

C 772 { Military Tattoo—Part I. (soloist Edward Halland)
Military Tattoo—Part II. (soloists Ernest Pike and Edward Halland)   *arr. by Mackenzie-Rogan*

LOVERS of Band Music will be pleased to see this double-sided record appear.

During the winter Dr. Rogan has performed his Military Tattoo at the London Opera House at several Charity Concerts.

Mr. Oswald Stoll was so pleased with the success that he persuaded Dr. Rogan to appear for a whole week at the Coliseum. A certain percentage of the receipts was given to the hospitals.

Many Londoners will remember this being performed at the Olympia each year during the Millitary Tournament. Dr. Rogan endeavoured to make the, records appear as realistic as possible.

To do this we not only had to have a Section of the Drum and Fife Corps of the Coldstream Guards, but also a Section of the Pipe and Drums of the Scots Guards, a choir and soloists, Dr. Rogan stage managing the whole proceedings. (*Speeds* 79)

Miss VIOLET OPPENSHAW (contralto)
with pianoforte accompaniment
10 inch double-sided record 2s. 6d

B 800
- Down here   *M. H. Brake*
  Published by Enoch & Sons
  ### Miss OLIVE KLINE (soprano)
- Charme d'Amour (Love's Spell)
  (with orchestral accompaniment)   *Kendall*

MISS VIOLET OPPENSHAW makes a fine record of the melodious "Down Here," while, on the reverse, the American Soprano gives a charming rendering of a real love song.

Mr. HUBERT EISDELL (tenor)
with orchestral accompaniment
10 inch double-sided record 2s. 6d.

B 799
- Until   *Sanderson*
  Published by Boosey & Co.
- So fair a flower   *Löhr*
  (with pianoforte accompaniment)
  Published by Chappell & Co., Ltd.

THE popular tenor's voice is at its best in these two delightful songs, sung as he alone can sing them. This record is a real object lesson in effective and tasteful ballad singing.

(*Speeds* 78)

OPAL MILITARY BAND
10 inch double-side record 2s. 6d.

B 797
- The London Scottish—March
  Published by Hawkes & Son   *H. E. Haines*
- Up Guards and at 'em   *Gordon Mackenzie*
  Published by Feldman & Co.

A STIRRING Scotch March written in honour of a Regiment of whom all Britons are rightly proud, and finely rendered by a first-rate Military Band.

(*Speeds* 79)

Mr. TOPLISS GREEN (baritone)

with orchestral accompaniment

12 inch double-sided record 4s. 0d.

C 775
{
The Last Call   *Sanderson*
Published by Boosey & Co.
Queen of my heart " Dorothy "   *Cellier*
Published by Chappell & Co., Ltd.
}

M R. TOPLISS GREEN'S virile baritone gives a perfect rendering of these two fine songs. There are many who will rejoice to hear once more, after many years, that fine ballad from " Dorothy," Cellier's tuneful opera which had such vogue in the last generation. We should not be in the least surprised if this tuneful English opera were to be revived very shortly.

(*Speeds* 79)

THE MAYFAIR ORCHESTRA

12 inch double-sided record 4s. 0d.

C 773
{
" SEE-SAW " — Selection I. cont. :—
Novello & Braham

Opening Chorus, See-Saw—The Nowhere Walk — The Ghost of Cleopatra — I can't find a place for that —The Automatic Wedding.

" SEE-SAW " — Selection II. cont :—
Novello & Braham

The Dream Boat—They called it London town — The Sandwichette—Jenny Johnson—Come and risk it.
Published by Ascherberg, Hopwood & Crew, Ltd.
}

T HE popular orchestra gives us all the gems from " SEE-SAW " and needless to say does full justice to all the tuneful numbers.

(*Speeds* 79)

Mr. SYDNEY REEVES and
Mr. BERNARD MOSS
with orchestral accompaniment
10 inch record 3s 6d.

2-4386 The Eton Boating Song *A.D.E.W*

A RECORD that will recommend itself not only to Etonians all the world over, but to all the "wet-bobs" wheresoever they be. It goes with a rare swing from beginning to end, and the chorus is a joy for ever. *(Speed 79)*

DE GROOT AND THE PICCADILLY ORCHESTRA
12 inch double-sided records 4s. 0d.

C 778
Some Sort of Somebody "Vanity Fair"
Published by Francis, Day & Hunter. **Kern**
Any time's Kissing time
"Chu Chin Chow" *F. Norton*
Published by Keith, Prowse & Co., Ltd.

C 774
Just my Love "Three Cheers"
H. Darewski
Published by the Herman Darewski Music Publishing Co.
JEAN LENSEN (conductor) AND THE TROCADERO ORCHESTRA
Désir Valse *D. Stone*

DE GROOT and LENSEN with their respective orchestras are in fine form in these four deservedly popular melodies. A very fine double-sided record which frequenters of the "Pic" and "Troc" will be eager to secure.

(Speeds 78)

Photo   Vandyck

Miss LOUISE LEIGH (soprano)
with orchestral accompaniment
12 inch double-sided record 4s. 0d.

C 776
Any place is Heaven if you are near me
Published by Chappell & Co., Ltd. *Löhr*
Miss VERA DESMOND (soprano)
Orpheus with his lute *Sullivan*

LOUISE LEIGH and VERA DESMOND, both excellent sopranos, give us these beautiful melodies which all singers love so well. Many excellent judges consider that "Orpheus and his Lute" is Sir Arthur Sullivan's masterpiece. and we believe that those who secure this fine record will endorse their opinion. (*Speeds* 78)

Miss LOUISE LEIGH and Chorus
with orchestral accompaniment
10 inch double-sided record 2s. 6d.

B 803
Luana Lou "Zig-Zag" *D. Stamper*
In Grandma's days they never did the
Fox–Trot "Zig-Zag" *D. Stamper*
Published by Francis, Day & Hunter

TWO catchy songs sung in Louise Leigh's inimitable style. We prophecy a big success for this double-sided record. (*Speeds* 78)

Miss OLIVE BURTON and Mr. ERIC COURTLAND
with orchestral accompaniment
10 inch double-sided record 2s. 6d.

B 802
Arizona *Melville Gideon*
There's a little bit of bad in every good little girl "Three Cheers"
Clarke & Darewski
Published by the Herman Darewski Music Publishing Co.

OLIVE BURTON and ERIC COURTLAND sing these two popular numbers with excellent taste and effect. Just the record to cheer you up if you feel a bit in the dumps. (*Speeds* 78)

HARRY WELDON
with orchestral accompaniment

12 inch double-sided record 4s. 0d.

C 777 {The Pastoral Song—Part I. *Tate & Harris*
{The Pastoral Song—Part II. *Tate & Harris*

Published by Francis, Day & Hunter

GOOD old Harry gives us a really first rate bit of rollicking fun. His idea of a Pastoral song is something that will fairly make your sides ache. This is a humorous record with a vengeance. (*Speeds* 78)

WALTON and CARTER
with orchestral accompaniment

10 inch double-sided record 2s. 6d.

B 801 {Morning Star *Thurban*
Published by Francis, Day & Hunter
{Dodo Dip *Tabbush*

Published by West & Co.

TWO ripping songs in the best rag-time style. This is indeed *some* record. (*Speeds* 79)

WARD BARTON and FRANK CARROLL (Yodling Duet)
with guitar accompaniment

10 inch double-sided record 2s. 6d.

B 796 {Hawaiian Love Song *Barton*
{Sleep, baby sleep (new version) *by Barton*

ALL lovers of yodling and that charming instrument the guitar will fairly rush to secure this record which is perfect of its kind.

(*Speeds* 78)

MARCH RECORDS

12-inch records 12s. 6d.

2-052107	Santa Lucia (Neapolitan Folk Song)	Caruso
2-033051	Romance—Elle a fui " Contes d'Hoffmann "	Lucrezia Bori

12-inch record 9s. 0d.

02628	The Pipes of Pan	De Gogorza

12-inch records 6s. 6d.

2-052047	O Paradiso " L'Africaine "	Ippolito Lazaro
03537	She wore a wreath of Roses	Madame Kirkby Lunn
03532	Listen to the Mocking Bird	Madame Alma Gluck
2-0702	Rouet d'Omphale, Op. 31 (poème Symphonique) (The Spinning Wheel of Omphale)	Royal Albert Hall Orchestra

12-inch records 5s. 6d.

04189	D'ye ken John Peel	The Gresham Singers
02703	Pro Peccatis " Stabat Mater "	Mr. Robert Radford
03538	The Green Hill o Somerset	Miss Carmen Hill
02706	Can't you hear me callin' (Caroline)	Mr. Charles Mott
02702	Molly Bawn	Mr. John Harrison
2-0703	The Butterfly's Ball—Overture	The Symphony Orchestra
05592	(a) Prelude in G flat	} Mr. Mark Hambourg
	(b) Etude in C sharp major	
02707	Somewhere in London Town	Mr. Tom Clare

10-inch record 4s. 6d.

4-7905	Chant d'Automne, Op. 37 No. 10	Efrem Zimbalist

12-inch double-sided records 4s. 0d.

C 757	" Maritana " Selection I. / " Maritana " Selection II.	} The Band of H.M. Coldstream Guards
C 762	Romeo and Juliet, Selection (Accordion solos) / The Barber of Seville-Overture	} Pietro Diero
C 763	Non è ver (Never more) / Death of Nelson	} Mr. Herbert Teale
C 758	God bring you home again / The Message	Miss Louise Leigh / Miss Ruby Helder
C 764	The White Hope Part I. / The White Hope Part II.	} Mr. Harry Weldon
C 765	Gems from " Theodore & Co. " Part I. / Gems from " Theodore & Co. " Part II.	} The Light Opera Company

10 inch record 3s. 6d.

2-4377	A Farewell	Miss Carmen Hill and Mr. Marcus Thomson

10-inch double sided records 2s. 6d.

B 771	Les Sylvains / Tarantelle	} Miss Una Bourne
B 770	Love, here is my heart / Arizona	} De Groot and the Piccadilly Orchestra
B 782	On the Plantation (Characteristic Piece) / The Irish Patrol	Descriptive / The Band of H.M. Coldstream Guards
B 783	Love me at Twilight / Melodie d'Amour	} The Mayfair Orchestra
B 784	Wait / Two Roses	Miss Ruby Heyl / Miss Elsie Baker
B 785	The Old Sexton / The Armourer's Song " Robin Hood "	} Mr. Peter Dawson
B 787	We'd better bide a wee / Lang Lang Syne	} Madame Lizzie Hunter
B 786	Oh how she could Yacki Hacki Wicki Wacki Woo / Come on to Nashville Tennessee	Mr. Olive Burton & / Mr. Eric Courtland
B 778	Oh Joe ! with your fiddle and your bow / That baby buffalo Rag	} Walton & Carter

NEW

RECORDS

for

June-July

1917

This list is Supplementary to
the Main Record Catalogue

TETRAZZINI

with orchestral accompaniment

12 inch record 12s. 6d.

2-053058   **Polonaise " Mignon "**   *Thomas*

WE are delighted to be able to announce to our subscribers that the Florentine nightingale has vouchsafed to give us a fresh record of what may be called her greatest triumph—the wonderful Polonaise from " Mignon." The great *diva's* wonderful voice is heard at its best in this beautiful melody which displays the perfect flexibility and " limpid sweetness long drawn out " which thrills the listener through and through. It would be difficult to find an aria better suited to display Tetrazzini's wondrous flexibility with its limpid trills and cadences. We prophesy an unprecedented rush for this splendid record.

(Speed **77**)

JOHN McCORMACK
with orchestral accompaniment

12 inch record 9s. 0d.

2-052111   Non é ver   *Mattet*

NON é ver ('Tis not true) is a lover's protest upon discovering that love is capricious. If the protest seems somewhat mild, it must be remembered that the song belongs to an era when a smooth-flowing melody was considered more important than dramatic force. John McCormack has adapted himself with admirable artistic discretion to the conditions and his protest is plaintive rather than vigorous. The volume and intensity of vocal beauty are quite remarkable. All lovers of a fine tenor voice will be proud possessors of this record.   (*Speed* **78**)

Published by Edwin Ashdown Ltd.

...ry VIII.

...an

...oser

...hestra

...Morris
...ward German

...hepherds'
...ward German

Photo   Elliott & Fry

...e Sir Henry Irving specially commissioned Edward German to write the inci-
...um production of Shakespeare's HENRY VIII.

...ser had never written anything since this, it would be safe to say that he would
..."Three Dances" which delight the ear no matter how often heard. Small
...ve become hugely popular. They display a vein of inspiration at once national
...he village green as it was in the days of Bluff King Hal, is caught and hauntingly
...hey are given to our subscribers by the Symphony Orchestra and we need not add
...oly of musicians, conducted by the composer himself, succeeds in investing the
...ty and atmosphere of the " Merrie England " of those peaceful days.

...ance " in all its graceful and rhythmic roundness ; then we are plunged into the
...ance " bringing a picture of passionate and even grotesque frenzy. But, of the
...ds' Dance " is the most enchanting in form of melody.   From this airy opening
...asure which enables one to visualize the merry footings of the country dancers.
...ery lover of British Music will hasten to secure these glorious records.

(Speeds 77)

Miss CARMEN HILL (mezzo-soprano)
with pianoforte accompaniment

10 inch record 3s. 6d.

2-3237   **John Anderson, My Jo**
(Old Scotch Air)

ANOTHER fine old Scottish song to which Carmen Hill does full justice. This gifted young artist gives the pathetic beauty of the lyric vocal treatment that is at the same time impressive and charming. Her perfect phrasing, delicate vocalization and the crystalline purity of her exquisite voice must be heard to be fully realised. This is a record that stands out conspicuously among Carmen Hill's many successes.

(Speed 79)

Mr. PETER DAWSON (baritone)
with orchestral accompaniment

12 inch double-sided records 4s. 0d.

C 790 {
   I'm a Roamer   *Mendelssohn*
   Mr. MAURICE BENSON (baritone)
   The Bo'sun, the gunner and me *Trotère*

Published by Ascherberg, Hopwood & Crew, Ltd.

FURTHER contributions of unusual merit by our two popular baritones. They impart real character and no little feeling to their singing of two rollicking songs of the sea.

(Speeds 79)

Miss PHYLLIS LETT (contralto)
with orchestral accompaniment

12 inch record 5s. 6d.

03557   Caller Herrin' (Old Scotch Air)

NO one could do greater justice to the pathos of this famous Scotch song. Miss Phyllis Lett's velvety, colourful voice is reproduced with a faithfulness that gives virtual possession of the singer and her art, alive and throbbing. It would be difficult, nay impossible, to give a finer rendering of this sad song that will bring tears to the eyes of the most unimpressionable.

(Speed 79)

Mr. HERBERT TEALE (tenor)
with orchestral accompaniment

12 inch double-sided record 4s. 0d.

C 789
{ **Love is waiting**   *W. H. Squire*
Published by Chappell & Co., Ltd.
Bantry Bay   *Molloy*
Published by Boosey & Co.

THIS greatly admired tenor scores new successes in two songs of great beauty by Squire and Molloy A real object-lesson in the art of tasteful singing.

(Speeds 77)

Mr. ERNEST BUTCHER (baritone)
with pianoforte accompaniment

12 inch record 5s. 6d.

02731 The Bulls won't bellow *Hetty Hocking*
Published by J. H. Larway

WE have been fortunate enough to secure the exclusive services of Ernest Butcher, whose special gift it is to render dialect songs in a way that is inimitably his own. He has many successes to his credit in London and is especially popular in the North.

This is a first-rate song with a fine chorus and we prophesy that ere long many a household will be singing its merry refrain.

More records of this artist's studies of country characters will be issued shortly.

(Speed 79)

Miss RUBY HEYL (contralto)
with orchestral accompaniment

10 inch double-sided record 2s. 6d.

B 816 { **You gave me comfort** *R. Wakley*
Published by West & Co.
{ **Humility** *D. Grant*
Published by Enoch & Sons

RUBY HEYL has a fine contralto voice full of that individuality that has made her so popular on the concert platform. In this double-sided record full scope is given to this gifted singer to show her charming talent. *(Speeds* 80)

ROYAL ALBERT HALL
O R C H E S T R A
conducted by LANDON RONALD

12 inch record 6s. 6d.

2-0740 Casse-Noisette Suite—Miniature
Overture   *Tschaikowsky*

Photo   Claude Harris, Ltd.

THIS is the Overture that opens the famous " Nut Cracker Suite " which has achieved such world-wide popularity. Our subscribers have already had the delight of hearing the March, the Danse Russe or Trepak, the lilting Valse des Fleurs, and last month the Danse Arabe. It opens pianissimo and maintains for a considerable time a gentle graceful rhythm. We call the attention to the extra-ordinary way Tschaikowsky succeeds in obtaining a miniature effect. It is a sweet dainty performance in which Landon Ronald's magnetic hold over his orchestra makes itself felt by the hearer at home.

(*Speed* 79)

Madame KIRKBY LUNN (contralto)

accompanied by the Band of H.M. COLDSTREAM GUARDS conducted by Capt. J. Macken: 'e-Rogan, M.V.O., Mus. Doc., Hon. R.A.M.

12 inch record 6s. 6d.

03556　　　　### Rule Britannia　　　*Arne*

Photo Claude Harris

THIS is a time when patriotic songs stir the hearts of Britons and spur them on to deeds of valour. To-day we are able to give a world-famed contralto's rendering of this national song which will appeal to the two great Sister Services. Added to this, Captain Rogan's splendid band of the Coldstream Guards, enhances the stirring strains by the support of his spirited conducting. A record that will be sought after by all who have their country's good at heart.　*(Speed 79)*

Mr. JOHN HARRISON (tenor)

with pianoforte accompaniment

10 inch record 3s. 6d.

4-2848　　　### My Lady Fair　　　*Gregh*

THIS dreamily beautiful song is perfectly rendered by John Harrison's golden voice. The suave qualities of rendition that distinguish this celebrated tenor are present in abounding measure in this perfect record.

There is deep emotion, pathos, tenderness and atmosphere in his interpretation. This is indeed well worthy to be added to our alre ady fine collection of records standing to John Harri son's name.

(Speed 78)

NEW RECORDS

Miss ROSINA BUCKMAN (soprano) and WALTER HYDE (tenor)

with orchestral accompaniment conducted by Mr. PERCY PITT

12 inch record 6s. 6d.

04195   **O Shrine of Beauty**
" Romeo and Juliet "   *Gounod*

O F all the gems from Gounod's beautiful opera, this is perhaps one of the most lovely. Rosina Buckman and Walter Hyde sing it with the delicacy and art which it deserves and their voices blend in thrilling harmony. These unequalled duettists have produced a splendid record which stands out conspicuously as one of their most finished efforts.

(Speed 78)

Mr. CHARLES MOTT (baritone)

with orchestral accompaniment

10 inch record 3s. 6d.

4-2849   **Curate's Song " The Sorcerer "**
Gilbert & Sullivan

Published by Metzler & Co., Ltd.

A L L admirers of Gilbert and Sullivan—and their name is legion—will rejoice to hear this old favourite sung by Charles Mott in his truly inimitable style. He does full justice to the humour of the song, which serves well to illustrate his fine vocal equipment and great range.   *(Speed* 78)

Miss UNA BOURNE (pianoforte)

12 inch double-sided record 4s. 0d.

C 787 {
Pas des Echarpes   *Chaminade*
Published by Enoch & Sons.
Air de Ballet   *Chaminade*
Published by Enoch & Sons.
}

THESE delightful Ballet airs, gracefully written by Chaminade, lend themselves to Una Bourne's exquisite touch and musical interpretation. She undoubtedly excels in the rendering of this kind of delicate music. (*Speeds* 78)

Photo   Elwin Neame

DE GROOT (violin)

with pianoforte and organ accompaniment

10 inch record 2s. 6d.

B 814 {
Auld Robin Gray (Old Scotch Song)
Bonnie Mary of Argyle (Old Scotch Song)
}

THE popular leader of the Piccadilly Orchestra charms us with his poetical rendering of two of the finest Old Scotch Songs. You couldn't wish for a more taking record.

Photo   Vandyk Ltd.

(*Speeds* 78)

NEW RECORDS

MARK HAMBOURG
(pianoforte)

12-inch record 5s. 6d.

05599 Sonata in C major Op. 2, No. 3
(last movement) *Beethoven*

THE renowned Russian pianist does full justice to the delicate charm of one of Beethoven's finest Sonatas. The colour which he imparts to the playing is a thing only to be realised by earnest hearing which this record richly merits. The great pianist makes a lovely spirit of grace and delicacy permeate his rendering, and when we state that this is a record worthy of Mark Hambourg's genius we have said sufficient.

(*Speed* **78**)

DE GROOT AND THE PICCADILLY ORCHESTRA

10 inch double-sided record 2s. 6d.

B 812
{
One hour of love with you " Hanky-Panky "   *M. Darewsk*·
Published by Francis, Day & Hunter
Come back to Ireland and me " Hanky-Panky "   *R. Wakley*
}

Published by West & Co.

HERE we have two of the most popular melodies from " Hanky-Panky " rendered in the famous Piccadilly Orchestra's unique style.

There will be a big demand for this excellent " double-sided." *(Speeds* 79)

THE MAYFAIR ORCHESTRA
conducted by Mr. JOHN ANSELL

10 inch double-sided record 2s. 6d.

B 810
{
Three Irish Pictures—No. 1   *J. Ansell*
Three Irish Pictures—No. 2   *J. Ansell*
}
Published by Hawkes & Son

WE call the special attention of music-lovers to the exquisite series of Irish Pictures arranged and conducted by Mr. John Ansell, the talented conductor of one of our deservedly popular orchestras. One of the most attractive of orchestral records.

(Speeds 79)

THE MAYFAIR ORCHESTRA

10 inch double-sided record 2s. 6d.

B 811
{
Poppies—A Japanese Intermezzo
N. Moret
When it's night-time in Dixieland
Irving Berlin
}

Published by Feldman & Co.

(Speeds 79)

THE BAND OF H.M. COLDSTREAM GUARDS

conducted by Capt. J. MACKENZIE-ROGAN
M.V.O., Mus. Doc., Hon. R.A.M.

12 inch double-sided record 4s. 0d.

C 786
{
Church Parade—Part I.
(soloist Mr. Peter Dawson)
Arr. by Mackenzie-Rogan

Church Parade—Part II.
(soloists Mr. Ernest Pike & Mr. Peter Dawson
Arr. by Mackenzie-Rogan
}

10 inch double-sided record 2s. 6d.

B 809
{
American National Airs (a) Yankee Doodle (b) Dixie (c) Hail Columbia
American National Airs (a) Red, White and Blue (b) The Star Spangled Banner
}

CAPTAIN ROGAN, just before leaving for his triumphant stay in Paris, gave us a magnificent Church Parade in two parts.

The splendid band of H.M. Coldstream Guards fairly surpasses itself, and its gifted conductor takes full advantage of the material he has so efficiently moulded in order to produce musical effects that must be heard to be believed. Then comes a splendid " double-sided " giving a fine selection of those splendid American National Airs that will soon strike terror into the Boche's heart—if he has one. These are military band records that will take a lot of beating. (*Speeds* **78**)

TOM CLARE
at the Piano
12 inch record 5s. 6d.

02726 The Gay River *Braham*

HERE we have the one and only Tom Clare at the Piano at his very best in one of his sauciest songs, and a very seasonable one too for it deals with the delights—and there are many—that are obtainable on the broad bosom of Old Father Thames. (*Speed* **78**)

Published by Ascherberg, Hopwood & Crew, Ltd.

JAY LAURIER
with orchestral accompaniment
10 inch double-sided record 2s. 6d.

B 819 {**Pudden !** *Blackmore & Gibson*
{**Nobody Loves me** *Lee & Grey*

TWO really subtle songs by that prince of Comedians, Jay Laurier. You can hear every single word he says and we advise you not to miss getting a record that will cheer you up in these strenuous times. (*Speeds* **79**)

Mr. ERIC COURTLAND and
Mr. WALTER JEFFERIES
with orchestral accompaniment
10 inch double-sided record 2s. 6d.

B 817 {**Mississippi Days** *Piantadosi*
{**We don't want a lot of flags a-flying**
{ **(When we all come marching home)**
Publish d by Feldman & Co. *Penso*

TWO very sprightly bits of the day delivered with dexterity, humour and harmonious effect by two past masters in the art of rag-time song. (*Speeds* **78**)

Published by Francis, Day & Hunter

THE ALBUM

of Eight Orchestral Records

of works of our

Great British Composers

conducted by themselves

SHOULD BE IN EVERY HOME

THE SYMPHONY ORCHESTRA conducted by
SIR EDWARD ELGAR, O.M.
12-inch records 5/6

2-0728 " Cockaigne Concert"—Overture   *Edward Elgar*
Published by Boosey & Co.

2-0729 " Wand of Youth"(a) The Tame Bear
             (b) The Wild Bear   *Edward Elgar*
(music to a child's play) Second Suite—Nos. 5 and 6
Published by Novello & Co., Ltd.

SIR ALEXANDER C. MACKENZIE
12-inch record 5/6

2-0719 " The Cricket on the Hearth "—Overture   *A. C. Mackenzie*
Published by Novello & Co., Ltd.

SIR CHARLES V. STANFORD
12-inch record 5/6

2-0718 " Suite of Ancient Dances "—(a) Sarabande
               (b) Morris Dance
Published by Boosey & Co.   *C. V. Stanford*

SIR FREDERIC H. COWEN
12-inch records 5/6

2-0714 " The Language of Flowers "—1st Set
             Gavotte—Yellow Jasmine   *F. H. Cowen*

2-0715 " The Language of Flowers "—2nd Set
Published by Metzler & Co., Ltd. —Waltz Viscaria   *F. H. Cowen*

EDWARD GERMAN
12-inch records 5/6

2-0716 " Much Ado About Nothing "—No. 1—Bourrèe
                            Edward German

2-0717 " Much Ado About Nothing "—No. 2—Gigue
Published by Novello & Co., Ltd.   *Edward German*

COMPLETE - £2 - 4 - 0

"His Master's Voice"

Miss OLIVE BURTON, Mr. ERIC COURTLAND and Mr. LLEWELLYN MORGAN

with orchestral accompaniment

10 inch double-sided record 2s. 6d.

B 818 { **Down Honolulu Way** *Burnett & Burke*
Published by Francis, Day & Hunter.
Baby (You're the sweetest baby I know)
Published by Feldman & Co. *Nat D. Ayer*

HERE you have a real galaxy of combined talent in two of the most catchy rag-songs you have ever heard. This record will have a big success.

(*Speeds* 79)

LIGHT OPERA COMPANY

12 inch double-sided record 4s. 0d.

C 791 {
" **Vanity Fair, Gems from—Part I. cont :**
The Kirchner Girl—Dashing Lady Vi—The Middy—The Rainbow Song—The Anzacs

" **Vanity Fair, Gems from–Part II. cont. :**
The Tanko—A little love—Some Sort of Somebody—Walkin' the Dog—Sunlight and shadow

EVERY single gem from one of the most successful " Revues " the Palace has ever produced. You have only to close your eyes and you will see the whole show from start to finish.

(*Speeds* 79)

ESTEY PIPE ORGAN
played by RICHARD K. BIGGS

12 inch double-sided record 4s. 0d.

C 788 { **Funeral March Op. 35, No. 2** *Chopin*
ESTEY AUTOMATIC PIPE ORGAN
Played by Mr. REGINALD L. McALL
Hallelujah Chorus "Messiah" *Handel*

TWO fine players on this noble instrument give us exquisite classical gems. You almost fancy you are listening to a full orchestra. A pleasant contrast to some of the lighter music in this catalogue. (*Speeds* 79)

HAWAIIAN GUITAR DUETS
played by HELEN LOUISE and FRANK FERERA

10 inch double-sided record 2s. 6d.

B 815 { **Hawaiian Hula Medley**
Pua Carnation

MISS HELEN LOUISE and Mr. FRANK FERERA show us what *can* be done on the guitar You must hear this record to believe it. A real revelation (*Speeds* 78)

MURRAY'S SAVOY QUARTETTE

10 inch double-sided record 2s. 6d.

B 813 { **Fancy you fancying me** *Lee & Weston*
Published by Francis, Day & Hunter
Hello! Hawaii, how are you? *Schwartz*
Published by Feldman & Co.

THIS record displays the special talents of Murray's celebrated Quartette to their fullest advantage. In their own way they display wonderful virtuosity. (*Speeds* 79)

APRIL-MAY RECORDS

12-inch record 9s. 0d.

| 2·063006 | La Partida Cancion Espanola | Amelita Galli-Curci |

12-inch records 6s. 6d.

2-032023	Piff! Paff! "Les Huguenots"	M. Murray-Davey
02529	The Holy City	Evan Williams
2-0720	Casse Noisette Suite—Danse Arabe	Royal Albert Hall Orchestra
05598	Nocturne (for the left hand only)	Benno Moiseiwitsch

10-inch records 6s. 0d.

| 7-52087 | Mattinata ('Tis the Day | Martinelli |

12-inch records 5s. 6d.

2-053127	Ah, che assorta (Forest Fairy)	Flora Woodman
02716	Mavis	Herbert Cave
03548	The Reason	Edith Evans
2-0721	Saltarello—Ballet Music from "Colomba"	The Symphony Orchestra
05593	(a) Prelude. Op. 28, No. 24 (b) Etude, Op. 10, No. 5	Vladimir de Pachmann

12-inch records 4s. 0d.

C 772	Military Tattoo—Part I. (soloist Edward Halland) Military Tattoo—Part II. (soloists Ernest Pike and Edward Halland)	The Band of H.M. Coldstream Guards
C 775	The Last Call Queen of my heart "Dorothy"	Topliss Green
C 773	"See-Saw"—Selection I. "See-Saw"—Selection II.	The Mayfair Orchestra
C 778	Some Sort of Somebody "Vanity Fair" Any time s Kissing time "Chu Chin Chow" Just my Love "Three Cheers"	De Groot and the Piccadilly Orchestra
C 744	Désir Valse	Jean Lenson and The Trocadero Orchestra
C 776	Any place is Heaven if you are near me Orpheus with his lute	Louise Leigh Vera Desmond
C 777	The Pastoral Song—Part I. The Pastoral Song—Part II.	Harry Weldon

10-inch records 3s. 6d.

2-3226	Time's Garden	Edna Thornton
4-2840	Bonnie Mary of Argyle (traditional)	Harry Lauder
4-2839	Uncle Tom Cobbley at War (Devonshire Folk Song)	Charles Tree
2-7853	When you're away	C. Warwick Evans
2-4386	The Eton Boating Song	Sydney Reeves and Bernard Moss

10-inch records 2s. 6d.

B 798	Rosemary (a) Sybilla (b) Pekinese	Helen Sealy
B 803	Luana Lou "Zig-Zag" In Grandma's days they never did the Fox-Trot "Zig-Zag"	Louise Leigh
B 800	Down here Charme d'Amour (Love's Spell)	Violet Oppenshaw Olive Kline
B 799	Until So Fair a Flower	Hubert Eisdell
B 797	The London Scottish March Up Guards and at 'em	Opal Military Band
B 801	Morning Star Dodo Dip	Walton & Carter
B 796	Hawaiian Love Song Sleep, baby sleep (new version)	Ward Barton and Frank Carrol
B 802	Arizona There's a little bit of bad in every good little girl "Three Cheers"	Olive Burton and Eric Courtland

THE SYMPHONY ORCHESTRA

conducted by Sir CHARLES V. STANFORD

12-inch record 5s. 6d.

2-0793   **Masque from " The Critic," Part I.**   *C. V. Stanford*

Published by Boosey & Co.

THE rare achievement of writing a successful British opera has certainly been accomplished by Sir Charles Stanford with " The Critic," which, produced a season or two ago by Sir Thomas Beecham, has been acknowledged as a remarkably fine work, and has already won great popularity with opera-lovers.

This delightful music is taken from the last act of the opera, and accompanies the masque, in 18th century style, that forms the finale to the whole work. In this olden-style pageant the English and Spanish fleets are seen approaching (it is the period of the Armada), they fight, and to wind up there is a grand procession, allegorical figures of rivers, sailors, and finally Britannia, accompanied by War and Peace.

The music, which recalls some of the chief themes of the opera, is notable for its grace and charm, and by its atmosphere and style skilfully suggests the quaint scenes on the stage. The music has been excellently recorded, with the composer conducting.

(Speed 78)

Saint-Saëns

Sir Chas. V. Stanford

THE ROYAL ALBERT HALL ORCHESTRA

conducted by LANDON RONALD

12-inch record 6s. 6d.

2-0792   **Marche Militaire Française**   *Saint-Saëns*
("Suite Algérienne," Op. 60, No. 4)

THIS brilliant march is one of a series of fascinating tone-pictures
of France's great African dominion that the genius of Saint-
Saëns has created for us.   In vivid music the composer suggests
a scene in which the bright uniforms of Zouave and Chasseur flash under
the blazing African sun.   The stirring opening phrases of the music
may be taken as representing the assembling of the soldiery, while the
fine swinging melody of the trio will possibly visualise for the imagina-
tive listener a long ride out into the desert on some reconnaissance or
manœuvre.

Beautifully orchestrated, the music is played with great dash and
finish by the Albert Hall Orchestra, under Landon Ronald.   The record
is a remarkably fine addition to the orchestral repertoire of " His
Master's Voice."

(Speed 79)

2

THE BAND OF H.M. COLDSTREAM GUARDS

conducted by Major J. MACKENZIE-ROGAN,
M.V.O., Mus.Doc., Hon. R.A.M.

12-inch double-sided record 5s.

C 837 { "**The Vikings**"—**Dramatic Overture, Part I.** *Hartmann*

"**The Vikings**"—**Dramatic Overture, Part II.** *Hartmann*

Published by Chappell & Co., Ltd.

THIS overture has a vigour and an open-air fr.shne.s most appropriate to its title. With vivid and picturesque descriptive
phrases the music conjures up to the mind a vision of those
grim old sea-raiders that the shores of Britain knew so well. The
opening is full of martial spirit and brilliant in instrumental colouring,
while the fine swinging melody next heard makes a very striking
contrast. These and other themes are skilfully treated, with much
variety of effect, making the Overture an uncommonly attractive piece.

The popular Guards' band is heard quite at its best in these records,
the playing being full of fire and notable for richness of tone.

(Speed 78)

10-inch double-sided record 3s.

B 891 {

Boston Tea Party—March   *Pryor*

Published by Hawkes & Son

Hands across the Sea—March   *Sousa*

HERE are a couple, of the jolliest marches imaginable, played in
spirited fashion. Both are by American composers. The
Pryor march, as its title shows, treats in a spirit of gaiety the
famous incident which resulted in America's independence as a nation.
Sousa's famous piece, a typical specimen of the March King's genius for
this kind of music, reminds us, on the other hand, of the kinship of our
American cousins, whose "hands across the sea" are particularly
welcome just now. *(Speed* 78)

3

Paderevski

PADEREVSKI

12-inch record 12s. 6d.

05567   **La Bandoline—Rondeau**   *Couperin*

IN this exquisite record the most famous living pianist has given
us a wonderful specimen of his great art that every music-lover
should possess. In each phrase one can feel the magnetic
personality of Paderevski, while its perfect technical finish and artistic
expression are alike remarkable. The music, a delightful little piece
by the famous French composer of the 17th century, is played with
surpassing grace and charm. Every note is perfectly poised and clear-
cut, and every phrase exquisitely polished, some of the pianissimos
being of extraordinary delicacy. From first to last we get the
impression of a master of his art, re-creating by his genius the
fascinating old-world atmosphere of this music of a past age.

(*Speed* 78)

O Music, sent to soothe and bless,
Vouchsafe me thy divine caress.—
Mary Cowden Clarke

Mischa Elman

ELMAN STRING QUARTETTE

MISCHA ELMAN
and Messrs. BAK, RISSLAND, and NAGEL of the
Boston Symphony Orchestra

12-inch record 9s.

08056   **Quartette in G Major—Andante**
C. von Dittersdorf

RARELY has one heard more perfect quartet playing than in
this beautiful Andante, performed by Mischa Elman and three
leading instrumentalists from the famous Boston Symphony
Orchestra of America. The exquisitely lovely melody with which the
movement commences is played by the first violin (Elman) while soft
rich harmonies are heard from the other instruments. This beautiful
theme is repeated again and again, during the movement, while a
graceful flowing tune is used to make an effective and welcome contrast.
The complete sympathy between the players has resulted in a most
artistically perfect ensemble, in which the tone of all four instruments
is blended to form a rich volume of sound as if one player alone
controlled them all, as indeed one may say that the famous violinist
actually does, for he is the ideal "leader" of the quartet.   (*Speed* 78)

Give me some music ; music, moody food
Of us that trade in love.—
Shakespeare

5

Beatrice Harrison

Miss BEATRICE HARRISON ('cello)

with orchestral accompaniment

10-inch record 3s. 6d.

2-7852   Orientale (Kaléidoscope, Op. 50, No. 9) *César Cui*

A REMARKABLY beautiful piece of 'cello playing has here been recorded by the gifted young English virtuoso of the instrument. The picturesque Eastern atmosphere of the music, by César Cui, who, like all Russian composers, excels in Oriental colouring, lends itself with uncommon effectiveness to the rich tone of the 'cello. Over a persistent throbbing of drums and *pizzicato* from the orchestra, the soloist plays the languorous phrases of a sensuous rich melody. With increasing intensity the music grows in richness and colour, but always with the faint undertone of melancholy so characteristic of the East. It is a fascinating little piece, and played to perfection by Miss Harrison.   (*Speed* 78)

I pant for the music which is divine. —
Shelley

Marie Hall

Una Bourne

Miss MARIE HALL (violin)

with pianoforte accompaniment

10-inch record 3s. 6d.

4-7931   Humoreske   *Dvořák*

MOST people know, and love, this beautiful little melody of Dvořák, and will welcome a record of the music by Marie Hall, who has brought all her perfectly finished art to bear upon it. The dainty, graceful tune, so familiar, is caressed with the greatest beauty of tone, every phrase clearcut, and the delicate sentiment of the music expressed to perfction. A record of unusual charm and one of the best the famous violinist has as yet given us.   (*Speed* 79)

Miss UNA BOURNE (pianoforte)

12-inch double-sided record 5s.

C 839 $\Big\{$ March—"Tannhäuser"   *Wagner, arr. Liszt*
         Liebestod "Tristan und Isolde"
                               Wagner, arr. Liszt

THAT genius of the pianoforte, Liszt, made many transcriptions of Wagnerian music, which recall in a wonderful way the orchestral effects of the original. To play them demands a considerable technique, and in these two famous numbers Miss Una Bourne shows her gifts in this direction with remarkable success. In each case the performance is brilliant and vivid, recalling to the mind the great scenes with which they are associated in the operas.   (*Speed* 79)

Music sweet as love.—
Shelley

Miriam Licette

Stewart Gardner

Madame LICETTE (soprano)

with orchestral accompaniment
conducted by Mr. PERCY PITT

12-inch record 6s. 6d.

**03596 Porgi amor qualche ristoro ("Nozze di Figaro")—
(sung in English) (Love I pray on me take pity)** *Mozart*

AMONG the many peerless melodies in Mozart's "Nozze di Figaro," which has been revived again with such success in recent operatic seasons, none is more beautiful than this little air in which the love-lorn Countess bewails her lot. Its pleading wistful phrases are tellingly sung by Madame Licette, the popular soprano who recently took the rôle in the Beecham production. The singer's fine treatment of the vocal phrases is enhanced by the excellent orchestral accompaniment, with Mr. Percy Pitt as conductor.
(Speed 78)

Mr. STEWART GARDNER (baritone)

with orchestral accompaniment

12-inch record 5s. 6d.

02779   Even bravest hearts may swell ("Faust") *Gounod*

THIS popular aria from "Faust" is universally recognised as one of the finest baritone songs ever written. Its stately opening phrases, so rich and glowing, and contrasting so effectively with the magnificent martial melody which follows, make it ideal for an artist who knows how to take full advantage of the opportunity it affords for fine singing. Mr. Stewart Gardner's rich resonant voice makes the familiar air unusually attractive by reason of his splendid manly delivery and power of dramatic expression. *(Speed* 79)

8

John McCormack

Rosina Buckman

Miss ROSINA BUCKMAN and Mr. WALTER HYDE
with orchestral accompaniment
conducted by Mr. PERCY PITT

12-inch record 6s. 6d.

04217   **Oh, Maritana ("Maritana")**   *Wallace*

THE tuneful music of "Maritana" will never fail in its hold on British folk. This fine duet, one of the best and most familiar numbers in the opera, is recorded splendidly by two of the most popular singers of the Beecham Company. The tenor phrases are most artistically sung by Mr. Walter Hyde, while Miss Buckman gives the soprano music with equal vocal beauty and expressiveness.

(Speed 78)

Mr. JOHN McCORMACK (tenor)
with male chorus and orchestral accompaniment

10-inch record 4s. 6d.

4-2886   **The Star-Spangled Banner**   *Key*

PERHAPS because of his recently attained American citizenship, John McCormack sings with unusually fine dignity and fervour the grand old national hymn of our Ally across the Atlantic. The melody is particularly effective for tenor, especially when the voice is such a glorious one as that of the famous Irish-American singer. An additionally impressive atmosphere is given to the music by the male-voice chorus which joins in at the end of each stanza in thrilling manner.

(Speed 78)

Carmen Hill   John Harrison

Miss CARMEN HILL (mezzo-soprano)
with pianoforte accompaniment

10-inch record 3s. 6d.

2-3287   **When the dream is there**   *Guy d'Hardelot*
Published by Chappell & Co., Ltd.

A NEW ballad record from such a favourite artist as Carmen Hill is always welcome. This graceful love-song of Guy d'Hardelot, so melodious and expressive, suits the singer's rich, warm voice and finished style perfectly ; in fact, it will rank as one of the best records she has made, delightful from beginning to end.   (*Speed* 78)

Mr. JOHN HARRISON (tenor)
with pianoforte accompaniment

12-inch record 5s. 6d.

02780   **I'll sing thee songs of Araby**   *Clay*
Published by Chappell & Co., Ltd.

HERE is a singularly fine record of one of the most famous English songs. Few composers have written a more beautiful melody than this lovely tenor air, so familiar to all and so universally popular. John Harrison sings it with that ringing tone and fervour of expression which has made him so noted as a ballad singer.   (*Speed* 78)

Herbert Teale

Edna Thornton

Madame EDNA THORNTON (contralto)

with orchestral accompaniment
conducted by Mr. HUBERT BATH

10-inch record 3s. 6d.

2-3286   **Dashing White Sergeant**   *Bishop*

THIS quaint and charming old 18th century song, by the composer of
the immortal " Home, Sweet Home," has a special appropriate-
ness to-day, except that the " red-coat " the lady's sweetheart
wore would now be khaki. Then, as now, the fair sex was always
susceptible to a soldier. The lilting melody, so piquant and fresh, is
delightfully sung by Mme. Edna Thornton, whose rich-toned voice
makes every phrase so effective.   (*Speed* 79)

Mr. HERBERT TEALE (tenor)

with orchestral accompaniment

12-inch double-sided record 5s.

C 838 {
    Whisper and I shall hear   *Piccolomini*
    Published by Ascherberg, Hopwood & Crew, Ltd.
    Mary of Allandale   *Hook, arr. Lane Wilson*
    Published by Boosey & Co.

TWO old favourites are here very artistically sung by the well-
known tenor. Piccolomini's popular song, with its haunting
refrain, is always welcome, and the exquisite century-old ballad
by Hook, one of the most graceful love-songs in English music, equally
so. The record of the latter is particularly fine, a song that can be
listened to again and again.   (*Speed* 77)

A MAGNIFICENT RECORD OF CHURCH MUSIC.

Mr. BEN MILLETT (alto vocalist)

Soloist : Church of the Immaculate Conception, Farm Street
(with Choir and Organ)

12-inch record 5s. 6d.

02787 **Pie Jesu** *Niedermeyer*

THIS music is by a composer whose merits deserve a wider appreciation. This number, one of his best, is a solo of unusual purity of style and variety of effect.

It rendering by Mr. Ben Millett, who has achieved a striking success with this, his first record, constitutes an extraordinarily beautiful piece of singing (accompanied by organ and choir) such as is not often heard. *(Speed* **79)**

THREE MINIATURE PIANOFORTE RECITALS.

I. By PADEREVSKI

1.	La Bandoline	*Couperin*
2.	Le Carillon de Cythère	*Couperin*
3.	Aufschwung	*Schumann*
4.	Minuet	*Paderevski*
5.	Serenade "Hark! Hark! the Lark"	*Schubert-Liszt*

II. By MARK HAMBOURG

1.	Moonlight Sonata (2 records)... ...	*Beethoven*
2.	(a) Nocturne in E flat ⎫ (b) Waltz in A flat ⎭	*Chopin*
3.	Polonaise in B flat	*Chopin*
4.	Étude	*Moszkowski*

III. By MOISEIWITSCH

1.	Le Coucou	*Daquin*
2.	Jardins sous la pluie	*Debussy*
3.	Jeux d'eau	*Ravel*
4.	Chant Polonais	*Chopin-Liszt*

THE "HOUSEHOLD INSTRUMENT."

MANY people are so accustomed to regard the pianoforte as a humble household instrument—even as a piece of furniture on which to place photos or objets d'art—that its wonderful capabilities for musical art are often forgotten. Yet in the hands of a great artist what a marvellous thing can this familiar object in the household become, almost a totally different instrument to that upon which we play accompaniments for singers or try over the latest musical comedy score.

A famous professor has stated that there are over two hundred varieties of "touch" in pianoforte playing, and when one listens to the performance of great virtuosi like Paderevski, Hambourg or Moiseiwitsch, one can at once realise this. Under the player's magic fingers the instrument at one moment may suggest to us the orchestra, at another the singing tone of violin or 'cello, the next moment the soft rich tones of the organ. In fact the pianoforte, with this magic power of suggestion, can cover the whole range of musical expression. Most of the greatest composers have given us some of their choicest inspirations in the form of pianoforte music. Chopin is a towering figure in the pianoforte world, while Schumann and Liszt are scarcely less notable. Among our composers of to-day the French musicians Debussy and Ravel have evolved many exquisitely beautiful new effects from the instrument.   H. C.

Mr. ERNEST BUTCHER and Miss MURIEL GEORGE

with pianoforte accompaniment

10-inch record 3s. 6d.

2-4474   **My Boy Billy**   *Butcher*

THE clever songs in folk-song style which Mr. Butcher writes are widely popular with audiences now-a-days. Here is a very taking number, delightful both in sentiment and music, and sung with delicious sparkle by the composer himself and that popular artist Muriel George.   *(Speed 79)*

Mr. TOM CLARE

with pianoforte accompaniment

12-inch record 5s. 6d.

02782   **Rumours**   *Lee & Weston*

Published by Francis, Day & Hunter

IN this clever ditty the popular comedian gives a humorous dissertation on rumour, which, as the proverb says, has "a thousand tongues." We are all familiar with the person "who knows someone who knows someone," &c., &c., that Tom Clare satirises so delightfully. It is one of his best and brightest songs.   *(Speed 77)*

COURTLAND and JEFFERIES

with orchestral accompaniment

10-inch double-sided records 3s.

B 898 {
Oh ! oh ! oh ! it's a lovely war   *Long & Scott*
Published by the Star Music Publishing Co.
Oh, boy ! when you're home on leave
Ayer, arr. Stoddon
Published by B. Feldman & Co.

B 895 {
For Me and My Gal ("Here and There")   *Meyer*
Published by B. Feldman & Co.
There's a girl for every Soldier   *Long & Scott*
Published by the Star Music Publishing Co.

HERE we have one of the brightest and best numbers from the popular Empire Revue. Another number tells of the fascinations of uniform for the fair sex, and has a refrain of a particularly catchy kind, while the other two are capital songs of topical interest.   *(Speed 79)*

THE MAYFAIR ORCHESTRA

12-inch double-sided record 5s.

C 840
{ **" Here and There "—Selection I. containing :**
Opening Chorus—Chunk-a-loo—The Petrol Patrol—Post Office Rag
—Omar Khayyam   *F. W. Chappelle*
" Here and There "—Selection II. containing :
Sporty Girlies—For Me and My Gal—Camouflage *F. W. Chappelle*
Published by Ascherberg, Hopwood & Crew, Ltd.

TO its bright melodious music the popularity of the Empire Revue owes not a little. In these two selections the Mayfair Orchestra gives us all the best features of the piece, played in very spirited style.
(Speed **78**)

DE GROOT AND THE PICCADILLY ORCHESTRA

10-inch double-sided records 3s.

B 892
{ **A Merry Farewell (Valse Song) (" Carminetta')** *Lassailly*
Published by the Herman Darewski Music Publishing Co.
Clicquot (" Carminetta ")   *H. Darewski*
Published by the Herman Darewski Music Publishing Co.

THESE two charming numbers from " Carminetta" sound wonderfully effective at the hands of De Groot and his clever instrumentalists. The dainty waltz and the appropriately sparkling music of " Clicquot " have both been recorded splendidly.
(Speed **77**)

B 893
{ **Didn't know the way to (" Arlette ")**
Novello, arr. Stoddon
Published by Ascherberg, Hopwood & Crew, Ltd.
Poor Butterfly !   *Hubbell*
Published by Francis, Day & Hunter

IVOR NOVELLO'S pretty song from " Arlette " makes a capital solo for De Groot, as does also the popular ballad of " Poor Butterfly ! "
(Speed **78**)

SAVOY QUARTETTE

10-inch double-sided record 3s.

B 896
{ **Down Texas Way** *Godfrey, Mills & Scott*
Published by the Star Music Publishing Co.
For Me and My Gal (" Here and There ")   *Meyer*
Published by B. Feldman & Co.

THESE two favourite numbers are given by the popular quartet in their own inimitable style, with brilliant playing and clever vocal effects. They are notable additions to the records made by the " Savoyards," and are certain to find wide favour.
(Speed **79**)

FEBRUARY RECORDS

12-inch record 12s. 6d.

2-053063 Ballata d' Ofelia (Mad Scene)—"Hamlet" Tetrazzini

12-inch record 9s.

2-034019 Parle-moi de ma mère—"Carmen"

John McCormack and Lucy Marsh

12-inch double-sided record 6s. 6d.

D 1 {
Appeal for £1,000,000 for maimed Scottish Soldiers and Sailors Harry Lauder
Shouther to Shouther (Shoulder to Shoulder) Harry Lauder
}

12-inch records 6s. 6d.

03591 Tacea la notte placida (The night calm and serene)—"Il Trovatore" (sung in English) Rosina Buckman
05613 Capriccio in B minor, Op. 76, No. 2 Moiseiwitsch
08055 Scherzo from Trio in D minor. Op. 49 Instrumental Trio
2-0782 "Lohengrin," Prelude, Part II The Royal Albert Hall Orchestra
2-032030 Don Juan's Serenade, Op. 38, No. 1 M. Murray-Davey

12-inch records 5s. 6d.

02770 Women's Work Tom Clare
03592 Rose softly blooming Dora Labbette
2-07951 "Carmen"—Selection II Tessie Thomas

12-inch double-sided records 5s.

C 825 {
A Comical Contest—Burlesque The Band of H.M. Coldstream Guards
American Fantasia—Happy Days in Dixie, or Life in the Old Plantation The Band of H.M. Coldstream Guards
}
C 826 {
"John and Jonathan"—Part I The Mayfair Orchestra
"John and Jonathan"—Part II The Mayfair Orchestra
}
C 828 {
"Arlette," Gems from—Part I The Light Opera Company
"Arlette," Gems from—Part II The Light Opera Company
}
C 829 {
Parted De Groot and the Piccadilly Orchestra
"The Maid of the Mountains"—Valse Song (Love will find a way) De Groot and the Piccadilly Orchestra
}
C 836 {
Roses of Picardy—in D, for soprano or tenor Pianoforte accompaniments
Love's Garden of Roses—in B flat, for soprano or tenor Pianoforte accompaniments
}

10-inch records 3s. 6d.

1473 A Message to the British Nation M. Venizelos
2-3277 The Lass with the delicate air Flora Woodman
2-3281 Your heart will call me home Phyllis Lett
2-4451 Down in a flow'ry vale The Gresham Singers
2-7854 Mon cœur s'ouvre à ta voix ("Samson et Delilah") C. Warwick Evans
4-2932 Derry Down Dale (Old English Song) Ernest Butcher
4-2933 Inside the Bar Charles Mott
4-2934 The Dream Cottage Herbert Cave

10-inch double-sided records 3s.

B 871 {
A Perfect Day The Band of H.M. Coldstream Guards
Until The Band of H.M. Coldstream Guards
}
B 872 {
Amerinda Intermezzo The Mayfair Orchestra
In a Monastery Garden The Mayfair Orchestra
}
B 873 {
The Wells of Sleep Hubert Eisdell and Bessie Jones
Down Zummerzet Way (We don't do things like that in Zummerzet) Ruby Heyl and Ernest Pike
}
B 874 {
The Green Hills o' Somerset Peter Dawson
The Soul of England Peter Dawson
}
B 875 {
Good Luck Vera Desmond
Fairy Revel Vera Desmond
}
B 876 {
Speak of Love again Hubert Eisdell
Steppin' down along the road Hubert Eisdell
}
B 878 {
Traumerie De Groot
The Bonnie Banks of Loch Lomond Helen Sealy
}
B 887 {
Shall us? Let's Jay Laurier
Top Hole Jay Laurier
}
B 889 {
On the other side of the big black cloud Eric Courtland
You taught me all I know Eric Courtland
}
B 890 {
Over There (the Great American War Song) Savoy Quartette
Oh, boy! when you're home on leave Savoy Quartette
}

Caruso

ENRICO CARUSO (tenor)

with orchestral accompaniment

10-inch record 8s.

7-52080 **Luna d'Estate (Summer moon)** *Tosti*

IT is a most fascinating little song that Caruso has chosen for his latest record—"Luna d'Estate," by his countryman Tosti, a composer who wrote some of the most enchantingly melodious songs in existence. This is a dainty ballad in the style of a Neapolitan serenade, words and music both describing eloquently the "Summer Moon" of the South, with its seductive charm and atmosphere of romance. Caruso, himself a Neapolitan, sings it in most delightful manner. He gives the lilting rhythm of the melody full play, while the touch of passion which now and again creeps into the music displays his wonderful voice at its very finest. The record is one which every admirer of the great tenor will want to possess. (*Speed* 79)

Radford as Boris

ROBERT RADFORD (bass)

with orchestral accompaniment
conducted by Mr. PERCY PITT
12-inch record 6s. 6d.

02792 My Power is absolute ("Boris Godounov") *Moussorgsky*

A NEW source of enjoyment has been afforded to opera-lovers in
recent years, by those magnificent Russian music-dramas,
which took all Western Europe by storm a few seasons back.
Amongst those which were performed here, at Covent Garden and
Drury Lane, "Boris Godounov" has been generally considered as the
masterpiece, and the most typical of the Russian operatic stage.   It
has already become a popular and permanent addition to our
operatic repertoire.   This solo, recorded so splendidly by Mr. Robert
Radford (whose appearances as Boris in the English production of the
opera have been strikingly successful) is a fine example of Moussorgsky's
music, so wonderfully dramatic and realistic.   The guilty Tsar,
occupying the throne by murdering the rightful heir (his nephew),
reflects upon his position, and betrays himself haunted by fear.   The
music portrays his panic-stricken mind in a vivid and intense way,
in phrases which have a peculiar charm derived from their Russian
colouring.   (*Speed* 79)

Galli-Curci   Rosina Buckman

AMELITA GALLI-CURCI (soprano)
with orchestral accompaniment
10-inch record 6s.

7-33017 Laughing Song (Bourbonnaise) " Manon Lescaut "—
(sung in French—L'Eclat de rire)   *Auber*

ONE cannot imagine a more perfect expression in music of the
spirit of laughter than this charming air by Auber.   The music
is the very essence of gaiety, while the dainty cadenza for the
voice at the end of each verse is an exquisite ripple of melody.
Mlle. Galli-Curci sings it with perfect art, and it is not too much to
describe the record as one of the most perfect of its kind ever made.
The exceptional purity and beauty of the vocalisation, especially in the
cadenza referred to, where every note is perfectly poised, with faultless
technique, makes it most delightful to listen to.   (*Speed* 79)

ROSINA BUCKMAN (soprano)
with orchestral accompaniment
conducted by Mr. PERCY PITT
12-inch record 6s. 6d.

03610   It was a dream   *Cowen*
Published by Boosey & Co.

SIR FREDERIC COWEN has given us many ballads of a
melodious and expressive character, and this well-known song is
a charming example of his genius in this direction, the melody
of the refrain being in his happiest vein. It has been excellently
recorded by Miss Rosina Buckman, who sings its graceful phrases
with great effect.   (*Speed* 79)

Arthur de Greef

ARTHUR DE GREEF (pianoforte)

12-inch record 5s. 6d.

05623   **Melody in F**   *Rubinstein*

THE distinguished Belgian pianist and composer, M. Arthur de Greef, is the latest recruit to the select company of famous pianoforte virtuosi who record only for "His Master's Voice." M. de Greef, who has long been a favourite with British audiences for his superbly artistic playing, has chosen for his first recording solo the ever-popular melody of Rubinstein, a little tune that is always welcome for its sunny charm and grace. The player caresses it with the true genius of the great artist, making the melody eloquent and expressive.   (*Speed* 79)

MARJORIE HAYWARD and UNA BOURNE
(violin and pianoforte)

12-inch double-sided record 5s.

C. 854 { Kreutzer Sonata : III. Andante, with variations, Part II.   *Beethoven*
Kreutzer Sonata : IV. Finale   *Beethoven*

THE Kreutzer sonata, one of Beethoven's finest works, is full of beauty and poetry from beginning to end. These two records, completing the earlier parts of the sonata (issued in two records in May) give us the last part of the beautiful variations in the Andante and the Finale, the brilliant music of the latter being played in fine style by the two talented instrumentalists.   (*Speed* 79)

"THE LILAC DOMINO"

THE MAYFAIR ORCHESTRA

12-inch double-sided records 5s.

C. 847 { "The Lilac Domino"—Selection I.   The Mayfair Orchestra
{ "The Lilac Domino"—Selection II.   The Mayfair Orchestra

C. 848 { For your love I am waiting (with chorus)   Louise Leigh
{ The Lilac Domino (with chorus)   Louise Leigh

C. 849 { Song of the Chimes   Louise Leigh and Randell Jackson
{ Where love is waiting   Louise Leigh and Randell Jackson

C. 850 { What is done you never can undo (with chorus) (Finale—Act II.)
{   Louise Leigh and Randell Jackson
{ The Land of Happy Memories   De Groot and the Piccadilly Orchestra

10-inch double-sided records 3s.

B. 906 { Carnival night (with chorus)   Eric Courtland
{ Consolation   Randell Jackson

B. 907 { For your love I am waiting   De Groot and the Piccadilly Orchestra
{ First love, last love, best love   De Groot and the Piccadilly Orchestra
{ ("The Bing Boys on Broadway")

The Music of "The Lilac Domino" is published by The Herman Darewski
Music Publishing Company.

"YES, UNCLE"

Accompanied by the Princes Theatre Orchestra, conducted by
Mr. WILLIE REDSTONE.

12-inch records 5s. 6d.

03609   Widows are wonderful   Julia James

02790   Ninny, Nonny, No   Norman Griffin

04231   Would you believe it?   Norman Griffin and Davy Burnaby

10-inch record 3s. 6d.

4-2965   Carry on the good work (with chorus)   Norman Griffin

10-inch double-sided records 3s.

B. 908 { Think of me (with chorus)   Henri Leoni and Mimi Crawford
{ You may take me round Paree   Henri Leoni and Mimi Crawford

B. 909 { Play me that marching melody (with chorus)   Henri Leoni
{ Widows are wonderful   De Groot and the Piccadilly Orchestra

12-inch double-sided records 5s.

C. 851 { The dear old days (with chorus)   Davy Burnaby
{ Some day I'll make you love me   De Groot and the Piccadilly Orchestra
{ "Round the Map"

C. 852 { "Yes, Uncle"—Selection I.   The Mayfair Orchestra
{ "Yes, Uncle"—Selection II.   The Mayfair Orchestra

The Music of 'Yes Uncle" is published by B. Feldman & Co.

Fraser Gange

Phyllis Lett

John Harrison

FRASER GANGE (baritone)
with pianoforte accompaniment
and violin obbligato, played by MARJORIE HAYWARD
12-inch record 5s. 6d.

| 02793 | **Beauty's Eyes** | *Tosti* |

Published by Chappell & Co., Ltd.

PHYLLIS LETT (contralto)
with organ (E. STANLEY ROPER) and pianoforte accompaniment
12-inch record 5s. 6d.

| 03611 | **The Pearl Cross** | *Marshall* |

Published by Boosey & Co.

JOHN HARRISON (tenor)
with pianoforte accompaniment
12-inch record 5s. 6d.

| 02794 | **Oft in the stilly night** | *Moore* |

PETER DAWSON (baritone)
with orchestral accompaniment
10-inch double-sided record 3s.

B 910	**Your England and mine**	*Simpson*
	Published by J. H. Larway	
	Home ! Canada ! Home !	*Hennessy*
	Published by the Canadian Gazette, Ltd.	

HERBERT TEALE (tenor)
with orchestral accompaniment
10-inch double-sided record 3s.

B 911	**She's the daughter of Mother Machree**	*Ball*
	Published by B. Feldman & Co.	
	When love is calling	*Brewer*
	Published by Chappell & Co., Ltd.	

(Speeds 79)

8

NEW BALLAD RECORDS

THERE are songs to please varied tastes in the selection issued this month, all recorded by popular artists. Those who love the old ballads—and what better choice could there be—will delight in one of Moore's beautiful melodies, "Oft in the Stilly Night," which Mr. John Harrison sings so charmingly and expressively in the remarkable record he has made of this old Irish ballad.

In charming contrast is an exquisite modern song, "Beauty's Eyes," by that master of melody, Tosti. This is very finely sung by the popular baritone, Fraser Gange, whose resonant voice is rendered still more effective by the violin obbligato so beautifully played by Miss Marjorie Hayward. Another very pleasing example of our modern ballads—Marshall's "The Pearl Cross," gives a fine opportunity to display Miss Phyllis Lett's richly-toned voice. Its melody is cleverly enhanced by the organ obbligato (played by Mr. Stanley Roper). Two pretty little songs are also artistically sung by Mr. Herbert Teale, a dainty love song by Brewer, and an Irish ditty with a charming bell effect in the orchestral accompaniment.

Last, but not least, come two stirring patriotic songs, sung by Mr. Peter Dawson with a vigour and vocal resonance that make them both most impressive. There is something of the atmosphere of the Dominion's vast plains in the stately melody of "Home, Canada, Home," while in "Your England and Mine" both words and music are worthy of the theme they express.

PROGRAMMES.

I.

1	Selection	"Madame Favart"	*Offenbach*
		COLDSTREAM GUARDS BAND	
2	Operatic Selection	Gems from "Aïda"	*Verdi*
		GRAND OPERA COMPANY	
3	Vocal Solo	"Vesti la giubba" ("Pagliacci")	*Leoncavallo*
		CARUSO	
4		Marche Militaire	*Saint-Saëns*
		ROYAL ALBERT HALL ORCHESTRA	
5	Humorous	"What is life without love"	
		W. H. BERRY	
6	Dance	"Shepherd's Hey"	*Grainger*
		ROYAL ALBERT HALL ORCHESTRA	
7		"Welsh Rhapsody"	*Edward German*
		THE MAYFAIR ORCHESTRA	

II.

1	March	"Tannhäuser"	*Wagner*
		COLDSTREAM GUARDS BAND	
2	Vocal Solo	"Eri tu" ("Ballo in Maschera")	*Verdi*
		BATTISTINI	
3	Dances	"Henry VIII"	*Edward German*
		THE SYMPHONY ORCHESTRA	
4	Operatic Selection	Gems from "Il Trovatore"	*Verdi*
		GRAND OPERA COMPANY	
5		Marche Militaire	*Schubert*
		ROYAL ALBERT HALL ORCHESTRA	
6	Humorous	"The Wedding of Sandy McNab"	
		HARRY LAUDER	
7	Selection	"La Bohême"	*Puccini*
		THE MAYFAIR ORCHESTRA	

MUSIC AL FRESCO

IN olden days our forefathers made much music in the open-air. On high-days and holidays the sounds of flute and viol would be heard on the village green, while man and maid footed it merrily in the Morris or other old English dances. Open-air music was not only popular with the rustics, but also with the aristocracy. The great Handel wrote his beautiful " Water-music " for performance on the river Thames as the Royal barge went by in pageant, and one might recall many other instances in which composers have sought the charm of open air for their compositions.

Music, indeed, has an attraction of its own in the open, and most of us have some delightful memories of al fresco performances. I always remember vividly an exquisite effect when, on the slopes of a Swiss mountain, there floated up to me the strains of a hymn sung by a religious procession in the valley far below, sounds to which distance certainly lent enchantment. Most of us can recall something of the kind—voices of Welsh miners heard far away on their hills, the stirring strains of a military band in a procession, the soft sound of an orchestra in some outdoor Continental café. Perhaps there may be something in the associations and surroundings that makes us remember these things, but there is no doubt that Nature's auditorium often gives to certain music a unique charm. Most of us have noticed, for instance, how remarkably fine many records sound when played from an instrument in a boat on a river or lake. The water, in fact, acts as a resonator, making the music more brilliant. Similarly, in a garden where there may be an arch or an aisle of trees or foliage, an instrument may be placed and sound wonderfully well to those listening at a distance. Under these circumstances, indeed, many records, particularly vocal examples, have a naturalness which often deceives experts into believing they are actually listening to the performers themselves. What music should we like best to hear for an outdoor performance? One can suggest many things—some of the fine military band or orchestral pieces, vocal solos by a great voice like Caruso's, which takes on a new beauty in open air, vocal quartets or choruses— a glance at the catalogue, in fact, will give one plenty of ideas for an al fresco concert. On the facing page are given some attractive programmes which will be found suitable.   HENRY COATES.

| Margaret Cooper | Jay Laurier |

MARGARET COOPER
with pianoforte accompaniment
12-inch record 5s. 6d.

03612   **Lonely**   *Foulde*
Published by Chappell & Co., Ltd.

THE GRESHAM SINGERS
10-inch record 3s. 6d.

2-4482   **The Mulligan Musketeers**   *Atkinson*
Published by J. Curwen & Sons, Ltd.

JAY LAURIER
with orchestral accompaniment
10-inch double-sided record 3s.

B 912 {
     I'd like to marry (but I couldn't leave the girls)
     Published by B. Feldman & Co.   *Nat D. Ayer*
     Long Boy   *Barclay Walker*
     Published by B. Feldman & Co.

COURTLAND and JEFFERIES
with orchestral accompaniment
10-inch double-sided records 3s.

B 913 {
     Lily, my water Lily   *J. W. Tate*
     Published by Francis, Day & Hunter
     Honey, will you miss me ?   *Wilbur & Rice*
     Published by the Herman Darewski Music Publishing Co.

B 916 {
     Southern Gals   *Gumble*
     Published by B. Feldman & Co.
     Where do we go from here ?   *Johnson & Wenrich*
     Published by the Herman Darewski Music Publishing Co.

(Speeds 79)

MUSIC AND MIRTH

THE delightful personality of Margaret Cooper has never been more charmingly expressed by the recording machine than in this new record of her latest success, "Lonely." Both words and music make an irresistible appeal, thanks to Miss Cooper's individuality and genius for expressing such pretty sentiments so perfectly. The record is one which everyone will want to get, after having heard it once.

Two capital records by that popular comedian, Jay Laurier, deserve special attention, for they are both full of fun. In one he gives a humorous account, with some excellent " patter," of fickle man contemplating matrimony. The other is a droll topical song of an American recruit, who somehow gets camouflaged in turn with Lancashire, Welsh and Scottish accents.

Another first-rate topical song is provided by those popular duettists, Courtland and Jefferies, with a merry ditty on the American catchphrase, " Where do we go from here," a song with a taking melody. These two artists have also recorded three more ditties in first-rate style—"Southern Gals," a pretty Haiwaiian, " Lily, my water Lily," a graceful sentimental number by J. W. Tate, and " Honey, will you miss me ? " a song with a melody of captivating character.

That famous vocal quartet " The Gresham Singers," whose exquisite art is so much admired, give us one of the most perfect specimens of their beautiful and artistic singing in the delightfully humorous partsong " The Mulligan Musketeers," some of the vocal effects being most ingenious and amusing.

LIGHT ORCHESTRAL MUSIC.

THE BAND OF H.M. COLDSTREAM GUARDS

conducted by Major J. MACKENZIE-ROGAN,
M.V.O., Mus.Doc., Hon. R.A.M.

10-inch double-sided record 3s.

B 915 {
Manhattan Beach March	*Sousa*
Uncle Sammy—March and Two-step	*Holzmann*

THE MAYFAIR ORCHESTRA

12-inch double-sided record 5s.

C 853 {
" The Beauty Spot "—Selection I, containing : My ideal husband—The flower that never dies—I do love the girls—Ribbons and frills.   *J. W. Tate*

" The Beauty Spot "—Selection II, containing : Myself and I—I wish I were a dog like you—Beauty spot of Asia—The kiss that you're going to get   *J. W. Tate*

Published by Francis, Day & Hunter

SAVOY QUARTET

10-inch double-sided record 3s.

B 914 {
Hello ! New York ("The Bing Boys on Broadway ")
Published by B. Feldman & Co.   *Nat D. Ayer*
Widows are wonderful (" Yes, Uncle ! ") *Nat D. Ayer*
Published by B. Feldman & Co.

(Speeds 79)

ONE can always rely upon the Coldstream Guards Band for fine records, and these two issued this month fully sustain the famous players' reputation. Sousa's swinging march "Manhattan Beach," one of the March King's most melodious pieces, is played by them with the utmost vigour and brilliance, a splendidly spirited piece of military band music. The clever march and two step "Uncle Sammy" with its breezy tunes is equally welcome, and is an uncommonly fine record.

The Mayfair Orchestra this month has chosen for recording a selection from "The Beauty Spot," the sparkling music of which is by that popular composer J. W. Tate, who has many of his best and happiest ideas in this score. Needless to add the orchestra plays it all with splendid spirit and excellent tone.

The popular Savoy Quartet of banjoists and singers have made attractive records of two popular successes, "Hello, New York," sung by Miss Vi Loraine in "The Bing Boys on Broadway," and "Widows are Wonderful," Miss Julia James' pretty number in "Yes, Uncle !" Each is played with much dash and brilliance by the Savoy Quartet.

14

MAY RECORDS

12-inch record 9s.

2-052119 Esultate—"Otello"   De Muro

12-inch records 6s. 6d.

2-0802 Scheherazade, Op. 35 (Suite Symphonique), Part I
                                                         The Royal Albert Hall Orchestra

10-inch record 6s.

7-52095 Il balen—"Il Trovatore"   De Luca

12-inch records 5s. 6d.

03603 Voi che sapete—"Nozze di Figaro" (sung in English) (Twilight)
                                                      Jeanne Brola
05622 Funeral March—Chopin   Irene Scharrer
2-0803 "Tom Jones" Dances. No. 1, Morris Dance. No. 2, Gavotte
                                                  The Symphony Orchestra

12-inch double-sided records 5s.

C 842 { Love's Garden of Roses   The Band of H.M. Coldstream Guards
     { Solveig's Song—"Peer Gynt"   The Band of H.M. Coldstream Guards
C 843 { "Any Old Thing"—Selection I   The Mayfair Orchestra
     { "Any Old Thing"—Selection II   The Mayfair Orchestra
C 844 { Kreutzer Sonata—I. First Movement
     {   Marjorie Hayward and Una Bourne
     { Kreutzer Sonata—II. Andante, with variations, Part I
                                      Marjorie Hayward and Una Bourne

10-inch records 4s. 6d.

2-3289 I bring you joy   Ruth Vincent
4-7930 Souvenir   Mischa Elman

10-inch records 3s. 6d

2-3288 A Pastoral   Flora Woodman
2-4475 Forty Years On ("Harrow School Song")
                                  Sydney Reeves and Bernard Moss
2-7856 Slumber Song   Cedric Sharpe
4-2962 The Company Sergeant-Major   Harry Dearth

10-inch double-sided records 3s.

B 894 { Till you come home again   Ruby Heyl
     { Before you came   Ruby Heyl
B 899 { Hullo! my dearie—"Zig-Zag"   De Groot and the Piccadilly Orchestra
     { Smoke Clouds—"Topsy Turvy"   De Groot and the Piccadilly Orchestra
B 900 { Roses of a summer day   Hubert Eisdell
     { Roses of memory   Hubert Eisdell
B 901 { 'Sno Use   Harry Weldon
     { Sleuthy, the dread of the heads   Harry Weldon
B 904 { Samoa, Samoa, some more   Courtland and Jefferies
     { Tommy over There   Courtland and Jefferies
B 905 { You oughtn't to do it, when you don't belong to me   Savoy Quartette
     { Honey, will you miss me?   Savoy Quartette

'HIS MASTER'S VOICE'
NEW RECORDS
for
SEPTEMBER
1918

THE SYMPHONY ORCHESTRA

conducted by SIR EDWARD ELGAR, O.M.

12-inch record 5s. 6d.

| 2-0824 | **Bavarian Dances, No. I, Op. 27** | *Elgar* |

THE beautiful Bavarian Dances by Sir Edward Elgar, the second and third of which have already been recorded, are amongst the composer's most popular compositions. They were written during a happy holiday spent by him, years ago, in the Tyrol, where picturesque peasant life is still to be seen. It is one of those famous Tyrolean fêtes, with sports, games and dances, which inspired the music, in which Elgar has made some use of the lovely folk-song idioms of the district. It breathes the very spirit of the mountains and the open-air, melody and rhythm giving the sense of light-hearted gaiety most delightfully. The almost boisterous jollity of the principal theme is charmingly set off by the dainty little phrase heard a little later, and the brilliant orchestration adds picturesqueness. It is a miniature masterpiece, beautifully recorded, under the composer's own direction, by the Symphony Orchestra. (*Speed* 79)

| 2-0519 | **Bavarian Dances, No. 2.** | *Elgar* |
| 2-0530 | **Bavarian Dances, No. 3.** | *Elgar* |

1

Sir Edward Elgar

Claude Debussy

THE ROYAL ALBERT HALL ORCHESTRA

conducted by LANDON RONALD

12-inch record 6s. 6d.

0723 " Prélude à l'après-midi d'un faune," **Part II** *Debussy*

NO work is more representative of Debussy's genius than this wonderful " Symphonic Prelude," which has already become a modern classic in the orchestral repertoire. It is a picture of pagan Greece—inspired by a poem of his countryman Mallarmé—that the composer has painted in tones. The music is a delicate iridescent web of sound which perfectly suggests the palpitating heat of the Southern sun under which the mythological figure of a faun drowses, in an ilex grove of ancient Greece. With masterly skill the composer evokes this shadowy picture of antiquity. This record, forming the second part of the Prelude (the first being issued recently), carries the elusively beautiful music to a close in which the picture seems to fade away slowly, leaving us the impression of an exquisite dream.

(*Speed* 79)

NEW QUEEN'S HALL LIGHT ORCHESTRA

(Proprietors—Messrs. Chappell & Co., Ltd.)

conducted by Mr. ALICK MACLEAN

12-inch double-sided record 6s. 6d.

D 29 { "Miniature Suite," No. I (Children's Dance) *Eric Coates*
{ "Miniature Suite," No. II (Intermezzo) *Eric Coates*
Published by Boosey & Co.

HERE are two splendid records by the famous Queen's Hall players, from a "Miniature Suite" by one of our cleverest young composers, Eric Coates, himself the leading viola player of the orchestra, and therefore actually taking a prominent part in the recording of his own music. No. I is a piece of music as quaint and ingenuous as its title suggests. The second (Intermezzo) is in more serious vein and is based upon a very expressive melody which the composer develops with much skill, culminating in a fine climax of emotional intensity. The very graceful orchestration is one of the charms of the music, which has been recorded with perfect tone and finished style. (*Speeds* 79)

THE MAYFAIR ORCHESTRA

12-inch double-sided record 5s.

C 863 { "Three Dale Dances," Nos. I & II (On Yorkshire
{ Folk Tunes) *Arthur Wood*
{ "Three Dale Dances," Nos. II (cont.) and III (On
{ Yorkshire Folk Tunes) *Arthur Wood*
(conducted by the Composer)

ALL who love fine old tunes will delight in these "Dale Dances," the melodies of which come from the sturdy old dalesmen of the North, old English yeomen so typical of the bull-dog breed. The composer has handled the tunes with much skill and brilliance. The first dance is built up from a very jolly theme, with a striking rhythm, and is a most vivacious movement. The second number, in minor key, provides an effective contrast by its slow and pensive melody. The finale is most exhilarating, with two or three themes of delightful freshness and gaiety, with which the composer makes alternate play in clever manner. The second of these themes is particularly taking, and all through the movement the instrumentation is captivating. The composer himself has conducted for these records, which are remarkably fine. (*Speeds* 79)

Chaliapin

CHALIAPIN (Russian bass)

with orchestral accompaniment

12-inch record 12s. 6d.

032260   **Pourquoi donc se taisent les voix**   *Glazounoff*

THE art of Chaliapin, the greatest living basso of to-day, and a singer without a rival on the operatic stage, is nowhere more widely appreciated than in this country. This fine record will recall vividly the marvellous voice and dominating personality of the famous Russian artist. It shows him in a new light, apart from opera, as a fascinating singer of songs. In this song of haunting beauty, by the well-known Russian composer Glazounoff, Chaliapin's interpretative genius has full scope. The expressive vocal phrases are given by him with remarkable dramatic intensity and expressive power. The song is a genuine little tone-poem for the voice, and the lovely orchestral colouring of the accompaniment gives it an added richness and beauty. The record is one that will appeal to all musical connoisseurs.

(Speed 79)

Boninsegna   Bolis

CELESTINA BONINSEGNA and LUIGI BOLIS

with orchestral accompaniment

12-inch record 9s.

2-054071   M'ami, M'ami (Duet, Act II) ("Un Ballo in Maschera")   *Verdi*

SOME of Verdi's most beautiful melodies are to be found in his opera "Un Ballo in Maschera," from which this fine love-duet is taken. It occurs in the second act of the opera, where the heroine, Amelia, has gone to visit a witch, to seek advice. Her admirer, Riccardo, also comes, disguised, on a similar errand. The two meet and declare their love, in music, which is one of Verdi's happiest inspirations in the expression of the "grand passion." The duet is begun by the tenor, whose passionate exclamations are soon merged into a rich sensuous melody. This is repeated by the soprano, while after a fine climax, the two voices join in a third repetition. Mme. Boninsegna, one of Italy's most famous sopranos, and the fine tenor, Signor Bolis, both sing the music with superb tone and brilliant vocalisation, and have made one of the finest operatic records ever issued.   (*Speed* 79)

Ruth Vincent   John McCormack

RUTH VINCENT (soprano)

with pianoforte accompaniment
10-inch record 4s. 6d.

2-3290   **In my Garden**   *Liddle*
Published by Boosey & Co.

THE very dainty and tuneful little song that Miss Ruth Vincent has here recorded so takingly has long been popular with both singers and public. Words and music are perfectly matched in their delicate sentiment, the expression of which is so beautifully reproduced by the popular soprano. It is one of the most brilliant records Miss Ruth Vincent has made.   (*Speed* 79)

JOHN McCORMACK (tenor)

with orchestral accompaniment
10-inch record 4s. 6d.

4-2482   **Bonnie Wee Thing**   *Lehmann*
Published by Boosey & Co.

THE famous Irish tenor has made an exquisite record of a very charming song, Mme. Liza Lehmann's setting of Burns' familiar poem. The music is in the style of an old folk-tune, the melody being very graceful and expressive. John McCormack, one of the world's greatest ballad-singers, invests both words and music with such a wonderful sincerity of emotion that the song will surely find its way to the hearts of everyone.   (*Speed* 79)

Marie Hall   Irene Scharrer

MARIE HALL (violin)

with pianoforte accompaniment

12-inch record 5s. 6d.

2-07953　　　　**Sarabande et Tambourin**　　　　*Leclaire*

THE music of our forefathers, with its exquisite grace and serenity, has a peculiarly restful charm in the storm and stress of the present time. These lovely little dance pieces of the famous French composer of the seventeenth century take us, in imagination, into a dream-world of the past. The slow and stately Sarabande is extremely beautiful, and the Tambourin is a brilliant movement of delightful quaintness. Both are perfectly recorded, with fine tone and finished technique.　　　　(*Speed* 79)

IRENE SCHARRER (pianoforte)

12-inch record 5s. 6d.

05625　　　　(a) **Étude in G flat**　　　　*Chopin*

　　　　　　　　(b) **Bees' Wedding**　　　　*Mendelssohn*

THESE two pieces, so familiar to all, and such universal favourites, are splendidly recorded by Miss Irene Scharrer. The wonderful Chopin Étude (often known as the "black-note study," because it is written for the black keys of the instrument) is played with unequalled brilliance and perfection, and the same may be said of the well-known Mendelssohn "Song without Words," the gossamer-like music of which fully justifies its title.

(*Speed* 79)

PROGRAMMES

I. Instrumental Works founded on Folk-Songs

1 Welsh Rhapsody   *Edward German*
       MAYFAIR ORCHESTRA (2 records)

2 Three Dale Dances   *A. Wood*
       MAYFAIR ORCHESTRA

3 Irish Rhapsody (No. 1 in D minor)   *Stanford*
       SYMPHONY ORCHESTRA

4 Bavarian Dances   *Elgar*
       SYMPHONY ORCHESTRA

5 Hungarian Rhapsody   *Liszt*
       ROYAL ALBERT HALL ORCHESTRA

II. Vocal Music selected from Folk-Songs

1 D'ye Ken John Peel   *Old English*
       GRESHAM SINGERS

2 Oh no, John   *Old English*
       CHARLES TREE

3 { The Pretty Creature   *Old English (arr. Lane Wilson)*
  { Banks of Allan Water   *Old Scottish*
       KIRKBY LUNN

4 The Lowland Sea   *Old English (arr. Eric Coates)*
       HARRY DEARTH

5 Danny Boy   *Old Irish*
       EDNA THORNTON

6 O good ale, thou art my darling   *Old English*
       ERNEST BUTCHER

7 Volga Boatmen's Song   *Old Russian*
       ST. PETERSBURG QUARTET

8

THE FASCINATION OF FOLK-SONG

EVERY country has its store of those sweet songs—centuries old —which have been handed down from generation to generation through the ages, and which we moderns know as folk-songs. Their origin no one can with certainty tell. Like Topsy, they "just growed." Their earliest beginnings must have been with our primitive forefathers, who would tell a simple tale in prose or rudimentary poetry, accompanying it with some sort of chant or simple vocal inflections. The idea would be handed on, improved and altered, preserved only by the bards themselves, for these folk-songs must have begun before ever music had a written notation, until at length some sort of actual melody was arrived at. That melody in turn would gradually change its shape, for modern researches into folk-song have brought to light many different versions of the same song existing in different parts of the same country, modified in each case, of course, by local conditions. To the strenuous and complex life of to-day, the sweet savour and simplicity of folk-song comes like a cool draught to parched lips. Much of the modern musical art has been founded upon it, for our musical master-minds have realised the significance and beauty of these melodies which have been forged by the ages out of the people themselves, and not created by any artificial process. One need only recall, for example, the wonderful " national " school of Russian music, to show what great musicians can do with this material. Those wonderful operas and symphonies which have delighted us in these past few years have all been built from this material. In our own country native composers have begun to do the same thing, and many a fine orchestral work has been written in the same way. England, Scotland, Wales and Ireland are all rich in folk-tunes of the most exquisite description, many of them amongst the finest examples of traditional music to be found anywhere in the world. Listen to the examples given on the opposite page and you will find a new delight in music, if you have not yet been fortunate enough to discover it.

HENRY COATES.

Carmen Hill

Ruby Heyl

CARMEN HILL (mezzo-soprano)

with pianoforte accompaniment

12-inch record 5s. 6d.

03618	**Flow down, cold rivulet**	*Graham Peel*
	Published by Chappell & Co., Ltd.	

JOHN and JOSEPH HARRISON

with pianoforte accompaniment

12-inch record 5s. 6d.

04244	**All's Well**	*Braham*

RUBY HEYL (contralto)

with orchestral accompaniment

10-inch double-sided record 3s.

B 964	**One little hour**	*Sharpe*
	Published by J. B. Cramer & Co., Ltd.	
	ERNEST PIKE (tenor)	
	with orchestral accompaniment	
	The heart of a rose	*Nicholls*
	Published by the Lawrence Wright Music Publishing Co.	

ERNEST BUTCHER (baritone)

with pianoforte accompaniment

10-inch record 3s. 6d.

4-2985	**O good ale, thou art my darling** (Old English song)

NEW BALLAD RECORDS

T HERE are some very charming songs to be found in the list given on the opposite page. Miss Carmen Hill, always such a delightful artist to hear in a ballad, has recorded a very effective song by Graham Peel, whose refined and graceful music is always welcome. The melody is smooth and flowing, with an exquisitely rippling accompaniment that suggests the atmosphere of the poem. Miss Carmen Hill's singing of it is remarkable for beauty of tone and expressive feeling.

It is a quaint and charming old English song that Mr. Ernest Butcher—always such an attractive· singer of folk-songs—has recorded in " O good ale, thou art my darling." The beverage that the ditty extols is evidently somewhat more inspiring than the brew known as " Government ale," judging by the words.

A pretty song of tender sentiment is the record, by Miss Ruby Heyl, of " One little hour," both the words and music of which are very expressive as sung by this popular young contralto. Its melodious phrases are very attractive.

" All's Well " is another old-world piece of music, by a composer (Braham) whose name will always be remembered by his famous song " The Death of Nelson." Himself a celebrated tenor of the day, Braham knew how to write effectively for the voice, as the phrases of this fine old duet show. The music, which describes the soldier on " sentry-go," is splendidly sung by Messrs. John and Joseph Harrison, whose voices blend to perfection.

Mr. Ernest Pike has recorded a song with a striking refrain, " The Heart of a Rose," both words and music of which are unusually attractive, the well-known tenor singing it most effectively.

(*Speeds* 79)

11

Tom Clare

Harry Weldon

TOM CLARE

with pianoforte accompaniment

12-inch record 5s. 6d.

02799   **Exemptions and otherwise**   *Lee, Weston & Hastings*
Published by Francis, Day & Hunter

HARRY WELDON

with orchestral accompaniment

12-inch double-sided record 5s.

C 864 { **Travesty on "What do you want to make those eyes at me for?"**   *J. Foley*
Published by the Herman Darewski Music Publishing Co.
Somebody's Baby   *H. Castling*

COURTLAND and JEFFERIES

with orchestral accompaniment

10-inch double-sided record 3s.

B 961 { **On the road to home, sweet home**   *Van Alstyne*
Published by B. Feldman & Co.
Some Sunday Morning   *Whiting*
Published by B. Feldman & Co.

MUSIC AND MIRTH

HARRY WELDON'S whimsicalities are always delightful medleys of fascinating nonsense. In these two songs you hear him at his funniest, in parodies of a mirth-making kind. The "patter" in "What do you want to make those eyes at me for?" is of a typically "Weldonian" kind and most laughable. In the other song there is a most amusing interlude in the shape of a number of nonsense rhymes, delivered in the comedian's inimitable way. Both records are wonderfully life-like in their reproduction of the artist's individual style.

Tom Clare's song, "Exemptions and Otherwise," is topical humour of a kind that will appeal to most of us, in its deft jokes on military matters. The song has a swinging tune and is recorded most effectively.

Two graceful light numbers are excellently recorded by Courtland and Jefferies, "Some Sunday Morning," with a lilting tune, and a sentimental ballad on the familiar theme of "Home, Sweet Home." Both are taking songs of the lighter type.

(*Speeds* 79)

OTHER TOM CLARE RECORDS
recently issued

4-2967	**The Hindenburg Trot**	10-in. 3s. 6d.
02782	**Rumours**	12-in. 5s. 6d.
02770	**Women's Work**	12-in. 5s. 6d.
02757	**Fritz**	12-in, 5s. 6d

LIGHT ORCHESTRAL
AND INSTRUMENTAL MUSIC

THE BAND OF H.M. COLDSTREAM GUARDS

conducted by Major J. MACKENZIE-ROGAN,
M.V.O., Mus. Doc., Hon. R.A.M.

12-inch double-sided record 5s.

C 862
- **Doges March ("Merchant of Venice")** *Rosse*
  Published by Hawkes & Son
- **"L'Italiana in Algeri"—Overture** *Rossini*

DE GROOT and THE PICCADILLY ORCHESTRA

10-inch double-sided record 3s.

B 963
- **Little Miss Melody ("The Boy")** *Monckton*
  Published by Chappell & Co., Ltd.
- **If you look in her eyes ("Going Up")** *L. A. Hirsch*
  Published by B. Feldman & Co.

HELEN LOUISE and FRANK FERERA
(Hawaiian Guitar Duet)

10-inch double-sided record 3s.

B 897
- **Waiu Luliluli (Old Hawaiian Melody)**
- **Kai Maia O Ka Maoli (Medley March)** *Kekupuchi*

SAVOY QUARTET

10-inch double-sided record 3s.

B 962
- **The wild women are making a wild man of me** *Piantadosi*
- **I don't want to get well** *H. Jentes*
  Published by the Herman Darewski Music Publishing Co.

THIS month's selection of light orchestral pieces is exceptionally
good. The Coldstreams' players, under Major Mackenzie-
Rogan, have turned out two capital records. The Doge's
March from Rosse's music to the "Merchant of Venice" is a striking
piece, with a stately march tune and a melodious trio theme. The
overture "L'Italiana in Algeri" is brilliant music, of a typically
Southern warmth in its sparkling phrases.

Some very quaint and charming melodies from Haiwaii have been
turned into captivating duets by those accomplished guitarists, Helen
Louise and Frank Ferera, the old melody "Waiu Luliluli" being
especially tuneful.

The Savoy Quartet has recorded two popular numbers in first-rate
style, both vocal and instrumental effects being striking.

Then the clever De Groot and his accomplished players give us two
very delightful versions of songs from topical theatrical pieces, "If you
look in her eyes" being a particularly brilliant transcription by the
famous Piccadilly Orchestra. (*Speeds* 79)

The New Records
OF
INSTRUMENTAL MUSIC

MOISEIWITSCH (pianoforte)
12-inch record 6s. 6d.

05624   Clair de Lune   *Debussy*

TESSIE THOMAS (violin)
with pianoforte accompaniment
12-inch record 5s. 6d.

2-07952   Polonaise   *Vieuxtemps*

PHILHARMONIC STRING QUARTET
10-inch double-sided record 4s. 6d.

E 1   { Cherry Ripe   *Cyril Scott, arr. by Frank Bridge*
         { Marche Militaire, Op. 51   *Schubert*

12-inch double-sided records 6s. 6d.

D 13   { Quartet in A Major, Op. 41, No. 3, Part I   *Schumann*
      { Quartet in A Major, Op. 41, No. 3, Part II   *Schumann*

D 14   { Sally in our Alley   *Levey, arr. by Frank Bridge*
      { Londonderry Air   *arr. by Frank Bridge*

D 15   { Irish Reel   *Holbrooke*
      { Quartet (3rd and 4th movements)   *Ravel*

CEDRIC SHARPE ('cello)
with pianoforte accompaniment
10-inch record 3s. 6d.

2-7857   A Memory   *Goring Thomas, arr. by Squire*

12-inch record 5s. 6d.

07896   Romanze (G), Op. 26   *Svendsen*

"GOING UP"

The Gaiety Theatre Success recorded exclusively
by the Original Artists

*All the songs are accompanied by the Orchestra of the Gaiety Theatre
conducted by Mr. ARTHUR WOOD*

JOSEPH COYNE and MARJORIE GORDON
12-inch records 5s. 6d.

04232   First Act, Second Act, Third Act   *Louis A. Hirsch*

MARJORIE GORDON

03613   The touch of a woman's hand (with chorus)   *Louis A. Hirsch*

MARJORIE GORDON (Dialogue—Franklyn Bellamy)
03614   The Tickle Toe (with chorus)   *Louis A. Hirsch*

MARJORIE GORDON and EVELYN LAYE
04233   If you look in her eyes (with chorus)   *Louis A. Hirsch*

MARJORIE GORDON and H. DE BRAY
04234   Kiss me!   *Louis A. Hirsch*

**JOSEPH COYNE, AUSTIN MELFORD, ROY BYFORD and
FRANKLYN BELLAMY**
04235   Down! Up! Left! Right! Finale, Act 2 (with dialogue and chorus)
                                     Louis A. Hirsch

EVELYN LAYE and AUSTIN MELFORD
12-inch double-sided records 5s.

       (Do it for me   *Louis A. Hirsch*
       { **JOSEPH COYNE, MARJORIE GORDON, EVELYN LAYE,**
C 860 { **H. DE BRAY (Solo), AUSTIN MELFORD and CLIFTON**
       { **ALDERSON**
      (Finale, Act I., "Going Up" (with dialogue and chorus) *Louis A. Hirsch*

GAIETY THEATRE ORCHESTRA
C 861 { "Going Up," Selection 1   *Louis A. Hirsch*
      { "Going Up," Selection 2   *Louis A. Hirsch*

The Music of "Going Up" is published by B. Feldman & Co.

JULY RECORDS

12-inch double-sided records 6s. 6d.

D 16 {
"Ballet Egyptien"—Suite, Part I   New Queen's Hall Light Orchestra
"Ballet Egyptien"—Suite, Part II   New Queen's Hall Light Orchestra
}

D 17 {
"Ballet Egyptien"—Suite, Part III   New Queen's Hall Light Orchestra
"Ballet Egyptien"—Suite, Part IV   New Queen's Hall Light Orchestra
}

12-inch records 6s. 6d.

0722	" Prélude à l'après-midi d'un faune," Part I	Royal Albert Hall Orchestra
02792	My Power is absolute (" Boris Godounov ")	Robert Radford
03610	It was a dream	Rosina Buckman

10-inch record 8s.

l-52080	**Luna d'Estate** (Summer moon)	Enrico Caruso

10-inch record 6s.

l-33017	**Laughing Song** (Bourbonnaise) " Manon Lescaut "—(sung in French—L'Eclat de rire)	Amelita Galli-Curci

12-inch records 5s. 6d.

02793	Beauty's Eyes	Fraser Gange
02794	Oft in the stilly night	John Harrison
03611	The Pearl Cross	Phyllis Lett
03612	Lonely	Margaret Cooper
05623	Melody in F	Arthur de Greef

12-inch double-sided records 5s.

C 853 {
"The Beauty Spot "—Selection I   The Mayfair Orchestra
"The Beauty Spot "—Selection II   The Mayfair Orchestra
}

C 854 {
Kreutzer Sonata : III. Andante, with variations, Part II
    Marjorie Hayward and Una Bourne
Kreutzer Sonata : IV. Finale   Marjorie Hayward and Una Bourne
}

10-inch record 3s. 6d.

2-4482	**The Mulligan Musketeers**	The Gresham Singers

10-inch double-sided records 3s.

B 910 {
Your England and mine   Peter Dawson
Home ! Canada ! Home !   Peter Dawson
}

B 911 {
She's the daughter of Mother Machree   Herbert Teale
When love is calling   Herbert Teale
}

B 912 {
I'd like to marry (but I couldn't leave the girls)   Jay Laurier
Long Boy   Jay Laurier
}

B 913 {
Lily, my water Lily   Courtland and Jefferies
Honey, will you miss me?   Courtland and Jefferies
}

B 914 {
Hello ! New York (" The Bing Boys on Broadway ")   Savoy Quartet
Widows are wonderful (" Yes, Uncle ! ")   Savoy Quartet
}

B 915 {
Manhattan Beach March   The Band of H.M. Coldstream Guards
Uncle Sammy—March and Two-step
    The Band of H.M. Coldstream Guards
}

B 916 {
Southern Gals   Courtland and Jefferies
Where do we go from here?   Courtland and Jefferies
}

16

'HIS MASTER'S VOICE'
NEW RECORDS
for
DECEMBER
1918

THE ROYAL ALBERT HALL ORCHESTRA

conducted by LANDON RONALD

12-inch record 7s.

2-0837	**Capriccio Italien, Op. 45, Part I.**	*Tchaikovsky*

A N interesting glimpse of Tchaikovsky composing this brilliant and genial Capriccio Italien is to be found in his letters. He had come from the Russian winter to Florence, where the Southern spring was already stirring. Opposite his rooms in the lovely city on the Arno was a cavalry barracks from which the bugle calls suggested the fanfares with which the piece begins. Down in the streets the gay Florentine crowd and its animation stamped upon the composer's mind a picture which inspired him to depict the scene in music. The opening phrases for trumpet recall the military pageant, then comes a vivacious movement, the lively *saltarello* rhythm of which evidently represents the throng in the streets of the famous city, while the melody which follows is in the style of a popular folk-song. From these ideas, and with masterly instrumentation, the composer has woven a work of which the Albert Hall Orchestra, under Landon Ronald, has made a wonderful record. It is, indeed, one of the finest orchestral numbers we have ever issued.　　　　(*Speed* 79)

Alick Maclean

Offenbach

NEW QUEEN'S HALL LIGHT ORCHESTRA

(Proprietors—Messrs. Chappell & Co., Ltd.)

conducted by Mr. ALICK MACLEAN

12-inch double-sided record 7s.

D 30 { **Orphée aux Enfers—Overture** *Offenbach*
Published by Lafleur & Sons.
"Miniature Suite," No. III (Scene du bal) *Eric Coates*
Published by Boosey & Co.

TRUE to its reputation the Queen's Hall Light Orchestra has produced yet another superb record of delicious sparkling music, played with all the artistic perfection of tone, technique and expression for which this famous body of players is so noted. The Offenbach overture, from one of the most delightful of his light operas—the successful revival of which, a few years ago at His Majesty's, will be remembered—is full of gay melody and piquant rhythm. In its dash and swing the music is typical of the genius of one of the greatest comic-opera composers the world has ever known. The charming little piece by Eric Coates, one of the cleverest young English composers (himself the leading viola player of the orchestra, and therefore actually taking a prominent part in the recording of his own music), is equally taking. The lively introduction, to which succeeds a graceful waltz melody, and then a dainty measure, in thirds, all suggest cleverly the brilliance and gaiety of the ball-room. (*Speeds* 79)

Caruso

ENRICO CARUSO

with orchestral accompaniment

10-inch record 8s.

7-52092 O sole mio (My sunshine) (Neapolitan Folk-Song)
di Capua

CARUSO in a Neapolitan folk-song—what more delightful record could the music-lover desire ! For the great operatic tenor sings these popular ballads of his own country—he is a Neapolitan, of course—with inimitable charm. He realizes perfectly their quaint sentiment and gives to them a miniature dramatic expression that is quite wonderful, while, needless to say, he sings the music with gorgeous beauty of tone. This record, too, is of a world-famous Neapolitan tune, " O sole mio," a song of life under the Southern sun. Many will recall the melody, especially as it has been used as a waltz in our ball-rooms, but to realize all its beauty you must hear the Caruso record. *(Speed 79)*

CARUSO RECORDS PREVIOUSLY ISSUED

7-52080	**Luna d'Estate (Summer Moon)**	*Tosti*
2-032022	**Noël (Christmas Hymn)**	*Adolphe Adam*
2-052108	**Tiempo Antico (Olden times)**	*Caruso*

Radford

ROBERT RADFORD (bass)
with orchestral accompaniment
conducted by Mr. PERCY PITT

12-inch record 7s.

02804 Ah! My pretty brace of fellows ("Il Seraglio")
Mozart

ONE of the most successful of the Beecham operatic productions has
been Mozart's "Il Seraglio," the immortal melodies and
amusing comedy of which have delighted thousands all over
the country recently. The comic figure of the Pasha's servant, Osmin
(which Mr. Radford plays so capitally), is heard, in this charming air,
gloating over the fate he has in store for the hero and his servant, who
are endeavouring to rescue the Pasha's fair captive, beloved of the hero.
The merry melody, with its many sly touches of humour, of which
Mozart was such a master, and the sparkling accompaniment make the
song quite irresistible, while Mr. Radford sings it with immense spirit.
It is, indeed, one of the finest records the popular English basso has
ever produced.   (*Speed* 79)

Kirkby Lunn

KIRKBY LUNN (contralto)

with pianoforte accompaniment
played by Mr. PERCY PITT
10-inch record 5s.

2-3311   **Now sleeps the crimson petal**   *Quilter*
Published by Boosey & Co.

A VERY beautiful example of a modern English song is this exquisite setting of Tennyson's familiar poem, by one of our most gifted native composers. It has found a place in the repertoire of most singers, for the softly sensuous melody suggests so perfectly the ecstasy of the magic hour the poet describes in his wonderful love-song. Mme. Kirkby Lunn has made a fine record of the song, singing it with beauty of tone and fervour of expression, the artistic accompaniment by Mr. Percy Pitt adding greatly to the effect.

(Speed 79)

BEN MILLETT (alto vocalist)

Soloist : Church of the Immaculate Conception, Farm Street.
(With choir and organ)
12-inch record 6s.

02805   **Adore Te Devote**   *Rev. F. M. de Zulueta*
Published by Cary & Co.

H ERE is a fine record of church music by the well-known priest-composer, Father de Zulueta. The lovely solo with which it commences is sung with devotional tone and fervour by Mr. Ben Millett, the alto soloist of the choir at the famous Farm Street Catholic Church. The choir itself joins in later, with grandiose effect, the music swelling out to a majestic pæan of praise.   *(Speed* 79)

Marjorie Hayward

Mark Hambourg

C. Warwick Evans

INSTRUMENTAL TRIO

MARK HAMBOURG,
MARJORIE HAYWARD and C. WARWICK EVANS

12-inch record 7s.

**08067 Theme and Variations from Trio in A minor,
Op. 50, Part I**   *Tchaikovsky*

THE magnificent A minor Trio by Tchaikovsky, in which the
three instruments—piano, violin, 'cello—are combined with
such masterly effect was dedicated by the composer, "to the
memory of a great artist," and intended as a musical tribute to his friend
and teacher, Nicholas Rubinstein. This act of homage inspired
Tchaikovsky to produce a work of the greatest beauty and one remarkable for its technical cleverness. The glorious theme and variations here
recorded form the second movement of the Trio. The exquisite melody
which the piano announces is said to be a reminiscence of a happy day
spent by Tchaikovsky with his friend. Its serenity and beauty are
enhanced by its repetition on the violin. Then begin some brilliant
variations, one of which, for the 'cello, is particularly beautiful.
Finally, piano and violin join together in repeating the theme. A wonderful performance of the music has been recorded, with Mark Hambourg
at the piano, Marjorie Hayward the violinist and Warwick Evans as
'cellist, these fine artists producing a singularly perfect ensemble.

(*Speed* 79)

Marie Hall   De Groot

MARIE HALL (violin)

with pianoforte accompaniment

12-inch record 6s.

2-07956   **Jota Arogonesa**   *Sarasate*

A NEW record by such a perfect player as Marie Hall is always sure of a welcome. Her remarkable technique and delicate beauty of tone are quite at their best in this picturesque piece by Sarasate. In the "Jota Arogonesa" the composer has created, from a popular dance of his native Spain, music that is fascinating alike in melody and rhythm, and admirable for a display of violin virtuosity. Marie Hall, one need scarcely say, makes light of its technical difficulties and plays the piece with the utmost spirit.   (*Speed* 79)

DE GROOT (violin)

with pianoforte accompaniment

played by Mr. PERCY KAHN

10-inch double-sided record 3s. 6d.

B 989 {
    "Roi d'Ys"—Aubade   *Lalo*
    Published by Heugel & Co., Paris
    Minuet   *Beethoven*
}

T HE popular conductor of the Piccadilly Orchestra shows himself as a remarkably fine violinist in these two delightful records. The little piece by Lalo, so charming and graceful, is played with rich tone and finish of phrase. Of the Beethoven minuet, too, de Groot gives a most artistic performance.   (*Speed* 79)

LIGHT OPERA PROGRAMMES

"THE MIKADO" (Gilbert and Sullivan)

Concert Performance

"MERRIE ENGLAND" (Edward German)

Concert Performance

A MISCELLANEOUS SELECTION

1 Overture	"Zampa" ROYAL ALBERT HALL ORCHESTRA	*Herold*
2 Selection	"Les Cloches de Corneville" COLDSTREAM GUARDS BAND	*Planquette*
3 Duet	Swing Song ("Veronique") CARMEN HILL and MARCUS THOMSON	*Messager*
4 Intermezzo	Barcarolle ("Hoffmann") METROPOLITAN ORCHESTRA	*Offenbach*
5 Song	Waltz Song ("Tom Jones") RUTH VINCENT	*Ed. German*
6 Selection	"La Fille de Madame Angot" COLDSTREAM GUARDS BAND	*Lecocq*
7 Selection	"Dorothy" LIGHT OPERA COMPANY	*Cellier*

LIGHT OPERA MUSIC

IN no country is the taste for light opera more widespread than in Britain. One may say that light opera is to us what lyric opera is to Italy—it is the form of theatre music which seems to appeal most generally to the national taste and temperament. If we consider musical comedy as a somewhat humble form of light opera, then one may say that the latter holds our stage very largely.

I do not mean to imply that grand opera is not appreciated or understood in this country : on the contrary, there is a very large and growing public for it. But light operatic pieces seem peculiarly suited to the average British taste. Perhaps it is because the self-consciousness of our national character finds the frank comedy of light opera more in keeping with the conventions and unrealities of the stage, whereas grand opera puts a greater strain upon those dramatic artificialities.

Moreover, light opera comes as a welcome relief from the mental strain of life that the war brought about. Sparkling melodies and light-hearted lyrics are a real tonic which can make us more ready to face sterner things.

The lover of light opera has a big field to choose from when it comes to gramophone records. There are not only the pieces at present popular, such as " The Lilac Domino," but the beautiful works of past generations, which, when revived from time to time nowadays, delight us as much as they did our fathers. First and foremost is the glorious French school—Offenbach, with his incomparable series of *opera-bouffe*, Auber, Audran, Lecocq, Planquette, Messager, and others. Then our own exquisite works, headed by the peerless Sullivan, to whom a worthy successor is Edward German, while such composers as Sidney Jones, Howard Talbot and Lionel Monckton have given us many charming pieces of a light character. The list of " His Master's Voice " light-opera records is so extensive that it is only possible to mention a few typical examples, which are given in the programmes printed on the opposite page. Realizing the popularity of light opera, the experiment—already very successful—has been made of issuing, in record form, complete operas, two delightful examples of which are mentioned. HENRY COATES.

CARMEN HILL (mezzo-soprano)

with pianoforte accompaniment

10-inch record 4s.

2-3312   **'Tis the hour of farewell**   *Lehmann*
Published by Chappell & Co., Ltd.

ERNEST BUTCHER (baritone)

with pianoforte accompaniment

10-inch record 4s.

5-2007   **Little Bridget Flynn**   *arr. by M. French*

PHYLLIS LETT (contralto)

with organ (E. STANLEY ROPER) and pianoforte

10-inch record 4s.

2-3313   **Ships that pass in the night**   *Stephenson*
Published by Boosey & Co.

HUBERT EISDELL (tenor)

with pianoforte accompaniment

10-inch double-sided record 3s. 6d.

B 990 {

A lesson in love   *Kitty Parker*
Published by Cary & Co.

As a star   *Kitty Parker*
Published by Augener, Ltd.

NEW BALLAD RECORDS

A SPLENDID record by Carmen Hill is among this month's ballads. The popular mezzo-soprano has chosen a very effective number of the late Liza Lehmann. It is a very exquisite love-song, the words of which are of tender sentiment, and the music, which matches them perfectly, in the style of an old folk-song. Most melodious are its phrases, and beautifully sung by the artist. A quaint, old traditional tune, splendidly recorded by Mr. Ernest Butcher, may next claim our attention. "Little Bridget Flynn" is a dainty ditty of a love-lorn youth, graceful and charming in the melody to which the words are set, and very attractively sung by this popular artist, who has made a speciality of old folk-tunes, which he sings most sympathetically.

A record by Miss Phyllis Lett shows off the well-known contralto's beautiful voice perfectly. The song, with its fanciful theme, has a broad, stately melody of a type ideally suited to the singer's rich, smooth tones. The striking close, in which Miss Lett's low notes are heard with telling effect, should be particularly noted.

The two songs recorded by Hubert Eisdell are well contrasted in style, and both exceedingly effective as sung by the popular tenor, who is such an accomplished ballad-singer. "As a Star" is deep in feeling, while "A lesson in love" is bright and piquant. Both are very melodious and vocally attractive. (*Speed* 79)

Lauder has a smile for the munitionettes

HARRY LAUDER

with orchestral accompaniment

12-inch record 6s.

02806   **When I was twenty-one**   *Lauder*

HERE is another splendid Lauder record to add to the unique series which the great Scottish comedian has already given to the world. The song in which he is heard has all that large-hearted humour and genial philosophy that have made him so universally popular. How delightful is this little story, set to a lively tune of the kind one knows so well, of the old man's reminiscences of his youth. The "patter" in between the verses of the song is delicious in its deft portraits of the old man wheezing and coughing, but still cheery, as he thinks of his gay past. Such a record is a real tonic, a sure cure for the blues.   (*Speed* 79)

COURTLAND and JEFFERIES

with orchestral accompaniment
10-inch double-sided records 3s. 6d.

B 992
It'll be nice to get back home again   *Cuthbert Clarke*
Published by the Newman Publishing Co.

Stick around for the New Jazz Band   *Tunbridge*
Published by the Star Music Publishing Co.

B 993
Oshkosh   *Weston & Lee*
Published by Francis, Day & Hunter

My Tennessee, is that you calling me ?   *Bennett Scott*
Published by the Star Music Publishing Co.

A SELECTION of popular songs are here recorded in capital style. The popular soldier-song, " It'll be nice to get back home again," has a sentiment that is especially appropriate just now, and a catchy tune to which to be " merry and bright again." The " Jazz Band " song gives us some weird orchestral effects, describing " rags in any old key," a most amusing number. " Oshkosh " is a melodious Hawaiian, as is also the American home song, " My Tennessee." *(Speeds 79)*

THE GRESHAM SINGERS

unaccompanied
10-inch record 4s.

3-4023   When for the world's repose   *Lord Mornington*

THE perfect ensemble of this popular vocal quartet is displayed to the best advantage in a fine old piece of English music, rich in harmonic effects. It shows off the voices admirably, and is beautifully sung by the Gresham Singers. *(Speed 79)*

AN HISTORICAL RECORD

which should be in every home

GAS SHELL BOMBARDMENT

12-inch record 6s.

09308   Actual recording of the Gas Shell Bombardment by The Royal Garrison Artillery (9th October, 1918), preparatory to the British Troops entering Lille

The profits derived from the sale of this record will be entirely devoted to

THE KING'S FUND FOR THE DISABLED

NEW DANCE RECORDS

THE GAIETY THEATRE ORCHESTRA
conducted by Mr. ARTHUR WOOD
10-inch double-sided record 3s. 6d.

B 988 $\left\{\begin{array}{l}\end{array}\right.$ **Medley Two-Step ("Going Up")** *L. A. Hirsch*
(*a*) **I'll bet you** (*b*) **The touch of a woman's hand**
("Going up") *L. A. Hirsch*
Published by B. Feldman & Co.

McKEE'S ORCHESTRA
12-inch double-sided record 5s. 6d.
Riverside Bells Waltz *McKee*

C 875 $\left\{\begin{array}{l}\end{array}\right.$

METROPOLITAN DANCE BAND
Have a heart—Medley Fox Trot

VESS OSSMAN'S BANJO ORCHESTRA
12-inch double-sided record 5s. 6d.
Merry Whirl—One Step *Lenzberg*

C 876 $\left\{\begin{array}{l}\end{array}\right.$

McKEE'S ORCHESTRA
Youth and Beauty Waltz *McKee*

SAVOY QUARTET
10-inch double-sided record 3s. 6d.

B 991 $\left\{\begin{array}{l}\end{array}\right.$ **I'm all bound 'round with the Mason Dixie Line**
Published by B. Feldman & Co. *Schwartz*
The Darktown Strutters' Ball (A Jazz Melody) *Brooks*
Published by the Herman Darewski Music Publishing Co.

SOME very taking dance music is a feature of the light orchestral records this month. Two very melodious waltzes first must be mentioned, "Youth and Beauty," a very captivating tune for dancing, a remark which applies equally well to the "Riverside Bells," with its picturesque bell effect. Both are excellently recorded by McKee's well-known New York Orchestra, while the Metropolitan Dance Band supplies a merry Fox-trot, very catchy in tune and rhythm. A lively one-step for banjo orchestra is a very pleasing novelty in records, and the medley two-step from the Gaiety success "Going Up," recorded by the Gaiety Orchestra, is one of the best of the dance numbers. This fine theatre orchestra also gives us another selection from the piece in excellent style. Finally, the popular Savoy quartet of banjoists have recorded two bright pieces, in each giving their characteristic orchestral and vocal effects. (*Speed's* 79)

NEW RECORDS OF SCOTTISH SONGS

12-inch record 6s.

02781 We all go hame the same way — Harry Lauder

10-inch record 4s.

4–2990 Border Ballad — Fraser Gange

10-inch double-sided records 3s. 6d.

B 969 { My ain wee house — Hugh Friel
       { Ae fond kiss — Hugh Friel
B 970 { Mary — Hugh Friel
       { The Scottish emigrant's farewell — Hugh Friel
B 971 { Afton Water — Jenny Black
       { Lochnagar — Jenny Black
B 972 { O, sing to me the auld Scotch songs — Jenny Black
       { Jock o' Hazeldean — Jenny Black
B 973 { The boatman (Fear à Bhata) (sung in Gaelic) — Phemie Marquis
       { Hebridean sea rievers' song (Na Reubairean) (sung in Gaelic) — Phemie Marquis
B 974 { The land of the mountains (An teid thu leam abighinn og) (sung in Gaelic) — Phemie Marquis
       { A fairy's love song (Tha mi sgith) (sung in Gaelic) — Phemie Marquis
B 975 { The nameless lassie — Alexander Macgreggor
       { There's a wee bit land — Alexander Macgreggor
B 976 { Rolling home to Bonnie Scotland — Alexander Macgreggor
       { Mary Morrison — Alexander Macgreggor
B 977 { Castles in the air — Jean Cross
       { Rothesay Bay — Jean Cross
B 978 { Psalm 118, verses 1 and 2 (" Kilmarnock ") (sung in Gaelic) — Roderick Macleod and Chorus
       { Psalm 103, verses 1 and 2 (" Coleshill ") (sung in Gaelic) — Roderick Macleod and Chorus
B 979 { Psalm 34, verses 1 and 2 (" St. David ") (sung in Gaelic) — Roderick Macleod and Chorus
       { Stornoway (Paraphrase 18, verse 4) (sung in Gaelic) — Roderick Macleod and Chorus
B 980 { Cock o' the North — Pipe-Major D. Smith (bagpipes) assisted by Corporal White
       { Hielan' Laddie — Pipe-Major D. Smith (bagpipes) assisted by Corporal White
       { Miss Drummond o' Perth (Highland fling) — Pipe-Major D. Smith (bagpipes) assisted by Corporal White
       { Reel of Tulloch (Reel) — Pipe-Major D. Smith (bagpipes) assisted by Corporal White

---

" AS YOU WERE "

12-inch double-sided records 5s. 6d.

C 874 { " As you were." Selection I. containing : Helen of Troy—I didn't arf larf—If you could care—Old man Adam — The Mayfair Orchestra
       { " As you were." Selection II. containing : Potsdam—Fritz—Live for all you're worth—The aeroplane walk — The Mayfair Orchestra

10-inch double-sided records 3s. 6d.

B 986 { Back to Blighty — Eric Courtland and Walter Jefferies
       { I'm the Great Big Pot of Potsdam — Eric Courtland and Walter Jefferies
B 987 { What ho ! Mr. Watteau (with chorus) — Blanche Dare
       { If you could care — Eric Courtland

" As you Were " is published by The Herman Darewski Music Publishing Company

15

NOVEMBER RECORDS

12-inch record 12s. 6d.

2-052090	Credo (" Otello ")	Titta Ruffo

12-inch records 7s.

03619	{ (a) Oh, tell me, nightingale	Olga Haley
	{ (b) Good morning, brother Sunshine	Olga Haley
03620	Hush'd is my lute	Olga Haley
03621	In the silent night	Olga Haley
03622	Annie Laurie	Olga Haley
2-0834	Slav March, Op. 31	The Royal Albert Hall Orchestra

10-inch and 12-inch records 6s.

8195	Quartet in E flat—Allegro (Finale)	Elman String Quartet
03627	The Children's Home	Edna Thornton
03628	I am only seven	Margaret Cooper
07897	Gigue in C major (unaccompanied)	Beatrice Harrison

12-inch double-sided records 5s. 6d.

C 870	{ "Aïda "—Selection I	The Band of H.M. Coldstream Guards
	{ "Aïda "—Selection II	The Band of H.M. Coldstream Guards
C 871	{ Songs my mother used to sing	Violet Essex
	{ Three wonderful letters from home	Violet Essex
C 872	{ The bellringer	Harry Talbot
	{ A farmer's boy (Old English song)	Harry Talbot
C 873	{ Adagio Religioso from 4th Concerto	Mary Law
	{ Fantaisie ou Scène de Ballet, Op. 100	Mary Law

10-inch records 5s.

2-3295	Song of love and June	Olga Haley
2-3308	Waiata Poi (A Maori love song)	Rosina Buckman

10-inch records 4s.

2-572	Intermezzo (" Monica's Blue Boy ")	The Symphony Orchestra
2-3309	A little twilight song	Alice Wilna
5-2003	To Mary	Fraser Gange
3-4015	Weep ye no more, sad fountains	Carmen Hill and Marcus Thomson
5334	Humoreske	Mark Hambourg

10-inch double-sided records 3s. 6d.

B 981	{ Marche Russe	The Band of H.M. Coldstream Guards
	{ Lorraine (March Majestic)	The Opal Military Band
B 982	{ The tickle toe (" Going Up! ')	De Groot and the Piccadilly Orchestra
	{ The Apache Rag (" Tails Up! ")	De Groot and the Piccadilly Orchestra
B 983	{ Bread ! Bread ! Bread !	Jay Laurier
	{ Why is Cecil selling sea shells?	Jay Laurier
B 984	{ Give me a little cosy corner	Louise Leigh, Eric Courtland and Walter Jefferies
	{ Indianapolis	Courtland and Jefferies
B 985	{ Some Sunday morning	Savoy Quartet
	{ Indian Rag	Savoy Quartet